Mathematical Methods in Physics-I

PHE-04

For

Bachelor of Science [B.Sc.]

Useful For

IGNOU, KSOU (Karnataka), Bihar University (Muzaffarpur), Nalanda University, National Open University of Nigeria, Jamia Millia Islamia, Vardhman Mahaveer Open University (Kota), Uttarakhand Open University, Kurukshetra University, Seva Sadan's College of Education (Maharashtra), Lalit Narayan Mithila University, Andhra University, Pt. Sunderlal Sharma (Open) University (Bilaspur), Annamalai University, Bangalore University, Bharathiar University, Bharathidasan University, HP University, Centre for distance and open learning, Kakatiya University (Andhra Pradesh), KOU (Rajasthan), MPBOU (MP), MDU (Haryana), Punjab University, Tamilnadu Open University, Sri Padmavati Mahila Visvavidyalayam (Andhra Pradesh), Sri Venkateswara University (Andhra Pradesh), UCSDE (Kerala), University of Jammu, YCMOU, Rajasthan University, UPRTOU, Kalyani University, Banaras Hindu University (BHU) and all other Indian Universities.

GULLYBABA PUBLISHING HOUSE (P) LTD.

ISO 9001 & ISO 14001 CERTIFIED CO.

Published by:

GullyBaba Publishing House Pvt. Ltd.

Regd. Office:
2525/193, 1st Floor, Onkar Nagar-A,
Tri Nagar, Delhi-110035
(From Kanhaiya Nagar Metro Station Towards Old Bus Stand)
Ph. 011-27387998, 27384836, 27385249

Branch Office:
1A/2A, 20, Hari Sadan,
Ansari Road, Daryaganj,
New Delhi-110002
Ph. 011-23289034
011-45794768

E-mail: hello@gullybaba.com, Website: GullyBaba.com

New Edition

Author: GullyBaba.Com Panel

ISBN: 978-93-82688-78-5

Preface

The advances of physical theories in the first half of the nineteenth century demonstrated to German physicists for their powerful mathematical techniques. Some of the techniques they owned to the German mathematician Gauss, who not only developed them but also applied them to physical problems. During Gauss's later years and after his death, other German mathematicians developed mathematical techniques useful in physics and, as Gauss did, applied them.

We all know the Newton's law of universal gravitation. There is indeed a fascinating interplay between physics and mathematics, which dates back to Newton's time. Newton developed calculus as a tool for calculating planetary orbits. In this case, the need to understand a physical problem provided a stimulus for developing mathematics. In many other cases, the mathematics already developed turned out to be tailor-made for physics. Thus, physics and mathematics are intimately linked.

In this book ***"Mathematical Methods in Physics-I (PHE-04)"*** various mathematical techniques are given which are very useful in Physics. The book is strictly based on IGNOU syllabus. We will study vector calculus, probability and statistics in this book.

Introductions and solved practical problems are given in each chapter, which will give you better understanding of chapters. Best point is that we have included previous years solved papers to help students to understand the unique examination structure.

We hope that this book will not only helpful for students but also for teachers.

We wish you great success. Feedback in this regard is solicited.

– GPH Panel of Expert

Acknowledgement

Our compliments go to the **GullyBaba Publishing House (P) Ltd.,** and its meticulous team who have been enthusiastically working towards the perfection of the book.

Their teamwork, initiative and research have been very encouraging. Had it not been for their unflagging support, this work wouldn't have been possible. The creative freedom provided by them along with their aim of presenting the best to the reader has been a major source of inspiration in this work. Hope that this book would be successful.

– GPH Panel of Expert

Publisher's Note

The present book of the PHE series is targeted for examination purpose as well as enrichment. With the advent of technology and the Internet, there has been no dearth of information available to all; however, finding the relevant and qualitative information, which is focused, is an uphill task.

We at **GullyBaba Publishing House (P) Ltd.,** have taken this step to provide quality material which can accentuate in-depth knowledge about the subject. GPH books are a pioneer in the effort of providing unique and quality material to its readers. With our books, you are sure to attain success by making use of this powerful study material. Provided book is just a reference book based on the syllabus of particular University/Board. For a profound information, see the textbooks recommended by the University/Board.

Our site **gullybaba.com** is a vital resource for your examination. The publisher wishes to acknowledge the significant contribution of the Team Members and our experts in bringing out this publication and highly thankful to Almighty God, without His blessings, this endeavor wouldn't have been successful.

– Publisher

Topics Covered

Block-1 Vector Calculus

Unit-1 Vector Algebra
Unit-2 Vector Differential Calculus
Unit-3 Coordinate Systems
Unit-4 Integration of Scalar and Vector Fields

Block-2 Probability and Statistics

Unit-5 Basic Concepts of Probability Theory
Unit-6 Probability Distributions
Unit-7 Applications in Physics

Contents

Chapter-1 Vector Algebra....................1-32
Chapter-2 Vector Differential Calculus....................33-64
Chapter-3 Coordinate Systems....................65-89
Chapter-4 Integration of Scalar and Vector Fields....................91-128
Chapter-5 Basic Concepts of Probability Theory....................129-158
Chapter-6 Probability Distributions....................159-182
Chapter-7 Applications in Physics....................183-213
Important Formulae....................217-223
Appendix Table....................227-234

Question Papers

(1) June: 2011 (Solved)....................237-239
(2) December: 2011 (Solved)....................240-242
(3) June: 2012 (Solved)....................243-245
(4) December: 2012 (Solved)....................246-248
(5) June: 2013 (Solved)....................249-250
(6) December: 2013....................251-252
(7) June: 2014....................253-254
(8) December: 2014....................255-256
(9) June: 2015....................257-258
(10) December: 2015....................259-260
(11) June: 2016....................261-262
(12) December: 2016 (Solved)....................263-265
(13) June: 2017 (Solved)....................266-273
(14) December: 2017....................274-275
(15) June: 2018 (Sample Paper)....................276-277
(16) June: 2018....................278-279
(17) December: 2018....................280-281
(18) June: 2019....................282-283
(19) December: 2019....................284-285

Chapter 1 Vector Algebra

An Overview

A vector V in the plane or in space is an arrow; it is determined by its length, denoted $|V|$ and its direction. Two arrows represent the same vector if they have the same length and are parallel. We use vectors to represent entities which are described by magnitude and direction. For example, a force applied at a point is a vector; it is completely determined by the magnitude of the force and the direction in which it is applied. An object moving in space has, at any given time, a direction of motion, and a speed. This is represented by the velocity vector of the motion. More precisely, the velocity vector at a point is an arrow of length of the speed (ds/dt), which lies on the tangent line to the trajectory. The success and importance of vector algebra derives from the interplay between geometric interpretation and algebraic calculation.

Scalar Quantity: Scalar quantity is completely specified by a single number (with a suitable choice of units).

Vector Quantity: Quantities which are specified by a magnitude and a direction in space are called vector quantities.

Notation of Vectors: We denote the vector in printed way by bold faces, e.g. v, a, f, etc. But in our written work, we should denote vectors by drawing arrows above them, e.g. $\vec{v}$, $\vec{a}$ or by drawing a line (straight or curly) below them, e.g. $\underline{v}$, $\underline{f}$ or $\underset{\sim}{v}$, $\underset{\sim}{f}$.

Representation of Vectors: Since a vector has both magnitude and direction so that it can be conveniently represented by a directed straight line segment.

Let O be an arbitrary point to the space and P be any other point. Then the straight line OP has magnitude as well as direction. Hence, the directed line segment OP is capable of representing a vector quantity. We denote this vector by $\overrightarrow{OP}$.

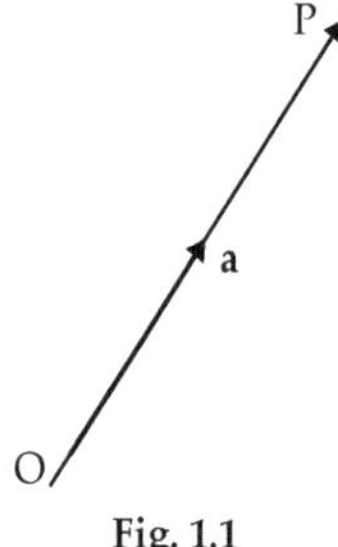

Fig. 1.1

Here O is the initial point and P is the terminal point.

Equal Vectors: Two vectors are said to be equal if they have equal magnitudes and are parallel and have the same sense of direction. They need not have the same origin. Thus, if AB and CDEF are two parallel lines and if AB=CD=EF then the vectors $\overrightarrow{AB}$, $\overrightarrow{CD}$, $\overrightarrow{EF}$ are equal, i.e. $\overrightarrow{AB} = \overrightarrow{CD} = \overrightarrow{EF}$

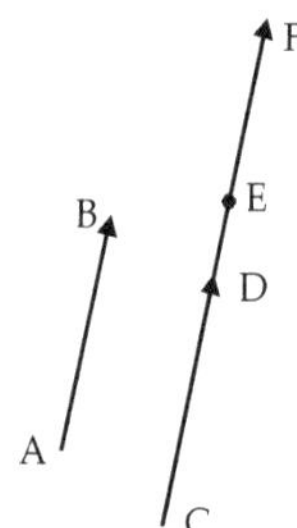

Fig. 1.2: Equal Vectors

Free Vectors: A vector whose direction in space is prescribed but whose point of application and line of application are not prescribed.

Sliding Vectors: If two vectors are equal only if they have same magnitude direction and the same line of action. Such vectors are called sliding vectors.

Bound Vectors: Sometimes even the point of action of a vector is fixed. Such vectors are called bound vectors. For example, the force applied at any point of an elastic body is a bound vector.

Addition of Vectors: Let $\vec{a}, \vec{b}$ be two given vectors. Take any point O and let $\overrightarrow{OA} = \vec{a}; \ \overrightarrow{AB} = \vec{b}$ so that the terminal point of $\vec{a}$ is the initial point of $\vec{b}$.

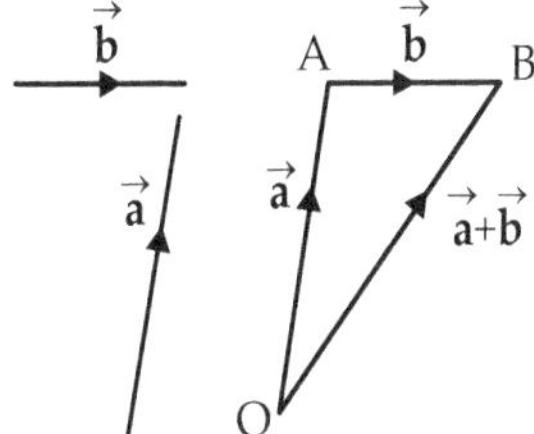

Fig. 1.3: Addition of Vectors

Then the vector $\overrightarrow{OB}$ is defined to be the sum of the vectors $\vec{a}$ and $\vec{b}$. If vector $\overrightarrow{OB}$ is represented by $\vec{c}$, then we write $\vec{c} = \overrightarrow{OB} = \overrightarrow{OA} + \overrightarrow{OB} = \vec{a} + \vec{b}$

This is known as the triangle law of vector addition. Vector addition obeys the commutative and associative laws.

Properties of Vector Addition

- **Commutative law:** If $\vec{a}, \vec{b}$ are two vectors, then $\vec{a} + \vec{b} = \vec{b} + \vec{a}$

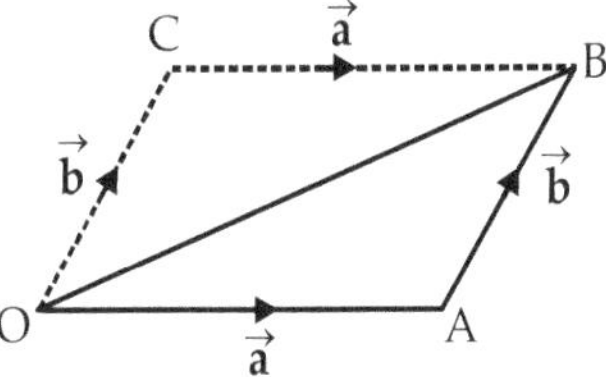

Fig. 1.4: Commutative Law

This is known as the parallelogram law of vectors.

- **Associative law:** If $\vec{a}, \vec{b}, \vec{c}$ are any three vectors, then

$\vec{a} + (\vec{b} + \vec{c}) = (\vec{a} + \vec{b}) + \vec{c}$

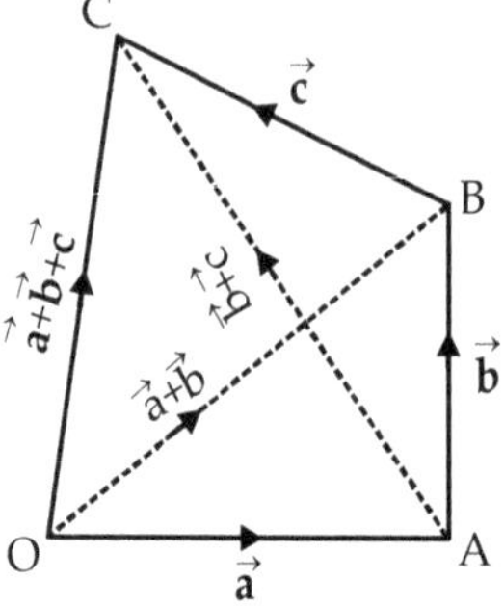

Fig. 1.5: Associative Law

Multiplication of a Vector by a Scalar: Let m be any scalar and $\vec{a}$ a vector, then $m\vec{a}$ is defined as a vector whose magnitude is m times the magnitude of $\vec{a}$ and whose direction is that of $\vec{a}$ or opposite to it according as m is positive or negative.

Some laws related to Multiplication of a Vector by a Scalar are stated below:

$$m(n\vec{a}) = (mn)\vec{a}$$

$$(m+n)\vec{a} = m\vec{a} + n\vec{a}$$

$$m(\vec{a}+\vec{b}) = m\vec{a} + m\vec{b}$$

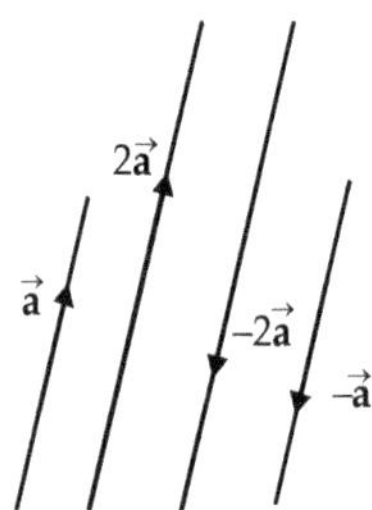

Fig. 1.6: Multiplication of a Vector by a Scalar

Subtraction of Vectors: To every vector $\vec{a}$ there corresponds the vector

$-\vec{a}$ such that $\vec{a} + (-\vec{a}) = 0$.

If $\overrightarrow{OA} = \vec{a}$, then $\overrightarrow{AO} = -\vec{a}$, so that $\overrightarrow{OA} + \overrightarrow{AO} = \overrightarrow{00} = 0$ or $\vec{a} + (-\vec{a}) = 0$.

The vector $-\vec{a}$ is called the inverse of the vector $\vec{a}$ for the operation of addition.

We know that $-\vec{b}$ is vector which has the same length as $\vec{b}$, but the opposite direction. The subtraction of $\vec{b}$ from $\vec{a}$ is to be understood as the addition of $-\vec{b}$ to $\vec{a}$. Thus, we write $\vec{a} - \vec{b} = \vec{a} + (-\vec{b})$

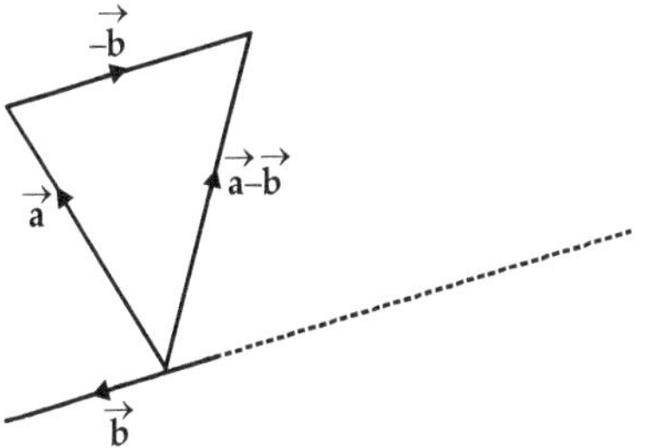

Fig. 1.7: Subtraction of Vectors

Null Vector: If the module (modulus) of a vector is zero then that vector is called a zero or Null Vector. A null vector is denoted by the bold face type 0 or $\vec{0}$. $\overrightarrow{AA}$ or $\overrightarrow{BB}$ is a zero vector.

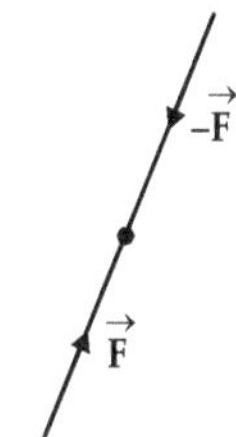

Fig. 1.8: Null Vector

Unit Vector: A unit vector is one whose module is unity. The unit vectors in the directions $\vec{a}, \vec{b}, \vec{c}$ are denoted by $\hat{a}, \hat{b}, \hat{c}$, respectively.

Thus, $\hat{a} = \frac{\vec{a}}{a}, \hat{b} = \frac{\vec{b}}{b}, \hat{c} = \frac{\vec{c}}{c}$

Scalar Product: The scalar product of two non-zero vectors $\vec{a}$ and $\vec{b}$ (written as $\vec{a}.\vec{b}$) is a scalar defined as $\vec{a}.\vec{b} = ab\cos\theta$

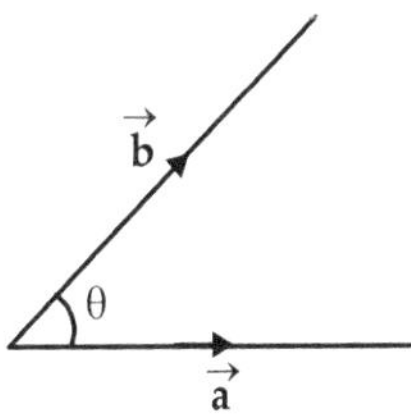

Fig. 1.9: Scalar Product of Two Vector

$\vec{a}.\vec{b}$ is also called the dot product.

Properties of the dot product:

- $\vec{a}.\vec{b}$ is a scalar
- $\vec{a}.\vec{b} = \vec{b}.\vec{a}$, i.e. the dot product is commutative.
- $\vec{a}.(\vec{b}+\vec{c}) = \vec{a}.\vec{b} + \vec{a}.\vec{c}$, i.e. the dot product is associative over addition.
- $(m\vec{a}).\vec{b} = m(\vec{a}.\vec{b}) = \vec{a}.(m\vec{b})$

- If $\vec{a}.\vec{b}=0$, and $\vec{a}$ and $\vec{b}$ are not zero vectors then $\vec{a}$ is perpendicular to $\vec{b}$.
- $|\vec{a}| = \sqrt{\vec{a}.\vec{a}}$
- $\vec{a}.\vec{a} > 0$ for non-zero vector $\vec{a}$.
- $\vec{a}.\vec{a} = 0$ only if $a = 0$.

Vector or Cross Product: The vector or cross product of $\vec{a}$ and $\vec{b}$, written as $\vec{a}\times\vec{b}$, is defined to be the vector as $\vec{c}=\vec{a}\times\vec{b}=(ab\sin\theta)\,\hat{c}$

Here $\hat{c}$ is a unit vector perpendicular to $\vec{a}$ and $\vec{b}$.

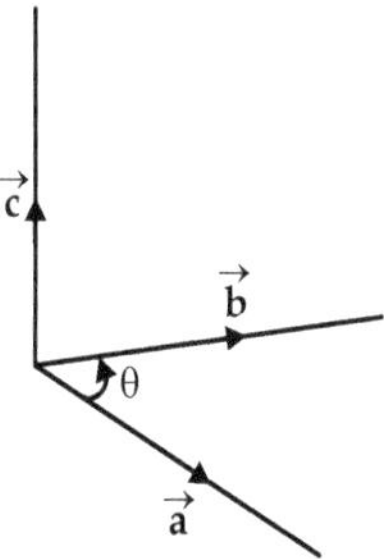

Fig. 1.10: Vector product of two vectors

The sense of $\hat{c}$ is given by the right-hand rule: Rotate the fingers of our right hand so that the fingertips point along the direction of rotation of $\vec{a}$ into $\vec{b}$ through $\theta(\leq\pi)$. The thumb gives the direction of $\hat{c}$ [Fig. 1.11]

Fig. 1.11: The right hand rule for finding the direction of $\vec{a}\times\vec{b}$. $\vec{a},\vec{b}$ and $\vec{c}$ are said to form a right-handed triple. The direction of $\vec{c}$ is also the direction in which a right-handed screw would move if it is rotated from $\vec{a}$ towards $\vec{b}$.

Note: $\vec{b}\times\vec{a}$ is not same vector as $\vec{a}\times\vec{b}$ [Fig. 1.12] here, $\vec{a}\times\vec{b} = -\vec{b}\times\vec{a}$

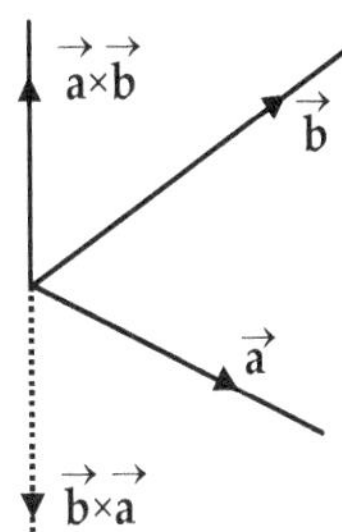

Fig. 1.12: The vector b×a is equal and opposite to a×b.

Properties of Vector Product:

- $\vec{a}\times\vec{b}$ is a vector
- $\vec{a}\times\vec{b} = -\vec{b}\times\vec{a}$
- If $\vec{a}$ and $\vec{b}$ are non-zero vectors, and $\vec{a}\times\vec{b} = 0$, then $\vec{a}$ is parallel to $\vec{b}$.
- $\vec{a}\times\vec{a} = 0$; for any vector $\vec{a}$
- $\vec{a}\times(\vec{b}+\vec{c}) = (\vec{a}\times\vec{b}) + (\vec{a}\times\vec{c})$
- $(\vec{a}+\vec{b})\times\vec{c} = (\vec{a}\times\vec{c}) + (\vec{b}\times\vec{c})$

  That is, the vector product is distributive over addition. The order in which these vectors appear remains the same.
- $(m\vec{a})\times\vec{b} = m(\vec{a}\times\vec{b}) = \vec{a}\times(m\vec{b})$

Vector Components Relative to a Coordinate System: Consider the two-dimensional Cartesian coordinate system [Fig. 1.13]. Here, OX and OY are two mutually perpendicular axes. Let us consider a vector $\vec{a}$ in the XY plane. Now draw perpendiculars from the ends of $\vec{a}$ on the OX and OY- axes. Then the projections a_x and a_y so formed on the x and y-axes are called, respectively, the x and y components of $\vec{a}$. From below [Fig. 1.13], we can see that

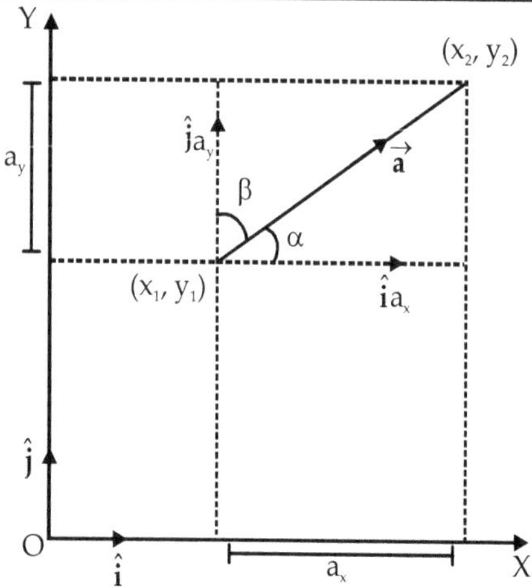

Fig. 1.13: Cartesian components a_x, a_y of a vector in two dimensions. $(x_1, y_1), (x_2, y_2)$ are the coordinates of the tail and head of $\vec{a}$ respectively. α and β are the angles which $\vec{a}$ makes with the x and y-axes, respectively.

$$a_x = x_2 - x_1,\ a_y = y_2 - y_1 \quad \text{...(i)}$$

$$a_x = a\cos\alpha,\ a_y = a\cos\beta = a\sin\alpha \quad \text{...(ii)}$$

$$a = \sqrt{a_x^{\ 2} + a_y^{\ 2}} \quad \text{...(iii)}$$

$$\tan\alpha = \frac{a_y}{a_x} \quad \text{...(iv)}$$

The angle α specifies the direction of $\vec{a}$ The cosines of the angles α and β, which $\vec{a}$ makes with the x and y -axes, respectively, are called **direction cosines** of $\vec{a}$ with respect to this co-ordinate system.

These are denoted by l and m. Thus $l = \cos\alpha = \frac{a_x}{a}$, $m = \cos\beta = \frac{a_y}{a}$

...(v)

Now, let $\hat{i}$ and $\hat{j}$ be the unit vectors in the positive x and positive y directions, respectively. Whereas a_x and a_y are the scalar components of $\vec{a}$ in the (x, y) plane, $a_x\hat{i}$ and $a_y\hat{j}$ are its vector components.

We can see from [fig. 1.13] that $\vec{a}$ is the sum of its vector components:

$$\vec{a} = a_x\hat{i} + a_y\hat{j} \quad \text{...(vi)}$$

Eq.(vi) represents a two-dimensional vector in terms of its components and the unit vector along the OX and OY.

Vector Components in three Dimensions: In this system, we have a set of three orthogonal (mutually perpendicular) axes. So a vector $\vec{a}$ has three components a_x, a_y, a_z along the x, y and z-axes [Fig. 1.14]. In terms of the coordinates of the tail (x_1, y_1, z_1) and head (x_2, y_2, z_2) of $\vec{a}$, these are

$$a_x = x_2 - x_1,\ a_y = y_2 - y_1,\ a_z = z_2 - z_1 \qquad \text{...(vii)}$$

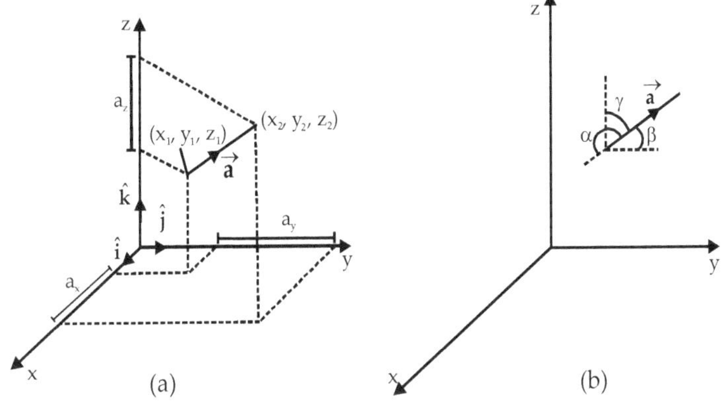

Fig. 1.14: (a) Cartesian components of a vector in three dimensions; (b) the angles α, β and γ.

The magnitude of $\vec{a}$ is the distance between the two points (x_1, y_1, z_1) and (x_2, y_2, z_2): $a = \sqrt{a_x^2 + a_y^2 + a_z^2}$

...(viii)

Now the direction of $\vec{a}$ is given by the angles α, β and γ between $\vec{a}$ and the positive x, y and z-axes, respectively. Generally, we use the cosines of these angles. These are $\cos\alpha = \frac{a_x}{a}$, $\cos\beta = \frac{a_y}{a}$, $\cos\gamma = \frac{a_z}{a}$

Where $\cos\alpha$, $\cos\beta$, $\cos\gamma$ are called the **direction cosines** of $\vec{a}$ in a three-dimensional orthogonal system. We denote $\cos\alpha$, $\cos\beta$, $\cos\gamma$ by *l*, m and n, respectively.

Let $\hat{i}, \hat{j}$ and $\hat{k}$ be the respective unit vectors in the positive x, y and z directions. Here $\hat{i}, \hat{j}, \hat{k}$ form a right-handed triple and the corresponding Cartesian coordinate system (x, y, z) is a right-handed system. Then

$a_x\hat{i}+a_y\hat{j}$ and $a_z\hat{k}$ are the vector components of $\vec{a}$ in the x, y and z directions, respectively, and $\vec{a}=a_x\hat{i}+a_y\hat{j}+a_z\hat{k}$ ...(ix)

Transformation of Coordinate System and Vector Components in two dimensional vector: Consider the displacement $\vec{d}$ of a particle of mass m with respect to the origin of a two dimensional (xy) Cartesian coordinate system. [Fig. 1.15]

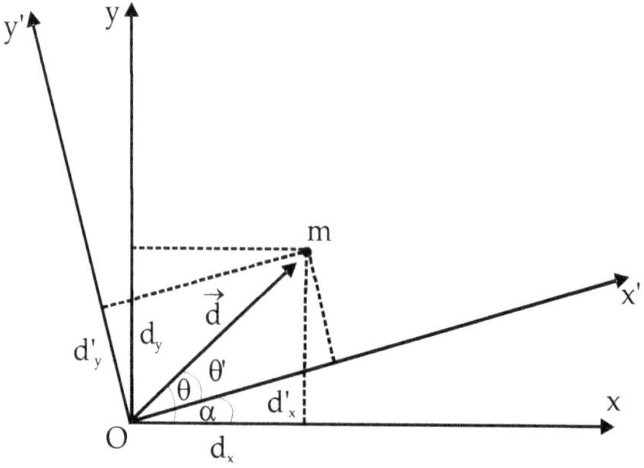

Fig. 1.15: A vector $\vec{d}$ represented in two different Cartesian coordinate systems.

In terms of its components in the xy coordinate system, we can write $\vec{d}$ as $\vec{d}=d_x\hat{i}+d_y\hat{j}$ ...(x)

Note: Scalar quantities remain invariant (unchanged) under any transformation of coordinate systems.

Now let us rotate the coordinate axes by an angle α so that we have a different Cartesian coordinate system (x'y'), i.e. we have transformed the (xy) system into the (x'y') system.

Its components d'_x, d'_y in the (x' y') system are different from d_x, d_y. If $\hat{i}', \hat{j}'$ denote unit vectors along x', y'-axes, then we have $d=d'_x\hat{i}'+d'_y\hat{j}'$

Now, we can see from [Fig. 1.15] that

$$d_x=d\cos\theta,\quad d_y=d\sin\theta$$

and $d'_x=d\cos\theta'=d\cos(\theta-\alpha)=d(\cos\theta\cos\alpha+\sin\theta\sin\alpha)$

$$=\cos\alpha d_x+\sin\alpha d_y$$

$$d'_y=d\sin\theta'=d\sin(\theta-\alpha)=d(\sin\theta\cos\alpha-\cos\theta\sin\alpha)$$

$= -\sin\alpha d_x + \cos\alpha d_y$

We can express these results in a general notation as

$d_x' = c_{11} d_x + c_{12} d_y$

$d_y' = c_{21} d_x + c_{22} d_y$

where $c_{11} = \cos\alpha$, $c_{12} = \sin\alpha$, $c_{21} = -\sin\alpha$, $c_{22} = \cos\alpha$

The Precise Definition of three-Dimensional Vectors: Let (x, y, z) and (x', y', z') be any two systems of Cartesian coordinates. Let the representation of a vector $\vec{a}$ in the two systems, respectively, be

$$\vec{a} = a_1\hat{i} + a_2\hat{j} + a_3\hat{k} \qquad \text{...(xi)}$$

and $\vec{a} = a_1'\hat{i}' + a_2'\hat{j}' + a_3'\hat{k}'$ ...(xii)

Here $\hat{i}, \hat{j}, \hat{k}$ and $\hat{i}', \hat{j}', \hat{k}'$ are the unit vectors in the positive x, y, z and x', y', z' directions, respectively. Then using associativity rules of dot product and eqs. (xi) & (xii) we obtain

$$\hat{i}'.\vec{a} = a_1\hat{i}'.\hat{i} + a_2\hat{i}'.\hat{j} + a_3\hat{i}'.\hat{k} \qquad \text{...(xiii)}$$

and also $\hat{i}'.\vec{a} = a_1'\hat{i}'.\hat{i}' + a_2'\hat{i}'.\hat{j}' + a_3'\hat{i}'.\hat{k}'$ ...(xiv)

Again using the definition of scalar product, we can see that $\hat{i}'.\vec{a} = a_1'$, since

$$\hat{i}'.\hat{i}' = 1.1\cos 0^\circ = 1, \hat{i}'.\hat{j}' = 1.1\cos 90^\circ = 0 \text{ and } \hat{i}'.\hat{k}' = 1.1\cos 90^\circ = 0.$$

Thus, we can write from Eqs. ((xiii) & (xiv)) that

$$a_1' = a_1\hat{i}'.\hat{i} + a_2\hat{i}'.\hat{j} + a_3\hat{i}'.\hat{k} \qquad \text{...(xv)}$$

Similarly, we can take the scalar products $\hat{j}'.\vec{a}$ and $\hat{k}'.\vec{a}$ to show that

$$a_2' = a_1\hat{j}'.\hat{i} + a_2\hat{j}'.\hat{j} + a_3\hat{j}'.\hat{k} \qquad \text{...(xvi)}$$

and $a_3' = a_1\hat{k}'.\hat{i} + a_2\hat{k}'.\hat{j} + a_3\hat{k}'.\hat{k}$ ...(xvii)

To write Eqs. ((xv) to (xvii)) in a compact form, we adopt the following notation

$$\hat{i}'.\hat{i} = c_{11},\ \hat{i}'.\hat{j} = c_{12},\ \hat{i}'.\hat{k} = c_{13}$$

$$\hat{j}'.\hat{i} = c_{21},\ \hat{j}'.\hat{j} = c_{22},\ \hat{j}'.\hat{k} = c_{23} \qquad \text{...(xviii)}$$

$\hat{k}'.\hat{i}=c_{31}$, $\hat{k}'.\hat{j}=c_{32}$, $\hat{k}'.\hat{k}=c_{33}$

These coefficients are nothing but the cosines of the angles between the respective positive axes. For example, c_{11} is the cosine of the angle between positive x' and x-axes, c_{12} is the cosine of the angle between positive x' and y-axes, and so on. Then we can write

$$a'_1 = c_{11}a_1 + c_{12}a_2 + c_{13}a_3 \quad \text{...(xix(a))}$$

$$a'_2 = c_{21}a_1 + c_{22}a_2 + c_{23}a_3 \quad \text{...(xix(b))}$$

$$a'_3 = c_{31}a_1 + c_{32}a_2 + c_{33}a_3 \quad \text{...(xix(c))}$$

In the matrix form: $$\begin{pmatrix} a'_1 \\ a'_2 \\ a'_3 \end{pmatrix} = \begin{pmatrix} c_{11} & c_{12} & c_{13} \\ c_{21} & c_{22} & c_{23} \\ c_{31} & c_{32} & c_{33} \end{pmatrix} \begin{pmatrix} a_1 \\ a_2 \\ a_3 \end{pmatrix} \quad \text{...(xix(d))}$$

We can similarly derive the inverse relations.

$$a_1 = c_{11}a'_1 + c_{21}a'_2 + c_{31}a'_3 \quad \text{...(xx(a))}$$

$$a_2 = c_{12}a'_1 + c_{22}a'_2 + c_{32}a'_3 \quad \text{...(xx(b))}$$

$$a_3 = c_{13}a'_1 + c_{23}a'_2 + c_{33}a'_3 \quad \text{...(xx(c))}$$

or $$\begin{pmatrix} a_1 \\ a_2 \\ a_3 \end{pmatrix} = \begin{pmatrix} c_{11} & c_{21} & c_{31} \\ c_{12} & c_{22} & c_{32} \\ c_{13} & c_{23} & c_{33} \end{pmatrix} \begin{pmatrix} a'_1 \\ a'_2 \\ a'_3 \end{pmatrix} \quad \text{...(xx(d))}$$

Now, we can give a **precise definition** of a **three-dimensional** vector:

A three-dimensional vector is defined as a set of three numbers (or components) referred to an orthogonal coordinate system. If a_1, a_2, a_3 are the components of $\vec{a}$ in one system and a'_1, a'_2, a'_3 are its components in another system, then these two sets of components are related by Eqs. (xix) and (vi). A physical quantity is called a vector if it transforms under a change of coordinate system in accordance with Eqs. (xviii), (xix) and (xx).

While the components of a vector are different in different coordinate systems, its magnitude remains the same in all systems:

$$a = a' = \sqrt{a_x^2 + a_y^2 + a_z^2} = \sqrt{a_x'^2 + a_y'^2 + a_z'^2} \quad \text{...(xxi)}$$

Thus, the magnitude of a vector remains invariant under any transformation of coordinate systems.

Vector Addition and Subtraction in component form: Suppose we have to add the two vectors $\vec{a}$ and $\vec{b}$ of equation $\vec{a} = a_x\hat{i} + a_y\hat{j} + a_z\hat{k}$ and $\vec{b} = b_x\hat{i} + b_y\hat{j} + b_z\hat{k}$. Let the resultant $\vec{c}$ of the vectors $\vec{a}$ and $\vec{b}$ have components c_x, c_y and c_z. Then,

$$\vec{c} = \vec{a} + \vec{b} \text{ or } c_x\hat{i} + c_y\hat{j} + c_z\hat{k} = a_x\hat{i} + a_y\hat{j} + a_z\hat{k} + b_x\hat{i} + b_y\hat{j} + b_z\hat{k}$$

$$= (a_x + b_x)\hat{i} + (a_y + b_y)\hat{j} + (a_z + b_z)\hat{k}$$

Hence, $c_x = a_x + b_x,\ c_y = a_y + b_y,\ c_z = a_z + b_z$

The same procedure applies to subtraction. So, we can say that, to add or subtract vectors, add or subtract their like components. This rule can be applied to add more than two vectors. We can also extend it to multiplication of a vector by a scalar, i.e.

$$ma = m(a_x\hat{i} + a_y\hat{j} + a_z\hat{k}) = ma_x\hat{i} + ma_y\hat{j} + ma_z\hat{k}$$

Scalar Product in Component form: If $\vec{a} = a_1\hat{i} + a_2\hat{j} + a_3\hat{k}$ and $\vec{b} = b_1\hat{i} + b_2\hat{j} + b_3\hat{k}$ than $\vec{a}.\vec{b} = a_1b_1 + a_2b_2 + a_3b_3$

$$\because \hat{i}.\hat{i} = \hat{j}.\hat{j} = \hat{k}.\hat{k} = 1 \text{ and } \hat{i}.\hat{j} = \hat{j}.\hat{i} = 0,\ \hat{j}.\hat{k} = \hat{k}.\hat{j} = 0,\ \hat{k}.\hat{i} = \hat{i}.\hat{k} = 0$$

Projection of a vector along another vector: We know that a_x, a_y, a_z in equation $\vec{a} = a_x\hat{i} + a_y\hat{j} + a_z\hat{k}$ are components of $\vec{a}$ along the x, y, z axes. We can also define the component or projection of $\vec{a}$ along any other vector $\vec{b}$ using the concept of scalar product.

Suppose $\vec{a}$ and $\vec{b}$ are non-zero vectors and the angle between them is θ. Then the real number $p = |\vec{a}|\cos\theta = \frac{\vec{a}.\vec{b}}{|\vec{b}|}$ is called the projection or component $\vec{a}$ of $\vec{a}$ in the direction of $\vec{b}$

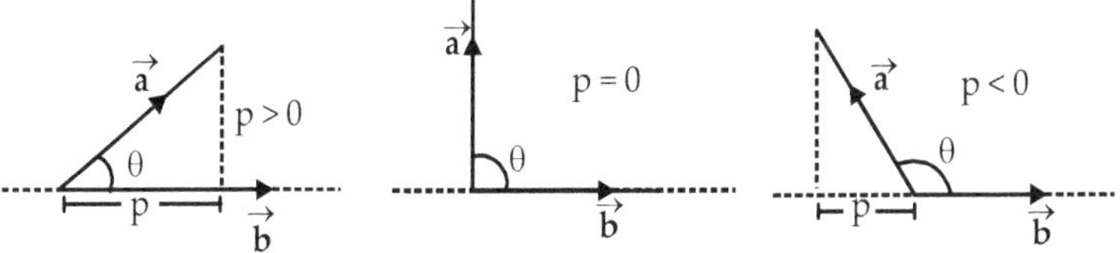

Fig. 1.16: Component of a vector $\vec{a}$ in the direction of a vector $\vec{b}$

If a=0, then θ is undefined and we get p=0.

Similarly, the projection of $\vec{b}$ on $\vec{a}$ is the real number $q = |\vec{b}|\cos\theta = \frac{\vec{a}.\vec{b}}{|\vec{a}|}$

Angle between two vectors: If $\vec{a}$ and $\vec{b}$ are two non-zero vectors, then an angle θ between them are $\theta = \cos^{-1}\left(\frac{\vec{a}.\vec{b}}{ab}\right)$ or $\theta = \cos^{-1}\left(\frac{\vec{a}.\vec{b}}{\sqrt{\vec{a}.\vec{a}}\sqrt{\vec{b}.\vec{b}}}\right)$

Vector Product in component form: Let two vectors $\vec{a}$ and $\vec{b}$ be given as $\vec{a} = a_1\hat{i} + a_2\hat{j} + a_3\hat{k}$, $\vec{b} = b_1\hat{i} + b_2\hat{j} + b_3\hat{k}$ then vector product in its component form, $\vec{a}\times\vec{b} = (a_2b_3 - a_3b_2)\hat{i} + (a_3b_1 - a_1b_3)\hat{j} + (a_1b_2 - a_2b_1)\hat{k}$

It is simply the expansion of a 3×3 determinant, $\vec{a}\times\vec{b} = \begin{vmatrix} \hat{i} & \hat{j} & \hat{k} \\ a_1 & a_2 & a_3 \\ b_1 & b_2 & b_3 \end{vmatrix}$

Scalar Triple Product $\vec{a}.(\vec{b}\times\vec{c})$: Consider the parallelogram whose concurrent edges OA, OB, OC have the lengths and directions of the vectors $\vec{a}, \vec{b}, \vec{c}$ respectively. Then the vector $\vec{b}\times\vec{c}$ denotes the vector area of the parallelogram with OB and OC as adjacent sides and is denoted by $n\hat{n}$ or $\hat{n}$ where n is the area of the parallelogram OBDC and

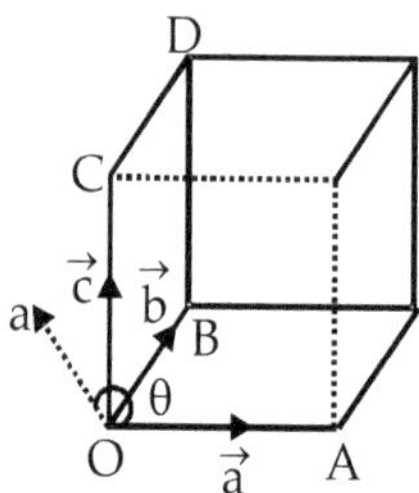

Fig. 1.17

$\hat{n}$ is a unit vector perpendicular to the parallelogram and in the positive sense of rotation from OB to OC.

If θ be the angle between $\hat{n}$ and $\vec{a}$, then $\vec{a}\cdot\hat{n} = a\cos\theta$ is the projection of OA along $\hat{n}$, i.e. $\vec{a}\cdot\hat{n}$ is the length of the perpendicular from A on the plane of the parallelogram OBDC.

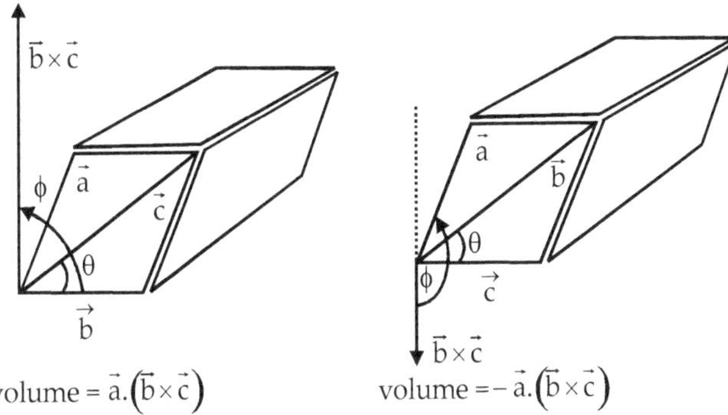

Fig. 1.18

Now, the volume V of parallelepiped is given by

V = Area OBDC × perpendicular from A on OBDC

$= na \quad \cos\theta = \vec{a}\cdot\hat{n} \; = \vec{a}.(\vec{b}\times\vec{c})$.

This is usually written as $[\vec{a}\vec{b}\vec{c}]$.

Thus, $V = \pm[\vec{a}\vec{b}\vec{c}]$ according as the angle θ is acute or obtuse.

Scalar triple product in component form: Taking $\vec{a} = a_1\hat{i} + a_2\hat{j} + a_3\hat{k}$, $\vec{b} = b_1\hat{i} + b_2\hat{j} + b_3\hat{k}$ and $\vec{c} = c_1\hat{i} + c_2\hat{j} + c_3\hat{k}$

we get $\vec{b}\times\vec{c} = (b_2c_3 - b_3c_2)\hat{i} + (b_3c_1 - b_1c_3)\hat{j} + (b_1c_2 - b_2c_1)\hat{k}$

$$\therefore \vec{a}\cdot(\vec{b}\times\vec{c}) = a_1(b_2c_3 - b_3c_2) + a_2(b_3c_1 - b_1c_3) + a_3(b_1c_2 - b_2c_1) = \begin{vmatrix} a_1 & a_2 & a_3 \\ b_1 & b_2 & b_3 \\ c_1 & c_2 & c_3 \end{vmatrix}$$

Similarly, $(\vec{a}\times\vec{b})\cdot\vec{c} = \begin{vmatrix} c_1 & c_2 & c_3 \\ a_1 & a_2 & a_3 \\ b_1 & b_2 & b_3 \end{vmatrix}$

Properties of the scalar triple product:

- Interchange of two rows reverses the sign of the determinant. $\vec{a}\cdot(\vec{b}\times\vec{c}) = -\vec{b}\cdot(\vec{c}\times\vec{a}) = -\vec{a}\cdot(\vec{c}\times\vec{b})$
- Interchanging the rows twice we get $\vec{a}\cdot(\vec{b}\times\vec{c}) = \vec{b}\cdot(\vec{c}\times\vec{a}) = \vec{c}\cdot(\vec{a}\times\vec{b})$
- Dot product is commutative, so $\vec{a}\cdot(\vec{b}\times\vec{c}) = (\vec{a}\times\vec{b})\cdot\vec{c}$

- For any constant k, $\left[k\vec{a}.(\vec{b}\times\vec{c})\right]=k\left[\vec{a}\cdot(\vec{b}\times\vec{c})\right]$
- If $\vec{a}\times\vec{b}$ is perpendicular to $\vec{a}$, we have $\vec{a}.(\vec{a}\times\vec{b})=0$

Vector Triple Product $\vec{a}\times(\vec{b}\times\vec{c})$: Let $\vec{P}=\vec{a}\times(\vec{b}\times\vec{c})$. Then $\vec{P}$ is a vector perpendicular to the vector $\vec{a}$ and also to $\vec{b}\times\vec{c}$. But $\vec{b}\times\vec{c}$ is normal to the plane of $\vec{b}$ and $\vec{c}$, so that $\vec{P}$ must lie in the plane of $\vec{b}$ and $\vec{c}$, and as such it can be written as $\vec{P}=\vec{a}\times(\vec{b}\times\vec{c})=l\vec{b}+m\vec{c}$ ...(xxii)

Multiplying both sides of (xxii) scalarly by $\vec{a}$, $\vec{P}\cdot\vec{a}=l\vec{b}\cdot\vec{a}+m\vec{c}\cdot\vec{a}$

...(xxiii)

Since $\vec{P}$ is perpendicular to $\vec{a}$, we have $\vec{P}\,.\vec{a}\ =0$ ...(xxiv)

$\therefore$ From (xxiii) and (xxiv), we get $\frac{l}{\vec{c}\cdot\vec{a}}=\frac{-m}{\vec{b}\cdot\vec{a}}=k$ (say)

Putting these values l, m in (xxii) we get $\vec{P}=\vec{a}\times(\vec{b}\times\vec{c})=k(c\cdot\vec{a}\vec{b}-\vec{b}\cdot\vec{a}\vec{c})$

...(xxv)

To find the value of k, we proceed as follows:

Let $\hat{j}$ be the unit vector along $\vec{b}$ and let $\hat{k}$ be perpendicular to $\vec{b}$ and in the plane of $\vec{b}$ and $\vec{c}$. Then $\vec{b}=b_2\hat{j}$, $\vec{c}=c_2\hat{j}+c_3\hat{k}$

Then let the third vector $\vec{a}$ in terms of $\hat{i},\hat{j},\hat{k}$ be $a_1\hat{i}+a_2\hat{j}+a_3\hat{k}$; $\hat{i},\hat{j},\hat{k}$ have been taken in a right handed system.

Then $\vec{b}\times\vec{c}=b_2\hat{j}\times\left(c_2\hat{j}+c_3\hat{k}\right)=b_2c_3\hat{j}\times\hat{k}=b_2c_3\hat{i}$.

Therefore, $\vec{a}\times(\vec{b}\times\vec{c})=\left(a_1\hat{i}+a_2\hat{j}+a_3\hat{k}\right)\times\left(b_2c_3\hat{i}\right)$

$=a_2b_2c_3\hat{j}\times\hat{i}+a_3b_2c_3\hat{k}\times\hat{i}\ =a_3b_2c_3\hat{j}-a_2b_2c_3\hat{k}$ ...(xxvi)

Also $\vec{c}\cdot\vec{a}\vec{b}-\vec{b}\cdot\vec{a}\vec{c}=\left(c_2\hat{j}+c_3\hat{k}\right)\cdot\left(a_1\hat{i}+a_2\hat{j}+a_3\hat{k}\right)b_3\hat{j}$

$-b_2\hat{j}\cdot\left(a_1\hat{i}+a_2\hat{j}+a_3\hat{k}\right)\left(c_2\hat{j}+c_3\hat{k}\right)$

$=(c_3a_2+c_3a_3)b_2\hat{j}-a_2b_2\left(c_2\hat{j}+c_3\hat{k}\right)\ =a_3c_3b_2\hat{j}-a_2b_2c_3\hat{k}$ ...(xxvii)

From (xxv), (xxvi), and (xxvii), we find that $k=1$

Hence, $\vec{a}\times(\vec{b}\times\vec{c})=\vec{a}.\vec{c}\vec{b}-\vec{a}.\vec{b}\vec{c}$

Similarly, $\vec{b}\times(\vec{c}\times\vec{a})=\vec{b}\cdot\vec{a}\vec{c}-\vec{b}\cdot\vec{c}\vec{a}$ and $\vec{c}\times(\vec{a}\times\vec{b})=\vec{c}\cdot\vec{b}\vec{a}-\vec{c}\cdot\vec{a}\vec{b}$

Quadruple Products of Vectors: Quadruple product means the product of four vectors. Some of the relevant quadruple products are $(\vec{a}\times\vec{b})\cdot(\vec{c}\times\vec{d}), (\vec{a}\times\vec{b})\times(\vec{c}\times\vec{d})$ and $\vec{a}\times[\vec{b}\times(\vec{c}\times\vec{d})]$. Here we will state their simplified expressions;

$$(a\times b).(c\times d)=(a.c)(b.d)-(a.d)(b.c)$$
$$(a\times b)\times(c\times d)=[a.(b\times d)]c-[a.(b\times c)]d$$
$$a\times[b\times(c\times d)]=(b.d)(a\times c)-(b.c)(a\times d)$$

Polar Vectors: If the direction of some of the vector quantities is clearly indicated by the direction of motion of a system then such vectors are called polar vectors. For example, displacement, velocity, acceleration, etc.

Axial Vectors: If the direction of some of the vector quantities does not indicate the direction of rotation of the body. Their direction is taken to be along the axis of rotation then such vectors are called axial vectors.

For example, angular velocity, angular acceleration, angular momentum, etc.

Note: If we transform like $x'=-x,\ y'=-y,\ z'=-z$

Such a transformation is called the parity transformation.

Therefore, if a vector changes sign under the parity transformation, it is called a proper or a polar vector and the vectors which do not change sign under a parity transformation are called axial vectors.

Solved Practical Problems

Q1. Draw a figure to show that

$$\vec{a}-(\vec{b}-\vec{c})=(\vec{a}-\vec{b})+\vec{c}$$

Ans.

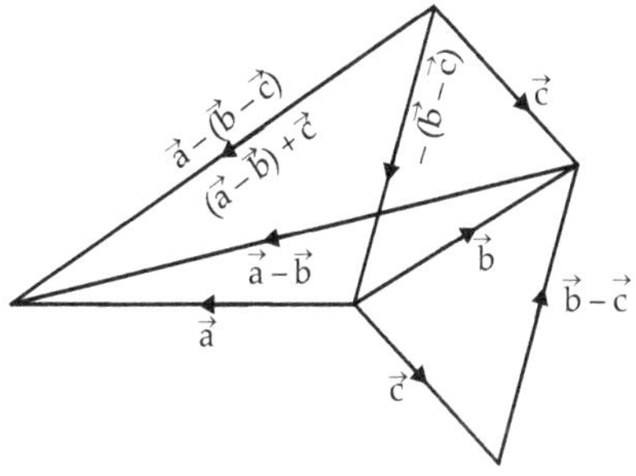

Fig. 1.19

Q2. Let $\vec{V}$ be the wind velocity of 50 $km\,h^{-1}$ from north-east. Write down the vector representing a wind velocity of (i) 75 $km\,h^{-1}$ from north-east, (ii) 100 $km\,h^{-1}$ from south-west, in terms of $\vec{V}$.

Ans.

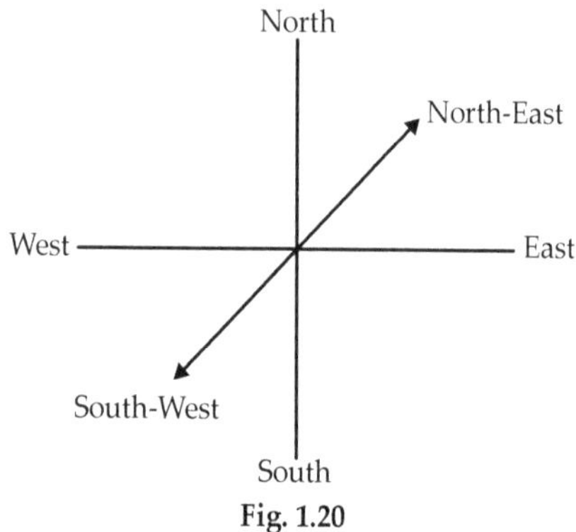

Fig. 1.20

(i) For 50 $km\,h^{-1}$ from North-East wind velocity is $= \vec{V}$

$\therefore$ For 75 $km\,h^{-1}$ from North-East wind velocity is $= \dfrac{\vec{V}\times 75}{50} = \dfrac{3}{2}\vec{V}$

(ii) South-West is opposite direction from North-East.

So for 100 $km\,h^{-1}$ from south-west wind

velocity is $= \dfrac{-\vec{V}\times 100}{50} = -2\vec{V}$

Q3. (a) Find the vectors in following figure equal to the vector $\vec{a}$ shown there.

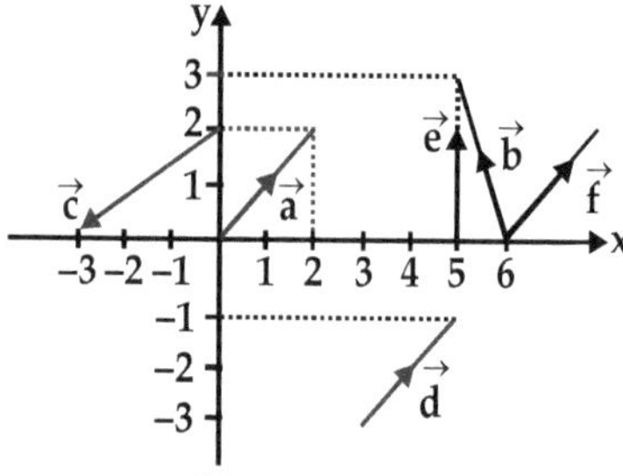

Ans. The vectors $\vec{d}$ and $\vec{f}$.

(b) Four forces, $\vec{F}_1, \vec{F}_2, \vec{F}_3$ and $\vec{F}_4$, all in the same plane, are applied at a point. (See following figure). Find graphically the resultant $\vec{F}$ of these forces through the point O. Show that it is always the same,

whatever be the order in which we add vectors. Draw at least two different sequences for adding these vectors.

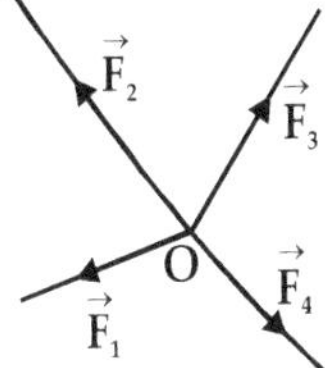

Ans. Two different sequences for obtaining the resultant $\vec{F}$ are shown in [Fig. 1.21(a),(b)]. The resultant is the same.

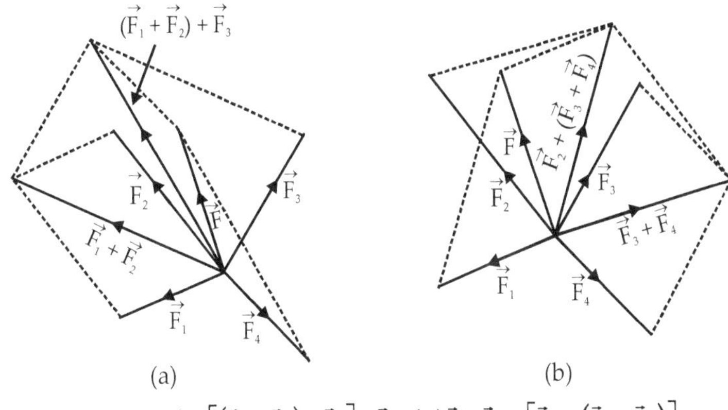

Fig. 1.21: (a) $\vec{F} = \left[\left(\vec{F}_1 + \vec{F}_2\right) + \vec{F}_3\right] + \vec{F}_4$; (b) $\vec{F} = \vec{F}_1 + \left[\vec{F}_2 + \left(\vec{F}_3 + \vec{F}_4\right)\right]$;

(c) **Consider two displacements, one of magnitude 3 m and another of magnitude 4 m. Show graphically how the displacement vectors may be combined to get a resultant displacement of magnitude (i) 7m, (ii) 1m and (iii) 5m**

Ans. The graphical addition of the two vectors is shown in [Fig. 1.22 (a), (b) and (c)].

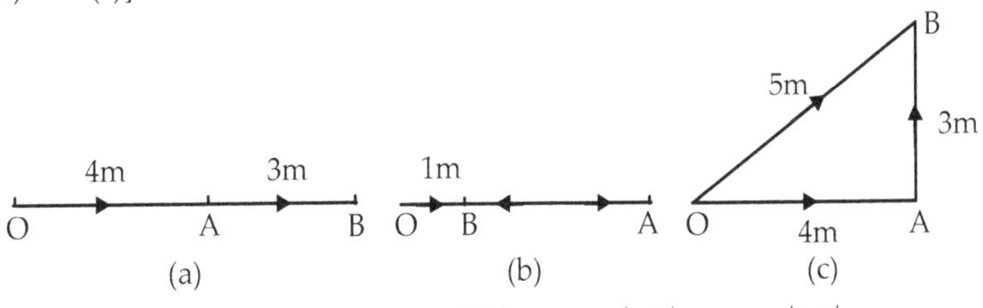

Fig. 1.22: $\vec{OB} = \vec{OA} + \vec{AB}$. (a) $|\vec{OB}| = 7m$; (b) $|\vec{OB}| = 1m$; (c) $|\vec{OB}| = 5m$;

Q4. A radar station detects an aeroplane approaching from the east. At first sighting, the aeroplane is 500m away at 30° above the horizon.

The aeroplane is tracked for another 120°in the vertical plane containing the east-west direction. At final sighting it is 1000m away from the radar (See following figure). Find the displacement of the aeroplane in component form during the period of observation.

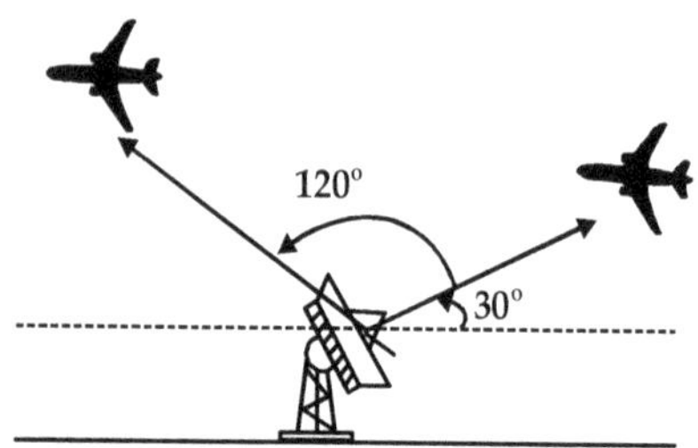

Ans. Taking the x-axis to be in the direction of east and the y-axis perpendicular to it in the vertical plane containing the aeroplane. Let the origin of the system be at point O of the radar dish. Let the displacement vector at initial sighting be $\vec{d}_1$. Then $d_1 = 500m$ and $\theta_1 = 30°$.

$$\therefore d_{x_1} = d_1 \cos\theta_1 = (500m)\cos 30° = 250\sqrt{3}m,$$

$$d_{y_1} = d_1 \sin\theta_1 = (500m)\sin 30° = 250m$$

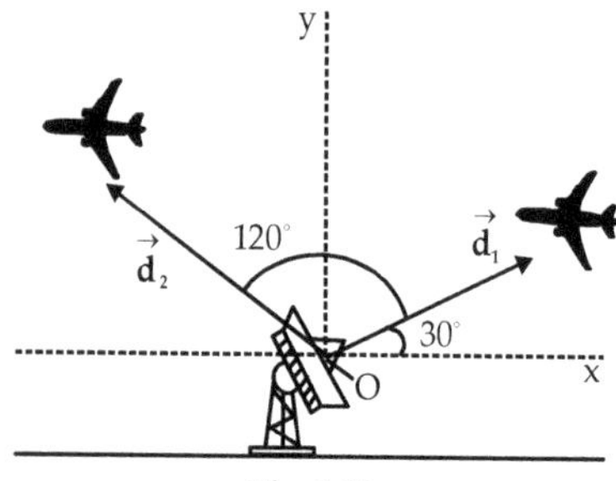

Fig. 1.23

Let $\vec{d}_2$ be its displacement vector at final sighting. Then

$$d_2 = 1000m, \theta_2 = 120° + 30° = 150°$$

$$\therefore d_{x_2} = d_2 \cos\theta_2 = (1000m)(\cos 150°) = -500\sqrt{3}m$$

$$d_{y_2} = d_2 \sin\theta_2 = (1000m)(\sin 150°) = 500m$$

The resultant displacement is then $\vec{d} = \vec{d}_2 - \vec{d}_1 = (d_{x_2} - d_{x_1})\hat{i} + (d_{y_2} - d_{y_1})\hat{j} = (-500\sqrt{3} - 250\sqrt{3})m\hat{i} + (500 - 250)m\hat{j}$.

$$\text{or } \vec{d} = \left[(-750\sqrt{3}m)\hat{i} + (250m)\hat{j}\right]$$

Q5. Show that for two vectors $\vec{a}$ and $\vec{b}$ given as

$$\vec{a} = a_1\hat{i} + a_2\hat{j} + a_3\hat{k}$$

$$\vec{b} = b_1\hat{i} + b_2\hat{j} + b_3\hat{k}$$

$$\vec{a}.\vec{b} = a_1b_1 + a_2b_2 + a_3b_3$$

Ans. Given, $\vec{a} = a_1\hat{i} + a_2\hat{j} + a_3\hat{k}$ and $\vec{b} = b_1\hat{i} + b_2\hat{j} + b_3\hat{k}$

Now, $\vec{a}.\vec{b} = a_1b_1(\hat{i}.\hat{i}) + a_1b_2(\hat{i}.\hat{j}) + a_1b_3(\hat{i}.\hat{k}) + a_2b_1(\hat{j}.\hat{i}) + a_2b_2(\hat{j}.\hat{j}) + a_2b_3(\hat{j}.\hat{k})$

$+a_3b_1(\hat{k}.\hat{i}) + a_3b_2(\hat{k}.\hat{j}) + a_3b_3(\hat{k}.\hat{k})$

Since, we know that, $\hat{i}.\hat{i} = \hat{j}.\hat{j} = \hat{k}.\hat{k} = 1$ and $\hat{i}.\hat{j} = \hat{j}.\hat{i} = \hat{j}.\hat{k} = \hat{k}.\hat{j} = \hat{k}.\hat{i} = \hat{i}.\hat{k} = 0$

$\Rightarrow \vec{a}.\vec{b} = a_1b_1 + a_2b_2 + a_3b_3$

Q6. Discuss magnetic and electric flux as a scalar product.

Ans. Consider the magnetic flux. Consider a surface of area A in a region where a magnetic field exists. The area could be a rectangle, a circle, or any other shape. Let the magnetic field $\vec{B}$ be perpendicular to the surface.

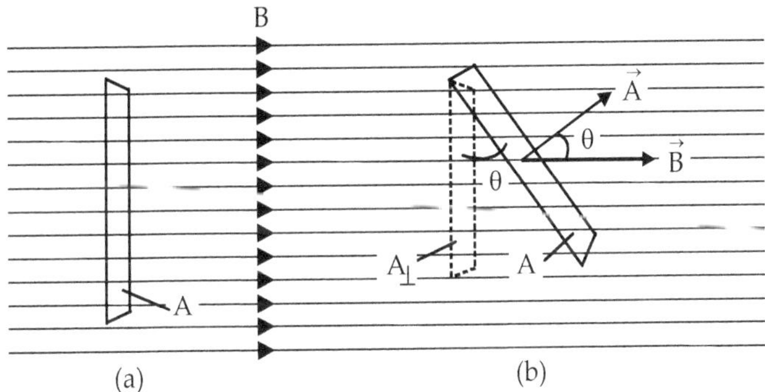

Fig. 1.24: A uniform magnetic field $\vec{B}$ (indicated by the parallel field lines) passing through a surface of area A which is (a) perpendicular to $\vec{B}$, (b) not perpendicular to $\vec{B}$. The dashed surface of area A in (b) is the projection of A perpendicular to field $\vec{B}$.

Then the magnetic flux Φ_B through this surface is defined as the product of $\vec{B}$ and $\vec{A}$, i.e. $\Phi_B = BA$

If the magnetic field $\vec{B}$ makes an angle θ with the normal to the surface [Fig. 1.24(b)] then Φ_B is defined as $\Phi_B = BA_{\perp} = BA\cos\theta$ ($\vec{B}$ uniform) where $A_{\perp}$ is the projection of the area A on a surface perpendicular to $\vec{B}$.

We can again represent the area A of a surface by a vector $\vec{A}$. The magnitude of $\vec{A}$ is A and its direction is perpendicular to the surface as shown in [Fig. 1.24(b)]. The angle θ is also the angle between $\vec{B}$ and $\vec{A}$ so we can write $\Phi_B = \vec{B}\bullet\vec{A}$ ($\vec{B}$ uniform) ...(i)

We can also interpret Φ_B in terms of the field lines associated with the magnetic field. The field lines can always be drawn so that B is proportional to the number of field lines passing through a unit area perpendicular to the field. Now, if N is the number of field lines through $A_\perp$, then $B \propto \frac{N}{A_\perp}$, i.e. $N \propto BA_\perp = \Phi_B$

Thus, the magnetic flux through an area is proportional to the number of magnetic field lines passing through the area. Of course, the number of field lines cannot be counted. It is mentioned here only for the sake of visualising the concept of flux.

In analogy to Eq. (i), we define the electric flux due to a uniform electric field $\vec{E}$ through a surface of area A as $\Phi_E = \vec{E}\bullet\vec{A}$ ...(ii)

Φ_E through an area is also proportional to the number of electric field lines passing through the area.

Q7. When will the work done on a particle by a force $\vec{F}$ be (i) zero, even when it undergoes a finite displacement, and (ii) maximum?

Ans. The work done will be

(i) zero when $\vec{F}$ is perpendicular to the displacement $\vec{d}$

(ii) maximum when $\vec{F}$ is along $\vec{d}$.

Q8. Vectors $\vec{a}$ and $\vec{b}$ are given by

$$\vec{a} = 3\hat{i} - 2\hat{j} + \hat{k} \text{ and } \vec{b} = -2\hat{i} + 2\hat{j} + 4\hat{k}$$

(i) Find the magnitudes of $\vec{a}$ and $\vec{b}$ and the angle between them.

Ans. $|\vec{a}| = \sqrt{\vec{a}\bullet\vec{a}} = \sqrt{a_1^2 + a_2^2 + a_3^2} = \sqrt{(3)^2 + (-2)^2 + (1)^2} = \sqrt{14}$

$$|\vec{b}| = \sqrt{\vec{b}\bullet\vec{b}} = \sqrt{b_1^2 + b_2^2 + b_3^2} = \sqrt{(-2)^2 + (2)^2 + (4)^2} = \sqrt{24} = 2\sqrt{6}$$

$$\theta = \cos^{-1}\frac{\vec{a}\cdot\vec{a}}{\vec{a}\vec{b}} = \cos^{-1}\left(\frac{-6-4+4}{\sqrt{14}2\sqrt{16}}\right) = \cos^{-1}\left(\frac{-6}{4\sqrt{21}}\right) = \cos^{-1}\left(\frac{-3}{2\sqrt{21}}\right)$$

(ii) Which of the following vectors is perpendicular to $\vec{a}$?

$$\vec{c} = -\hat{i} - 4\hat{j} + 2\hat{k},\ \vec{d} = -3\hat{i} + \hat{k},\ \vec{e} = 2\hat{i} + 2\hat{j} - 2\hat{k}$$

Ans. Consider $\vec{a}.\vec{c}$, $\vec{a}.\vec{d}$ and $\vec{a}.\vec{e}$:

$$\vec{a}.\vec{c} = -3 + 8 + 2 = 7$$

$$\vec{a}.\vec{d} = -9 + 1 = -8$$

$\vec{a}.\vec{e} = 6 - 4 - 2 = 0$

$\because \vec{a}.\vec{e} = 0, \vec{e}$ is perpendicular to $\vec{a}$.

(iii) Find the projection of the vector $\vec{a} + \frac{1}{2}\vec{b}$ onto $\vec{a}$.

Ans. The projection p is

$$p = \frac{\left(\vec{a} + \frac{1}{2}\vec{b}\right).\vec{a}}{|\vec{a}|} = \frac{\vec{a}.\vec{a} + \frac{1}{2}\vec{b}.\vec{a}}{|\vec{a}|} = \frac{14 + \frac{1}{2}(-6)}{\sqrt{14}} = \frac{11}{\sqrt{14}}$$

Q9. Discuss Area as a vector.

Ans. Consider the area A of the parallelogram formed by the vectors $\vec{c}$ and $\vec{d}$ [Fig. 1.25]. It is given by

$$A = \text{base} \times \text{height} = c\, d \sin\theta = |\vec{c} \times \vec{d}|$$

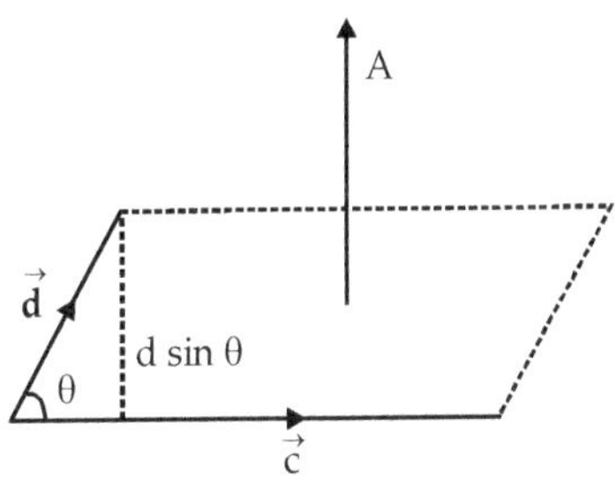

Fig. 1.25: Area as a vector

If we think of $\vec{A}$ as a vector then we can write $\vec{A} = \vec{c} \times \vec{d}$

By this definition, the direction of area is perpendicular to the plane of the area and is given by the right-hand rule. Thus, $\vec{A}$ is parallel to a normal to the surface (Fig. 1.25). The sense of $\vec{A}$ is arbitrary because we could also have defined $\vec{A} = \vec{d} \times \vec{c}$. However, once we choose the sense, it is unique.

Q10. (a) Find x and y such that the vectors $\vec{B} = x\hat{i} + 3\hat{j}$ and $\vec{C} = 2\hat{i} + y\hat{j}$ are each parallel to $\vec{A} = 5\hat{i} + 6\hat{j}$

Ans. If $\vec{B}$ and $\vec{C}$ are to be parallel to $\vec{A}$ then $\vec{B} \times \vec{A} = 0$, $\vec{C} \times \vec{A} = 0$

Now, $\vec{B} \times \vec{A} = (x\hat{i} + 3\hat{j}) \times (5\hat{i} + 6\hat{j}) = 6x\hat{k} - 15\hat{k} = (6x - 15)\hat{k} = \vec{0}, \Rightarrow 6x - 15 = 0$

$\because \hat{k} \neq 0$

$\therefore x = \frac{15}{6} = 2.5$

$\vec{C}\times\vec{A} = (2\hat{i}+y\hat{j})\times(5\hat{i}+6\hat{j}) = 12\hat{k}-5y\hat{k} = \vec{0} \Rightarrow 12-5y=0. \because \hat{k}\neq 0$

$$\therefore\ y = \frac{12}{5} = 2.4$$

(b) Consider a force $\vec{F} = (-3\hat{i}+\hat{j}+5\hat{k})$ newton, acting at a point P $(7\hat{i}+3\hat{j}+\hat{k})$ m. What is the torque in Nm about the origin?

Ans. The displacement of P with respect to O is $\vec{r}$ where $\vec{r} = 7\hat{i}+3\hat{j}+\hat{k}$ m

$$\therefore \vec{\tau} = \vec{r}\times\vec{F} = (7\hat{i}+3\hat{j}+\hat{k})\text{m}\times(-3\hat{i}+\hat{j}+5\hat{k})\text{N}$$

Hence, $\vec{\tau} = \left[\hat{i}(15-1)+\hat{j}(-3-35)+\hat{k}(7+9)\right]\text{Nm} = (14\hat{i}-38\hat{j}+16\hat{k})\text{Nm}$

Q11. Let $\vec{a} = a_1\hat{i}+a_2\hat{j}+a_3\hat{k}$, $\vec{b} = b_1\hat{i}+b_2\hat{j}+b_3\hat{k}$, and $\vec{c} = c_1\hat{i}+c_2\hat{j}+c_3\hat{k}$ Fill up the following blank spaces and express $\vec{a}.(\vec{b}\times\vec{c})$ in terms of the components of a, b and c.

(a) $\vec{b}\times\vec{c}$ =....

Ans. $\vec{b}\times\vec{c} = \hat{i}(b_2c_3-b_3c_2)+\hat{j}(b_3c_1-b_1c_3)+\hat{k}(b_1c_2-b_2c_1)$

(b) $\vec{a}.(\vec{b}\times\vec{c})$= ...

Ans. $\vec{a}\cdot(\vec{b}\times\vec{c}) = (a_1\hat{i}+a_2\hat{j}+a_3\hat{k}).\left[\hat{i}(b_2c_3-b_3c_2)+\hat{j}(b_3c_1-b_1c_3)+\hat{k}(b_1c_2-b_2c_1)\right]$

$$= a_1(b_2c_3-b_3c_2)+a_2(b_3c_1-b_1c_3)+a_3(b_1c_2-b_2c_1)$$

Q12. The volume of a tetrahedron is one-sixth of the volume of a parallelepiped. The three sides of a tetrahedron are given to be $\vec{a} = 2\hat{i}+3\hat{j}-4\hat{k}$, $\vec{b} = \hat{i}+2\hat{j}-\hat{k}$, $\vec{c} = 2\hat{i}+3\hat{j}+4\hat{k}$

Find the volume of the tetrahedron.

Ans. $V = \frac{1}{6}\left|\vec{a}.(\vec{b}\times\vec{c})\right|.$

Therefore, $$V = \frac{1}{6}\begin{vmatrix} 2 & 3 & -4 \\ 1 & 2 & -1 \\ 2 & 3 & 4 \end{vmatrix}$$

$$= \frac{1}{6}[2\times(2\times4+1\times3)+3\times(-1\times2-1\times4)-4(1\times3-2\times2)]$$

Or $V = \frac{1}{6}[22-18+4] = \frac{8}{6} = \frac{4}{3}$

Q13. Discuss forces on current carrying conductors.

Ans. Consider two wires 1 and 2 carrying currents i_1 and i_2, respectively [Fig. 1.26]. Let $d\vec{l}_1$ and $d\vec{l}_2$ be infinitesimal elements of the wires in the direction of current flow. The force experienced by an infinitesimal element $d\vec{l}_2$ due to $d\vec{l}_1$ is given by $\vec{F} = \frac{\mu_0}{4\pi} i_1 i_2 \frac{d\vec{l}_2 \times (d\vec{l}_1 \times \vec{r})}{r^3}$

Here μ_0 is the permeability of free space and $\vec{r}$ is the position vector of $d\vec{l}_2$ with respect to $d\vec{l}_1$. We can understand this rather complicated expression from [Fig. 1.26]. Here $d\vec{l}_1 \times \vec{r}$ is a vector perpendicular to the plane of this paper and points into it. So $d\vec{l}_2 \times (d\vec{l}_1 \times \vec{r})$ is a vector along BA. This means that parallel wires carrying current in the same direction attract each other.

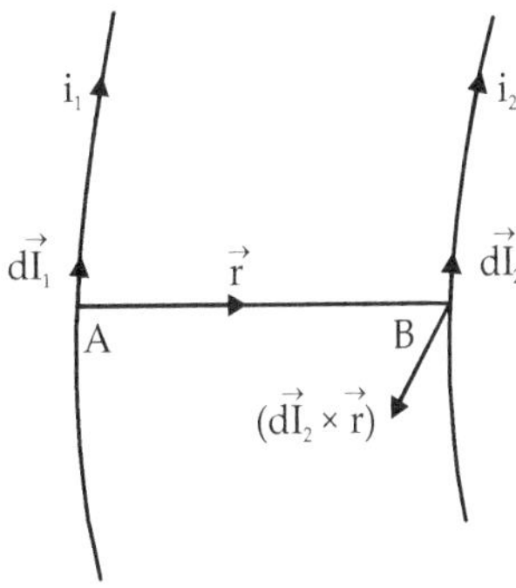

Fig. 1.26: Forces on current-carrying conductor. If the direction of any one of the currents is reversed, then either $d\vec{l}_1$ or $d\vec{l}_2$ will be in the opposite direction. So the force will be in such a direction that the wires repel each other. Thus, parallel wires carrying currents in opposite directions repel each other.

Q14. Prove that the value of the scalar triple product of $\vec{a}, \vec{b}, \vec{c}$ remains unchanged if the cyclic order of the vectors is maintained, i.e. prove that

$$\vec{a} \cdot (\vec{b} \times \vec{c}) = \vec{b} \cdot (\vec{c} \times \vec{a}) = \vec{c} \cdot (\vec{a} \times \vec{b}).$$

Ans. Let $\vec{a} = a_1 \hat{i} + a_2 \hat{j} + a_3 \hat{k}$, $\vec{b} = b_1 \hat{i} + b_2 \hat{j} + b_3 \hat{k}$, $\vec{c} = c_1 \hat{i} + c_2 \hat{j} + c_3 \hat{k}$.

$$\Rightarrow \vec{a}.(\vec{b} \times \vec{c}) = a_1(b_2c_3 - b_3c_2) - a_2(b_1c_3 - b_3c_1) + a_3(b_1c_2 - b_2c_1)$$

$$= \begin{vmatrix} a_1 & a_2 & a_3 \\ b_1 & b_2 & b_3 \\ c_1 & c_2 & c_3 \end{vmatrix} = - \begin{vmatrix} b_1 & b_2 & b_3 \\ a_1 & a_2 & a_3 \\ c_1 & c_2 & c_3 \end{vmatrix}, \text{ interchanging } R_1 \text{ and } R_2$$

$$= \begin{vmatrix} b_1 & b_2 & b_3 \\ c_1 & c_2 & c_3 \\ a_1 & a_2 & a_3 \end{vmatrix}, \text{ interchanging } R_2 \text{ and } R_3$$

$= \vec{b}.(\vec{c}\times\vec{a}).$ ...(i)

Again $\begin{vmatrix} a_1 & a_2 & a_3 \\ b_1 & b_2 & b_3 \\ c_1 & c_2 & c_3 \end{vmatrix} = -\begin{vmatrix} c_1 & c_2 & c_3 \\ b_1 & b_2 & b_3 \\ a_1 & a_2 & a_3 \end{vmatrix}$, interchanging R_1 and R_3

$= \begin{vmatrix} c_1 & c_2 & c_3 \\ a_1 & a_2 & a_3 \\ b_1 & b_2 & b_3 \end{vmatrix}$, interchanging R_2 and R_3

$= \vec{c}.(\vec{a}\times\vec{b}).$ ...(ii)

From (i) and (ii), we have

$\vec{a}.(\vec{b}\times\vec{c}) = \vec{b}.(\vec{c}\times\vec{a}) = \vec{c}.(\vec{a}\times\vec{b}).$

Q15. Prove that

(a) $\vec{a}\cdot\vec{b}\times\vec{c} = \vec{a}\times\vec{b}\cdot\vec{c}.$

Ans. We have $\vec{a}\cdot\vec{b}\times\vec{c} = \vec{a}\cdot(\vec{b}\times\vec{c})$

$= \vec{c}\cdot(\vec{a}\times\vec{b})$ [$\because$ scalar triple product is unchanged if the cyclic order of the vectors is maintained]

$= (\vec{a}\times\vec{b})\cdot\vec{c}$ [$\because$ dot product of two vectors is commutative]

(b) Show that $\hat{i}\cdot\hat{j}\times\hat{k} = 1.$

Ans. We have $\hat{i}\cdot\hat{j}\times\hat{k} = \hat{i}\cdot(\hat{j}\times\hat{k}) = \hat{i}\cdot\hat{i}$ [$\because \hat{j}\times\hat{k} = \hat{i}$]

$= 1.$

(c) Show that $[\lambda\vec{a}+\mu\vec{b}, \vec{c}, \vec{d}] = \lambda[\vec{a}, \vec{c}, \vec{d}] + \mu[\vec{b}, \vec{c}, \vec{d}].$

Ans. We have $[\lambda\vec{a}+\mu\vec{b}, \vec{c}, \vec{d}] = (\lambda\vec{a}+\mu\vec{b})\cdot(\vec{c}\times\vec{d})$

$= \lambda\vec{a}\cdot(\vec{c}\times\vec{d}) + \mu\vec{b}\cdot(\vec{c}\times\vec{d})$, by distributive law for dot product

$= \lambda[\vec{a}, \vec{c}, \vec{d}] + \mu[\vec{b}, \vec{c}, \vec{d}].$

(d) Prove that $[\hat{i}-\hat{j}, \hat{j}-\hat{k}, \hat{k}-\hat{i}] = 0.$

Ans. We have $[\hat{i}-\hat{j}, \hat{j}-\hat{k}, \hat{k}-\hat{i}]$

$= (\hat{i}-\hat{j})\cdot\{(\hat{j}-\hat{k})\times(\hat{k}-\hat{i})\} = (\hat{i}-\hat{j})\cdot(\hat{j}\times\hat{k} - \hat{j}\times\hat{i} - \hat{k}\times\hat{k} + \hat{k}\times\hat{i})$

$= (\hat{i}-\hat{j})\cdot(\hat{i}+\hat{k}+\hat{j}) = \hat{i}\cdot\hat{i}+\hat{i}\cdot\hat{k}+\hat{i}\cdot\hat{j}-\hat{j}\cdot\hat{i}-\hat{j}\cdot\hat{k}-\hat{j}\cdot\hat{j}$

$= 1+0+0-0-0-1=0.$

Q16. Find the volume of the parallelepiped whose edges are represented by $\vec{a}=2\hat{i}-4\hat{j}+5\hat{k}, \vec{b}=\hat{i}-\hat{j}+\hat{k}, \vec{c}=3\hat{i}-5\hat{j}+2\hat{k}$.

Ans. The required volume of the parallelepiped is equal to the absolute value of $[\vec{a}\vec{b}\vec{c}]$.

$$\text{Now, } [\vec{a}\ \vec{b}\ \vec{c}] = \begin{vmatrix} 2 & -4 & 5 \\ 1 & -1 & 1 \\ 3 & -5 & 2 \end{vmatrix} = 2(-2+5)+4(2-3)+5(-5+3) = 6-4-10 = -8.$$

Neglecting the negative sign, we get the volume of the parallelepiped = 8 cubic units.

Q17. Find the volume of the parallelepiped whose edges are represented by

(i) $\vec{a}=2\hat{i}-3\hat{j}+4\hat{k}, \vec{b}=\hat{i}+2\hat{j}-\hat{k}, \vec{c}=3\hat{i}-\hat{j}+2\hat{k}$

Ans. The required volume of the parallelepiped is equal to the absolute value of $[\vec{a}\ \vec{b}\ \vec{c}]$. we have $[\vec{a}\vec{b}\vec{c}] = \begin{vmatrix} 2 & -3 & 4 \\ 1 & 2 & -1 \\ 3 & -1 & 2 \end{vmatrix}$

$= 2(4-1)+3(2+3)+4(-1-6)$, expanding the determinant along R_1

$= 2\times3+3\times5+4\times(-7) = 6+15-28 = -7$

Neglecting the negative sign, we get the volume of the parallelepiped = 7 cubic units.

(ii) $\vec{a}=\hat{i}-2\hat{j}+3\hat{k}, \vec{b}=2\hat{i}+\hat{j}-\hat{k}, \vec{c}=\hat{j}+\hat{k}$

Ans. The required volume $= \begin{vmatrix} 1 & -2 & 3 \\ 2 & 1 & -1 \\ 0 & 1 & 1 \end{vmatrix} = \begin{vmatrix} 1 & -2 & 3 \\ 0 & 5 & -7 \\ 0 & 1 & 1 \end{vmatrix}$, by R_2-2R_1

$= 1\times(5+7) = 12$ cubic units.

Q18. Prove that $\vec{a}\times(\vec{b}\times\vec{c})+\vec{b}\times(\vec{c}\times\vec{a})+\vec{c}\times(\vec{a}\times\vec{b})=0$.

Ans. We have $\vec{a}\times(\vec{b}\times\vec{c}) = (\vec{a}\cdot\vec{c})\vec{b}-(\vec{a}\cdot\vec{b})\vec{c}, \vec{b}\times(\vec{c}\times\vec{a}) = (\vec{b}\cdot\vec{a})\vec{c}-(\vec{b}\cdot\vec{c})\vec{a}$

and $\vec{c}\times(\vec{a}\times\vec{b}) = (\vec{c}\cdot\vec{b})\vec{a}-(\vec{c}\cdot\vec{a})\vec{b}$.

Adding these three expressions, we get $\vec{a}\times(\vec{b}\times\vec{c})+\vec{b}\times(\vec{c}\times\vec{a})+\vec{c}\times(\vec{a}\times\vec{b})$

$$=(\vec{a}\cdot\vec{c})\vec{b}-(\vec{a}\cdot\vec{b})\vec{c}+(\vec{b}\cdot\vec{a})\vec{c}-(\vec{b}\cdot\vec{c})\vec{a}+(\vec{c}\cdot\vec{b})\vec{a}-(\vec{c}\cdot\vec{a})\vec{b}$$

$$=\vec{0}.\ \left[\because \vec{a}\cdot\vec{c}=\vec{c}\cdot\vec{a}, \vec{a}\cdot\vec{b}=\vec{b}\cdot\vec{a}, \vec{b}\cdot\vec{c}=\vec{c}\cdot\vec{b}\right]$$

Q19. Verify the formula for vector triple product $\vec{a}\times(\vec{b}\times\vec{c})=(\vec{a}\cdot\vec{c})\vec{b}-(\vec{a}\cdot\vec{b})\vec{c}$

by taking $\vec{a}=\hat{i}+\hat{j}, \vec{b}=-\hat{i}+2\hat{k}, \vec{c}=\hat{j}+\hat{k}$.

Ans. We have $\vec{b}\times\vec{c}=(-\hat{i}+2\hat{k})\times(\hat{j}+\hat{k})$

$$=\begin{vmatrix}\hat{i} & \hat{j} & \hat{k}\\ -1 & 0 & 2\\ 0 & 1 & 1\end{vmatrix}=(0-2)\hat{i}-(-1-0)\hat{j}+(-1-0)\hat{k}=-2\hat{i}+\hat{j}-\hat{k}.$$

$$\therefore \vec{a}\times(\vec{b}\times\vec{c})=(\hat{i}+\hat{j})\times(-2\hat{i}+\hat{j}-\hat{k})=\begin{vmatrix}\hat{i} & \hat{j} & \hat{k}\\ 1 & 1 & 0\\ -2 & 1 & -1\end{vmatrix}$$

$$=(-1-0)\hat{i}-(-1-0)\hat{j}+(1+2)\hat{k}=-\hat{i}+\hat{j}+3\hat{k}. \qquad ...(i)$$

Again $(\vec{a}\cdot\vec{c})\vec{b}-(\vec{a}\cdot\vec{b})\vec{c}=\left[(\hat{i}+\hat{j})\cdot(\hat{j}+\hat{k})\right](-\hat{i}+2\hat{k})-\left[(\hat{i}+\hat{j})\cdot(-\hat{i}+2\hat{k})\right](\hat{j}+\hat{k})$

$$=(0+1+0)(-\hat{i}+2\hat{k})-(-1+0+0)(\hat{j}+\hat{k})=1(-\hat{i}+2\hat{k})+(\hat{j}+\hat{k})=-\hat{i}+\hat{j}+3\hat{k}. \qquad ...(ii)$$

From (i) and (ii), we see that $\vec{a}\times(\vec{b}\times\vec{c})=(\vec{a}\cdot\vec{c})\vec{b}-(\vec{a}\cdot\vec{b})\vec{c}$.

Q20. Show that $\hat{i}\times(\vec{a}\times\hat{i})+\hat{j}\times(\vec{a}\times\hat{j})+\hat{k}\times(\vec{a}\times\hat{k})=2\vec{a}$.

Ans. We have $\hat{i}\times(\vec{a}\times\hat{i})=(\hat{i}\cdot\hat{i})\vec{a}-(\hat{i}\cdot\vec{a})\hat{i}=\vec{a}-(\hat{i}\cdot\vec{a})\hat{i}$ $\quad[\because \hat{i}\cdot\hat{i}=1]$

$$\hat{j}\times(\vec{a}\times\hat{j})=(\hat{j}\cdot\hat{j})\vec{a}-(\hat{j}\cdot\vec{a})\hat{j}=\vec{a}-(\hat{j}\cdot\vec{a})\hat{j}\quad[\because \hat{j}\cdot\hat{j}=1]$$

and $\hat{k}\times(\vec{a}\times\hat{k})=(\hat{k}\cdot\hat{k})\vec{a}-(\hat{k}\cdot\vec{a})\hat{k}=\vec{a}-(\hat{k}\cdot\vec{a})\hat{k}\quad[\because \hat{k}\cdot\hat{k}=1]$

Adding these three expressions, we get

$$\hat{i}\times(\vec{a}\times\hat{i})+\hat{j}\times(\vec{a}\times\hat{j})+\hat{k}\times(\vec{a}\times\hat{k})=3\vec{a}-(\hat{i}\cdot\vec{a})\hat{i}-(\hat{j}\cdot\vec{a})\hat{j}-(\hat{k}\cdot\vec{a})\hat{k}$$

$= 3\vec{a} - \left[\left(\vec{a}\cdot\hat{i}\right)\hat{i} + \left(\vec{a}\cdot\hat{j}\right)\hat{j} + \left(\vec{a}\cdot\hat{k}\right)\hat{k}\right]$ $[\because \vec{a}\cdot\hat{j} = \hat{j}\cdot\vec{a}]$

Now, we shall show that $\vec{a} = \left(\vec{a}\cdot\hat{i}\right)\hat{i} + \left(\vec{a}\cdot\hat{j}\right)\hat{j} + \left(\vec{a}\cdot\hat{k}\right)\hat{k}$.

Let $\vec{a} = x\hat{i} + y\hat{j} + z\hat{k}$.

Taking dot product of both sides with $\hat{i}, \hat{j}$ and $\hat{k}$ successively, we get

$x = \vec{a}\cdot\hat{i}, y = \vec{a}\cdot\hat{j}, z = \vec{a}\cdot\hat{k}$.

$\therefore \vec{a} = \left(\vec{a}\cdot\hat{i}\right)\hat{i} + \left(\vec{a}\cdot\hat{j}\right)\hat{j} + \left(\vec{a}\cdot\hat{k}\right)\hat{k}$.

Hence $\hat{i}\times\left(\vec{a}\times\hat{i}\right) + \hat{j}\times\left(\vec{a}\times\hat{j}\right) + \hat{k}\times\left(\vec{a}\times\hat{k}\right) = 3\vec{a} - \vec{a} = 2\vec{a}$.

Q21. (a) Find a unit vector in the yz plane such that it is perpendicular to the vector $\vec{a} = \hat{i} + \hat{j} + \hat{k}$.

Ans. Since the unit vector is in yz plane, its components will be along the positive y and z directions. Let it be the vector $\hat{b} = m\hat{j} + n\hat{k}$, where m and n are numbers. Since $\hat{b}$ is a unit vector, its magnitude

$\left|\hat{b}\right| = \sqrt{m^2 + n^2} = 1$ or $m^2 + n^2 = 1$

Since $\hat{b}$ is perpendicular to $\vec{a} = \hat{i} + \hat{j} + \hat{k} \Rightarrow \vec{a}\cdot\vec{b} = \left(\hat{i} + \hat{j} + \hat{k}\right).\left(m\hat{j} + n\hat{k}\right) = 0$ or $m + n = 0$.

Substituting $m = -n$ in $m^2 + n^2 = 1$ we have $m^2 + n^2 = 2n^2 = 1$, or $n = \frac{1}{\sqrt{2}}$

$\therefore m = -\frac{1}{\sqrt{2}}$ Thus $\hat{b} = -\frac{1}{\sqrt{2}}\hat{j} + \frac{1}{\sqrt{2}}\hat{k}$

We can see that it can also be the vector $\hat{b} = +\frac{1}{\sqrt{2}}\hat{j} - \frac{1}{\sqrt{2}}\hat{k}$.

(b) A proton having a speed of 5.0×10^6 ms^{-1} in a uniform magnetic field feels a force of 8.0×10^{-14}N towards west when it moves vertically upward. When moving horizontally in a northerly direction it feels zero force. What is the magnitude and direction of the magnetic field in this region? Change on the proton = 1.6×10^{-19}C.

Ans. The force on the proton is given by $\vec{F} = q\vec{v}\times\vec{B}$

When the proton's velocity is in the north direction in the horizontal plane, the force on it is zero. This implies that $\vec{v}$ is parallel to $\vec{B}$. The direction of $\vec{B}$ is then in the north direction in the horizontal plane.

Therefore, when the proton moves vertically upward $\vec{v}$ is perpendicular to $\vec{B}$ and $\vec{F} = q\,v\,\vec{B}$

$$\text{or } \vec{B} = \frac{\vec{F}}{qv} = \frac{8\times10^{-14}\,\text{N}}{1.6\times10^{-19}\,\text{C}\times5.0\times10^{6}\,\text{ms}^{-1}} = 10^{-1}\,\text{Tesla}$$

Q22. Consider a current circuit in a prescribed magnetic field. The magnetic force on each circuit element $d\vec{l}$ is given by I ($d\vec{l}$ × B). Let the circuit be allowed to move under the influence of magnetic forces, such that an element is displaced by $d\vec{r}$ and at the same time I is held constant. Show that the mechanical work done by the force is dW = Id Φ_B where d Φ_B is the additional flux through the circuit.

Ans. Here, work done $dW = \vec{F}\,.\,d\vec{r} = I\left(d\vec{l}\times\vec{B}\right).d\vec{r} = d\vec{r}.I\left(d\vec{l}\times\vec{B}\right)$

Since, $\vec{a}\cdot\left(\vec{b}\times\vec{c}\right) = \left(\vec{a}\times\vec{b}\right)\cdot\vec{c}$

Hence, we have $dW = \vec{I}\left(d\vec{r}\times d\vec{l}\right).\vec{B}$

Now let $d\vec{A}$ define the area formed by $d\vec{r}$ and $d\vec{l}$, then $d\vec{A} = \left(d\vec{r}\times d\vec{l}\right)$

$\therefore\ dW = Id\vec{A}.\vec{B} = Id\Phi_B$ where $d\Phi_B = d\vec{A}.\vec{B}$.

Here $d\Phi_B$ is the flux of the magnetic field through $d\vec{A}$, i.e. It is the additional flux through the circuit.

Q23. Determine the angle between the vectors

$\vec{A} = -6\hat{i} - 4\hat{j} + 2\hat{k}$ and $\vec{B} = \hat{i} - 2\hat{j} - \hat{k}$ [June-2012, Q.No.-1(a)]

Ans. We have, $\vec{A} = -6\hat{i} - 4\hat{j} + 2\hat{k}$ and $\vec{B} = \hat{i} - 2\hat{j} - \hat{k}$

Now, $\vec{A}.\vec{B} = \left(-6\hat{i} - 4\hat{j} + 2\hat{k}\right).\left(\hat{i} - 2\hat{j} - \hat{k}\right) = -6 + 8 - 2 = 0$

and $\left|\vec{A}\right| = \sqrt{36+16+4} = \sqrt{56}$ and $\left|\vec{B}\right| = \sqrt{1+4+1} = \sqrt{6}$

We know that $\vec{A}.\vec{B} = \left|\vec{A}\right|\left|\vec{B}\right|\cos\theta \Rightarrow \cos\theta = \dfrac{\vec{A}.\vec{B}}{\left|\vec{A}\right|\left|\vec{B}\right|}$

$$\Rightarrow \theta = \cos^{-1}\left(\frac{\vec{A}.\vec{B}}{\left|\vec{A}\right|\left|\vec{B}\right|}\right) \Rightarrow \theta = \cos^{-1}\left(\frac{0}{\sqrt{56}\sqrt{6}}\right)$$

$$\Rightarrow \theta = \cos^{-1}(0) \Rightarrow \theta = \cos^{-1}\left(\cos\frac{\pi}{2}\right) \Rightarrow \theta = \frac{\pi}{2}$$

Q24. Show that $\left(\vec{a}\times\vec{b}\right)\cdot\left(\vec{c}\times\vec{d}\right)=\left(\vec{a}\cdot\vec{c}\right)\left(\vec{b}\cdot\vec{d}\right)-\left(\vec{a}\cdot\vec{d}\right)\left(\vec{b}\cdot\vec{c}\right)$

[June-2011, Q.No.-1(a)]

Ans. Let $\vec{a}\times\vec{b}=\vec{r}$. Then $\left(\vec{a}\times\vec{b}\right)\cdot\left(\vec{c}\times\vec{d}\right)=\vec{r}\cdot\left(\vec{c}\times\vec{d}\right)$

Now, in a scalar triple product, the position of dot and cross may be interchanged without altering the value of the product.

Therefore, $\vec{r}\cdot\left(\vec{c}\times\vec{d}\right)=\left(\vec{r}\times\vec{c}\right)\cdot\vec{d}$

$\therefore$ L.H.S. $=\left(\vec{a}\times\vec{b}\right)\cdot\left(\vec{c}\times\vec{d}\right)=\left[\left(\vec{a}\times\vec{b}\right)\times\vec{c}\right]\cdot\vec{d}$

$=\left[\left(\vec{c}\cdot\vec{a}\right)\vec{b}-\left(\vec{c}\cdot\vec{b}\right)\vec{a}\right]\cdot\vec{d}=\left(\vec{c}\cdot\vec{a}\right)\left(\vec{b}\cdot\vec{d}\right)-\left(\vec{c}\cdot\vec{b}\right)\left(\vec{a}\cdot\vec{d}\right)=$ R.H.S.

Q25. Calculate the area of a parallelogram having diagonals $\vec{A}=3\hat{i}+\hat{j}-2\hat{k}$ **and** $\vec{B}=\hat{i}-3\hat{j}+4\hat{k}$. **[Dec-2011, Q.No.-1(a)]**

Ans. We have $\vec{A}=3\hat{i}+\hat{j}-2\hat{k}$ and $\vec{B}=\hat{i}-3\hat{j}+4\hat{k}$

Now, area of parallelogram, $\vec{A}\times\vec{B}=\begin{vmatrix}\hat{i} & \hat{j} & \hat{k}\\ 3 & 1 & -2\\ 1 & -3 & 4\end{vmatrix}$

$=\hat{i}(4-6)-\hat{j}(12+2)+\hat{k}(-9-1)=-2\hat{i}-14\hat{j}-10\hat{k}$

$\rightarrow\left|\vec{A}\times\vec{B}\right|=\sqrt{4+196+100}=\sqrt{300}=10\sqrt{3}$

$\Rightarrow$ area of parallelogram $=10\sqrt{3}$ sq. unit.

Q26. Determine the vector $\vec{A}$ **perpendicular to the vectors** $\vec{B}=2\hat{i}+\hat{j}-\hat{k}$ **and** $\vec{C}=\hat{i}-\hat{j}+\hat{k}$. **[Dec-2012, Q.No.-1(a)]**

Ans. Given vectors are $\vec{B}=2\hat{i}+\hat{j}-\hat{k}$ and $\vec{C}=\hat{i}-\hat{j}+\hat{k}$

It is also given that vector $\vec{A}$ is perpendicular to $\vec{B}$ and $\vec{C}$.

So, we have $\vec{A}.\vec{B}=0$ and $\vec{A}.\vec{C}=0$

Let $\vec{A}=a\hat{i}+b\hat{j}+c\hat{k}$ $\Rightarrow$ $\left(a\hat{i}+b\hat{j}+c\hat{k}\right).\left(2\hat{i}+\hat{j}-\hat{k}\right)=0$

$\Rightarrow\quad 2a+b-c=0$ ...(i)

and $\left(a\hat{i}+b\hat{j}+c\hat{k}\right).\left(\hat{i}-\hat{j}+\hat{k}\right)=0\Rightarrow\quad a-b+c=0$ ...(ii)

After solving (i) and (ii), we find that $a=b=c=0$

Hence, $\vec{A}=\vec{0}$ or $\vec{A}=0\hat{i}+0\hat{j}+0\hat{k}$.

Q27. Show that $(\vec{A}\times\vec{B}).(\vec{A}\times\vec{B}) = A^2B^2 - (\vec{A}\vec{B})^2$. **[Dec-2012, Q.No.-1(b)]**

Ans. L. H. S. $= (\vec{A}\times\vec{B}).(\vec{A}\times\vec{B}) = \left[(\vec{A}\times\vec{B})\times\vec{A}\right].\vec{B} = \left[(\vec{A}.\vec{A})\vec{B} - (\vec{A}.\vec{B})\vec{A}\right].\vec{B}$

$= (\vec{A}.\vec{A})(\vec{B}.\vec{B}) - (\vec{A}.\vec{B})(\vec{A}.\vec{B}) = A^2B^2 - (\vec{A}.\vec{B})^2 =$ R.H.S.

$\Rightarrow$ L. H. S. = R. H. S.

Q28. Determine the unit vector perpendicular to the plane formed by the two vectors:

$\vec{a} = 2\hat{i} - \hat{k},\ \vec{b} = 3\hat{j} + 2\hat{k}$ **[June-2013, Q.No.-1(a)]**

Ans. The equation of plane formed by $\vec{a} = 2\hat{i} - \hat{k}$ and $\vec{b} = 3\hat{i} + 2\hat{k}$ is $(\vec{r} - \vec{a}).\vec{b} = 0 \Rightarrow \left[x\hat{i} + y\hat{j} + z\hat{k} - 2\hat{i} + \hat{k}\right].(3\hat{j} + 2\hat{k}) = 0$

$\Rightarrow \left[(x-2)\hat{i} + y\hat{j} + (z+1)\hat{k}\right].(3\hat{j} + 2\hat{k}) = 0$

$\Rightarrow \quad 3y + 2z + 2 = 0$

This is the equation of plane.

Now, let vector perpendicular to the above plane is $\vec{n}$.

Hence, direction ratios of $\vec{n}$ are 0, 3, 2.

Hence, $\vec{n} = 3\hat{j} + 2\hat{k}$

Therefore, unit vector $\hat{n} = \frac{\vec{n}}{|\vec{n}|} = \frac{3\hat{j} + 2\hat{k}}{\sqrt{9+4}} = \frac{1}{\sqrt{13}}(3\hat{j} + 2\hat{k})$.

The book you can believe most – GPH book.

Chapter 2

Vector Differential Calculus

An Overview

Vector calculus (or vector analysis) is a branch of mathematics concerned with differentiation and integration of vector fields, primarily in three dimensional Euclidean space R^3. The term "vector calculus" is sometimes used as a synonym for the broader subject of multivariable calculus, which includes vector calculus as well as partial differentiation and multiple integration. Vector calculus plays an important role in differential geometry and in the study of partial differential equations. It is used extensively in physics and engineering, especially in the description of electromagnetic fields, gravitational fields and fluid flow.

Scalar Function: Let D be any subset of the set of all real numbers. If to each element t of D, we associate by some rule a unique real number f (t), then this rule defines a scalar function of the scalar variable t. Here f (t) is a scalar quantity and thus f is a scalar function.

Vector Function: Let D be any subset of the set of all real numbers. If to each element t of D, we associate by some rule a unique vector $\vec{f}$ (t), then this rule defines a vector function of the scalar variable t. Here $\vec{f}$ (t) is a vector quantity and thus $\vec{f}$ is a vector function.

Differentiating Vector functions: We know that from the first principle of differentiation, the derivative of a scalar function f(t) with respect to t is defined as $\frac{df(t)}{dt} = \lim_{\Delta t \to \circ} \frac{f(t+\Delta t) - f(t)}{\Delta t}$

In the same way, we define the derivative of a vector function $\vec{f}$ (t) with respect to t as follows: $\frac{d\vec{f}(t)}{dt} \lim_{\Delta t \to 0} \frac{\vec{f}(t+\Delta t) - \vec{f}(t)}{\Delta t}$

Rate of change of a vector: Let a vector $\vec{f}$ (t) at any instant t. We now increase the scalar t by an amount Δt. The vector corresponding to the scalar $t+\Delta t$ is $\vec{f}(t+\Delta t)$. The change in $\vec{f}$ (t) corresponding to the change Δt in t is then $\Delta \vec{f} = \vec{f}(t+\Delta t) - \vec{f}(t)$

Since $\vec{f}$ (t) is a vector, It can change both in magnitude and direction, where as a scalar function changes only in magnitude.

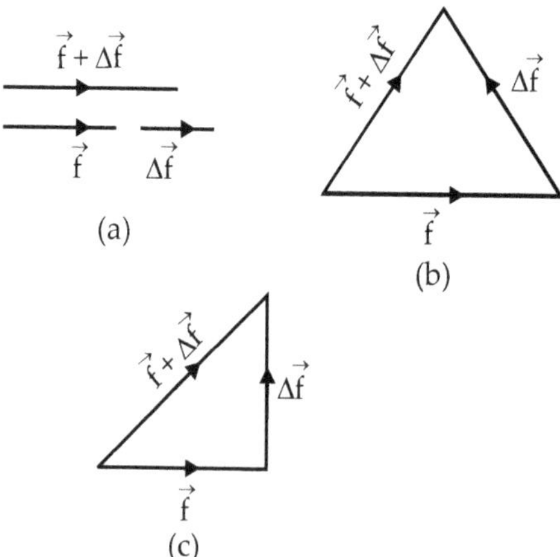

Fig. 2.1: Derivative of a vector function when there is a change in (a) magnitude only, (b) direction only (c) both magnitude and direction.

Derivative of a Vector Function in Component Form: Let $\vec{r}$ be a vector function of the scalar variable t.

Let $\vec{r} = x\hat{i} + y\hat{j} + z\hat{k}$ where the components x, y, z are scalar function of the scalar variable t and $\hat{i}, \hat{j}, \hat{k}$ are fixed unit vectors.

We have $\vec{r} + \delta\vec{r} = (x + \delta x)\hat{i} + (y + \delta y)\hat{j} + (z + \delta z)\hat{k}$.

$\therefore\ \delta\vec{r} = (\vec{r} + \delta\vec{r}) - \vec{r} = \delta x\,\hat{i} + \delta y\,\hat{j} + \delta z\,\hat{k}$.

$$\therefore\ \frac{\delta\vec{r}}{\delta t} = \frac{\delta x}{\delta t}\hat{i} + \frac{\delta y}{\delta t}\hat{j} + \frac{\delta z}{\delta t}\hat{k}.$$

$$\therefore\ \lim_{\delta t \to 0}\frac{\delta\vec{r}}{\delta t} = \lim_{\delta t \to 0}\left\{\frac{\delta x}{\delta t}\hat{i} + \frac{\delta y}{\delta t}\hat{j} + \frac{\delta z}{\delta t}\hat{k}\right\}$$

$$\therefore\ \frac{d\vec{r}}{dt} = \frac{dx}{dt}\hat{i} + \frac{dy}{dt}\hat{j} + \frac{dz}{dt}\hat{k}.$$

Thus, in order to differentiate a vector we should differentiate its components.

Note: If $\vec{r} = x\hat{i} + y\hat{j} + z\hat{k}$, then sometimes we also write it as $\vec{r} = (x, y, z)$.

In this notation, $\frac{d\vec{r}}{dt} = \left(\frac{dx}{dt}, \frac{dy}{dt}, \frac{dz}{dt}\right), \frac{d^2\vec{r}}{dt^2} = \left(\frac{d^2x}{dt^2}, \frac{d^2y}{dt^2}, \frac{d^2z}{dt^2}\right)$, and so on.

Alternative Method

We have $\vec{r} = x\hat{i} + y\hat{j} + z\hat{k}$, where $\hat{i}, \hat{j}, \hat{k}$ are constant vectors and so their derivatives will be zero.

Now, $\frac{d\vec{r}}{dt} = \frac{d}{dt}\left(x\hat{i} + y\hat{j} + z\hat{k}\right) = \frac{d}{dt}\left(x\hat{i}\right) + \frac{d}{dt}\left(y\hat{j}\right) + \frac{d}{dt}\left(z\hat{k}\right)$

$$= \frac{dx}{dt}\hat{i} + x\frac{d\hat{i}}{dt} + \frac{dy}{dt}\hat{j} + y\frac{d\hat{j}}{dt} + \frac{dz}{dt}\hat{k} + z\frac{d\hat{k}}{dt}$$

$= \frac{dx}{dt}\hat{i} + \frac{dy}{dt}\hat{j} + \frac{dz}{dt}\hat{k}$, Since $\frac{d\hat{i}}{dt}$, etc. vanish.

Differentiation formulae: If $\vec{a}, \vec{b}$ and $\vec{c}$ are differentiable vector functions of a scalar t and Φ is a differentiable scalar function of the same variable t, then

- $\frac{d}{dt}\left(\vec{a} + \vec{b}\right) = \frac{d\vec{a}}{dt} + \frac{d\vec{b}}{dt}$
- $\frac{d}{dt}\left(\vec{a} \cdot \vec{b}\right) = \vec{a} \cdot \frac{d\vec{b}}{dt} + \frac{d\vec{a}}{dt} \cdot \vec{b}$

- $\frac{d}{dt}(\vec{a}\times\vec{b}) = \vec{a}\times\frac{d\vec{b}}{dt}+\frac{d\vec{a}}{dt}\times\vec{b}$
- $\frac{d}{dt}(\Phi\vec{a}) = \Phi\frac{d\vec{a}}{dt}+\frac{d\Phi}{dt}\vec{a}$
- $\frac{d}{dt}\left[\vec{a}\vec{b}\vec{c}\right] = \left[\frac{d\vec{a}}{dt}\vec{b}\vec{c}\right]+\left[\vec{a}\frac{d\vec{b}}{dt}\vec{c}\right]+\left[\vec{a}\vec{b}\frac{d\vec{c}}{dt}\right]$
- $\frac{d}{dt}\left\{\vec{a}\times(\vec{b}\times\vec{c})\right\} = \frac{d\vec{a}}{dt}\times(\vec{b}\times\vec{c})+\vec{a}\times\left(\frac{d\vec{b}}{dt}\times\vec{c}\right)+\vec{a}\times\left(\vec{b}\times\frac{d\vec{c}}{dt}\right)$

Scalar field: Let ϕ be a function which associates a unique scalar with each point in a given region. Then ϕ is called a scalar field function, or a scalar field. For example, the resistance R (x, y, z) of a cylindrical wire with a non-uniform cross-sectional area is a scalar field.

Contour curves and contour surfaces: For a two-dimensional scalar field ϕ (x, y), contour curves are defined by the equation ϕ (x, y) = constant, i.e. they are the curves along which ϕ has a constant value, say ϕ_0. In the same way, for a three-dimensional scalar field, we define contour surfaces as if we join all the points for which ϕ (x, y, z) has the same value, we obtain a contour surface with equation ϕ (x, y, z) = C, where C is a constant.

Partial Derivatives: The partial derivative of a function f (x, y, z, t) with respect to x is $\frac{\partial f}{\partial x} = \lim_{\Delta x\to 0}\frac{f(x+\Delta x,y,z,t)-f(x,y,z,t)}{\Delta x}$ ...(i)

To calculate the partial derivative of a function f(x, y, z, t) with respect to x, for all practical purposes. We have to differentiate f with respect to x, holding other variables y, z and t to be constant.

For example, consider f (x, y, z, t) = $2x^2yzt^3$

we have $\frac{\partial f}{\partial x} = \left[\frac{\partial}{\partial x}(x^2)\right](2yzt^3) = 4xyzt^3$

Similarly, for the partial derivative with respect to any other variable, keep the remaining variables as constant:

$$\frac{\partial f}{\partial y} = \left[\frac{\partial}{\partial y}(y)\right](2x^2zt^3) = 2x^2zt^3$$

$$\frac{\partial f}{\partial z} = \left[\frac{\partial}{\partial z}(z)\right](2x^2yt^3) = 2x^2yt^3$$

$$\frac{\partial f}{\partial t} = \left[\frac{\partial}{\partial t}\left(t^3\right)\right]\left(2x^2yz\right) = 6x^2yzt^2$$

The Vector Differential Operator Del(∇): The vector differential operator ∇ (read as del or nabla) is defined as

$$\nabla \equiv \frac{\partial}{\partial x}\hat{i} + \frac{\partial}{\partial y}\hat{j} + \frac{\partial}{\partial z}\hat{k} \equiv \hat{i}\frac{\partial}{\partial x} + \hat{j}\frac{\partial}{\partial y} + \hat{k}\frac{\partial}{\partial z}$$ and operates distributively.

The vector operator ∇ can generally be treated to behave as on ordinary vector. It possesses properties like ordinary vectors. The symbols $\frac{\partial}{\partial x}, \frac{\partial}{\partial y}, \frac{\partial}{\partial z}$ can be treated as its components along $\hat{i}, \hat{j}, \hat{k}$.

The Gradient of a Scalar field: Let f (x, y, z) be defined and differentiable at each point (x, y, z) in a certain region of space (i.e. defines a differentiable scalar field). Then the gradient of f, written as ∇f or grad f, is defined as $\nabla f = \left(\frac{\partial}{\partial x}\hat{i} + \frac{\partial}{\partial y}\hat{j} + \frac{\partial}{\partial z}\hat{k}\right)f = \frac{\partial f}{\partial x}\hat{i} + \frac{\partial f}{\partial y}\hat{j} + \frac{\partial f}{\partial z}\hat{k}$

It should be noted that ∇f is a vector whose three successive components are $\frac{\partial f}{\partial x}, \frac{\partial f}{\partial y}$ and $\frac{\partial f}{\partial z}$. Thus, the gradient of a scalar field defines a vector field. If f is a scalar point function, then ∇f is a vector point function.

Geometrical Interpretation of the Gradient: Grad f or ∇f is a vector and so it has a magnitude and a direction. To understand the geometrical meaning of ∇ f, we write the scalar product ($\nabla f . d\vec{r}$) in the form

$$df = \nabla f . d\vec{r} = |\nabla f||d\vec{r}|\cos\theta \qquad \text{...(ii)}$$

where θ is the angle between ∇ f and $d\vec{r}$.

Now consider [Fig. 2.2] showing two contour surface S_1 and S_2 of the scalar field f. The scalar field f is constant over S_1 and S_2. Examples are the surfaces of constant temperature in a room or surfaces of constant gravitational potential due to a point mass. Let the surface S_1 be defined by $f = c_1$ and S_2 by $f = c_2$. The point P is on S_1 and Q is on S_2.

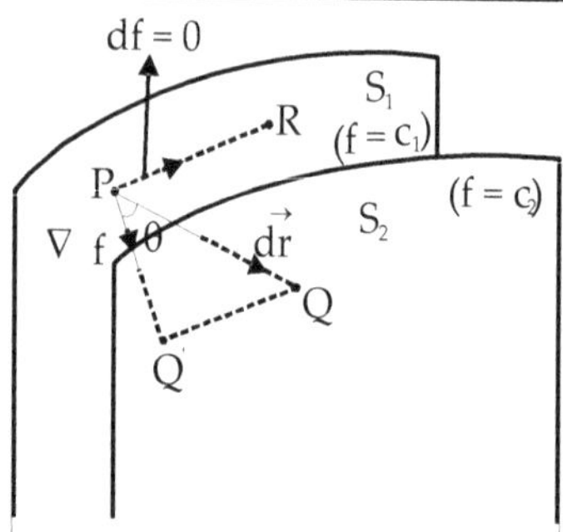

Fig. 2.2: Geometrical Interpretation of the Gradient.

Now suppose we move between points P and R on the surface S_1. Since f is constant on this surface, df = 0 as one goes from P to R. Since $d\vec{r} \equiv \overline{PR}$ in this case the result df = 0 in Eq. (ii) implies that ∇ f is perpendicular to $d\vec{r}$, i.e. to the surface S_1.

Thus, the vector ∇ f is perpendicular to the surface f = constant

Properties of Grad $f(\overline{\nabla} f)$:

- The components of grad f at any point are the rates of change of the function f along the direction of the coordinate axes at that point.
- Grad f is, at any point, perpendicular to the line (in two dimensions) or surface (in three dimensions) for which f is constant.
- The magnitude of grad f at any point is the maximum space rate of change of f.
- The direction of grad f is that in which f changes most rapidly.
- The sense of its direction is such that grad f points towards larger values of f.

Directional Derivative: Let Q be a point at a distance s from P in the direction of $\hat{n}$ [Fig. 2.2]. Then if the limit

$$\lim_{s\to 0}\frac{f(Q)-f(P)}{s}, \text{ (s = distance QP)} \qquad ...(iii)$$

exists, it is called the directional derivative of f at P in the direction of $\hat{n}$. Let us denote it by $\frac{\partial f}{\partial s}$. We can see that $\frac{\partial f}{\partial s}$ is the rate of change of f at P in the direction of $\hat{n}$. It can be $\frac{\partial f}{\partial s} = \hat{n}.\Delta f.$ ...(iv)

Vector Field: Let $\vec{F}$ be a function which associates a unique vector with every point in a given region. Then $\vec{F}$ is called a vector field function or a vector field.

Vector Field Lines: A more complete picture of a vector field $\vec{F}$ is obtained by drawing vector field lines. These are continuous curves in the region over which $\vec{F}$ is defined. The curves are such that at any point the tangent to the curve gives the direction of the vector field function at that point. The tangent is drawn in the same sense as that of the lines.

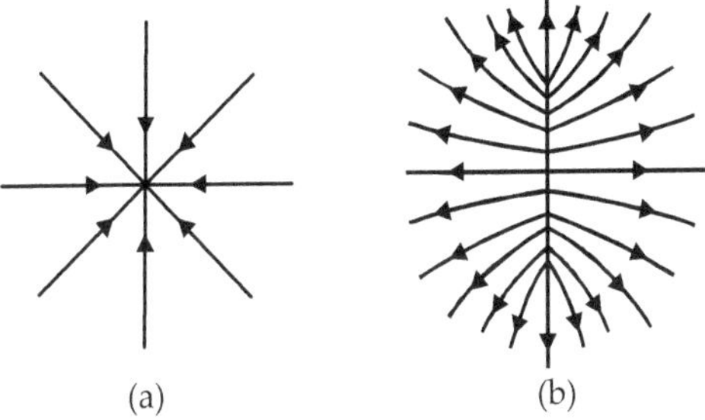

Fig. 2.3: Vector field lines for (a) gravitational force field, (b) uniformly charged disc.

Divergence of a Vector Field: Let $\vec{F}$ (x, y, z) be a differentiable vector field having component scalar fields

$F_x(x,y,z), F_y(x,y,z), F_z(x,y,z)$, i.e.

$$\vec{F}(x,y,z) = F_x(x,y,z)\hat{i} + F_y(x,y,z)\hat{j} + F_z(x,y,z)\hat{k} \qquad \text{...(v)}$$

Then the divergence of the vector field $\vec{F}$ is defined as

$$\text{div } \vec{F} = \nabla \cdot \vec{F} = \left(\hat{i}\frac{\partial}{\partial x} + \hat{j}\frac{\partial}{\partial y} + \hat{k}\frac{\partial}{\partial z}\right) \cdot \left(F_x\hat{i} + F_y\hat{j} + F_z\hat{k}\right)$$

$$\text{or } \nabla \cdot \vec{F} = \frac{\partial F_x}{\partial x} + \frac{\partial F_y}{\partial y} + \frac{\partial F_z}{\partial z} \qquad \text{...(vi)}$$

Note: If div V = 0, then vector V is solenoid.

The Curl of a Vector Field: If $\vec{f}$ is any given continuously differentiable vector point function, then the vector function defined by

$$\nabla \times \vec{f} = \hat{i} \times \frac{\partial \vec{f}}{\partial x} + \hat{j} \times \frac{\partial \vec{f}}{\partial y} + \hat{k} \times \frac{\partial \vec{f}}{\partial z}$$

is called the curl of $\vec{f}$ and is written as curl $\vec{f}$. We read it as del cross $\vec{f}$ or curl of $\vec{f}$.

Expression of curl f in terms of the components of f: Let $\vec{f} = f_x\hat{i} + f_y\hat{j} + f_z\hat{k}$.

$$\text{Then curl } \vec{f} = \hat{i} \times \frac{\partial \vec{f}}{\partial x} + \hat{j} \times \frac{\partial \vec{f}}{\partial y} + \hat{k} \times \frac{\partial \vec{f}}{\partial z} = \sum \hat{i} \times \left(\hat{i}\frac{\partial f_x}{\partial x} + \hat{j}\frac{\partial f_y}{\partial y} + \hat{k}\frac{\partial f_z}{\partial z}\right)$$

$$= \hat{i}\left(\frac{\partial f_z}{\partial y} - \frac{\partial f_y}{\partial z}\right) + \hat{j}\left(\frac{\partial f_x}{\partial z} - \frac{\partial f_z}{\partial x}\right) + \hat{k}\left(\frac{\partial f_y}{\partial x} - \frac{\partial f_x}{\partial y}\right) = \begin{vmatrix} \hat{i} & \hat{j} & \hat{k} \\ \frac{\partial}{\partial x} & \frac{\partial}{\partial y} & \frac{\partial}{\partial z} \\ f_x & f_y & f_z \end{vmatrix}$$

From the above result, the curl $\vec{f}$ has the following components along the co-ordinate axes: $\left(\frac{\partial f_z}{\partial y} - \frac{\partial f_y}{\partial z}\right), \left(\frac{\partial f_x}{\partial z} - \frac{\partial f_z}{\partial x}\right), \left(\frac{\partial f_y}{\partial x} - \frac{\partial f_x}{\partial y}\right)$

The Laplacian Operators ∇^2: The operator ∇^2 is defined by the equation $(\nabla \cdot \nabla)f = \nabla \cdot (\nabla f)$

The operator ∇^2 is called the Laplacian.

Now $\nabla^2 f = \nabla \cdot (\nabla f)$

$$= \left(\hat{i}\frac{\partial}{\partial x} + \hat{j}\frac{\partial}{\partial y} + \hat{k}\frac{\partial}{\partial z}\right) \cdot \left(\hat{i}\frac{\partial f}{\partial x} + \hat{j}\frac{\partial f}{\partial y} + \hat{k}\frac{\partial f}{\partial z}\right) = \frac{\partial^2 f}{\partial x^2} + \frac{\partial^2 f}{\partial y^2} + \frac{\partial^2 f}{\partial z^2} \qquad \text{...(vii)}$$

since $\hat{i} \cdot \hat{i} = 1, \hat{i} \cdot \hat{j} = 0$, etc.

Again $\nabla . \nabla f = \left(\hat{i}\frac{\partial}{\partial x} + \hat{j}\frac{\partial}{\partial y} + \hat{k}\frac{\partial}{\partial z}\right) \cdot \left(\hat{i}\frac{\partial}{\partial x} + \hat{j}\frac{\partial}{\partial y} + \hat{k}\frac{\partial}{\partial z}\right) f$

$$= \left(\frac{\partial^2}{\partial x^2} + \frac{\partial^2}{\partial y^2} + \frac{\partial^2}{\partial z^2}\right) f = \frac{\partial^2 f}{\partial x^2} + \frac{\partial^2 f}{\partial y^2} + \frac{\partial^2 f}{\partial z^2} \qquad \text{...(viii)}$$

Hence from (vii) and (viii)

$\nabla \cdot \nabla f = \nabla \cdot (\nabla f)$.

Note:

- $\nabla^2 f$ is read as del square of f.
- If $\nabla^2 f = 0$, then $\nabla^2 f_x = 0, \nabla^2 f_y = 0, \nabla^2 f_z = 0$.

Identities involving the del operator:

Identity I: grad (uv) = v grad u + u grad v

Since, grad (uv) = $\sum \hat{i}\frac{\partial}{\partial x}(uv) = \sum \hat{i}\left(u\frac{\partial v}{\partial x} + v\frac{\partial u}{\partial x}\right)$

$= u\sum \hat{i}\frac{\partial v}{\partial x} + v\sum \hat{i}\frac{\partial u}{\partial x}$ = u grad v + v grad u

i.e. $\nabla(uv) = u\nabla v + v\nabla u$.

Identity II: $\mathbf{grd}(\vec{a} \cdot \vec{b}) = \vec{a} \times \mathbf{curl}\vec{b} + \vec{b} \times \mathbf{curl}\vec{a} + (\vec{a} \cdot \nabla)\vec{b} + (\vec{b} \cdot \nabla)\vec{a}$

Since, $\text{grad}(\vec{a} \cdot \vec{b}) = \sum \hat{i}\frac{\partial}{\partial x}(\vec{a} \cdot \vec{b}) = \sum \hat{i}\left(\vec{a} \cdot \frac{\partial \vec{b}}{\partial x} + \vec{b} \cdot \frac{\partial \vec{a}}{\partial x}\right)$

$$= \sum \hat{i}\left(\vec{a}.\frac{\partial \vec{b}}{\partial x}\right) + \sum \hat{i}\left(\vec{b}.\frac{\partial \vec{a}}{\partial x}\right) \qquad ...(ix)$$

Now $\vec{a}\times\left(\hat{i}\times\frac{\partial \vec{b}}{\partial x}\right) = \left(\vec{a}.\frac{\partial \vec{b}}{\partial x}\right)\hat{i} - \left(\vec{a}.\hat{i}\right)\frac{\partial \vec{b}}{\partial x}$ or $\left(\vec{a}.\frac{\partial \vec{b}}{\partial x}\right)\hat{i} = \vec{a}\times\left(\hat{i}.\frac{\partial \vec{b}}{\partial x}\right) + \left(\vec{a}.\hat{i}\right)\frac{\partial \vec{b}}{\partial x}$

$$\therefore \sum\left(\vec{a}.\frac{\partial \vec{b}}{\partial x}\right)\hat{i} = \vec{a}\times\left(\sum \hat{i}\times\frac{\partial \vec{b}}{\partial x}\right) + \sum\left(\vec{a}.\hat{i}\right)\frac{\partial \vec{b}}{\partial x} = \vec{a}\times \text{curl}\vec{b} + \left(\vec{a}.\nabla\right)\vec{b}. \qquad ...(x)$$

Similarly $\sum\left(\vec{b}.\frac{\partial \vec{a}}{\partial \vec{b}}\right)\hat{i} = \vec{b}\times \text{curl}\vec{a} + \left(\vec{b}.\nabla\right)\vec{b}$ ...(xi)

Therefore, from (ix), (x) and (xi), we obtain,

$\text{grad}\left(\vec{a}.\vec{b}\right) = \vec{a}\times\text{curl}\vec{b} + \vec{b}\times\text{curl}\vec{a} + \left(\vec{a}.\nabla\right)\vec{b} + \left(\vec{b}.\nabla\right)\vec{a}.$

Identity III: $\text{div}\left(u\vec{a}\right) = u\,\text{div}\,\vec{a} + \vec{a}\bullet\text{grad}\,u$.

Since, $\text{div}\,(u\,\vec{a}\,) = \nabla\cdot(u\,\vec{a}\,) = \hat{i}.\frac{\partial}{\partial x}\left(u\vec{a}\right) + \hat{j}.\frac{\partial}{\partial y}\left(u\vec{a}\right) + \hat{k}.\frac{\partial}{\partial z}\left(u\vec{a}\right)$

$$= \hat{i}.\left(\vec{a}\frac{\partial u}{\partial x} + u\frac{\partial \vec{a}}{\partial x}\right) + \hat{j}.\left(\vec{a}\frac{\partial u}{\partial y} + u\frac{\partial \vec{a}}{\partial y}\right) + \hat{k}.\left(\vec{a}\frac{\partial u}{\partial z} + u\frac{\partial \vec{a}}{\partial z}\right)$$

$$= \hat{i}\cdot\left(\vec{a}\frac{\partial u}{\partial x}\right) + \hat{j}\cdot\left(\vec{a}\frac{\partial u}{\partial y}\right) + \hat{k}\cdot\left(\vec{a}\frac{\partial u}{\partial z}\right) + u\left(\hat{i}\frac{\partial \vec{a}}{\partial x} + \hat{j}\cdot\frac{\partial \vec{a}}{\partial y} + \hat{k}\frac{\partial \vec{a}}{\partial z}\right)$$

$$= \vec{a}.\left(\hat{i}\frac{\partial u}{\partial x} + \hat{j}\frac{\partial u}{\partial y} + \hat{k}\frac{\partial u}{\partial z}\right) + u\left(\hat{i}\frac{\partial \vec{a}}{\partial x} + \hat{j}.\frac{\partial \vec{a}}{\partial y} + \hat{k}.\frac{\partial \vec{a}}{\partial z}\right) = \vec{a}\cdot\text{grad}\,u + u\,\text{div}\,\vec{a}\,.$$

Identity IV: $\text{div}\left(\vec{a}\times\vec{b}\right) = \vec{b}\bullet\text{curl}\vec{a} - \vec{a}\bullet\text{curl}\vec{b}$

Since, $\text{div}\left(\vec{a}\times\vec{b}\right) = \hat{i}.\frac{\partial}{\partial x}\left(\vec{a}\times\vec{b}\right) + \hat{j}.\frac{\partial}{\partial y}\left(\vec{a}\times\vec{b}\right) + \hat{k}.\frac{\partial}{\partial z}\left(\vec{a}\times\vec{b}\right) = \sum \hat{i}.\left(\frac{\partial \vec{a}}{\partial x}\times\vec{b} + \vec{a}\times\frac{\partial \vec{b}}{\partial x}\right)$

$$= \sum \hat{i}.\frac{\partial \vec{a}}{\partial x}\times\vec{b} + \sum \hat{i}.\vec{a}\times\frac{\partial \vec{b}}{\partial x} = \left(\sum \hat{i}\times\frac{\partial \vec{a}}{\partial x}\right).\vec{b} - \left(\sum \hat{i}\times\frac{\partial \vec{b}}{\partial x}\right).\vec{a},$$

i.e. $\vec{b}\bullet\text{curl}\vec{a} - \vec{a}\bullet\text{curl}\vec{b}$

Identity V: $\text{curl}\left(u\vec{a}\right) = \left(\text{grad}\,u\right)\times\vec{a} + u\,\text{curl}\,\vec{a}$

Since, $\text{curl}\,(u\,\vec{a}\,) = \hat{i}\times\frac{\partial}{\partial x}\left(u\vec{a}\right) + \hat{j}\times\frac{\partial}{\partial y}\left(u\vec{a}\right) + \hat{k}\times\frac{\partial}{\partial z}\left(u\vec{a}\right) = \sum \hat{i}\times\left(\frac{\partial u}{\partial x}\vec{a} + u\frac{\partial \vec{a}}{\partial x}\right)$

$$= \sum \hat{i} \times \left(\frac{\partial u}{\partial x}\vec{a}\right) + \sum \hat{i} \times u \frac{\partial \vec{a}}{\partial x} = \sum \left(\hat{i}\frac{\partial u}{\partial x}\right) \times \vec{a} + \left(\sum \hat{i} \times \frac{\partial \vec{a}}{\partial x}\right) u = \text{grad } u \times \vec{a} + u$$

$\text{curl}\, \vec{a}$

Identity VI: $\text{curl}\left(\vec{a} \times \vec{b}\right) = \vec{a}\, \text{div}\, \vec{b} - \vec{b}\, \text{div}\, \vec{a} + \left(\vec{b}.\nabla\right)\vec{a} - \left(\vec{a}.\nabla\right)\vec{b}$

Since, $\text{curl}\left(\vec{a} \times \vec{b}\right) = \hat{i} \times \frac{\partial}{\partial x}\left(\vec{a} \times \vec{b}\right) + \hat{j} \times \frac{\partial}{\partial y}\left(\vec{a} \times \vec{b}\right) + \hat{k} \times \frac{\partial}{\partial z}\left(\vec{a} \times \vec{b}\right)$

$$= \sum \hat{i} \times \left(\vec{a} \times \frac{\partial \vec{b}}{\partial x} + \frac{\partial \vec{a}}{\partial x} \times \vec{b}\right) = \sum \hat{i} \times \left(\vec{a} \times \frac{\partial \vec{b}}{\partial x}\right) + \sum \hat{i} \times \left(\frac{\partial \vec{a}}{\partial x} \times \vec{b}\right)$$

$$= \sum \left(\hat{i}.\frac{\partial \vec{b}}{\partial x}\vec{a} - \sum \left(\hat{i}.\vec{a}\right)\frac{\partial \vec{b}}{\partial x} + \sum \left(\hat{i}.\vec{b}\right)\frac{\partial \vec{a}}{\partial x} - \sum \hat{i}.\frac{\partial \vec{a}}{\partial x}\right)\vec{b}$$

as $\vec{a} \times \left(\vec{b} \times \vec{c}\right) = \left(\vec{a}.\vec{c}\right)\vec{b} - \left(\vec{a}.\vec{b}\right)\vec{c}$

$$= \sum \hat{i}.\left(\frac{\partial \vec{b}}{\partial x}\right)\vec{a} - \left(\sum \hat{i}.\frac{\partial \vec{a}}{\partial x}\right)\vec{b} + \sum \left(\hat{i}.\vec{b}\right)\frac{\partial \vec{a}}{\partial x} - \sum \left(\hat{i}.\vec{a}\right)\frac{\partial \vec{b}}{\partial x}$$

$$= \vec{a}\, \text{div}\, \vec{b} - \vec{b}\, \text{div}\, \vec{a} + \left(\vec{b}.\nabla\right)\vec{a} - \left(\vec{a}.\nabla\right)\vec{b}$$

Successive Applications of the Del Operator (Second order differential function):

Property I: $\text{div grad } f = \nabla \cdot (\nabla f) = \frac{\partial^2 f}{\partial x^2} + \frac{\partial^2 f}{\partial y^2} + \frac{\partial^2 f}{\partial z^2} = \nabla^2 f$

We have $\nabla f = \hat{i}\frac{\partial f}{\partial x} + \hat{j}\frac{\partial f}{\partial y} + \hat{k}\frac{\partial f}{\partial z}$

$$\therefore\ \nabla.\nabla f = \left(\hat{i}\frac{\partial}{\partial x} + \hat{j}\frac{\partial}{\partial y} + \hat{k}\frac{\partial}{\partial z}\right).\left(\hat{i}\frac{\partial f}{\partial x} + \hat{j}\frac{\partial f}{\partial y} + \hat{k}\frac{\partial f}{\partial z}\right) = \frac{\partial^2 f}{\partial x^2} + \frac{\partial^2 f}{\partial y^2} + \frac{\partial^2 f}{\partial z^2} = \nabla^2 f$$

Property II: $\text{curl grad } f = \nabla \times \nabla f = \vec{0}$

We have $\nabla \times \nabla f = \sum \hat{i}\frac{\partial}{\partial x} \times \left(\hat{i}\frac{\partial f}{\partial x} + \hat{j}\frac{\partial f}{\partial y} + \hat{k}\frac{\partial f}{\partial z}\right) = \sum \hat{i} \times \frac{\partial}{\partial x}\left(\hat{i}\frac{\partial f}{\partial x} + \hat{j}\frac{\partial f}{\partial y} + \hat{k}\frac{\partial f}{\partial z}\right)$

$$= \sum \hat{i} \times \left(\hat{i}\frac{\partial^2 f}{\partial x^2} + \hat{j}\frac{\partial^2 f}{\partial x \partial y} + \hat{k}\frac{\partial^2 f}{\partial x \partial z}\right) = \sum \left(\hat{k}\frac{\partial^2 f}{\partial x \partial y} - \hat{j}\frac{\partial^2 f}{\partial x \partial z}\right)$$

$= 0$, as terms will cancel in pairs.

Property III: div curl $\vec{f}=\nabla\cdot\left(\nabla\times\vec{f}\right)=0$

We have $\nabla\bullet\left(\nabla\times\vec{f}\right)=\sum\hat{i}\bullet\frac{\partial}{\partial x}\left(\hat{i}\times\frac{\partial\vec{f}}{\partial x}+\hat{j}\times\frac{\partial\vec{f}}{\partial y}+\hat{k}\times\frac{\partial\vec{f}}{\partial z}\right)$

$$=\sum\hat{i}\bullet\left(\hat{i}\times\frac{\partial^2\vec{f}}{\partial x^2}+\hat{j}\times\frac{\partial^2\vec{f}}{\partial x\partial y}+\hat{k}\times\frac{\partial^2\vec{f}}{\partial x\partial z}\right)$$

$$\sum\left(\hat{i}\times\hat{i}\bullet\frac{\partial^2\vec{f}}{\partial x^2}+\hat{i}\times\hat{j}\bullet\frac{\partial^2\vec{f}}{\partial x\partial y}+\hat{i}\times\hat{k}\bullet\frac{\partial^2\vec{f}}{\partial x\partial z}\right)=\sum\left(\hat{k}.\frac{\partial^2\vec{f}}{\partial x\partial y}-\hat{j}.\frac{\partial^2\vec{f}}{\partial x\partial z}\right)$$

$=0$, as terms will cancel in pairs.

Property IV: grad div $\vec{f}=$ curl curl$\vec{f}+\frac{\partial^2\vec{f}}{\partial x^2}+\frac{\partial^2\vec{f}}{\partial y^2}+\frac{\partial^2\vec{f}}{\partial z^2}$

i.e. $\nabla\left(\nabla.\vec{f}\right)=\nabla\times\left(\nabla\times\vec{f}\right)+\nabla.\nabla\vec{f}.$

We have $\nabla\times\left(\nabla\times\vec{f}\right)=\sum\hat{i}\frac{\partial}{\partial x}\times\left(\hat{i}\times\frac{\partial\vec{f}}{\partial x}+\hat{j}\times\frac{\partial\vec{f}}{\partial y}+\hat{k}\times\frac{\partial\vec{f}}{\partial z}\right)$

$$=\sum\hat{i}\times\left(\hat{i}\times\frac{\partial^2\vec{f}}{\partial x^2}+\hat{j}\times\frac{\partial^2\vec{f}}{\partial x\partial y}+\hat{k}\times\frac{\partial^2\vec{f}}{\partial x\partial z}\right)$$

$$=\sum\left[\left(\hat{i}.\frac{\partial^2\vec{f}}{\partial x^2}\hat{i}-\hat{i}.\hat{i}\frac{\partial^2\vec{f}}{\partial x^2}\right)+\left(\hat{i}.\frac{\partial^2\vec{f}}{\partial x\partial y}\hat{j}-\hat{i}.\hat{j}\frac{\partial^2\vec{f}}{\partial x\partial y}\right)+\left(\hat{i}.\frac{\partial^2\vec{f}}{\partial x\partial z}\hat{k}-\hat{i}.\hat{k}\frac{\partial^2\vec{f}}{\partial x\partial z}\right)\right]$$

$$=\sum\left(\hat{i}\cdot\frac{\partial^2\vec{f}}{\partial x^2}\hat{i}+\hat{i}\cdot\frac{\partial^2\vec{f}}{\partial x\partial y}\hat{j}+\hat{i}\cdot\frac{\partial^2\vec{f}}{\partial x\partial z}\hat{k}\right)-\sum\frac{\partial^2\vec{f}}{\partial x^2}\qquad\text{...(xii)}$$

Again $\nabla\left(\nabla.\vec{f}\right)=\sum\hat{i}\frac{\partial}{\partial x}\left(\hat{i}.\frac{\partial\vec{f}}{\partial x}+\hat{j}.\frac{\partial\vec{f}}{\partial y}+\hat{k}.\frac{\partial\vec{f}}{\partial z}\right)$

$$=\sum\hat{i}\left(\hat{i}.\frac{\partial^2\vec{f}}{\partial x^2}+\hat{j}.\frac{\partial^2\vec{f}}{\partial x\partial y}+\hat{k}.\frac{\partial^2\vec{f}}{\partial x\partial z}\right)=\sum\left(\hat{i}.\frac{\partial^2\vec{f}}{\partial x^2}\hat{i}+\hat{i}.\frac{\partial^2\vec{f}}{\partial x\partial y}\hat{j}+\hat{i}.\frac{\partial^2\vec{f}}{\partial x\partial z}\hat{k}\right)$$

$$=\nabla\times\left(\nabla\times\vec{f}\right)+\sum\frac{\partial^2\vec{f}}{\partial x^2}$$

$\therefore$ grad div $\vec{f}$ = curl curl $\vec{f}$ + $\sum\frac{\partial^2\vec{f}}{\partial x^2}$

This result can be put in the following form also:

curl curl $\vec{f}$ = grad div $\vec{f}$ = $\nabla^2\vec{f}$

Solved Practical Problems

Q1. **A particle P moves on a rotating disc towards the edge. Its position vector is given by $\vec{r}(t) = bt\left(\cos\omega t\,\hat{i} + \sin\omega t\,\hat{j}\right)$, where ω is the angular speed of the disc rotating anti-clockwise. Find the acceleration $\vec{a}$ of P.**

Ans. Here, $\vec{a} = \dfrac{d^2\vec{r}}{dt^2} = \dfrac{d}{dt}\left(\dfrac{d\vec{r}}{dt}\right)$.

Now, $\dfrac{d\vec{r}}{dt} = b\left(\cos\omega t\,\hat{i} + \sin\omega t\,\hat{j}\right) + bt\omega\left(-\sin\omega t\,\hat{i} + \cos\omega t\,\hat{j}\right)$

and

$$\vec{a} = \frac{d^2\vec{r}}{dt^2} = b\omega\left(-\sin\omega t\,\hat{i} + \cos\omega t\,\hat{j}\right) + b\omega\left(-\sin\omega t\,\hat{i} + \cos\omega t\,\hat{j}\right) + bt\omega^2\left(-\cos\omega t\,\hat{i} - \sin\omega t\,\hat{j}\right)$$

or $\vec{a} = 2b\omega\left(-\sin\omega t\,\hat{i} + \cos\omega t\,\hat{j}\right) - \omega^2\vec{r}$

Q2. **The nuclear force between two neutrons in a nucleus is described roughly by the Yukawa potential $U(r) = -U_0\dfrac{r_0}{r}\exp\left(\dfrac{r}{r_0}\right)$ where r is the distance between neutrons and U_0 and r_0 are constants. Determine the force $\vec{F}(r) = -\dfrac{dU}{dr}\hat{r}$**

Ans. We have, $\vec{F}(r) = -\dfrac{dU}{dr}\hat{r}, U = -U_0\dfrac{r_0}{r}\exp\left(\dfrac{r}{r_0}\right)$

Now, $$\frac{dU}{dr} = U_0\frac{r_0}{r^2}\exp\left(-\frac{r}{r_0}\right) + U_0\frac{r_0}{r}\frac{1}{r_0}\exp\left(-\frac{r}{r_0}\right) = U_0\frac{r_0}{r}\exp\left(-\frac{r}{r_0}\right)\left(\frac{1}{r} + \frac{1}{r_0}\right)$$

Therefore, $$\vec{F}(r) = -\frac{U_0 r_0}{r}\exp\left(-\frac{r}{r_0}\right)\left(\frac{1}{r} + \frac{1}{r_0}\right)\hat{r}.$$

Q3. **If the vectors $\vec{a}$ and $\vec{b}$ are functions of the scalar t, show that**

$$\frac{d}{dt}\left(\vec{a}\times\vec{b}\right) = \frac{d\vec{a}}{dt}\times\vec{b} + \vec{a}\times\frac{d\vec{b}}{dt}$$

Ans. Let $\vec{a} = a_1\hat{i} + a_2\hat{j} + a_3\hat{k}$, $\vec{b} = b_1\hat{i} + b_2\hat{j} + b_3\hat{k}$. Then

$\vec{a}\times\vec{b} = \hat{i}(a_2b_3 - a_3b_2) + \hat{j}(a_3b_1 - a_1b_3) + \hat{k}(a_1b_2 - a_2b_1)$

Now, $\frac{d}{dt}(\vec{a}\times\vec{b}) = \hat{i}\frac{d}{dt}(a_2b_3 - a_3b_2) + \hat{j}\frac{d}{dt}(a_3b_1 - a_1b_3) + \hat{k}\frac{d}{dt}(a_1b_2 - a_2b_1)$

$$= \hat{i}(a'_2\,b_3 + a_2b'_3 - a'_3\,b_2 - a_3b'_2) + \hat{j}(a'_3\,b_1 + a_3b'_1 - a'_1\,b_3 - a_1b'_3)$$
$$+ \hat{k}(a'_1\,b_2 + a_1b'_2 + a'_2\,b_1 - a_2b'_1)$$

where $a'_i = \frac{da_i}{dt}$ and $b'_i = \frac{db_i}{dt}$, for i = 1, 2, 3.

or $\frac{d}{dt}(\vec{a}\times\vec{b}) = \hat{i}\left(\frac{da_2}{dt}b_3 - \frac{da_3}{dt}b_2\right) + \hat{i}\left(a_2\frac{db_3}{dt} - a_3\frac{db_2}{dt}\right)$

$$+\hat{j}\left(\frac{da_3}{dt}b_1 - \frac{da_1}{dt}b_3\right) + \hat{j}\left(a_3\frac{db_1}{dt} - a_1\frac{db_3}{dt}\right)$$

$$+\hat{k}\left(\frac{da_1}{dt}b_2 - \frac{da_2}{dt}b_1\right) + \hat{k}\left(a_1\frac{db_2}{dt} - a_2\frac{db_1}{dt}\right)$$

Collecting first, third, fifth terms and second, fourth, sixth terms we have

$$= \hat{i}\left(\frac{da_2}{dt}b_3 - \frac{da_3}{dt}b_2\right) + \hat{j}\left(\frac{da_3}{dt}b_1 - \frac{da_1}{dt}b_3\right) + \hat{k}\left(\frac{da_1}{dt}b_2 - \frac{da_2}{dt}b_1\right)$$

$$+\hat{i}\left(a_2\frac{db_3}{dt} - a_3\frac{db_2}{dt}\right) + \hat{j}\left(a_3\frac{db_1}{dt} - a_1\frac{db_3}{dt}\right) + \hat{k}\left(a_1\frac{db_2}{dt} - a_2\frac{db_1}{dt}\right)$$

Using the definition of cross product, we get $\frac{d}{dt}(\vec{a}\times\vec{b}) = \frac{d\vec{a}}{dt}\times\vec{b} + \vec{a}\times\frac{d\vec{b}}{dt}$

Q4. Under the influence of a force field $\vec{F}$, a particle of constant mass m moves along an ellipse. Its position vector is $\vec{r}$ = a cos ωt $\hat{i}$ + b sin ωt $\hat{j}$.

Compute the instantaneous power $\vec{P} = \frac{d}{dt}(\vec{F}\cdot\vec{r})$ applied to the particle, given $\vec{F} = m\frac{d^2\vec{r}}{dt^2}$.

Ans. Given, $\vec{r}$ = a cos ωt $\hat{i}$ + b sin ωt $\hat{j}$

Therefore, $\frac{d\vec{r}}{dt} = \omega\,(-a \sin \omega t\ \hat{i} + b \cos \omega t\ \hat{j})$,

Since, $\vec{F} = m\frac{d^2\vec{r}}{dt^2} = m\,\omega^2\,(-a\cos \omega t\ \hat{i} - b\sin \omega t\ \hat{j}) = -m\omega^2\,\vec{r}$

Hence, $\vec{P} = \frac{d}{dt}(\vec{F}.\vec{r}) = \frac{d\vec{F}}{dt}.\vec{r} + \vec{F}.\frac{d\vec{r}}{dt} = -m\omega^2\frac{d\vec{r}}{dt}.\vec{r} - m\omega^2\vec{r}.\frac{d\vec{r}}{dt} = -2m\omega^2\vec{r}.\frac{d\vec{r}}{dt}$

or $\vec{P} = -2m\omega^2$ (a cos ωt $\hat{i}$ + b sin ωt $\hat{j}$) . (– aω sinωt $\hat{i}$ + bω cosωt $\hat{j}$)

$= -2m\omega^2\ (-a^2\omega\cos\omega t\sin\omega t + b^2\omega\sin\omega t\cos\omega t)$

$= +2m\omega^3\sin\omega t\cos\omega t\left(a^2 - b^2\right) = m\omega^3\left(a^2 - b^2\right)\sin 2\omega t$

Q5. Give two examples of scalar fields from physics.

Ans. Examples of Scalar Fields are:

(i) The intensity of a light source, such as a small light bulb, at a point at a distance $r = \sqrt{x^2 + y^2 + z^2}$ from the centre of the bulb's filament is $I = \frac{I_0}{x^2 + y^2 + z^2}$. I is a scalar field defined in the whole of space except the origin (0, 0, 0)

(ii) The gravitational potential V(x,y,z) at a point P(x,y,z) due to a point mass m at the origin is a scalar field: $V = -\frac{Gm}{\left(x^2 + y^2 + z^2\right)^{1/2}}$

Q6. (a) Compute $\frac{\partial f}{\partial x}$ and $\frac{\partial f}{\partial y}$ at (x, y) where $f(x,y) = x^2y^3 + \exp(x^2y)$

Ans. Here, $\frac{\partial f}{\partial x} = \frac{\partial}{\partial x}\left[x^2y^3 + \exp(x^2y)\right] = 2xy^3 + 2x\exp(x^2y)$

and $\frac{\partial f}{\partial y} = 3x^2y^2 + \exp(x^2y)$

(b) For a scalar field u(x,y,z) = 2x + yz - xy, evaluate $\frac{\partial u}{\partial x}, \frac{\partial u}{\partial y}$ and $\frac{\partial u}{\partial z}$ at the point (1,-1,1).

Ans. Here, $\frac{\partial u}{\partial x} = 2 - y, \frac{\partial u}{\partial y} = z - x, \frac{\partial u}{\partial z} = y.$

Now, at the point (1,–1,1), $\frac{\partial u}{\partial x} = 2 - (-1) = 3,\ \frac{\partial u}{\partial y} = 0$, and $\frac{\partial u}{\partial z} = -1.$

Q7. Compute ∇ f for $f = \frac{k}{\left(x^2 + y^2 + z^2\right)}$

Ans. Here, $\nabla f = \left(\hat{i}\frac{\partial}{\partial x} + \hat{j}\frac{\partial}{\partial y} + \hat{k}\frac{\partial}{\partial z}\right)\left(\frac{k}{x^2 + y^2 + z^2}\right)$

$$= \hat{i}\left[\frac{-2x}{\left(x^2 + y^2 + z^2\right)^2}\right] + \hat{j}\left[\frac{-2y}{\left(x^2 + y^2 + z^2\right)^2}\right] + \hat{k}\left[\frac{-2z}{\left(x^2 + y^2 + z^2\right)^2}\right]$$

Therefore, $\overline{\nabla}f = \dfrac{-2\left(x\hat{i}+y\hat{j}+z\hat{k}\right)}{\left(x^2+y^2+z^2\right)}$

Q8. Find the directional derivative of $V = \dfrac{k}{\left(x^2+y^2+z^2\right)^{1/2}}$ at the point (3, 4, 0) in the direction $\hat{n} = \dfrac{1}{\sqrt{6}}\left(\hat{i}+\hat{j}-2\hat{k}\right)$.

Ans. We know that $\dfrac{\partial f}{\partial s} = \hat{n}.\nabla f$

Hence, the required directional derivative is

$$\frac{\partial \overline{V}}{\partial s} = -\frac{k}{\sqrt{6}}\left(\hat{i}+\hat{j}-2\hat{k}\right).\left[\frac{x\hat{i}+y\hat{j}+z\hat{k}}{\left(x^2+y^2+z^2\right)^{3/2}}\right] = -\frac{k}{\sqrt{6}}\frac{x+y-2z}{\left(x^2+y^2+z^2\right)^{3/2}}$$

At the point (3, 4, 0) it is

$$\frac{\partial \overline{V}}{\partial s} = -\frac{k}{\sqrt{6}}\frac{3+4-0}{(9+16+0)^{3/2}} = -\frac{7k}{\sqrt{6}(25)^{3/2}} = -\frac{7k}{125\sqrt{6}}.$$

Q9. The temperature (in degrees Celsius) in a room is described as a scalar field by $T(x,y,z) = Ax^2 - By^2 + Cxyz + 273$.

Here x, y, and z are measured in metres. A, B, C are constants having appropriate dimensions.

(a) Determine the maximum rate of change of temperature with distance.

Ans. The maximum rate of change of temperature is $|(\nabla T)|$

$$\text{Now, } \nabla T = \left(\hat{i}\frac{\partial}{\partial x}+\hat{j}\frac{\partial}{\partial y}+\hat{k}\frac{\partial}{\partial z}\right)\left(Ax^2 - By^2 + Cxyz + 273\right)$$

$$= \hat{i}\left(2Ax+Cyz\right)+\hat{j}\left(-2By+Cxz\right)+\hat{k}\left(Cxy\right)$$

$$\text{Therefore, } |(\nabla T)| = \left[\left(2Ax+Cyz\right)^2+\left(-2By+Cxz\right)^2+C^2x^2y^2\right]^{1/2}$$

(b) Determine the unit vector in the direction of maximum temperature change at the point (–1, 2, 3).

Ans. Required unit vector $\hat{n} = \dfrac{\nabla T}{|(\nabla T)|}$ at the point (-1,2,3),

$$\text{or } \hat{n} = \frac{\hat{i}\left(2Ax+Cyz\right)+\hat{j}\left(-2By+Cxz\right)+\hat{k}\left(Cxy\right)}{\left[\left(2Ax+Cyz\right)^2+\left(-2By+Cxz\right)^2+C^2x^2y^2\right]^{1/2}}$$

At the point (–1,2,3), i.e. for $x = -1, y = 2, z = 3$.

$$\text{We get, } \hat{n} = \frac{\left[\hat{i}(-2A+6C)+\hat{j}(-4B-3C)-\hat{k}2C\right]}{\left[(-2A+6C)^2+(-4B-3C)^2+4C^2\right]^{1/2}}$$

(c) **Calculate the rate of change of temperature in the direction of $(\hat{i}+\hat{j}+\hat{k})$.**

Ans. Rate of change of temperature in the direction of $\hat{i}+\hat{j}+\hat{k}$ is $\hat{a}\,.\,\nabla T$ where $\hat{a}$ is the unit vector in this direction.

$$\text{i.e. } \hat{a} = \frac{\hat{i}+\hat{j}+\hat{k}}{|\hat{i}+\hat{j}+\hat{k}|} = \frac{\hat{i}+\hat{j}+\hat{k}}{\sqrt{3}}$$

$$\text{Therefore, } \hat{a}.\nabla T = \left(\frac{\hat{i}+\hat{j}+\hat{k}}{\sqrt{3}}\right)\cdot\left[\hat{i}(2Ax+Cyz)+\hat{j}(-2By+Cxz)+\hat{k}(Cxy)\right]$$

$$\text{i.e. } \hat{a}.\nabla T = \frac{1}{\sqrt{3}}\cdot(2Ax+Cyz-2By+Cxz+Cxy)$$

Q10. What do you mean by the Divergence and the net outward flux in fluid flow?

Or

Give the physical meaning of divergence.

Ans. Consider a region of fluid flow. Let dV = dx dy dz be a rectangular volume element located at the origin O (x,y,z). Let the faces of this element be normal to the three axes, as shown in Fig. 2.4.

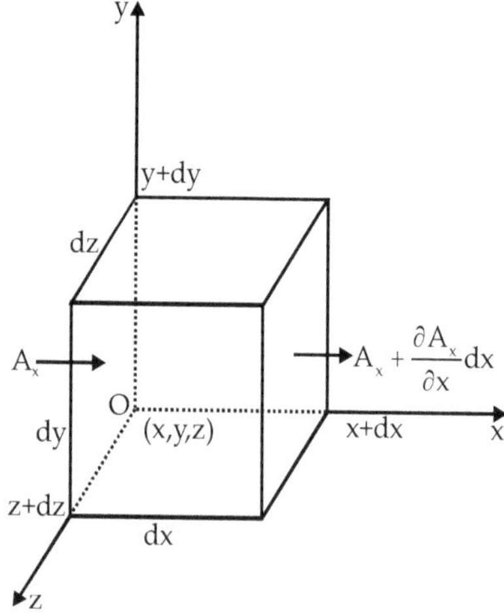

Fig. 2.4: Physical meaning of the divergence for fluid flow

Let $\vec{v}$ be velocity of fluid flow and ρ its density. Then the amount of fluid crossing an area $\vec{S}$ perpendicular to its flow in time t is (vt) $(\vec{S})\rho$.

If A is the amount of fluid crossing per unit area per unit time then $A = v\rho$. Now let $\vec{A} = \vec{v}\ \rho$. Let $\vec{A}$ be directed normal to the area S. Then $\vec{A}$ is the amount of fluid flowing per unit area per unit time in a direction normal to the area $\vec{S}$. Let us assume that the volume element dV is very small. Then $\vec{A}$, i.e. the flow rate per unit area, will be constant over each face. Let A_x, A_y, A_z be the components of $\vec{A}$, i.e. they are the flow rates per unit area in the x, y, z direction, respectively. Now if A_x (x) is the flow rate per unit area at x, then its change over a small distance dx is $dA_x = \frac{\partial A_x}{\partial x}dx$

Thus, the net flow rate per unit area at $x + dx$ is $A_x(x+dx) \approx A_x(x) + \frac{\partial A_x}{\partial x}dx$

So the rate of fluid flow at x into the volume element at the face normal to x-axis is $I_x = A_x\ dy\ dz$

The rate of fluid flowing at x + dx out of the volume element at the face normal to x-axis is $O_x = \left(A_x + \frac{\partial A_x}{\partial x}dx\right)dy\ dz$

The net outward flow rate along the x-axis through volume element $dV = dxdydz$ is $O_x - I_x = \frac{\partial A_x}{\partial x}dxdydz = \frac{\partial A_x}{\partial x}dV$ ...(i)

Similarly, the net outward flow rate parallel to the y and z-axes through the volume element dV are, respectively

$$O_y - I_y = \frac{\partial A_y}{\partial y}dV \qquad \text{...(ii)}$$

$$O_z - I_z = \frac{\partial A_z}{\partial z}dV \qquad \text{...(iii)}$$

Hence, the net outward flow rate through the volume element dV is the sum of the three Eqs. (i), (ii) and (iii).

Thus, Net outward flow rate F from $dV = \left(\frac{\partial A_x}{\partial x} + \frac{\partial A_y}{\partial y} + \frac{\partial A_z}{\partial z}\right)dV$

or $F = (\nabla.\vec{A})dV$. ...(iv)

Now make dV smaller and smaller so that it still encloses the point (x,y,z), i.e. shrink dx dy dz to a point. Then in the limit of infinitesimal dV we get

Net outward flow rate per unit volume, at a point (x,y,z) $= \nabla.\vec{A}$ ...(v)

Eq. (v) gives us the physical meaning of divergence; it is the net rate of fluid outflow from dV, per unit volume in the limit of infinitesimal dV. It may vary from point to point. Its value at the point (x,y,z) is given by Eq. (v) as dV is made smaller and smaller while always enclosing that point. This is the net outward flow of actual substance for liquids, gases and particles; it is called the flux for electric and magnetic fields. It could be different from zero because of a change in density.

Q11. (a) Given that $\vec{E} = -\nabla\Phi$ and $\nabla.\vec{E} = \frac{\rho}{\varepsilon_0}$, determine the electric field and the charge distribution that correspond to the following potential

$$\Phi = k_0\left(x^2+y^2+z^2\right) \text{ for } x^2+y^2+z^2 < a^2$$

$$\Phi = k_0\left[-a^2 + \frac{2a^3}{\left(x^2+y^2+z^2\right)^{1/2}}\right] \text{ for } a^2 < x^2+y^2+z^2$$

Ans. We have $\vec{E} = -\nabla\phi$

For $x^2+y^2+z^2 < a^2$

$$\vec{E} = -\left(\hat{i}\frac{\partial}{\partial x}+\hat{j}\frac{\partial}{\partial y}+\hat{k}\frac{\partial}{\partial z}\right)\left[k_0\left(x^2+y^2+z^2\right)\right]$$

$$= -k_0\left(2x\hat{i}+2y\hat{j}+2z\hat{k}\right) = -2k_0\left(x\hat{i}+y\hat{j}+z\hat{k}\right)$$

For $a^2 < x^2+y^2+z^2$

$$\vec{E} = -\left(\hat{i}\frac{\partial}{\partial x}+\hat{j}\frac{\partial}{\partial y}+\hat{k}\frac{\partial}{\partial z}\right)\left(-a^2k_0 + \frac{2a^3k_0}{\left(x^2+y^2+z^2\right)^{1/2}}\right)$$

$$= -2a^3k_0\left(-\frac{\hat{i}}{2}\frac{2x}{\left(x^2+y^2+z^2\right)^{3/2}} - \frac{\hat{j}}{2}\frac{2y}{\left(x^2+y^2+z^2\right)^{3/2}} - \frac{\hat{k}}{2}\frac{2z}{\left(x^2+y^2+z^2\right)^{3/2}}\right)$$

$$= \frac{2a^3k_0}{(x^2+y^2+z^2)^{3/2}}\left(x\hat{i}+y\hat{j}+z\hat{k}\right),$$

Now, $\rho = \varepsilon_0(\nabla.\vec{E})$

For $x^2+y^2+z^2 < a^2$

$$\rho(x,y,z) = \varepsilon_0\left(\hat{i}\frac{\partial}{\partial x}+\hat{j}\frac{\partial}{\partial y}+\hat{k}\frac{\partial}{\partial z}\right)\cdot\left[k_0\left(-2x\hat{i}-2y\hat{j}-2z\hat{k}\right)\right]$$

$$\rho(x,y,z) = -2\varepsilon_0 k_0(3) = -6\varepsilon_0 k_0$$

For $a^2 < x^2+y^2+z^2$

$$\rho(x,y,z) = \varepsilon_0\left(\frac{\partial E_x}{\partial x}+\frac{\partial E_y}{\partial y}+\frac{\partial E_z}{\partial z}\right)$$

$$= \varepsilon_0 k_0 2a^3\left[\frac{1}{(x^2+y^2+z^2)^{3/2}} - 3\frac{x^2}{(x^2+y^2+z^2)^{5/2}}\right]+\left[\frac{1}{(x^2+y^2+z^2)^{3/2}} - 3\frac{y^2}{(x^2+y^2+z^2)^{5/2}}\right]$$

$$+\left[\frac{1}{(x^2+y^2+z^2)^{3/2}} - 3\frac{z^2}{(x^2+y^2+z^2)^{5/2}}\right]$$

$$-\varepsilon_0 k_0 2a^3\left[\frac{3}{(x^2+y^2+z^2)^{3/2}} - 3\frac{(x^2+y^2+z^2)}{(x^2+y^2+z^2)^{5/2}}\right] \text{ or } \rho(x,y,z) = 0$$

(b) **The velocity vector field $\vec{v}$ of a rigid body rotating about a fixed axis (say z-axis) in space with a constant angular speed ω is given by $\vec{v} = \vec{\omega} \times \vec{r}$. Here $\vec{\omega}$ is the angular velocity of rotation. Show that the divergence of $\vec{v}$ is zero.**

Ans. Here $\vec{\omega} = \omega\hat{k}, \vec{v} = \vec{\omega}\times\vec{r} = \omega\hat{k}\times\left(x\hat{i}+y\hat{j}+z\hat{k}\right) = \omega\left(x\hat{j}-y\hat{i}\right)$

Therefore, $\nabla.\vec{v} = \left(\hat{i}\frac{\partial}{\partial x}+\hat{j}\frac{\partial}{\partial y}+\hat{k}\frac{\partial}{\partial z}\right).\left(\omega x\hat{j}-\omega y\hat{i}\right)$

$$= \frac{\partial}{\partial y}(\omega x) - \frac{\partial}{\partial x}(\omega y) = 0$$

Q12. Discuss the Rotation of a Rigid Body.

Ans. We know that the rotation of a rigid body about a fixed axis in space can be described by a vector $\vec{\omega}$ of constant magnitude ω. The direction of $\vec{\omega}$ is along the axis of rotation and its sense is determined by the right-hand rule. The velocity field of rotation is given by $\vec{v} = \vec{\omega} \times \vec{r}$ where $\vec{r}$ is the position vector of a point on the body with respect to a Cartesian coordinate system having the origin on the axis of rotation.

Let the axis of rotation be along the z-axis.

Then $\vec{\omega} = \omega\hat{k}$ and $\vec{v} = \vec{\omega} \times \vec{r} = \omega\hat{k} \times \left(x\hat{i} + y\hat{j} + z\hat{k}\right) = \left(-\omega y\hat{i} - \omega x\hat{j}\right)$.

Let us now calculate curl of $\vec{v}$:

$$\nabla \times \vec{v} = \begin{vmatrix} \hat{i} & \hat{j} & \hat{k} \\ \frac{\partial}{\partial x} & \frac{\partial}{\partial y} & \frac{\partial}{\partial z} \\ v_x & v_y & v_z \end{vmatrix} = \begin{vmatrix} \hat{i} & \hat{j} & \hat{k} \\ \frac{\partial}{\partial x} & \frac{\partial}{\partial y} & \frac{\partial}{\partial z} \\ -\omega y & \omega x & 0 \end{vmatrix}$$

In the expanded form, we can write

$$\nabla \times \vec{v} = \hat{i}\left[\frac{-\partial}{\partial z}(\omega x)\right] + \hat{j}\left[\frac{\partial}{\partial z}(-\omega y)\right] + \hat{k}\left[\frac{\partial}{\partial x}(\omega x) + \frac{\partial}{\partial y}(\omega y)\right]$$

$$= \vec{0} + \vec{0} + \hat{k}(2\omega) \quad [\because \frac{\partial x}{\partial z} = 0 \text{ and } \frac{\partial y}{\partial z} = 0 \text{ and } \omega \text{ is constant}]$$

$$\therefore \nabla \times \vec{v} = (2\omega)\hat{k} = 2\vec{\omega}$$

So for the rotation of a rigid body, the curl of the velocity field has the direction of the axis of rotation. Its magnitude equals twice the angular speed of rotation. So we can say that the curl of a velocity vector field at a point represents twice the rate at which a material element occupying the point is rotating.

Q13. Use Product rule, $\nabla(fg) = f\nabla g + g\nabla f$ to find $\nabla\left[\frac{1}{\left(x^2+y^2+z^2\right)^{3/2}}\right]$.

Ans. From given rule $\nabla(fg) = f.\nabla g + g\nabla f$,

$$\text{We get, } \nabla\left[\frac{1}{\left(x^2+y^2+z^2\right)^{3/2}}\right] = \nabla\left[\frac{1}{\left(x^2+y^2+z^2\right)} \cdot \frac{1}{\left(x^2+y^2+z^2\right)^{1/2}}\right]$$

$$= \frac{1}{\left(x^2+y^2+z^2\right)}\left[\nabla\frac{1}{\left(x^2+y^2+z^2\right)^{1/2}}\right] + \frac{1}{\left(x^2+y^2+z^2\right)^{1/2}}\left[\nabla\frac{1}{\left(x^2+y^2+z^2\right)}\right]$$

Hence, we get

$$\nabla\left[\frac{1}{\left(x^2+y^2+z^2\right)^{3/2}}\right]=-\left[\frac{x\hat{i}+y\hat{j}+z\hat{k}}{\left(x^2+y^2+z^2\right)\left(x^2+y^2+z^2\right)^{3/2}}\right]-\left[\frac{2\left(x\hat{i}+y\hat{j}+z\hat{k}\right)}{\left(x^2+y^2+z^2\right)^{1/2}\left(x^2+y^2+z^2\right)^2}\right]$$

$$=\frac{-3\left(x\hat{i}+y\hat{j}+z\hat{k}\right)}{\left(x^2+y^2+z^2\right)^{5/2}}$$

Q14. The position vector of a particle moving on an ellipse is given by

$r = (c \sin \omega t)\hat{i} + (d \cos \omega t)\hat{j}$.

Calculate (i) $\frac{d}{dt}(\vec{r}.\vec{v})$ and (ii) $\frac{d}{dt}(\vec{r}\times\vec{a})$.

Ans. We have, $\vec{r} = c \sin \omega t\,\hat{i} + d \cos \omega t\,\hat{j}$

Therefore, $\vec{v}=\frac{d\vec{r}}{dt} = c\,\omega \cos \omega t\,\hat{i} - d\omega \sin \omega t\,\hat{j}$

Hence, $\frac{d}{dt}\left(\vec{r}.\vec{v}\right)=\frac{d\vec{r}}{dt}.\vec{v}+\vec{r}.\frac{d\vec{v}}{dt}=\vec{v}.\vec{v}+\vec{r}.\vec{a}$

where $\vec{a}=\frac{d\vec{v}}{dt}=-c\,\omega^2\sin \omega t\,\hat{i}-d\,\omega^2\cos \omega t\,\hat{j}=-\omega^2\,\vec{r}$

$$\therefore\frac{d}{dt}\left(\vec{r}.\vec{v}\right)=c^2\omega^2\cos^2\omega t+d^2\omega^2\sin^2\omega t-\left(c^2\omega^2\sin^2\omega t+d^2\omega^2\cos^2\omega t\right)$$

$$=\omega^2\cos^2\omega t\left(c^2-d^2\right)+\omega^2\sin^2\omega t\left(d^2-c^2\right)$$

$$=\omega^2\left(c^2-d^2\right)\left(\cos^2\omega t-\sin^2\omega t\right)=\omega^2\left(c^2-d^2\right)\cos 2\omega t$$

and $\frac{d}{dt}\left(\vec{r}\times\vec{a}\right)=\frac{d\vec{r}}{dt}\times\vec{a}+\vec{r}\times\frac{d\vec{a}}{dt}=\vec{v}\times\vec{a}+\vec{r}\times\frac{d\vec{a}}{dt}$

Now, $\frac{d\vec{a}}{dt}=-\omega^2\frac{d\vec{r}}{dt}=-c\omega^3\cos\omega t\hat{i}+d\omega^3\sin\omega t\hat{j}$

$$\therefore\frac{d}{dt}\left(\vec{r}\times\vec{a}\right)=\left(-cd\omega^3\cos^2\omega t\hat{k}-cd\omega^3\sin^2\omega t\hat{k}\right)+\left(cd\omega^3\sin^2\omega t\hat{k}+cd\omega^3\cos^2\omega t\hat{k}\right)$$

$$=-cd\omega^3\hat{k}+cd\omega^3\hat{k}=0$$

Q15. If $\vec{r}=x\hat{i}+y\hat{j}+z\hat{k}$, show that $\nabla\vec{r}=\frac{\vec{r}}{r}$ and $\nabla r^n = nr^{n-2}\vec{r}$.

Ans. We have $\vec{r}=x\hat{i}+y\hat{j}+z\hat{k}$

$$\therefore\ \vec{r}=\sqrt{\vec{r}.\vec{r}}=\left(x^2+y^2+z^2\right)^{1/2}$$

Now, $\nabla \vec{r} = \left(\hat{i}\frac{\partial}{\partial x} + \hat{j}\frac{\partial}{\partial y} + \hat{k}\frac{\partial}{\partial z}\right)(x^2+y^2+z^2)^{1/2}$

$$= \hat{i}\left[\frac{1}{2}(x^2+y^2+z^2)^{-1/2}.2x\right] + \hat{j}\left[\frac{1}{2}(x^2+y^2+z^2)^{-1/2}.2y\right] + \hat{k}\left[\frac{1}{2}(x^2+y^2+z^2)^{-1/2}.2z\right]$$

$$= \frac{x\hat{i}+y\hat{j}+z\hat{k}}{(x^2+y^2+z^2)^{1/2}} = \frac{\vec{r}}{r}.$$

Now, $\nabla r^n = (x^2+y^2+z^2)^{n/2} = \left(\hat{i}\frac{\partial}{\partial x} + \hat{j}\frac{\partial}{\partial y} + \hat{k}\frac{\partial}{\partial z}\right)(x^2+y^2+z^2)^{n/2}$

$$= \hat{i}\left[\frac{n}{2}(x^2+y^2+z^2)^{\frac{n}{2}-1}.2x\right] + \hat{j}\left[\frac{n}{2}(x^2+y^2+z^2)^{\frac{n}{2}-1}.2y\right] + \hat{k}\left[\frac{n}{2}(x^2+y^2+z^2)^{\frac{n}{2}-1}.2z\right]$$

$$= n(x^2+y^2+z^2)^{\frac{n-2}{2}}(x\hat{i}+y\hat{j}+z\hat{k}) = nr^{n-2}\vec{r}.$$

Q16. A scalar field f is said to be harmonic if div grad f = 0. Show that

(a) $f(x,y,z) = \frac{1}{(x^2+y^2+z^2)^{1/2}}$, **for** $x\hat{i}+y\hat{j}+z\hat{k} \neq 0$ **is harmonic.**

(b) $v(x,y) = \frac{y\hat{i}}{(x^2+y^2)} - \frac{x\hat{j}}{(x^2+y^2)}$ **is solenoidal.**

v approximates the horizontal part of the velocity field of water flowing down the drain.

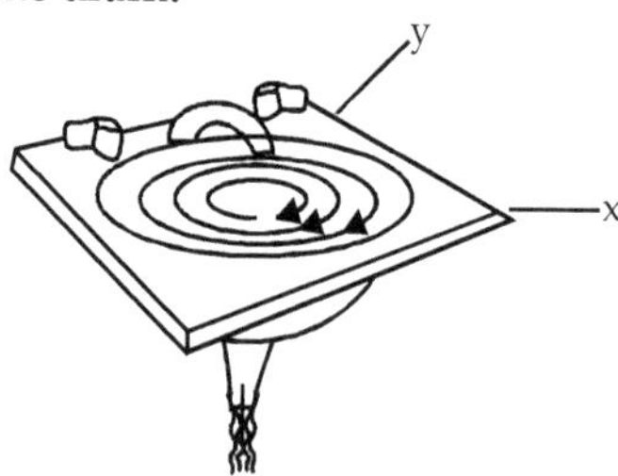

Ans. (a) Given, $f(x,y,z) = \frac{1}{(x^2+y^2+z^2)^{1/2}}, x\hat{i}+y\hat{j}+z\hat{k} \neq 0$

Here, $\nabla f = -\frac{(x\hat{i}+y\hat{j}+z\hat{k})}{(x^2+y^2+z^2)^{3/2}}$

Since, div grad $f = \nabla.(\nabla f)$

$$= -\frac{\partial}{\partial x}\left[\frac{x}{\left(x^2+y^2+z^2\right)^{3/2}}\right] - \frac{\partial}{\partial y}\left[\frac{y}{\left(x^2+y^2+z^2\right)^{3/2}}\right] - \frac{\partial}{\partial z}\left[\frac{z}{\left(x^2+y^2+z^2\right)^{3/2}}\right]$$

$$= -\frac{1}{\left(x^2+y^2+z^2\right)^{3/2}} + \frac{3}{2}\frac{2x^2}{\left(x^2+y^2+z^2\right)^{5/2}} - \frac{1}{\left(x^2+y^2+z^2\right)^{3/2}} + \frac{3}{2}\frac{2y^2}{\left(x^2+y^2+z^2\right)^{5/2}}$$

$$-\frac{1}{\left(x^2+y^2+z^2\right)^{3/2}} + \frac{3}{2}\frac{2z^2}{\left(x^2+y^2+z^2\right)^{5/2}} = -\frac{3}{\left(x^2+y^2+z^2\right)^{3/2}} + \frac{3\left(x^2+y^2+z^2\right)}{\left(x^2+y^2+z^2\right)^{5/2}} = 0$$

$\therefore$ $f(x,y,z)$ is harmonic.

(b) If $\vec{v}$ is solenoidal, then $\nabla.\vec{v} = 0$

Here, $\nabla.\vec{v} = \frac{\partial v_x}{\partial x} + \frac{\partial v_y}{\partial y} = -\frac{y.2x}{\left(x^2+y^2\right)^2} + \frac{x.2y}{\left(x^2+y^2\right)^2} = 0$

$\therefore$ $f(x,y,z)$ is solenoidal.

Q17. A particular electromagnetic field in free space is given by

$$\mathbf{E_x = 0, E_y = E_0 \sin(kx + \omega t), E_z = 0}$$

$$\mathbf{B_x = 0, B_y = 0, B_z = -E_0 \sin(kx + \omega t)}$$

Find the relation between ω and k for which each of the following equations hold: (i) curl $\vec{E} = -\frac{1}{c}\frac{\partial \vec{B}}{\partial t}$; (ii) curl $\vec{B} = \frac{1}{c}\frac{\partial \vec{E}}{\partial t}$

Ans. (i) We have $\vec{\nabla} \times \vec{E} = -\frac{1}{c}\frac{\partial \vec{B}}{\partial t}$

or $\hat{i}\left(\frac{\partial E_z}{\partial y} - \frac{\partial E_y}{\partial z}\right) + \hat{j}\left(\frac{\partial E_x}{\partial z} - \frac{\partial E_z}{\partial x}\right) + \hat{k}\left(\frac{\partial E_y}{\partial x} - \frac{\partial E_x}{\partial y}\right) = -\frac{1}{c}\frac{\partial}{\partial t}\left(\hat{i}B_x + \hat{j}B_y + \hat{k}B_z\right)$

or $\hat{i}(0-0) + \hat{j}(0-0) + \hat{k}\left[kE_0 \cos(kx+\omega t)\right] = \frac{E_0}{c}\hat{k}\,\omega \cos(kx+\omega t)$

or $kE_0 = \frac{E_0\omega}{c}$, or $k = \frac{\omega}{c}$.

(ii) We have $\nabla \times \vec{B} = \frac{1}{c}\frac{\partial \vec{E}}{\partial t}$, or

$\hat{i}\left(\frac{\partial B_z}{\partial y} - \frac{\partial B_y}{\partial z}\right) + \hat{j}\left(\frac{\partial B_x}{\partial z} - \frac{\partial B_z}{\partial x}\right) + \hat{k}\left(\frac{\partial B_y}{\partial x} - \frac{\partial B_x}{\partial y}\right) = \frac{1}{c}\frac{\partial}{\partial t}\left(\hat{i}E_x + \hat{j}E_y + \hat{k}E_z\right)$

or $\hat{i}(0-0) + \hat{j}kE_0 \cos(kx+\omega t) + \hat{k}(0-0) = \frac{\omega}{c}\hat{j}E_0 \cos(kx+\omega t)$ or $k = \frac{\omega}{c}$

Q18. Find grad e^{r^2}.

Ans. We know that, $r^2 = x^2 + y^2 + z^2$

$$\therefore \text{grad}\left\{e^{(x^2+y^2+z^2)}\right\} = \sum i\frac{\partial}{\partial x}e^{x^2+y^2+z^2}$$

$$= \sum \hat{i}\, e^{x^2+y^2+z^2}.2x = 2e^{x^2+y^2+z^2}\left(x\hat{i}+y\hat{j}+j\hat{k}\right) = 2e^{x^2+y^2+z^2}\vec{r}.$$

Q19. If $\phi(x,y,z) = 3x^2y - y^3z^2$, find $\nabla\phi$ at the point (1,-2, 1).

Ans. Here, $\nabla\phi = \left(\hat{i}\frac{\partial}{\partial x} + \hat{j}\frac{\partial}{\partial y} + \hat{k}\frac{\partial}{\partial z}\right)(3x^2y - y^3z^2)$

$$= \hat{i}\frac{\partial}{\partial x}(3x^2y - y^3z^2) + \hat{j}\frac{\partial}{\partial y}(3x^2y - y^3z^2) + \hat{k}\frac{\partial}{\partial z}(3x^2y - y^3z^2)$$

$$= 6xy\hat{i} + (3x^2 - 3y^2z^2)\hat{j} - 2y^3z\hat{k}$$

$$= -12\hat{i} - 9\hat{j} - 16\hat{k}, \text{ at the point } x = 1, y = -2, z = -1.$$

Q20. Find the directional derivative of the function

$f = x^2 - y^2 + 2z^2$ at the point P (1, 2, 3) in the direction of the line PQ, where Q is the point (5, 0, 4).

Ans. Here, the position vectors of P and Q are respectively

$$\hat{i} + 2\hat{j} + 3\hat{k} \text{ and } 5\hat{i} + 0\hat{j} + 4\hat{k}$$

$$\therefore \overrightarrow{PQ} = \left(5\hat{i} + 0\hat{j} + 4\hat{k}\right) - \left(\hat{i} + 2\hat{j} + 3\hat{k}\right) = 4\hat{i} - 2\hat{j} + \hat{k}.$$

If $\hat{a}$ be the unit vector along PQ, then

$$\hat{a} = \frac{4\hat{i} - 2\hat{j} + \hat{k}}{\sqrt{4^2 + 2^2 + 1^2}} = \frac{4\hat{i} - 2\hat{j} + \hat{k}}{\sqrt{21}}$$

Also, grad $f = \hat{i}\frac{\partial f}{\partial x} + \hat{j}\frac{\partial f}{\partial y} + \hat{k}\frac{\partial f}{\partial z} = 2x\hat{i} - 2y\hat{j} + 4z\hat{k}.$

Hence, directional derivative $\frac{df}{ds} = \hat{a}.$

$$\text{grad } f = \frac{4\hat{i} - 2\hat{j} + \hat{k}}{\sqrt{21}}.\left(2x\hat{i} - 2y\hat{j} + 4z\hat{k}\right)$$

$$= \frac{8x + 4y + 4z}{\sqrt{21}} = \frac{8.1 + 4.2 + 4.3}{\sqrt{21}}, \text{ at } (1, 2, 3) = \frac{28}{\sqrt{21}} = 4\sqrt{\frac{7}{3}}$$

Q21. What is the greatest rate of increase of u $= xyz^2$ at (1, 0, 3).

Ans. Here, grad u $= \frac{\partial u}{\partial x}\hat{i} + \frac{\partial u}{\partial y}\hat{j} + \frac{\partial u}{\partial z}\hat{k}$

$$= yz^2\hat{i} + xz^2\hat{j} + 2xyz\hat{k} = 0\hat{i} + 9\hat{j} + 0\hat{k} = 9\hat{j}, \text{ at the point } (1, 0, 3)$$

$\therefore$ The greatest rate of u at (1, 0, 3) $= |\text{grad}\, u| = |9\hat{i}| = 9$

Q22. Find curl $\vec{V}$, where $\vec{V} = e^{xyz}\left(\hat{i} + \hat{j} + \hat{k}\right)$.

Ans. Here, curl $\vec{V} = \nabla \times \vec{V} = \begin{vmatrix} \hat{i} & \hat{j} & \hat{k} \\ \frac{\partial}{\partial x} & \frac{\partial}{\partial y} & \frac{\partial}{\partial z} \\ e^{xyz} & e^{xyz} & e^{xyz} \end{vmatrix}$

$$= \hat{i}\left\{\frac{\partial}{\partial y}\left(e^{xyz}\right) - \frac{\partial}{\partial z}\left(e^{xyz}\right)\right\} + \hat{j}\left\{\frac{\partial}{\partial z}\left(e^{xyz}\right) - \frac{\partial}{\partial x}\left(e^{xyz}\right)\right\} + \hat{k}\left\{\frac{\partial}{\partial x}\left(e^{xyz}\right) - \frac{\partial}{\partial y}\left(e^{xyz}\right)\right\}$$

$$= e^{xyz}\left\{x(z-y)\hat{i} + y(x-z)\hat{j} + z(y-x)\hat{k}\right\}$$

Q23. If $\vec{f}$ = xy sin z$\hat{i}$ + y^2 sin x$\hat{j}$ + z^2 sin xy $\hat{k}$, find $\nabla.\vec{f}$ at the point $\left(0, \frac{1}{2}\pi, \frac{1}{2}\pi\right)$.

Ans. Here, $\nabla.\vec{f} = \left(\frac{\partial}{\partial x}\hat{i} + \frac{\partial}{\partial y}\hat{j} + \frac{\partial}{\partial z}\hat{k}\right).\left(xy \sin z\hat{i} + y^2 \sin x\hat{j} + z^2 \sin xy\hat{k}\right)$

$$= \frac{\partial}{\partial x}\left(xy \sin z\right) + \frac{\partial}{\partial y}\left(y^2 \sin x\right) + \frac{\partial}{\partial z}\left(z^2 \sin xy\right)$$

$$= y \sin z + 2y \sin x + 2z \sin xy = \frac{1}{2}\pi \text{ at the point } \left(0, \frac{1}{2}\pi, \frac{1}{2}\pi\right).$$

Q24. Prove that

(i) div grad $r^m = \nabla \cdot \nabla r^m = m(m+1)r^{m-2}$

Ans. Here, $\nabla r^m = mr^{m-2}\vec{r} = mr^{m-2}\left(x\hat{i} + y\hat{j} + z\hat{k}\right)$

Therefore, $\nabla.\nabla r^m = \left(\hat{i}\frac{\partial}{\partial x} + \hat{j}\frac{\partial}{\partial y} + \hat{k}\frac{\partial}{\partial z}\right) mr^{m-2}\left(\hat{i}x + \hat{j}y + z\hat{k}\right)$

$$= \frac{\partial}{\partial x}\left(mr^{m-2}x\right) + \frac{\partial}{\partial y}\left(mr^{m-2}y\right) + \frac{\partial}{\partial z}\left(mr^{m-2}z\right)$$

Now, $\frac{\partial}{\partial x}\left(mr^{m-2}x\right) = m.(m-2)r^{m-3}\frac{\partial r}{\partial x}x + mr^{m-2}$

$= m(m-2)r^{m-4}x^2 + mr^{m-2}$, as $\partial r/\partial x = x/r$.

Similarly, we get other two expressions.

$\therefore\ \nabla\cdot\nabla r^m = m(m-2)r^{m-4}(x^2+y^2+z^2) + 3mr^{m-2}$

$= m(m-2)r^{m-2} + 3mr^{m-2}$, as $x^2+y^2+z^2 = r^2$

$= m(m+1)r^{m-2}$

(ii) curl grad $\mathbf{r^m = \overline{\nabla}\times\overline{\nabla}r^m = 0}$

Ans. $\nabla\times\nabla r^m = \nabla\times mr^{m-2}(\hat{i}x+\hat{j}y+\hat{k}z)$

$$= \begin{vmatrix} \hat{i} & \hat{j} & \hat{k} \\ \dfrac{\partial}{\partial x} & \dfrac{\partial}{\partial y} & \dfrac{\partial}{\partial z} \\ mr^{m-2}x & mr^{m-2}y & mr^{m-2}z \end{vmatrix} = \sum\hat{i}\left\{\frac{\partial}{\partial y}(mr^{m-2}z) - \frac{\partial}{\partial z}(mr^{m-2}y)\right\}$$

$$= \sum\hat{i}\left\{m(m-2)r^{m-3}\frac{\partial r}{\partial y}z - m(m-2)r^{m-3}\frac{\partial r}{\partial z}y\right\}$$

$$= \sum\hat{i}\left\{m(m-2)r^{m-3}\frac{y}{r}z - m(m-2)r^{m-3}\frac{z}{r}y\right\} = \vec{0}.$$

Q25. Prove that div $\mathbf{\hat{r} = \dfrac{2}{r}}$.

Ans. Here, div $\hat{r} = \nabla\cdot\dfrac{\vec{r}}{r} = \left(\hat{i}\dfrac{\partial}{\partial x} + \hat{j}\dfrac{\partial}{\partial y} + \hat{k}\dfrac{\partial}{\partial z}\right)\cdot\dfrac{(\hat{i}x+\hat{j}y+\hat{k}z)}{r}$

$$= \frac{\partial}{\partial x}\left(\frac{x}{r}\right) + \frac{\partial}{\partial y}\left(\frac{y}{r}\right) + \frac{\partial}{\partial z}\left(\frac{z}{r}\right) = \frac{1}{r} - \frac{x}{r^2}\frac{\partial r}{\partial x} + \frac{1}{r} - \frac{y}{r^2}\frac{\partial r}{\partial y} + \frac{1}{r} - \frac{z}{r^2}\frac{\partial r}{\partial z}$$

$$= \frac{3}{r} - \frac{x}{r^2}\frac{x}{r} - \frac{y}{r^2}\frac{y}{r} - \frac{z}{r^2}\frac{z}{r} = \frac{3}{r} - \frac{1}{r^3}(x^2+y^2+z^2) = \frac{3}{r} - \frac{1}{r^3}r^2 = \frac{2}{r}$$

Q26. Prove that $\mathbf{\nabla\int f(u)du = f(u)\nabla u}$.

Ans. Let $\int f(u)du = F$, a function of u so that $\dfrac{\partial F}{\partial u} = f(u)$.

Then, $\nabla\int f(u)\,du = \left(\hat{i}\dfrac{\partial}{\partial x} + \hat{j}\dfrac{\partial}{\partial y} + \hat{k}\dfrac{\partial}{\partial z}\right)F$

$$= \hat{i}\frac{\partial F}{\partial x} + \hat{j}\frac{\partial F}{\partial y} + \hat{k}\frac{\partial F}{\partial z} = \hat{i}\frac{\partial F}{\partial u}\frac{\partial u}{\partial x} + \hat{j}\frac{\partial F}{\partial u}\frac{\partial u}{\partial y} + \hat{k}\frac{\partial F}{\partial u}\frac{\partial u}{\partial z} = \frac{\partial F}{\partial u}\left(\hat{i}\frac{\partial u}{\partial x} + \hat{j}\frac{\partial u}{\partial y} + \hat{k}\frac{\partial u}{\partial z}\right)$$

$= f(u)\ \nabla\ u.$

Q27. Prove that $\nabla\cdot(f\vec{f}) = f(\nabla\cdot\vec{f}) + \vec{f}\cdot\nabla f$.

(div $(f\vec{f})$ = f div $\vec{f}$ + $\vec{f}\cdot$ grad f)

Ans. Here $\nabla\cdot f\vec{f} = \left(\hat{i}\frac{\partial}{\partial x}+\hat{j}\frac{\partial}{\partial y}+\hat{k}\frac{\partial}{\partial z}\right)\left(ff_x\hat{i}+ff_y\hat{j}+ff_z\hat{k}\right)$

$$=\frac{\partial}{\partial x}(ff_x)+\frac{\partial}{\partial y}(ff_y)+\frac{\partial}{\partial z}(ff_z)$$

$$=f_x\frac{\partial f}{\partial x}+f\frac{\partial f_x}{\partial x}+f_y\frac{\partial f}{\partial y}+f\frac{\partial f_y}{\partial y}+f_z\frac{\partial f}{\partial z}+f\frac{\partial f_z}{\partial z}$$

$$=f\left(\frac{\partial f_x}{\partial x}+\frac{\partial f_y}{\partial y}+\frac{\partial f_z}{\partial z}\right)+f_x\frac{\partial f}{\partial x}+f_y\frac{\partial f}{\partial y}+f_z\frac{\partial f}{\partial z}=f(\nabla\cdot\vec{f})+\vec{f}\cdot\nabla f.$$

Q28. Prove that curl $\frac{\vec{a}\times\vec{r}}{r^3}=-\frac{\vec{a}}{r^3}+\frac{3\vec{r}}{r^5}(\vec{a}\cdot\vec{r})$, where $\vec{a}$ is a constant vector.

Ans. We know that, curl $\frac{\vec{a}\times\vec{r}}{r^3}=\nabla\times\frac{\vec{a}\times\vec{r}}{r^3}=\sum\hat{i}\times\frac{\partial}{\partial x}\left(\frac{\vec{a}\times\vec{r}}{r^3}\right)$

Now $\frac{\partial}{\partial x}\left(\frac{\vec{a}\times\vec{r}}{r^3}\right)=-\frac{3}{r^4}\frac{\partial r}{\partial x}(\vec{a}\times\vec{r})+\frac{1}{r^3}\left(\vec{a}\times\frac{\partial\vec{r}}{\partial x}\right)=-\frac{3x}{r^5}(\vec{a}\times\vec{r})+\frac{1}{r^3}\vec{a}\times\hat{i}$

$$\left\{\text{since}\frac{\partial r}{\partial x}=\frac{x}{r},\frac{\partial\vec{r}}{\partial x}=\frac{\partial}{\partial x}\left(x\hat{i}+y\hat{j}+z\hat{k}\right)=\hat{i}\right\}$$

$$\therefore\ \hat{i}\times\frac{\partial}{\partial x}\left(\frac{\vec{a}\times\vec{r}}{r^3}\right)=\frac{-3x}{r^5}\left(\hat{i}\times\vec{a}\times\vec{r}\right)+\frac{1}{r^3}\left[\hat{i}\times\vec{a}\times\hat{i}\right]$$

$$=\frac{-3x}{r^5}\left[\hat{i}.\vec{r}\vec{a}-\hat{i}.\vec{a}\vec{r}\right]+\frac{1}{r^3}\left[\hat{i}.\hat{i}\vec{a}-\hat{i}.\vec{a}\hat{i}\right]=-\frac{3x^3}{r^3}\vec{a}+\frac{3\vec{r}}{r^5}\left(\hat{i}x.\vec{a}\right)+\frac{1}{r^3}\vec{a}-\frac{1}{r^3}\left(\hat{i}.\vec{a}\right)\hat{i}$$

$$\therefore\sum\hat{i}\times\frac{\partial}{\partial x}\left(\frac{\vec{a}\times\vec{r}}{r^3}\right)=-\frac{3\vec{a}}{r^5}.r^2+\frac{3\vec{r}}{r^3}\vec{r}.\vec{a}+\frac{3}{r^3}\vec{a}-\frac{1}{r^3}\vec{a},$$

$$\left\{\text{since}\sum\hat{i}x=\vec{r},\sum\left(\hat{i}.\vec{a}\right)\hat{i}=\sum a_1\hat{i}=\vec{a}\right\}=-\frac{\vec{a}}{r_3}+\frac{3\vec{r}}{r^5}(\vec{a}.\vec{r}).$$

Q29. A particle moves along a curve whose parametric equations are $x=e^{-t}, y=2\cos 3t, z=2\sin 3t$, where t is the time. Determine the magnitude of the velocity and acceleration at t = 0.

[June-2011, Q.No.-1(b)]

Ans. Let $\vec{r}$ be the position vector of the particle at time t.

Then $\vec{r}=x\hat{i}+y\hat{j}+z\hat{k}=e^{-t}\hat{i}+2\cos 3t\,\hat{j}+2\sin 3t\,\hat{k}$.

If $\vec{v}$ is the velocity of the particle at time t and $\vec{a}$ its acceleration at that time, then $\vec{v} = \frac{d\vec{r}}{dt} = -e^{-t}\,\hat{i} - 6\sin 3t\,\hat{j} + 6\cos 3t\,\hat{k}$,

and $\vec{a} = \frac{d^2\vec{r}}{dt^2} = -e^{-t}\,\hat{i} - 18\cos 3t\,\hat{j} - 18\sin 3t\,\hat{k}$.

Putting t = 0 in the above relations, the velocity at t = 0 is $-\hat{i} + 6\hat{k}$, and the acceleration at t = 0 is $\hat{i} - 18\hat{j}$.

Hence, at t = 0, the magnitude of velocity

$$= \left|-\hat{i} + 6\hat{k}\right| = \sqrt{\left[(-1)^2 + 6^2\right]} = \sqrt{37},$$

and the magnitude of acceleration $= \left|\hat{i} - 18\hat{j}\right| = \sqrt{\left[1^2 + (-18)^2\right]} = \sqrt{(325)}$.

Q30. Prove that $\nabla^2\left(\frac{1}{r}\right) = 0$ or $\mathrm{div}\left(\mathrm{grad}\frac{1}{r}\right) = 0$.

Ans. We have $\nabla^2\left(\frac{1}{r}\right) = \nabla\cdot\left(\nabla\frac{1}{r}\right) = \mathrm{div}\left(\mathrm{grad}\frac{1}{r}\right) = \mathrm{div}\left(-\frac{1}{r^2}\mathrm{grad}\,r\right) = \mathrm{div}$ $\left(-\frac{1}{r^2}\frac{1}{r}\vec{r}\right) = \mathrm{div}\left(-\frac{1}{r^3}\vec{r}\right) = \left(-\frac{1}{r^3}\right)\mathrm{div}\,\vec{r} + \vec{r}\bullet\mathrm{grad}\left(-\frac{1}{r^3}\right) = -\frac{3}{r^3} + \vec{r}\bullet\left[\frac{d}{dr}\left(-\frac{1}{r^3}\right)\mathrm{grad}\,r\right]$

$$= -\frac{3}{r^3} + \vec{r}\bullet\left(\frac{3}{r^4}\frac{1}{r}\vec{r}\right) = -\frac{3}{r^3} + \frac{3}{r^5}\left(\vec{r}\bullet\vec{r}\right) = -\frac{3}{r^3} + \frac{3}{r^5}r^2 = 0.$$

Q31. Find a unit normal vector to the level surface $x^2y + 2xz = 4$ at the point (2, –2, 3).

Ans. The equation of the level surface is $f(x, y, z) \equiv x^2y + 2xz = 4$.

The vector grad f is along the normal to the surface at the point (x, y, z).

We have, grad $f = \nabla\left(x^2y + 2xz\right) = (2xy + 2z)\hat{i} + x^2\hat{j} + 2x\hat{k}$

$\therefore$ At the point (2, –2, 3), grad $f = -2\hat{i} + 4\hat{j} + 4\hat{k}$.

$\therefore -2\hat{i} + 4\hat{j} + 4\hat{k}$ is a vector along the normal to the given surface at the point (2, –2, 3). Hence, a unit normal vector to the surface at this point

$$= \frac{-2\hat{i}+4\hat{j}+4\hat{k}}{\left|-2\hat{i}+4\hat{j}+4\hat{k}\right|} = \frac{-2\hat{i}+4\hat{j}+4\hat{k}}{\sqrt{(4+16+16)}} = -\frac{1}{3}\hat{i} + \frac{2}{3}\hat{j} + \frac{2}{3}\hat{k}$$

The vector $-\left(-\frac{1}{3}\hat{i}+\frac{2}{3}\hat{j}+\frac{2}{3}\hat{k}\right)$, i.e. $\frac{1}{3}\hat{i}-\frac{2}{3}\hat{j}-\frac{2}{3}\hat{k}$ is also a unit normal vector to the given surface at the point (2, –2, 3).

Q32. A particle moves along the curve $x = t^3+1, y = t^2, z = 2t+5$, where t is the time. Find the components of its velocity and acceleration at $t=1$ in the direction $\hat{i}+\hat{j}+3\hat{k}$.

Ans. If $\vec{r}$ is the position vector of any point (x,y,z) on the given curve, then

$\vec{r} = x\hat{i}+y\hat{j}+z\hat{k} = (t^3+1)\hat{i}+t^2\hat{j}+(2t+5)\hat{k}.$

Now, velocity $=\vec{v} = \frac{d\vec{r}}{dt} = 3t^2\hat{i}+2t\hat{j}+2\hat{k} = 3\hat{i}+2\hat{j}+2\hat{k}$ at $t=1$

and Acceleration $=\vec{a} = \frac{d^2\vec{r}}{dt^2} = \frac{d}{dt}\left(\frac{d\vec{r}}{dt}\right) = 6t\hat{i}+2\hat{j} = 6\hat{i}+2\hat{j}$ at $t=1$.

Now, the unit vector in the given direction $\hat{i}+\hat{j}+3\hat{k}$

$$= \frac{\hat{i}+\hat{j}+3\hat{k}}{\left|\hat{i}+\hat{j}+3\hat{k}\right|} = \frac{\hat{i}+\hat{j}+3\hat{k}}{\sqrt{11}} = \vec{b}, \text{ say.}$$

∴ The component of velocity in the given direction

$$= \vec{v}\bullet\vec{b} = \frac{\left(3\hat{i}+2\hat{j}+2\hat{k}\right)\left(\hat{i}+\hat{j}+3\hat{k}\right)}{\sqrt{11}} = \frac{11}{\sqrt{11}} = \sqrt{(11)};$$

and the component of acceleration in the given direction

$$= \vec{a}\bullet\vec{b} = \frac{\left(6\hat{i}+2\hat{j}\right)\bullet\left(\hat{i}+\hat{j}+3\hat{k}\right)}{\sqrt{11}} = \frac{8}{\sqrt{11}}.$$

Q33. Prove that $\nabla\times(\nabla\times A) = \nabla(\nabla\bullet A) - \nabla^2 A$.

Ans. Let $\vec{A} = A_1\hat{i}+A_2\hat{j}+A_3\hat{k}$.

Then,

$$\nabla\times\vec{A} = \begin{vmatrix} \hat{i} & \hat{j} & \hat{k} \\ \frac{\partial}{\partial x} & \frac{\partial}{\partial y} & \frac{\partial}{\partial z} \\ A_1 & A_2 & A_3 \end{vmatrix} = \left(\frac{\partial A_3}{\partial y} - \frac{\partial A_2}{\partial z}\right)\hat{i} + \left(\frac{\partial A_1}{\partial z} - \frac{\partial A_3}{\partial x}\right)\hat{j} + \left(\frac{\partial A_2}{\partial x} - \frac{\partial A_1}{\partial y}\right)\hat{k}.$$

$$\therefore \nabla\times(\nabla\times A)=\begin{vmatrix}\hat{i} & \hat{j} & \hat{k}\\ \frac{\partial}{\partial x} & \frac{\partial}{\partial y} & \frac{\partial}{\partial z}\\ \frac{\partial A_3}{\partial y}-\frac{\partial A_2}{\partial z} & \frac{\partial A_1}{\partial z}-\frac{\partial A_3}{\partial x} & \frac{\partial A_2}{\partial x}-\frac{\partial A_1}{\partial y}\end{vmatrix}$$

$$=\sum\left[\left\{\frac{\partial}{\partial y}\left(\frac{\partial A_2}{\partial x}-\frac{\partial A_1}{\partial y}\right)-\frac{\partial}{\partial z}\left(\frac{\partial A_1}{\partial z}-\frac{\partial A_3}{\partial x}\right)\right\}\hat{i}\right]$$

$$=\sum\left[\left\{\left(\frac{\partial^2 A_2}{\partial y\partial x}+\frac{\partial^2 A_3}{\partial z\partial x}\right)-\left(\frac{\partial^2 A_1}{\partial y^2}+\frac{\partial^2 A_1}{\partial z^2}\right)\right\}\hat{i}\right]$$

$$=\sum\left[\left\{\frac{\partial}{\partial x}\left(\frac{\partial A_2}{\partial y}+\frac{\partial A_3}{\partial z}\right)-\left(\frac{\partial^2 A_1}{\partial y^2}+\frac{\partial^2 A_1}{\partial z^2}\right)\right\}\hat{i}\right]$$

$$=\sum\left[\left\{\frac{\partial}{\partial x}\left(\frac{\partial A_1}{\partial x}+\frac{\partial A_2}{\partial y}+\frac{\partial A_3}{\partial z}\right)-\left(\frac{\partial^2 A_1}{\partial x^2}+\frac{\partial^2 A_1}{\partial y^2}+\frac{\partial^2 A_1}{\partial z^2}\right)\right\}\hat{i}\right]$$

$$=\sum\left[\left\{\frac{\partial}{\partial x}(\nabla.\vec{A})-(\nabla^2 A_1)\right\}\hat{i}\right]=\sum\left[\left\{\frac{\partial}{\partial x}(\nabla.\vec{A})\right\}\hat{i}\right]-\nabla^2\sum A_1\hat{i}=\nabla(\nabla.\vec{A})-\nabla^2\vec{A}.$$

Q34. Find the constants a, b, c so that the vector

$\vec{F}=(x+2y+az)\hat{i}+(bx-3y-z)\hat{j}+(4x+cy+2z)\hat{k}$ is irrotational.

Ans. The vector $\vec{F}$ is irrotational if curl $\vec{F}=0$.

We have curl $\vec{F}=\nabla\times\vec{F}$ $\begin{vmatrix}\hat{i} & \hat{j} & \hat{k}\\ \frac{\partial}{\partial x} & \frac{\partial}{\partial y} & \frac{\partial}{\partial z}\\ x+2y+az & bx-3y-z & 4x+cy+2z\end{vmatrix}$

$$=\left[\frac{\partial}{\partial y}(4x+cy+z)-\frac{\partial}{\partial z}(bx-3y-z)\right]\hat{i}$$

$$+\left[\frac{\partial}{\partial z}(x+2y+az)-\frac{\partial}{\partial x}(4x+cy+2z)\right]\hat{j}$$

$$+\left[\frac{\partial}{\partial x}(bx-3y-z)-\frac{\partial}{\partial y}(x+2y+az)\right]\hat{k}=(c+1)\hat{i}+(a-4)\hat{j}+(b-2)\hat{k}.$$

$\therefore$ curl $\vec{F}=0\Rightarrow(c+1)\hat{i}+(a-4)\hat{j}+(b-2)\hat{k}=0$

$\Rightarrow c+1=0, a-4=0, b-2=0$

$\Rightarrow c=-1, a=4, b=2$

Hence, the vector $\vec{F}$ is irrotational if a = 4, b = 2, c = -1.

Q35. Determine the constant a so that the vector

$$\vec{V} = (x+3y)\hat{i} + (y-2z)\hat{j} + (x+az)\hat{k} \text{ is solenoidal.}$$

Ans. A vector $\vec{V}$ is said to be solenoidal if div $\vec{V} = 0$.

We have div

$$\vec{V} = \nabla \cdot \vec{V} = \frac{\partial}{\partial x}(x+3y) + \frac{\partial}{\partial y}(y-2z) + \frac{\partial}{\partial z}(x+az) = 1+1+a = 2+a.$$

Now div $\vec{V} = 0$ if $2 + a = 0$, i.e., if $a = -2$.

Q36. A frictionless bead slides down a vertical helix of radius R such that its position vector at time t is given by:

$$\vec{r}(t) = a\left(\cos\omega t\ \hat{i} + \sin\omega t\ \hat{j}\right) - \frac{1}{2}gt^2\hat{k}$$

Determine its velocity and acceleration. **[June-2012, Q.No.-1(d)]**

Ans. Given, $\vec{r}(t) = a\left(\cos\omega t\ \hat{i} + \sin\omega t\ \hat{j}\right) - \frac{1}{2}gt^2\hat{k}$

Now, velocity $\vec{v} = \frac{d\vec{r}}{dt} \Rightarrow \frac{d\vec{r}}{dt} = a\left[-\omega \sin\omega t\ \hat{i} + \omega \cos\omega t\ \hat{j}\right] - \frac{1}{2}g\hat{k}2t$

$$\Rightarrow \frac{d\vec{r}}{dt} = a\left(\omega \cos\omega t\ \hat{j} - \omega \sin\omega t\ \hat{i}\right) - gt\hat{k}$$

Hence, velocity $= a\left(\omega \cos\omega t\ \hat{j} - \omega \sin\omega t\ \hat{i}\right) - gt\hat{k}$

Now, acceleration $\vec{a} = \frac{d^2\vec{r}}{dt^2}$ So, now $\frac{d\vec{r}}{dt} = a\left(\omega \cos\omega t\ \hat{j} - \omega \sin\omega t\ \hat{i}\right) - gt\hat{k}$

$$\Rightarrow \frac{d^2\vec{r}}{dt^2} = a\left[\omega^2(-\sin\omega t\ \hat{j}) - \omega^2 \cos\omega t\ \hat{i}\right] - g\hat{k}$$

$$\Rightarrow \frac{d^2\vec{r}}{dt^2} = -a\left(\omega^2 \sin\omega t\ \hat{j} + \omega^2 \cos\omega t\ \hat{i}\right) - g\hat{k}$$

Hence, acceleration $= -a\omega^2\left(\sin\omega t\ \hat{j} + \cos\omega t\ \hat{i}\right) - g\hat{k}$

Q37. Determine the directional derivative of the scalar field $f = x^2 + yz$ at the point (1, 2, 2) in the direction of the unit vector $\hat{A} = \frac{1}{\sqrt{6}}\left(2\hat{i} + \hat{j} - \hat{k}\right)$. **[Dec-2012, Q.No.-1(c)]**

Ans. Given, scalar field is $f = x^2 + yz$ and unit vector is $\hat{A} = \frac{1}{\sqrt{6}}\left(2\hat{i} + \hat{j} - \hat{k}\right)$.

We know that, the directional derivative of field is $\frac{\partial f}{\partial s} = \hat{A}.\nabla f$

Now, $\nabla f = \hat{i}\frac{\partial f}{\partial x} + \hat{j}\frac{\partial f}{\partial y} + \hat{k}\frac{\partial f}{\partial z} = \hat{i}(2x) + \hat{j}(z) + \hat{k}(y)$

$\Rightarrow \qquad \nabla f = 2x\hat{i} + z\hat{j} + y\hat{k}$

Now, $\frac{\partial f}{\partial s} = \hat{A}.\nabla f \Rightarrow \qquad \frac{\partial f}{\partial s} = \frac{1}{\sqrt{6}}\left(2\hat{i} + \hat{j} - \hat{k}\right).\left(2x\hat{i} + z\hat{j} + y\hat{k}\right)$

$\Rightarrow \qquad \frac{\partial f}{\partial s} = \left(\frac{2}{\sqrt{6}}\hat{i} + \frac{1}{\sqrt{6}}\hat{j} - \frac{1}{\sqrt{6}}\hat{k}\right).\left(2x\hat{i} + z\hat{j} + y\hat{k}\right)$

$\Rightarrow \qquad \frac{\partial f}{\partial s} = \frac{4}{\sqrt{6}}x + \frac{1}{\sqrt{6}}z - \frac{1}{\sqrt{6}}y$

$\Rightarrow \qquad \frac{\partial f}{\partial s} = \frac{1}{\sqrt{6}}(4x + z - y)$

Now, $\left.\frac{\partial f}{\partial s}\right]_{at(1,2,2)} = \frac{1}{\sqrt{6}}(4\times 1 + 2 - 2) = \frac{1}{\sqrt{6}}(4)$

Hence, the directional derivative of given scalar field is $\frac{4}{\sqrt{6}}$.

The main aim of GPH book is to provide knowledge as well as good marks in exams.

Chapter 3 Coordinate Systems

An Overview

A coordinate system is a system which uses one or more numbers, or coordinates, to uniquely determine the position of a point or other geometric element on a manifold such as Euclidean space. The prototypical example of a coordinate system is the Cartesian coordinate system. In the plane, two perpendicular lines are chosen and the coordinates of a point are taken to be the signed distances to the lines. In three dimensions, three perpendicular planes are chosen and the three coordinates of a point are the signed distances to each of the planes. This can be generalised to create n coordinates for any point in n-dimensional Euclidean space.

Plane Polar Coordinate System:

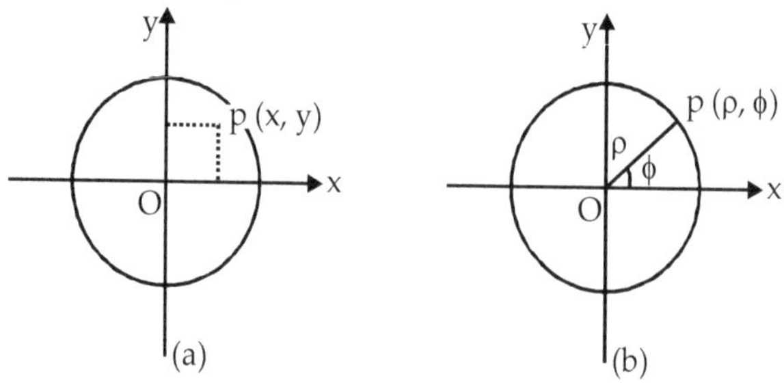

Fig. 3.1: Specification of a point in (a) Cartesian and (b) polar coordinates.

In [Fig. 3.1 (b)], Point O is called pole. The distance ρ is called the radius vector of the point P and ϕ is its polar angle. These two co-ordinates taken together are called plane polar coordinates of P. Now, we arrive at following results.

- Any point can be represented uniquely by specifying its distance from the origin and the angle radius vector makes with the x-axis.
- The Cartesian coordinates are uniquely related to plane polar coordinates of a point $x = \rho\cos\phi \quad y = \rho\sin\phi$
- The polar coordinates form an orthogonal coordinate system in a plane.
- The directions of coordinate axes are not the same for all points.

Cylindrical Coordinate System:

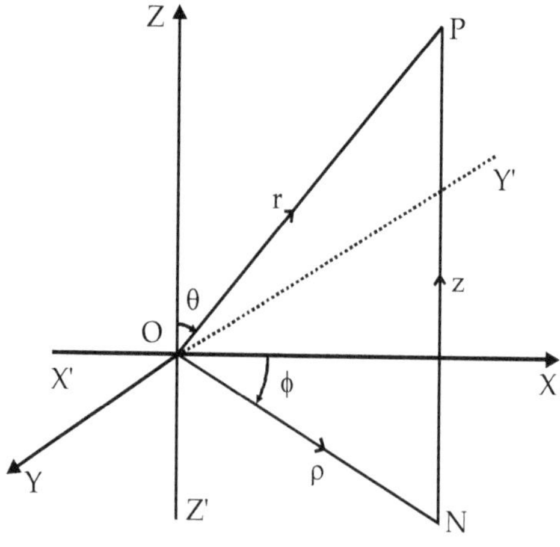

Fig. 3.2

Let P be a point in space. The position of P can also be determined if the measures of ON, $\angle XON$ and NP are known. Suppose ON $=\rho$, $\angle XON=\phi, NP=z$. The quantities ρ, ϕ, z are called the cylindrical co-ordinates of P and are written as (ρ,ϕ,z).

Let (x, y, z) be the Cartesian co-ordinates of P, then N has the co-ordinates (x, y, 0). Hence, we have $x=ON\cos\phi=\rho\cos\phi, y=\rho\sin\phi, z=z$.

Also $\rho^2=x^2+y^2, \tan\phi=y/x$.

We observe that the z-coordinate is the same in the two systems, i.e. Cartesian and cylindrical.

Spherical Polar Coordinate System: In spherical polar coordinate system, the position of a point is specified by the radial distance r, the polar angle θ and the azimuthal angle ϕ as shown in Fig. 3.3. We can see that while θ is measured in the clockwise direction from the z-axis, ϕ is measured in the anti-clockwise direction from the x-axis.

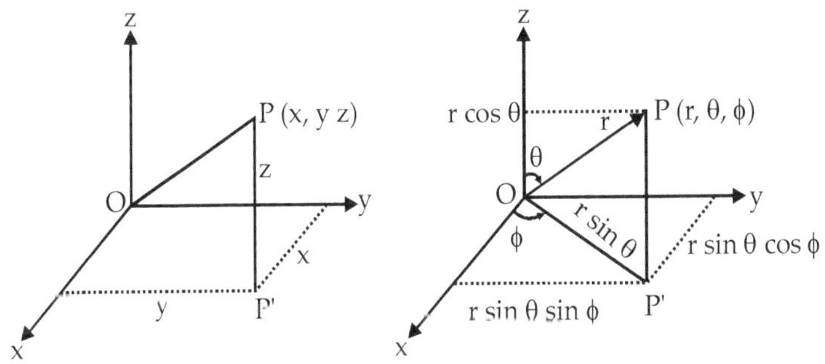

Fig. 3.3: Representation of a point in Cartesian and spherical polar coordinate system.

In fig. 3.3, we can see that the projection of OP onto the x – y plane, OP' = r sinθ while its projection on z-axis is r cos θ. The components of OP' along x and y-axes are OP' cos ϕ and OP' sin ϕ. Hence, for a point P having Cartesian coordinates (x, y, z) and spherical polar coordinate (r, θ, ϕ), we can write

$$x=OP'\cos\phi=r\sin\theta\cos\phi \quad (-\infty<x<\infty)$$

$$y=OP'\sin\phi=r\sin\theta\sin\phi \quad (-\infty<y<\infty)$$

$$z=OP\cos\theta=r\cos\theta \quad (-\infty<z<\infty)$$

By inverting the expressions for x, y and z, we can find spherical polar coordinates. For this, we should compute squares in each case and add the result. Then use of the identity $\sin^2\theta+\cos^2\theta=1$ simplifies the resultant expression. The results are $r=\sqrt{x^2+y^2+z^2} \quad (0\le r<\infty)$,

$$\theta = \tan^{-1}\frac{\sqrt{x^2+y^2}}{z} \ (0 \le \theta \le \pi), \text{ and } \phi = \tan^{-1}\left(\frac{x}{y}\right) \ (0 \le \phi \le 2\pi).$$

Expressing a vector in polar coordinates: We can resolve a vector $\vec{A}$ in Cartesian coordinate as $\vec{A} = A_x\hat{i} + A_y\hat{j} + A_z\hat{k}$ ...(i)

where $\hat{i}, \hat{j}, \hat{k}$ are unit vectors along the x, y and z-axes respectively. This means that to express $\vec{A}$ in polar coordinates, we must first relate $\hat{i}, \hat{j}, \hat{k}$ with the unit vectors associated with the system of interest. Let us first consider the cylindrical coordinate system.

Cylindrical Coordinate System:

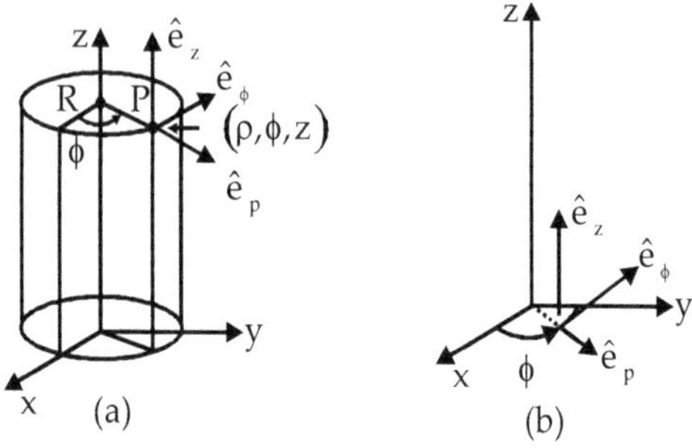

Fig. 3.4

For cylindrical coordinate system, we define the unit vectors $\hat{e}_\rho, \hat{e}_\phi$ and $\hat{e}_z$ at a given point P as follows: Let R be the point on the z-axis with the same z-coordinate as P. Then we define $\hat{e}_\rho$ to be the unit vector at P which is normal to the cylindrical surface ρ = constant through P. So $\hat{e}_\rho$ will be in the direction of RP, i.e. along the direction of increasing ρ, as shown in Fig. 3.4a. Similarly, we define $\hat{e}_\phi$ to be the unit vector normal to the half plane ϕ = constant through P in the direction of increasing ϕ. The unit vector $\hat{e}_z$ is defined normal to the plane z = constant through P in the direction of increasing z. Now, refer to [Fig. 3.4(b)]. We will note that $\hat{e}_\rho$ makes an angle ϕ with the x-axis, $\frac{\pi}{2} - \phi$ with the y-axis and $\frac{\pi}{2}$ with the z-axis. So the components of $\hat{e}_\rho$ along the directions of $\hat{i}, \hat{j}, \hat{k}$ are, respectively

$$\hat{e}_\rho.\hat{i} = \cos\phi\,; \hat{e}_\rho.\hat{j} = \cos\left(\frac{\pi}{2} - \phi\right) = \sin\phi\,; \text{ and } \hat{e}_\rho.\hat{k} = \cos\left(\frac{\pi}{2}\right) = 0 \quad ...(ii)$$

On combining these results, we can write

$$\hat{e}_\rho = \cos\phi\hat{i} + \sin\phi\hat{j} \quad \text{...(iii)}$$

Again, by looking at [Fig. 3.4(b)], we will note that $\hat{e}_\phi$ makes an angle $\left(\frac{\pi}{2}+\phi\right)$ with the x-axis, ϕ with the y-axis and $\frac{\pi}{2}$ with the z-axis. Now, we can compute the components of $\hat{e}_\phi$ along the directions of $\hat{i}, \hat{j}$ and $\hat{k}$ following the procedures outlined for $\hat{e}_\rho$.

The result is $\hat{e}_\phi = -\sin\phi\hat{i} + \cos\phi\hat{j}$ ...(iv)

Since $\hat{e}_z$ is parallel to z-axis, its projection along the x and y-axes will be zero. Hence, $\hat{e}_z = \hat{k}$ ...(v)

These relations can readily be inverted. To this end, we have to multiply Eq. (iii) by cos ϕ and Eq. (iv) by sin ϕ. Add the resulting expressions and use the identity, $\cos^2\phi + \sin^2\phi = 1$. On simplification we will get

$$\hat{i} = \cos\phi\,\hat{e}_\rho - \sin\phi\,\hat{e}_\phi \quad \text{...(vi)}$$

we can similarly write

$$\hat{j} = \sin\phi\,\hat{e}_\rho + \cos\phi\,\hat{e}_\phi \quad \text{...(vii)}$$

and $\hat{k} = \hat{e}_z$ ...(viii)

Spherical Coordinate System:

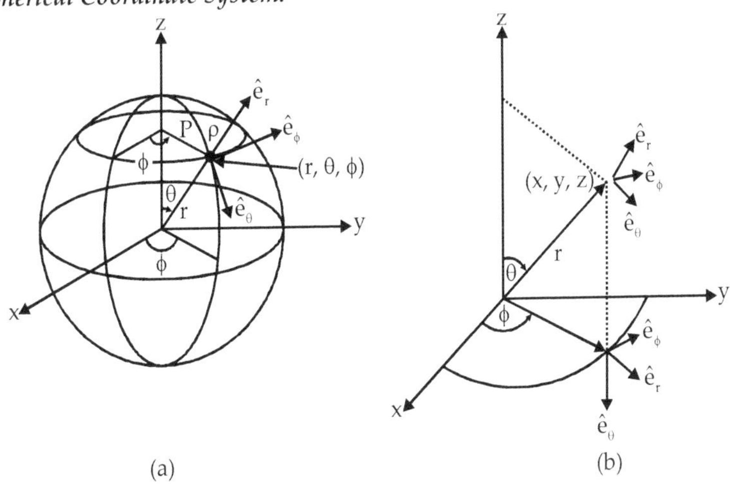

Fig. 3.5

For spherical polar coordinates, we define the unit vectors as follows: At the point $P(r,\theta,\phi)$, the unit vector $\hat{e}_r$ is normal to the surface r = constant, $\hat{e}_\theta$ is normal to the surface θ = constant and $\hat{e}_\phi$ is normal to the surface defined by ϕ = constant through the given point. Their direction are along increasing r, θ and ϕ respectively as shown in [Fig. 3.5(a)]. By considering the components of the unit vectors $\hat{e}_r, \hat{e}_\theta, \hat{e}_\phi$ in the directions of unit vectors $\hat{i}, \hat{j}, \hat{k}$ [Fig. 3.5(b)] we would like to show that

$$\hat{e}_r = \sin\theta\cos\phi\,\hat{i} + \sin\theta\sin\phi\,\hat{j} + \cos\theta\,\hat{k}$$

$$\hat{e}_\theta = \cos\theta\cos\phi\,\hat{i} + \cos\theta\sin\phi\,\hat{j} - \sin\theta\,\hat{k}$$

$$\hat{e}_\phi = -\sin\phi\,\hat{i} + \cos\phi\,\hat{j} \qquad \text{...(ix)}$$

Conversely,

$$\hat{i} = \sin\theta\cos\phi\,\hat{e}_r + \cos\theta\cos\phi\,\hat{e}_\theta - \sin\phi\,\hat{e}_\phi$$

$$\hat{j} = \sin\theta\sin\phi\,\hat{e}_r + \cos\theta\sin\phi\,\hat{e}_\theta + \cos\phi\,\hat{e}_\phi$$

$$\hat{k} = \cos\theta\,\hat{e}_r - \sin\theta\,\hat{e}_\theta \qquad \text{...(x)}$$

Differential Element of Vector Length in spherical polar coordinates: In spherical polar coordinates, the position vector of a point moving through space is given by $\vec{r} = r\,\hat{e}_r$

On substituting for $\hat{e}_r$ from Eq. (ix), we have

$$\vec{r} = r\left(\hat{i}\sin\theta\cos\phi + \hat{j}\sin\theta\sin\phi + \hat{k}\cos\theta\right)$$

Hence, we can write $d\vec{r} = dr\left(\hat{i}\sin\theta\cos\phi + \hat{j}\sin\theta\sin\phi + \hat{k}\cos\theta\right)$

$$+r\left(\hat{i}\cos\theta\cos\phi d\theta - \hat{i}\sin\theta\sin\phi d\phi + \hat{j}\sin\theta\cos\phi d\phi + \hat{j}\cos\theta\sin\phi d\theta - \hat{k}\sin\theta d\theta\right)$$

In spherical coordinates, small line elements along $\hat{e}_r, \hat{e}_\theta$ and $\hat{e}_\phi$ are given by dr, r$d\theta$ and r sinθ dϕ, respectively. On collecting coefficients of dr, r$d\theta$ and rsinθ dϕ, this expression becomes

$$d\vec{r} = \left(\hat{i}\sin\theta\cos\phi + \hat{j}\sin\theta\sin\phi + \hat{k}\cos\theta\right)dr$$

$$+\left(\hat{i}\cos\theta\cos\phi + \hat{j}\cos\theta\sin\phi - \hat{k}\sin\theta\right)rd\phi \; +\left(-\hat{i}\sin\phi + \hat{j}\cos\phi\right)r\sin\theta d\phi$$

Combining this with Eq. (ix), we find that differential element of vector length in spherical polar coordinates can be written as

$$d\vec{r} = \hat{e}_r\,dr + \hat{e}_\theta\,rd\theta + \hat{e}_\phi\,r\sin\theta d\theta \qquad \text{...(xi)}$$

Note: In cylindrical polar coordinates, the position vector of a point moving through space is given by $\vec{r}=\rho\hat{e}_\rho+z\hat{e}_z$ then a small change $d\vec{r}$ in the position vector can be written as $d\vec{r}=\hat{e}_\rho d\rho+\hat{e}_\phi \rho d\phi+\hat{e}_z dz$ ...(xii)

Differential Element of Vector Area: In Cartesian coordinate system, the area of the face normal to x-axis is given by $dA_x = dy\, dz$

We can use the same definition for non-Cartesian coordinates as well. In terms of cylindrical coordinates, we can write $dA_\rho = (d\vec{r})_\phi (d\vec{r})_z$

$$= \rho d\phi\, dz \qquad ...(xiii)$$

Similarly, $dA_\phi = (d\vec{r})_\rho (d\vec{r})_z = d\rho\, dz$ ...(xiv)

and $dA_z = \rho d\rho d\phi$ ...(xv)

On combining Eqs. (xiii), (xiv), (xv), we can express the differential element of vector area in cylindrical coordinates as $d\vec{A} = dA_\rho \hat{e}_\rho + dA_\phi \hat{e}_\phi + dA_z \hat{e}_z$

or $d\vec{A}=\rho d\phi dz\hat{e}_\rho+d\rho dz\hat{e}_\phi+\rho d\rho d\phi\hat{e}_z$ ...(xiv)

We can follow the same procedure and show that differential element of vector area in spherical coordinates can be expressed as

$$d\vec{A} = r^2 \sin\theta d\theta d\phi\hat{e}_r + r\sin\theta dr d\phi\hat{e}_\theta + r d\theta dr\hat{e}_\phi \qquad ...(xvii)$$

Note: The volume element in cylindrical and spherical polar coordinates can be written as $dV = \rho d\rho d\phi dz$ ...(xviii)

$$dV = r^2 dr \sin\theta d\theta d\phi \qquad ...(xix)$$

Gradient of a Scalar Field in cylindrical coordinates: To express gradient of a scalar field f in cylindrical coordinates, we first write ∇f in terms of its components:

$$\nabla f = g_\rho \hat{e}_\rho + g_\phi \hat{e}_\phi + g_z \hat{e}_z \qquad ...(xx)$$

where g_ρ, g_ϕ and g_z are unknown functions and we have to determine them. To this end, let us compute the dot product of $\hat{e}_\rho$ and ∇f. Since $\hat{e}_\rho, \hat{e}_\phi$ and $\hat{e}_z$ are orthogonal, we get $g_\rho = \hat{e}_\rho.\nabla f$

That is, g_ρ is the spatial rate of change of f in the direction of unit vector $\hat{e}_\rho$ At the point $P(\rho,\phi,z)$, g_ρ signifies the rate of changes of f in the direction of increasing ρ (with ϕ and z held constant). Refer to Fig. 3.6a.

We will observe that the distance between the points (ρ,ϕ,z) and $(\rho+\Delta\rho,\phi,z)$ is $\Delta\rho$ So when these points are close together, we can write

$$\lim_{\Delta\rho\to 0}\frac{f(\rho+\Delta\rho,\phi,z)-f(\rho,\phi,z)}{\Delta\rho}=\frac{\partial f}{\partial\rho}$$

where ∂ denotes partial derivative with respect to ρ .

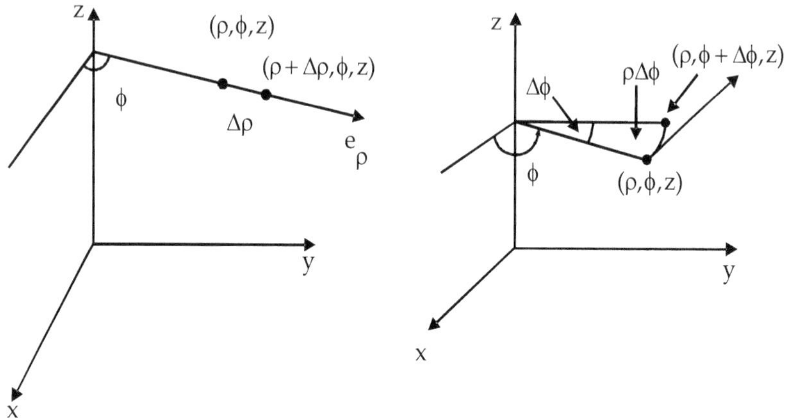

(a) (b)

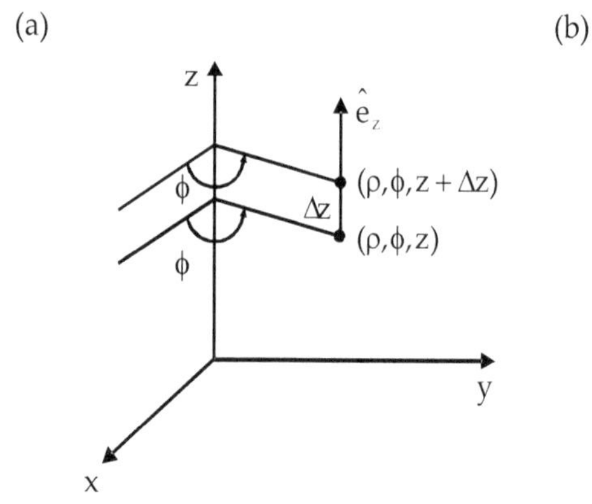

(c)

Fig. 3.6

Thus, the component of ∇f in the $\hat{e}_\rho$ direction is

$$g_\rho=\frac{\partial f}{\partial\rho} \qquad ...(xxi)$$

Similarly, g_ϕ is the components of ∇f in the $\hat{e}_\phi$ direction, i.e. $g_\phi = \hat{e}_\phi \cdot \nabla f$. But $\hat{e}_\phi . \nabla f$ denotes the rate of change of f in the direction of the unit vector $\hat{e}_\phi$, which is equal to $\lim\limits_{\Delta\phi \to 0} \frac{f(\rho,\phi+\Delta\phi,z)-f(\rho,\phi,z)}{\rho\Delta\phi} = \frac{1}{\rho}\frac{\partial f}{\partial \phi}$

This form of the term in the denominator of this limit arises because the distance between the point (ρ,ϕ,z) and $(\rho,\phi+\Delta\phi,z)$ is $\rho\Delta\phi$ [Fig. 3.6(b)].

Hence, $$g_\phi = \frac{1}{\rho}\frac{\partial f}{\partial \phi} \qquad \text{...(xxii)}$$

Finally, we can write the component of ∇f in the $\hat{e}_z$ direction, $g_z\left(=\hat{e}_z.\nabla f\right)$ as [Fig. 3.6(c)]: $$g_z = \frac{\partial f}{\partial z} \qquad \text{...(xxiii)}$$

On combining Eqs. (xx) and (xxi), (xxii), (xxiii), we will obtain

$$\nabla f = \frac{\partial f}{\partial \rho}\hat{e}_\rho + \frac{1}{\rho}\frac{\partial f}{\partial \phi}\hat{e}_\phi + \frac{\partial f}{\partial z}\hat{e}_z \qquad \text{...(xxiv)}$$

Curvilinear Coordinate System: Consider a 3-D space. A point P in 3-D space can be defined using Cartesian coordinates (x, y, z) [Equivalently written (x_1,x_2,x_3)], or in another system (q_1,q_2,q_3), as shown in [Fig. 3.7].

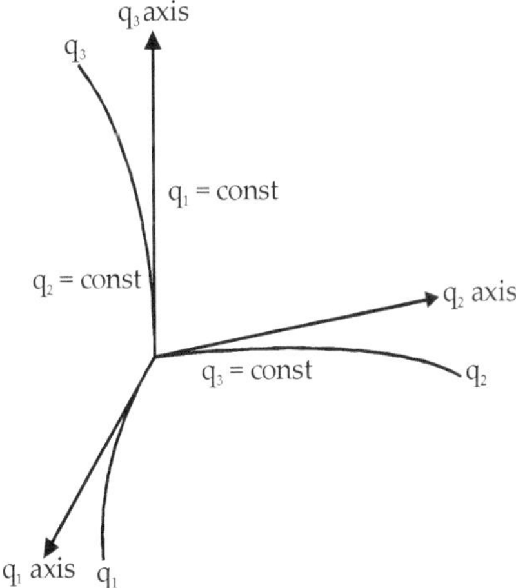

Fig. 3.7: Co-ordinate surfaces, coordinate lines, and coordinate axis of general curvilinear coordinates.

The surfaces q_1 = constant, q_2 = constant, q_3 = constant are called the curvilinear coordinate surfaces, and the space curves formed by their intersection in pairs are called the curvilinear coordinate curves.

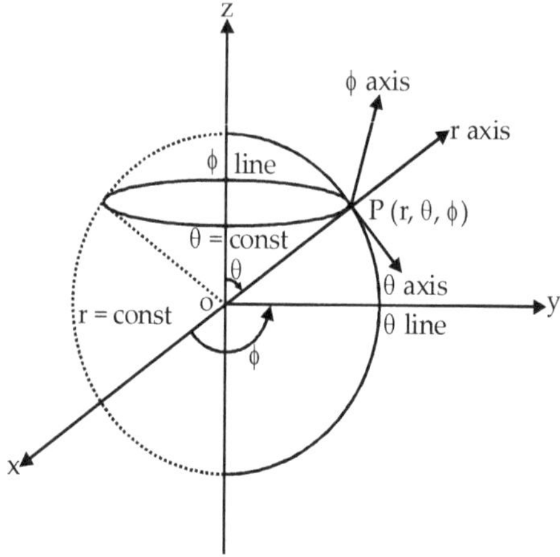

Fig. 3.8

The relation between the coordinates is given by the invertible transformation: $x = x(q_1, q_2, q_3)$; $y = y(q_1, q_2, q_3)$; $z = z(q_1, q_2, q_3)$;

$q_1 = q_1(x, y, z)$; $q_2 = q_2(x, y, z)$ and $q_3 = q_3(x, y, z)$

Any point can be written as a position vector $\vec{r}$ in Cartesian coordinates $\vec{r} = x\ \vec{e}_x + y\ \vec{e}_y + z\vec{e}_z$ where x, y, z are the co-ordinates of the position vector with respect to the standard basis vectors $\vec{e}_x, \vec{e}_y, \vec{e}_z$.

Here, $\vec{e}_x = \frac{\partial \vec{r}}{\partial x}, \vec{e}_y = \frac{\partial \vec{r}}{\partial y}, \vec{e}_z = \frac{\partial \vec{r}}{\partial z}$

Note: A vector $\vec{F}$ may be written in terms of its components F_1, F_2, F_3 as $\vec{F} = F_1 \hat{e}_1 + F_2 \hat{e}_2 + F_3 \hat{e}_3$

Orthogonality conditions for the curvilinear coordinate system: Consider a point P (x, y, z) in Cartesian space. If its position vector is $\vec{r}$, then, $d\vec{r} = \hat{i}\,dx + \hat{j}\,dy + \hat{k}\,dz$ and square of the distance between two neighbouring points along a curve is given by

$$(ds)^2 = d\vec{r}.d\vec{r} = (dx)^2 + (dy)^2 + (dz)^2 \qquad ...(xxv)$$

Now, we can express dx, dy, dz in terms of u_1, u_2, u_3 through the relations; $dx = \left(\frac{\partial x}{\partial u_1}\right) du_1 + \left(\frac{\partial x}{\partial u_2}\right) du_2 + \left(\frac{\partial x}{\partial u_3}\right) du_3$,

$$dy = \left(\frac{\partial y}{\partial u_1}\right) du_1 + \left(\frac{\partial y}{\partial u_2}\right) du_2 + \left(\frac{\partial y}{\partial u_3}\right) du_3,$$

and $dz = \left(\frac{\partial z}{\partial u_1}\right) du_1 + \left(\frac{\partial z}{\partial u_2}\right) du_2 + \left(\frac{\partial z}{\partial u_3}\right) du_3$

For convenience, we have dropped the subscripts u_1, u_2, u_3.

On substituting for $(dx)^2, (dy)^2$ and $(dz)^2$ in Eq. (xxv) and collecting the coefficients of $du_i du_j$ (i, j = 1, 2, 3) we can rewrite Eq. (xxv) as

$$(ds)^2 = g_{11}(du_1)^2 + 2g_{12}du_1du_2 + g_{22}(du_2)^2$$

$$+2g_{23}du_2du_3 + g_{33}(du_3)^2 + 2g_{31}du_3du_1 \quad \text{...(xxvi)}$$

where

$$g_{ij} = \frac{\partial x}{\partial u_i}\frac{\partial x}{\partial u_j} + \frac{\partial y}{\partial u_i}\frac{\partial y}{\partial u_j} + \frac{\partial z}{\partial u_i}\frac{\partial z}{\partial u_j} \quad \text{...(xxvii)}$$

are referred to as the metric coefficients of the curvilinear coordinate system.

Now the condition for a curvilinear coordinate system to be orthogonal is $g_{ij} = 0$ for $i \neq j$ ...(xxviii)

So for an orthogonal curvilinear coordinate system, Eq. (xxvi) for square of arc length takes a very compact form:

$$d\vec{r}.d\vec{r} = (ds)^2 = g_{11}(du_1)^2 + g_{22}(du_2)^2 + g_{33}(du_3)^2$$

$$= (h_1du_1)^2 + (h_2du_2)^2 + (h_3du_3)^2 \quad \text{...(xxix)}$$

where we have put $g_{ii} = h_i^2 (i = 1,2,3)$.

This means that for cylindrical polar coordinate system

$$h_1 \equiv h_\rho = 1;\ h_2 \equiv h_\phi = \rho;\ \text{and}\ h_3 \equiv h_z = 1 \quad \text{...(xxx)}$$

We can show that for spherical polar coordinate system

$$h_1 \equiv h_r = 1;\ h_2 \equiv h_\theta = r;\ \text{and}\ h_3 \equiv h_\phi = r\sin\theta \quad \text{...(xxxi)}$$

We note that when an element of arc ds is directed along the u_1 coordinate line, $du_2 = du_3 = 0$. Then Eq. (xxix) gives

$$(ds)^2 \equiv (ds_1)^2 = h_1^2(du_1)^2 \text{ so that, } ds_1 = h_1du_1 \quad \text{...(xxxii)}$$

That is, the length of the arc ds along the u_1- coordinate line is the product of h_1 and the differential of u_1. Similarly, we can show that the components of length of arc ds along the u_2 and u_3 coordinate lines are

$$ds_2 = h_2 du_2 \qquad ...(xxxiii)$$

$$ds_3 = h_3 du_3 \qquad ...(xxxiv)$$

Since ds_i and du_i are real, we can say that $h_i(i=1,2,3)$ are positive quantities. To get success in your studies, read only GPH Book.

Unit Vectors: Let us express the position vector $\vec{r}$ in terms of u_1, u_2, u_3 :

$$d\vec{r} = \left(\frac{\partial r}{\partial u_1}\right)du_1 + \left(\frac{\partial \vec{r}}{\partial u_2}\right)du_2 + \left(\frac{\partial \vec{r}}{\partial u_3}\right)du_3 = \sum_{i=1}^{3}\left(\frac{\partial \vec{r}}{\partial u_i}\right)du_i \qquad ...(xxxv)$$

We will recognise that the symbol $\frac{\partial \vec{r}}{\partial u_i}$ denotes the derivative of $\vec{r}$ with respect to a particular variable $u_i (i=1,2,3)$. This implies that if we fix u_2 and u_3, $\vec{r}$ becomes a function of u_1 alone. That is, the terminus of $\vec{r}$ will move along the u_1 coordinate line in the u-coordinate system. So the vector $\frac{\partial \vec{r}}{\partial u_1} = \lim_{\substack{\Delta u_1 \to 0 \\ u_2, u_3 = \text{const.}}} \frac{\Delta \vec{r}}{\Delta u_1}$

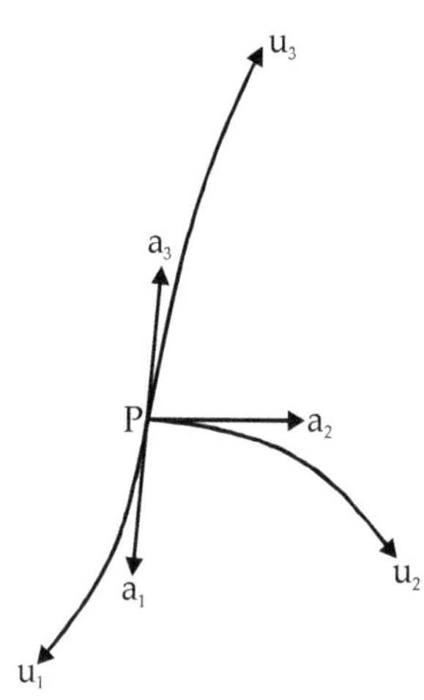

Fig. 3.9

will be tangent to the coordinate line u_1 at point P. Similarly, we can say that vector $\frac{\partial \vec{r}}{\partial u_2}$ and $\frac{\partial \vec{r}}{\partial u_3}$ are, respectively, tangent to u_2 and u_3 -coordinate lines, as shown in [Fig. 3.9]. If we denote these vectors by $\vec{a}_i$, i.e.

$$\vec{a}_i = \frac{\partial \vec{r}}{\partial u_i} \qquad \text{...(xxxvi)}$$

Eq. (xxxvi) can be rewritten as

$$d\vec{r} = \sum_{i=1}^{3} \vec{a}_i du_i \qquad \text{...(xxxvii)}$$

The vectors $\vec{a}_i$ are called base vectors in the curvilinear coordinate system. The two sets of vectors are analogous in that we can resolve any vector $\vec{F}$ into its components F_1, F_2, F_3, as shown in [Fig. 3.9]. However $\vec{a}_1, \vec{a}_2, \vec{a}_3$ are not unique; these are defined at a point and vary from point to point. Now, we compute the dot product $d\vec{r}.d\vec{r}$. Since we are considering an orthogonal coordinate system, $\vec{a}_i.\vec{a}_j = u \quad i \neq j$

Then, on comparing the coefficients of $(du_1)^2, (du_2)^2$ and $(du_3)^2$ with Eq. (xxix), we will get $|\vec{a}_i| = h_i (i = 1,2,3)$

so that the base vector $\vec{a}_i$ can be written as

$$\vec{a}_i = h_i \hat{e}_i (i = 1,2,3) \qquad \text{...(xxxviii)}$$

where $\hat{e}_i$ is a unit vector along u_1 coordinate line.

Using this result in Eq. (xxxvii), we find that

$$d\vec{r} = \sum_{i=1}^{3} h_i du_i \hat{e}_i \qquad \text{...(xxxix)}$$

For a given i, $\hat{e}_i$ can be expressed as $\hat{e}_i = \frac{1}{h_i} \frac{\partial \vec{r}}{\partial u_i}$ ...(xxxx)

Vector Differential Operators: Vector differential operators are defined in terms of divergence, curl and Laplace operator.

(i) Divergence: Consider a vector field $\vec{F}$. We can express it in terms of its components F_1, F_2, F_3 along $\hat{e}_1, \hat{e}_2, \hat{e}_3$ as $\vec{F}(u_1, u_2, u_3) = \vec{F}_1 \hat{e}_1 + \vec{F}_2 \hat{e}_2 + \vec{F}_3 \hat{e}_3$

In summation notation, it can be written in a compact form:

$$\vec{F}(u_1, u_2, u_3) = \sum_{i=1}^{3} \vec{F}_i \hat{e}_i$$

It could be more elegant. The divergence of $\vec{F}$ is then given by

$$\nabla.\vec{F} = \nabla.\sum_{i=1}^{3} \vec{F}_i \hat{e}_i \qquad \text{...(xxxxi)}$$

or $\nabla.\vec{F} = \frac{1}{h_1 h_2 h_3} \sum_{\substack{i=1 \\ i\neq j\neq k}}^{3} \left(h_j h_k F_i\right)$ ...(xxxxii)

(ii) *Curl:* $\nabla \times \vec{F} = \frac{1}{h_1 h_2 h_3} \begin{vmatrix} \hat{e}_1 h_1 & \hat{e}_2 h_2 & \hat{e}_3 h_3 \\ \frac{\partial}{\partial u_1} & \frac{\partial}{\partial u_2} & \frac{\partial}{\partial u_3} \\ h_1 F_1 & h_2 F_2 & h_3 F_3 \end{vmatrix}$ ...(xxxxiii)

In cylindrical and spherical polar coordinates, Eq. (xxxxiii) taken the form

$$\nabla \times \vec{F} = \frac{1}{\rho} \begin{vmatrix} \hat{e}_\rho & \rho\hat{e}_\phi & \hat{e}_z \\ \frac{\partial}{\partial \rho} & \frac{\partial}{\partial \phi} & \frac{\partial}{\partial z} \\ F_\rho & \rho F\phi & F_z \end{vmatrix} \quad ...(xxxxiv)$$

and $\nabla \times \vec{F} = \frac{1}{r^2 \sin\theta} \begin{vmatrix} \hat{e}_r & r\hat{e}_\phi & r\sin\theta\hat{e}_\phi \\ \frac{\partial}{\partial r} & \frac{\partial}{\partial \theta} & \frac{\partial}{\partial \phi} \\ F_r & rF_\theta & r\sin\theta F_\phi \end{vmatrix}$ ...(xxxxv)

(iii) Laplace Operator: Like the del operator, the Laplace operator also finds applications in fluid mechanics, electromagnetism, elasticity, propagation of waves and quantum mechanics. It is therefore important to give expressions for $\overline{V}^2$ in curvilinear, spherical and cylindrical coordinates.

We know that $\overline{V}^2 f = \overline{V}.\overline{V}f$ where f is a scalar.

Now, we have $\nabla^2 f = \nabla \cdot \sum_{i=1}^{3} \frac{1}{h_i} \frac{\partial f}{\partial u_i} \hat{e}_i$

Inserting the result contained in Eq. (xxxxii), this expression becomes

$$\nabla^2 f = \frac{1}{h_1 h_2 h_3} \sum_{\substack{i=1 \\ i\neq j\neq k}}^{3} \frac{\partial}{\partial u_i} \left(\frac{h_j h_k}{h_i} \frac{\partial f}{\partial u_i} \right)$$

In the expanded form, we can write

$$\nabla^2 f = \frac{1}{h_1 h_2 h_3} \left[\frac{\partial}{\partial u_1} \left(\frac{h_2 h_3}{h_1} \frac{\partial f}{\partial u_1} \right) + \frac{\partial}{\partial u_2} \left(\frac{h_3 h_1}{h_2} \frac{\partial f}{\partial u_2} \right) + \frac{\partial}{\partial u_3} \left(\frac{h_1 h_2}{h_3} \frac{\partial f}{\partial u_3} \right) \right]$$

Solved Practical Problems

Q1. Draw $\phi - z$ surface for the cylindrical coordinate system.

Ans. The $\phi - z$ surface for the cylindrical coordinate system are coaxial right circular cylinders having the z-axis for their common axis. This is shown in the [fig. 3.10].

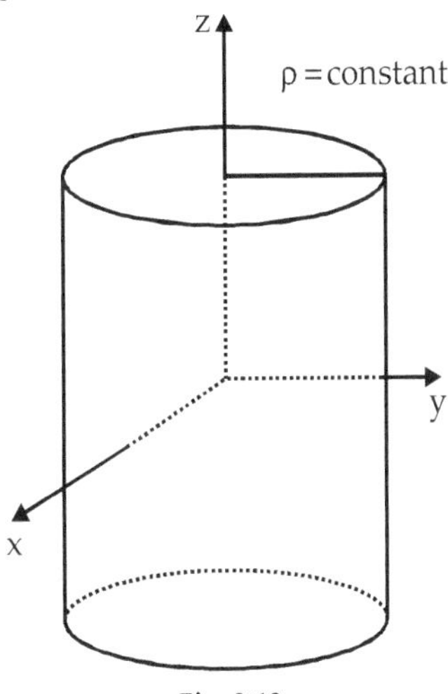

Fig. 3.10

Q2. The Cartesian coordinates of a point are (2, -2, 3) in arbitrary units. Compute its (i) cylindrical and (ii) spherical polar coordinates.

Ans. (i) Cylindrical coordinate:

$$\rho = \sqrt{x^2 + y^2} = \sqrt{2^2 + (-2)^2} = 2\sqrt{2}$$

$\phi = \tan^{-1}\left(\frac{y}{x}\right) = \tan^{-1}(-1) = 3\pi/4$ or $7\pi/4$. But x is positive and y is negative. Therefore, $3\pi/4$ is inadmissible. Hence, $\phi = 7\pi/4$ and $z = 3$.

(ii) Spherical polar coordinates:

$$r = \sqrt{x^2 + y^2 + z^2} = \sqrt{2^2 + (-2)^2 + 3^2} = \sqrt{17}$$

$$\theta = \tan^{-1}\frac{\sqrt{x^2 + y^2}}{z} = \tan^{-1}\left(\frac{2\sqrt{2}}{3}\right) \text{ and } \phi = \tan^{-1}\left(\frac{y}{x}\right) = \tan^{-1}(-1) = 7\pi/4$$

Q3. In Cartesian coordinates, the position vector is given by $\vec{r} = x\hat{i} + y\hat{j} + z\hat{k}$. Express it in terms of cylindrical coordinates (ρ, ϕ, z) and the associated unit vectors $\hat{e}_\rho, \hat{e}_\phi, \hat{e}_z$.

Ans. The position vector is given by $\vec{r} = x\hat{i} + y\hat{j} + z\hat{k}$

On substituting for x, y and z from cylindrical coordinate system and $(\hat{i}, \hat{j}, \hat{k})$ from Eqs. $\left(\hat{i} = \cos\phi\,\hat{e}_\rho - \sin\phi\,\hat{e}_\phi\right)$, $\left(\hat{j} = \sin\phi\,\hat{e}_\rho + \cos\phi\,\hat{e}_\phi\right)$, $\hat{k} = \hat{e}_z$ we get $\vec{r} = \rho\cos\phi\left(\cos\phi\hat{e}_\rho - \sin\phi\hat{e}_\phi\right) + \rho\sin\phi\left(\sin\phi\hat{e}_\rho + \cos\phi\hat{e}_\phi\right) + z\hat{e}_z$

On collecting the coefficients of $\hat{e}_\rho, \hat{e}_\phi$ and $\hat{e}_z$, we get $\vec{r} = \rho\hat{e}_\rho + z\hat{e}_z$

Q4. A particle is moving through space. Compute the components of its velocity in cylindrical coordinates.

Ans. We know that position vector of a particle moving through space is given by $\vec{r}(t) = \rho\hat{e}_\rho + z\hat{e}_z$. On substituting for $\hat{e}_\rho$ from $\hat{e}_\rho = \cos\phi\,\hat{i} + \sin\phi\,\hat{j}$ we have $\vec{r}(t) = \left(\hat{i}\cos\phi + \hat{j}\sin\phi\right) + \hat{k}z$ ...(i)

since $\hat{e}_z = \hat{k}$.

To compute the velocity of this particle, we have to keep in mind that ρ as well as ϕ change with time as $\vec{r}$ changes. So on differentiating (i) with respect to time, we get

$$\vec{v} = \dot{\vec{r}} = \left(\hat{i}\cos\phi + \hat{j}\sin\phi\right)\dot{\rho} + \left(-\hat{i}\sin\phi + \hat{j}\cos\phi\right)\rho\,\dot{\phi} + \hat{k}\,\dot{z}$$

$= \hat{e}_\rho\dot{\rho} + \hat{e}_\phi\rho\dot{\phi} + \hat{e}_z\dot{z}$ where dot over $\vec{r}, \rho$, ϕ and z denotes their respective first time derivatives.

On comparing this expression with the equation $\vec{v} = v_\rho\hat{e}_\rho + v_\phi\hat{e}_\phi + v_z\hat{e}_z$ we find that $v_\rho = \dot{\rho}, v_\phi = \rho\dot{\phi}$, and $v_z = \dot{z}$

Q5. A particle is moving in space. Express its position vector and components of its velocity in spherical coordinates.

Ans. The position vector of a particle moving in space is written as $\vec{r} = x\,\hat{i} + y\,\hat{j} + z\,\hat{k}$

Substituting $x = r\sin\theta\cos\phi, y = r\sin\theta\sin\phi, z = r\cos\theta$ and

$\hat{i} = \sin\theta\cos\phi\,\hat{e}_r + \cos\theta\cos\phi\,\hat{e}_\theta - \sin\phi\,\hat{e}_\phi$,

$\hat{j} = \sin\theta\sin\phi\,\hat{e}_r + \cos\theta\sin\phi\,\hat{e}_\theta + \cos\phi\,\hat{e}_\phi$,

$\hat{k} = \cos\theta \hat{e}_r - \sin\theta \hat{e}_\theta$,

we get $\vec{r} = r\sin\theta\cos\phi(\sin\theta\cos\phi\hat{e}_r + \cos\theta\cos\phi\hat{e}_\theta - \sin\phi\hat{e}_\phi)$

$+r\sin\theta\sin\phi(\sin\theta\sin\phi\hat{e}_r + \cos\theta\sin\phi\hat{e}_\theta + \cos\phi\hat{e}_\phi)$

$+r\cos\theta(\cos\theta\hat{e}_r - \sin\theta\hat{e}_\theta)$

On collecting the coefficients of $\hat{e}_r, \hat{e}_\theta$ and $\hat{e}_\phi$, this expression gives us the required result: $\vec{r} = \hat{e}_r(r\sin^2\theta\cos^2\phi + r\sin^2\theta\sin^2\phi + r\cos^2\theta)$

$+\hat{e}_\theta(r\sin\theta\cos^2\phi\cos\theta + r\sin\theta\cos\theta\sin^2\phi - r\cos\theta\sin\theta)$

$+\hat{e}_\phi(-r\sin\theta\cos\phi\sin\phi + r\sin\theta\sin\phi\cos\phi)$

$= \hat{e}_r\left[r\sin^2\theta(\cos^2\phi + \sin^2\phi) + r\cos^2\theta\right] = r\hat{e}_r$

In spherical polar coordinates, the position vector of a particle moving in space is given by $\vec{r} = r\,\hat{e}_r = r(\sin\theta\cos\phi\hat{i} + \sin\theta\sin\phi\hat{j} + \cos\theta\hat{k})$

Differentiating it with respect to time, we will get

$\vec{v} = \dot{r}\hat{e}_r + \hat{i}r(\cos\theta\cos\phi\dot{\theta} - \sin\theta\sin\phi\dot{\phi}) + r\hat{j}(\cos\theta\sin\phi\dot{\theta} + \sin\theta\cos\phi\dot{\phi}) - r\hat{k}\sin\theta\dot{\theta}$

$= \dot{r}\hat{e}_r + r\dot{\theta}(\cos\theta\cos\phi\hat{i} + \cos\theta\sin\phi\hat{j} - \hat{k}\sin\theta) + r\dot{\phi}(-\hat{i}\sin\theta\sin\phi + \hat{j}\sin\theta\cos\phi)$

$= \dot{r}\hat{e}_r + r\dot{\theta}\hat{e}_\theta + r\sin\theta\dot{\phi}\hat{e}_\phi$

where dot over r, θ, ϕ denotes their respective first time derivatives.

Q6. Obtain the components of acceleration in cylindrical coordinates for a particle moving in space. [June-2013, Q.No.-1(b)]

Ans. We know that the velocity of a particle moving through space in cylindrical coordinates is given by $\vec{v} = \dot{\rho}\,\hat{e}_\rho + \rho\dot{\phi}\,\hat{e}_\phi + \dot{z}\,\hat{e}_z$ ...(i)

On differentiating this with respect to time, we get

$\vec{a} = \dot{\vec{v}} = \ddot{\rho}\hat{e}_\rho + \dot{\rho}\dot{\hat{e}}_\rho + \rho\dot{\phi}\dot{\hat{e}}_\phi + \rho\ddot{\phi}\hat{e}_\phi + \dot{\rho}\dot{\phi}\hat{e}_\phi + \ddot{z}\hat{e}_z + \dot{z}\dot{\hat{e}}_z$ ...(ii)

Since, $\hat{e}_\rho = \hat{i}\cos\phi + \hat{j}\sin\phi$; $\hat{e}_\phi = -\hat{i}\sin\phi + \hat{j}\cos\phi$; $\hat{e}_z = \hat{k}$

Hence, $\dot{\hat{e}}_\rho = (-\hat{i}\sin\phi + \hat{j}\cos\phi)\dot{\phi} = \hat{e}_\phi\dot{\phi}$;

$\dot{\hat{e}}_\phi = (-\hat{i}\cos\phi - \hat{j}\sin\phi)\dot{\phi} = -\hat{e}_\rho\dot{\phi}$ and $\dot{\hat{e}}_z = 0$

Using these results in (ii), we get $\vec{a}=\left[\ddot{\rho}-\rho\left(\dot{\phi}\right)^2\right]\hat{e}_\rho+\left(\rho\ddot{\phi}+2\dot{\rho}\dot{\phi}\right)\hat{e}_\phi+\ddot{z}\hat{e}_z$

$$=\left[\ddot{\rho}-\rho\left(\dot{\phi}\right)^2\right]\hat{e}_\rho+\frac{1}{\rho}\frac{d}{dt}\left(\rho^2\dot{\phi}\right)\hat{e}_\phi+\ddot{z}\hat{e}_z \qquad ...(iii)$$

Hence, the cylindrical components of acceleration of a particle moving in space are $a_\rho=\ddot{\rho}-\rho\left(\dot{\phi}\right)^2$, $a_\phi=\rho\ddot{\phi}+2\dot{\rho}\dot{\phi}$ and $a_z=\ddot{z}$ ...(iv)

Q7. The cylindrical coordinates $u_1=\rho, u_2=\phi, u_3=z$ are related to the Cartesian coordinates x, y and z as follows:

$x=\rho\cos\phi$

$y=\rho\sin\phi$

$z=z$

Show that the cylindrical coordinate system is orthogonal, i.e. $g_{ij}(i\neq j)=0$ for all i and j. **[June-2012, QNo.-1(e)]**

Ans. From $g_{ij}=\frac{\partial x}{\partial u_i}\frac{\partial x}{\partial u_j}+\frac{\partial y}{\partial u_i}\frac{\partial y}{\partial u_j}+\frac{\partial z}{\partial u_i}\frac{\partial z}{\partial u_j}$, we have

$$g_{11}=\left(\frac{\partial x}{\partial u_1}\right)^2+\left(\frac{\partial y}{\partial u_1}\right)^2+\left(\frac{\partial z}{\partial u_1}\right)^2=\left(\frac{\partial x}{\partial \rho}\right)^2+\left(\frac{\partial y}{\partial \rho}\right)^2+\left(\frac{\partial z}{\partial \rho}\right)^2$$

$$=\cos^2\phi+\sin^2\phi+0=1;$$

$$g_{12}=\frac{\partial x}{\partial u_1}\frac{\partial x}{\partial u_2}+\frac{\partial y}{\partial u_1}\frac{\partial y}{\partial u_2}+\frac{\partial z}{\partial u_1}\frac{\partial z}{\partial u_2}=\frac{\partial x}{\partial \rho}\frac{\partial x}{\partial \phi}+\frac{\partial y}{\partial \rho}\frac{\partial y}{\partial \phi}+\frac{\partial z}{\partial \rho}\frac{\partial z}{\partial \phi}$$

$$=\cos\phi(-\rho\sin\phi)+\sin\phi(\rho\cos\phi)+0=0;$$

$$g_{22}=\left(\frac{\partial x}{\partial u_2}\right)^2+\left(\frac{\partial y}{\partial u_2}\right)^2+\left(\frac{\partial z}{\partial u_2}\right)^2=\left(\frac{\partial x}{\partial \phi}\right)^2+\left(\frac{\partial y}{\partial \phi}\right)^2+\left(\frac{\partial z}{\partial \phi}\right)^2$$

$$=\rho^2\sin^2\phi+\rho^2\cos^2\phi+0=\rho^2;$$

$$g_{33}=\left(\frac{\partial x}{\partial u_3}\right)^2+\left(\frac{\partial y}{\partial u_3}\right)^2+\left(\frac{\partial z}{\partial u_3}\right)^2=\left(\frac{\partial x}{\partial z}\right)^2+\left(\frac{\partial y}{\partial z}\right)^2+\left(\frac{\partial z}{\partial z}\right)^2=0+0+1=1;$$

Similarly, we will find that $g_{23}=g_{31}=0$. A coordinate system is said to be orthogonal if $g_{ij}=0,\ \forall i\neq j$.

Hence, cylindrical coordinate system is orthogonal because g_{12}, g_{23} and g_{31} are zero.

Q8. In spherical polar coordinates, $u_1 = r, u_2 = \theta, u_3 = \phi$. Using equation $(ds)^2 = g_{11}(du_1)^2 + 2g_{12}du_1du_2 + g_{22}(du_2)^2 + 2g_{23}du_2du_3 + g_{33}(du_3)^2 + 2g_{31}du_3du_1$, show that the expression for square of the arc element is given by $(ds)^2 = (dr)^2 + r^2(d\theta)^2 + r^2\sin^2\theta(d\phi)^2$

Ans. From equation $g_{ij} = \frac{\partial x}{\partial u_i}\frac{\partial x}{\partial U_j} + \frac{\partial y}{\partial u_i}\frac{\partial y}{\partial u_j} + \frac{\partial z}{\partial u_i}\frac{\partial z}{\partial u_j}$, we know that the metric coefficients are given by

$$g_{11} = \left(\frac{\partial x}{\partial u_1}\right)^2 + \left(\frac{\partial y}{\partial u_1}\right)^2 + \left(\frac{\partial z}{\partial u_1}\right)^2 = \left(\frac{\partial x}{\partial r}\right)^2 + \left(\frac{\partial y}{\partial r}\right)^2 + \left(\frac{\partial z}{\partial r}\right)^2$$

$$= \sin^2\theta\cos^2\phi + \sin^2\theta\sin^2\phi + \cos^2\theta = \sin^2\theta + \cos^2\theta = 1$$

$$g_{22} = \left(\frac{\partial x}{\partial u_2}\right)^2 + \left(\frac{\partial y}{\partial u_2}\right)^2 + \left(\frac{\partial z}{\partial u_2}\right)^2 = \left(\frac{\partial x}{\partial \theta}\right)^2 + \left(\frac{\partial y}{\partial \theta}\right)^2 + \left(\frac{\partial z}{\partial \theta}\right)^2$$

$$= r^2\cos^2\theta\cos^2\phi + r^2\cos^2\theta\sin^2\phi + r^2\sin^2\theta$$

$$= r^2\cos^2\theta\left(\cos^2\phi + \sin^2\phi\right) + r^2\sin^2\theta = r^2$$

$$g_{33} = \left(\frac{\partial x}{\partial u_3}\right)^2 + \left(\frac{\partial y}{\partial u_3}\right)^2 + \left(\frac{\partial z}{\partial u_3}\right)^2 = \left(\frac{\partial x}{\partial \phi}\right)^2 + \left(\frac{\partial y}{\partial \phi}\right)^2 + \left(\frac{\partial z}{\partial \phi}\right)^2$$

$$= r^2\sin^2\theta\sin^2\phi + r^2\sin^2\theta\cos^2\phi + 0 = r^2\sin^2\theta$$

$$g_{12} = \frac{\partial x}{\partial u_1}\frac{\partial x}{\partial u_2} + \frac{\partial y}{\partial u_1}\frac{\partial y}{\partial u_2} + \frac{\partial z}{\partial u_1}\frac{\partial z}{\partial u_2} = \frac{\partial x}{\partial r}\frac{\partial x}{\partial \theta} + \frac{\partial y}{\partial r}\frac{\partial y}{\partial \theta} + \frac{\partial z}{\partial r}\frac{\partial z}{\partial \theta}$$

$$= (\sin\theta\cos\phi)(r\cos\theta\cos\phi) + (\sin\theta\sin\phi)(r\cos\theta\sin\phi) + \cos\theta(-r\sin\theta)$$

$$= r\sin\theta\cos\theta - r\sin\theta\cos\theta = 0$$

Similarly, we can show that $g_{13} = g_{23} = 0$.

Hence, $d\vec{r} = g_{11}(du_1)^2 + g_{22}(du_2)^2 + g_{33}(du_3)^2$

$$= g_{11}(dr)^2 + g_{22}(d\theta)^2 + g_{33}(d\phi)^2 = (dr)^2 + r^2(d\theta)^2 + r^2\sin^2\theta(d\phi)^2$$

Q9. Evaluate $\hat{e}_i$'s for cylindrical and spherical polar coordinate systems.

Ans. The cylindrical polar coordinate system is defined by $u_1 = \rho, u_2 = \phi, u_3 = z$, $h_1 = 1, h_2 = \rho$, and $h_3 = 1$. So from equation $\hat{e}_i = \frac{1}{h_i}\frac{\partial \vec{r}}{\partial u_i}$, we can write $\hat{e}_1 = \hat{e}_\rho = \frac{1}{h_1}\frac{\partial \vec{r}}{\partial \rho} = \frac{\partial}{\partial \rho}\left(\hat{i}\rho\cos\phi + \hat{j}\rho\sin\phi + \hat{k}z\right)$

$= \hat{i}\cos\phi + \hat{j}\sin\phi$ ...(i)

$$\hat{e}_2 = \hat{e}_\phi = \frac{1}{h_2}\frac{\partial \vec{r}}{\partial \phi} = \frac{1}{\rho}\frac{\partial}{\partial \phi}\left(\hat{i}\rho\cos\phi + \hat{j}\rho\sin\phi + \hat{k}z\right) = -\hat{i}\sin\phi + \hat{j}\cos\phi \quad \text{...(ii)}$$

and $\hat{e}_3 = \hat{e}_z = \frac{1}{h_1}\frac{\partial \vec{r}}{\partial z} = \frac{\partial}{\partial z}\left(\hat{i}\rho\cos\phi + \hat{j}\rho\sin\phi + \hat{k}z\right) = \hat{k}$ ...(iii)

Q10. Prove that $\nabla \times \hat{\mathbf{e}}_3 = \frac{1}{\mathbf{h}_3}\left(\frac{\hat{\mathbf{e}}_1}{\mathbf{h}_2}\frac{\partial}{\partial \mathbf{u}_2} - \frac{\hat{\mathbf{e}}_2}{\mathbf{h}_1}\frac{\partial}{\partial \mathbf{u}_1}\right)\mathbf{h}_3$

Ans. We know that $\nabla \times \hat{e}_3 = -\frac{1}{h_3}\hat{e}_3 \times \nabla h_3$

Substituting for ∇h_3, we find that

$$\nabla \times \hat{e}_3 = -\frac{1}{h_3}\hat{e}_3 \times \left(\frac{\hat{e}_1}{h_1}\frac{\partial}{\partial u_1} + \frac{\hat{e}_2}{h_2}\frac{\partial}{\partial u_2} + \frac{\hat{e}_3}{h_3}\frac{\partial}{\partial u_3}\right)h_3 = -\frac{1}{h_3}\left(\frac{\hat{e}_2}{h_1}\frac{\partial}{\partial u_1} - \frac{\hat{e}_1}{h_2}\frac{\partial}{\partial u_2}\right)h_3$$

$$= \frac{1}{h_3}\left(\frac{\hat{e}_1}{h_2}\frac{\partial h_3}{\partial u_2} - \frac{\hat{e}_2}{h_1}\frac{\partial h_3}{\partial u_1}\right)$$

Q11. Show that in Cartesian coordinates, cylindrical coordinates and spherical polar coordinates, divergence of a vector can be expressed as $\nabla.\vec{\mathbf{F}} = \frac{\partial \mathbf{F}_x}{\partial \mathbf{x}} + \frac{\partial \mathbf{F}_y}{\partial \mathbf{y}} + \frac{\partial \mathbf{F}_z}{\partial \mathbf{z}}$, $\nabla.\vec{\mathbf{F}} = \frac{1}{\rho}\frac{\partial}{\partial \rho}(\rho \mathbf{F}_\rho) + \frac{1}{\rho}\frac{\partial \mathbf{F}_\phi}{\partial \phi} + \frac{\partial \mathbf{F}_z}{\partial \mathbf{z}}$ **and**

$$\nabla.\vec{\mathbf{F}} = \frac{1}{\mathbf{r}^2\sin\theta}\left[\sin\theta\frac{\partial}{\partial \mathbf{r}}(\mathbf{r}^2\mathbf{F}_r) + \mathbf{r}\frac{\partial}{\partial \theta}(\sin\theta\,\mathbf{F}_\theta) + \mathbf{r}\frac{\partial \mathbf{F}_\phi}{\partial \phi}\right].$$

Ans. We know that in curvilinear coordinates,

$$\nabla.\vec{F} = \frac{1}{h_1h_2h_3}\left[\frac{\partial}{\partial u_1}(h_2h_3F_1) + \frac{\partial}{\partial u_2}(h_3h_1F_2) + \frac{\partial}{\partial u_3}(h_1h_2F_3)\right]$$

In Cartesian coordinates,

$h_1 = h_2 = h_3 = 1, u_1 = x, u_2 = y, u_3 = z, F_1 = F_x, F_2 = F_y$ and $F_3 = F_z$.

Hence, $\nabla.\vec{F} = \frac{\partial}{\partial x}F_x + \frac{\partial}{\partial y}F_y + \frac{\partial}{\partial z}F_z$

In cylindrical coordinates, $h_1 = h_\rho = 1, h_2 = h_\phi = \rho, h_3 = h_z = 1$,

$u_1 = \rho, u_2 = \phi, u_3 = z, F_1 = F_\rho, F_2 = F_\phi$ and $F_3 = F_z$.

Hence, $\nabla.\vec{F} = \frac{1}{\rho}\left[\frac{\partial}{\partial \rho}(\rho F_\rho) + \frac{\partial F_\phi}{\partial \phi} + \frac{\partial}{\partial z}(\rho F_z)\right] = \frac{1}{\rho}\frac{\partial}{\partial \rho}(\rho F_\rho) + \frac{1}{\rho}\frac{\partial F_\phi}{\partial \phi} + \frac{\partial}{\partial z}F_z$

In spherical coordinates, $h_1 = h_r = 1, h_2 = h_\theta = r, h_3 = h_\phi = r\sin\theta,$

$u_1 = r, u_2 = \theta, u_3 = \phi, F_1 = F_r, F_2 = F_\theta,$ and $F_3 = F_\phi$.

$$\text{Hence, } \nabla.\vec{F} = \frac{1}{r^2\sin\theta}\left[\frac{\partial}{\partial r}\left(r^2\sin\theta F_r\right) + \frac{\partial}{\partial\theta}\left(r\sin\theta F_\theta\right) + \frac{\partial}{\partial\phi}\left(rF_\phi\right)\right]$$

$$= \frac{1}{r^2\sin\theta}\left[\sin\theta\frac{\partial}{\partial r}\left(r^2F_r\right) + r\frac{\partial}{\partial\theta}\left(\sin\theta F_\theta\right) + r\frac{\partial F_\phi}{\partial\phi}\right]$$

Q12. A particle is moving in space. Show that divergence of its position vector is invariant under coordinate transformation.

Ans. Let us compute $\nabla.\vec{r}$ for Cartesian, cylindrical and spherical polar coordinates.

In Cartesian coordinates, $\vec{r} = \hat{i}\,x + \hat{j}\,y + \hat{k}\,z$ so that

$$\nabla.\vec{r} = \left(\hat{i}\frac{\partial}{\partial x} + \hat{j}\frac{\partial}{\partial y} + \hat{k}\frac{\partial}{\partial z}\right).\left(\hat{i}\,x + \hat{j}\,y + \hat{k}\,z\right) = \left(\frac{\partial x}{\partial x} + \frac{\partial y}{\partial y} + \frac{\partial z}{\partial z}\right) = 3$$

In cylindrical coordinates, $\vec{r} = \rho\,\hat{e}_\rho + z\,\hat{e}_z$ and $\nabla.\vec{r} = \frac{1}{\rho}\frac{\partial}{\partial\rho}\left(\rho r_\rho\right) + \frac{1}{\rho}\frac{\partial r_\phi}{\partial\phi} + \frac{\partial r_z}{\partial z}$

In this case, $r_\rho = \rho, r_\phi = 0$ and $r_z = z$.

$$\text{Hence, } \nabla.\vec{r} = \frac{1}{\rho}\frac{\partial}{\partial\rho}\left(\rho^2\right) + 0 + 1 = 2 + 1 = 3.$$

Similarly, in spherical polar coordinates, $\vec{r} = r\,\hat{e}_r$

$$\text{and } \nabla.\vec{r} = \frac{1}{r^2\sin\theta}\left[\sin\theta\frac{\partial}{\partial r}\left(r^2r_r\right) + r\frac{\partial}{\partial\theta}\left(\sin\theta\, r_\theta\right) + r\frac{\partial r_\phi}{\partial\phi}\right]$$

Here, $r_r = r, r_\theta = r_\phi = 0.$

$$\text{Hence, } \nabla.\vec{r} = \frac{1}{r^2\sin\theta}\left[\sin\theta\frac{\partial}{\partial r}\left(r^3\right)\right] = \frac{1}{r^2\sin\theta}\left[3r^2\sin\theta\right] = 3$$

Since that value of $\nabla.\vec{r}$ comes out to be the same in all coordinate systems, we say that it is invariant.

Q13. The magnetic potential of a single current loop in the xy-plane is given by $\vec{V} = \nabla\times\left[\nabla\times\hat{e}_\phi A_\phi(r,\theta)\right]$. Express it in spherical polar coordinates.

$$\textbf{Ans. } \text{Here, } \vec{V} = \nabla\times\frac{1}{r^2\sin\theta}\begin{vmatrix} \hat{e}_r & r\hat{e}_\theta & r\sin\theta\,\hat{e}_\phi \\ \frac{\partial}{\partial r} & \frac{\partial}{\partial\theta} & \frac{\partial}{\partial\phi} \\ 0 & 0 & r\sin\theta A_\phi(r,\theta) \end{vmatrix}$$

$$= \nabla \times \frac{1}{r^2 \sin\theta}\left[\hat{e}_r \frac{\partial}{\partial\theta}\left(r \sin\theta A_\phi\right) - r\ \hat{e}_\theta \frac{\partial}{\partial r}\left(r\sin\theta A_\phi\right)\right]$$

Taking the curl again, we obtain

$$\vec{V} = \frac{1}{r^2 \sin\theta}\begin{vmatrix} \hat{e}_r & r\hat{e}_\theta & r\sin\theta\hat{e}_\phi \\ \frac{\partial}{\partial r} & \frac{\partial}{\partial\theta} & \frac{\partial}{\partial\phi} \\ \frac{1}{r^2 \sin\theta}\frac{\partial}{\partial\theta}\left(r\sin\theta A_\phi\right) & -\frac{1}{r\sin\theta}\frac{\partial}{\partial r}\left(r\sin\theta A_\phi\right) & 0 \end{vmatrix}$$

By expanding the determinant, we get

$$\vec{V} = -\hat{e}_\phi\left\{\frac{1}{r}\frac{\partial}{\partial r}\left[\frac{1}{r}\frac{\partial}{\partial r}\left(rA_\phi\right)\right] + \frac{1}{r^2}\frac{\partial}{\partial\theta}\left[\frac{1}{\sin\theta}\frac{\partial}{\partial\theta}\left(\sin\theta A_\phi\right)\right]\right\}$$

Q14. Show that $\frac{d\hat{e}_\rho}{dt} = \dot{\phi}\,\hat{e}_\phi$, $\frac{d\hat{e}_\phi}{dt} = -\hat{e}_\rho\dot{\phi}$, $\frac{d\hat{e}_r}{dt} = \dot{\theta}\,\hat{e}_\theta + \sin\theta\,\dot{\phi}\,\hat{e}_\phi$, $\frac{d\hat{e}_\theta}{dt} = -\dot{\theta}\,\hat{e}_r + \dot{\phi}\cos\theta\,\hat{e}_\phi$ **and** $\frac{d\hat{e}_\phi}{dt} = -\sin\theta\,\dot{\phi}\,\hat{e}_r - \cos\theta\,\dot{\phi}\,\hat{e}_\theta$.

Ans. We know that $\hat{e}_\rho = \cos\phi\ \hat{i} + \sin\phi\ \hat{j}$ ...(i)

and $\hat{e}_\phi = -\sin\phi\ \hat{i} + \cos\phi\ \hat{j}$ ...(ii)

Then $\frac{d\hat{e}_\rho}{dt} = \left[-\sin\phi\hat{i} + \cos\phi\hat{j}\right]\dot{\phi} = \dot{\phi}\,\hat{e}_\phi$

and $\frac{d\hat{e}_\phi}{dt} = \left[-\cos\phi\ \hat{i} - \sin\phi\ \hat{j}\right]\dot{\phi} = -\hat{e}_\rho\dot{\phi}$

Now, we know that $\hat{e}_r = \sin\theta\cos\phi\ \hat{i} + \sin\theta\sin\phi\ \hat{j} + \cos\theta\ \hat{k}$ ...(iii)

$\hat{e}_\theta = \cos\theta\cos\phi\ \hat{i} + \cos\theta\sin\phi\ \hat{j} - \sin\theta\ \hat{k}$ ...(iv)

and $\hat{e}_\phi = -\sin\phi\ \hat{i} + \cos\phi\ \hat{j}$ ...(v)

Hence, $\frac{d\hat{e}_r}{dt} = \cos\theta\cos\phi\ \hat{i}\dot{\theta} - \sin\theta\sin\phi\ \hat{i}\ \dot{\phi} + \cos\theta\sin\phi\,\hat{j}\,\dot{\theta} + \sin\theta\cos\phi\,\hat{j}\dot{\phi} - \sin\theta\ \hat{k}\dot{\theta}$

$= \left(\cos\theta\cos\phi\ \hat{i} + \cos\theta\sin\phi\ \hat{j} - \sin\theta\ \hat{k}\right)\dot{\theta} + \sin\theta\dot{\phi}\left(-\sin\phi\ \hat{i} + \cos\phi\,\hat{j}\right)$

$= \dot{\theta}\,\hat{e}_\phi + \sin\theta\,\dot{\phi}\,\hat{e}_\phi$

and

$\frac{d\hat{e}_\theta}{dt} = -\sin\theta\cos\phi\ \hat{i}\dot{\theta} - \cos\theta\sin\phi\ \hat{i}\ \dot{\phi} - \sin\theta\sin\phi\,\hat{j}\ \dot{\theta} + \cos\theta\cos\phi\,\hat{j}\ \dot{\phi} - \cos\theta\ \hat{k}\dot{\theta}$

$$= -\dot{\theta}\,\hat{e}_r + \dot{\phi}\cos\theta\,\hat{e}_\phi$$

and $\dfrac{d\hat{e}_\phi}{dt} = -\left(\cos\phi\,\hat{i} + \sin\phi\,\hat{j}\right)\dot{\phi}$

Multiply (iii) by sinθ and (iv) by cosθ. We will get

$$\hat{e}_r\sin\theta = \sin^2\theta\cos\phi\,\hat{i} + \sin^2\theta\sin\phi\,\hat{j} + \cos\theta\sin\theta\,\hat{k}$$

$$\cos\theta\,\hat{e}_\theta = \cos^2\theta\cos\phi\,\hat{i} + \cos^2\theta\sin\phi\,\hat{j} - \cos\theta\sin\theta\,\hat{k}$$

On adding these, we find that $\sin\theta\,\hat{e}_r + \cos\theta\,\hat{e}_\theta = \cos\phi\,\hat{i} + \sin\phi\,\hat{j}$

Hence, $\dfrac{d\hat{e}_\phi}{dt} = -\left(\sin\theta\,\hat{e}_r + \cos\theta\,\hat{e}_\theta\right)\dot{\phi}$

Q15. A rigid body is rotating about a fixed axis with a constant angular velocity ω. Take ω to be along the z-axis. Using spherical polar coordinates, calculate (i) $\vec{v} = \omega \times \vec{r}$ and (ii) $\nabla \times \vec{v}$.

Ans. (i) In spherical polar coordinates, $\vec{r} = r\,\hat{e}_r$ and $\vec{\omega} = \omega\left(\cos\theta\,\hat{e}_r - \sin\theta\,\hat{e}_\theta\right)$

Hence, $\vec{v} = \vec{\omega}\times\vec{r} = \omega r\left(\cos\theta\,\hat{e}_r - \sin\theta\,\hat{e}_\theta\right)\times\hat{e}_r = -r\,\omega\sin\theta\left(\hat{e}_\theta\times\hat{e}_r\right)$

$= \omega\, r\sin\theta\,\hat{e}_\phi$

(ii) $$\nabla\times v = \frac{1}{r^2\sin\theta}\begin{bmatrix} \hat{e}_r & r\,\hat{e}_\theta & r\sin\theta\,\hat{e}_\phi \\ \dfrac{\partial}{\partial r} & \dfrac{\partial}{\partial\theta} & \dfrac{\partial}{\partial\phi} \\ 0 & 0 & \omega r^2\sin^2\theta \end{bmatrix}$$

$$= \frac{1}{r^2\sin\theta}\left[\hat{e}_r\,2\omega r^2\sin\theta\cos\theta - \hat{e}_\theta\,2\omega r^2\sin^2\theta\right] = 2\hat{e}_r\,\omega\cos\theta - 2\omega\,\hat{e}_\theta\sin\theta$$

$$= 2\omega\left(\hat{e}_r\cos\theta - \hat{e}_\theta\sin\theta\right) = 2\omega\,\hat{k} = 2\vec{\omega}$$

Q16. A central force field is given by

$$\vec{F} = \hat{e}_r\frac{2r_0\cos\theta}{r^3} + \hat{e}_\theta\frac{r_0}{r^3}\sin\theta.\ \textbf{Calculate } \nabla\times\vec{F}.$$

Ans. We have $\vec{F} = \hat{e}_r\dfrac{2r_0\cos\theta}{r^3} + \hat{e}_\theta\dfrac{r_0}{r^3}\sin\theta$

Hence, $$\nabla\times\vec{F} = \frac{1}{r^2\sin\theta}\begin{vmatrix} \hat{e}_r & \hat{e}_\theta & r\sin\theta\,\hat{e}_\phi \\ \dfrac{\partial}{\partial r} & \dfrac{\partial}{\partial\theta} & \dfrac{\partial}{\partial\phi} \\ \dfrac{2r_0\cos\theta}{r^3} & \dfrac{r_0}{r^3}\sin\theta & 0 \end{vmatrix}$$

$$= \frac{1}{r^2 \sin\theta}\left[r\sin\theta\, \hat{e}_\phi \left(-\frac{3r_0}{r^4}\sin\theta + \frac{2r_0}{r^3}\sin\theta \right)\right] = \hat{e}_\phi \frac{\sin\theta}{r^4}\left(2r_0 - 3\frac{r_0}{r}\right)$$

$$= \hat{e}_\phi \sin\theta \left(\frac{2r\, r_0 - 3r_0}{r^5} \right)$$

Q17. Express the following vector field in spherical polar coordinates.

$$\vec{F} = \frac{k\left(x\,\hat{j} - y\,\hat{i}\right)}{x^2 + y^2 + z^2}$$

[June-2011, Q.No.-1(d)]

Ans. Given, $\vec{F} = \dfrac{k\left(x\,\hat{j} - y\,\hat{i}\right)}{x^2 + y^2 + z^2}$

Substituting, $x = r\sin\theta\cos\phi$; $y = r\sin\theta\sin\phi$; $z = r\cos\theta$

and $\hat{i} = \sin\theta\cos\phi\,\hat{e}_r + \cos\theta\cos\phi\,\hat{e}_\theta - \sin\phi\,\hat{e}_\phi$;

$\hat{j} = \sin\theta\sin\phi\,\hat{e}_r + \cos\theta\sin\phi\,\hat{e}_\theta + \cos\phi\,\hat{e}_\phi$; $\hat{k} = \cos\theta\,\hat{e}_r - \sin\theta\,\hat{e}_\theta$

$$\text{We get, } \vec{F} = \frac{k\left[r\sin\theta\cos\phi\left(\sin\theta\sin\phi\,\hat{e}_r + \cos\theta\sin\phi\,\hat{e}_\theta + \cos\phi\,\hat{e}_\phi\right) - r\sin\theta\sin\phi\left(\sin\theta\cos\phi\,\hat{e}_r + \cos\theta\cos\phi\,\hat{e}_\theta - \sin\phi\,\hat{e}_\phi\right)\right]}{r^2\sin^2\theta\cos^2\phi + r^2\sin^2\theta\sin^2\phi + r^2\cos^2\theta}$$

$$\vec{F} = \frac{k\left[r\sin^2\theta\sin\phi\cos\phi\,\hat{e}_r + r\sin\theta\cos\theta\sin\phi\cos\phi\,\hat{e}_\theta + r\sin\theta\cos^2\phi\,\hat{e}_\phi - r\sin^2\theta\sin\phi\cos\phi\,\hat{e}_r - r\sin\theta\cos\theta\sin\phi\cos\phi\,\hat{e}_\theta + r\sin\theta\sin^2\phi\,\hat{e}_\phi\right]}{r^2}$$

$$\Rightarrow \quad \vec{F} = \frac{k\left[r\sin\theta\cos^2\phi\,\hat{e}_\phi + r\sin\theta\sin^2\phi\,\hat{e}_\phi\right]}{r^2}$$

$$\Rightarrow \quad \vec{F} = \frac{kr\sin\theta\;\hat{e}_\phi\left(\cos^2\phi + \sin^2\phi\right)}{r^2}$$

$$\Rightarrow \quad \vec{F} = \frac{k\sin\theta\,\hat{e}_\phi}{r} \Rightarrow \quad \vec{F} = \frac{k}{r}\left(\sin\theta\,\hat{e}_\phi\right)$$

Q18. Express the force field $\vec{F} = \dfrac{z\,\hat{i} + x\,\hat{j} + y\,\hat{k}}{x^2 + y^2 + z^2}$ in cylindrical polar coordinates. **[Dec-2011, Q.No.-1(c)]**

Ans. Given, $\vec{F} = \dfrac{z\,\hat{i} + x\,\hat{j} + y\,\hat{k}}{x^2 + y^2 + z^2}$

Substituting, $x = \rho\cos\phi$; $y = \rho\sin\phi$; $z = z$

and $\hat{i} = \cos\phi\, \hat{e}_\rho - \sin\phi\, \hat{e}_\phi$; $\hat{j} = \sin\phi\, \hat{e}_\rho + \cos\phi\, \hat{e}_\phi$; $\hat{k} = \hat{e}_z$

$$\Rightarrow \vec{F} = \frac{z\left(\cos\phi\, \hat{e}_\rho - \sin\phi\, \hat{e}_\phi\right) + x\left(\sin\phi\, \hat{e}_\rho + \cos\phi\, \hat{e}_\phi\right) + y\, \hat{e}_z}{\rho^2 \cos^2\phi + \rho^2 \sin^2\phi + z^2}$$

$$\Rightarrow \vec{F} = \frac{z\left(\cos\phi\, \hat{e}_\rho - \sin\phi\, \hat{e}_\phi\right) + \rho\cos\phi\left(\sin\phi\, \hat{e}_\rho + \cos\phi\, \hat{e}_\phi\right) + \rho\sin\phi\, \hat{e}_z}{\rho^2 + z^2}$$

$$\Rightarrow \vec{F} = \frac{z\cos\phi\, \hat{e}_\rho - z\sin\phi\, \hat{e}_\phi + \rho\cos\phi\sin\phi\, \hat{e}_\rho + \rho\cos^2\phi\, \hat{e}_\phi + \rho\sin\phi\, \hat{e}_z}{\rho^2 + z^2}$$

$$\Rightarrow \vec{F} = \frac{\left(z\cos\phi + \rho\cos\phi\sin\phi\right)\hat{e}_\rho + \left(\rho\cos^2\phi - z\sin\phi\right)\hat{e}_\phi + \rho\sin\phi\, \hat{e}_z}{\rho^2 + z^2}$$

Q19. Spherical polar coordinates $u_1 = r, u_2 = \theta, u_3 = \phi$ are related to the Cartesian coordinates x, y and z as follows:

$x = r\sin\theta\cos\phi$

$y = r\sin\theta\sin\phi$

$z = r\cos\theta$.

Calculate g_{12}, g_{13} and g_{23} to show that the spherical coordinate system is orthogonal. **[Dec-2012, Q.No.-1(e)]**

Ans. We know that $g_{ij} = \frac{\partial x}{\partial u_i}\frac{\partial x}{\partial u_j} + \frac{\partial y}{\partial u_i}\frac{\partial y}{\partial u_j} + \frac{\partial z}{\partial u_i}\frac{\partial z}{\partial u_j}$

Now $g_{12} = \frac{\partial x}{\partial u_1}\frac{\partial x}{\partial u_2} + \frac{\partial y}{\partial u_1}\frac{\partial y}{\partial u_2} + \frac{\partial z}{\partial u_1}\frac{\partial z}{\partial u_2} = \frac{\partial x}{\partial r}\frac{\partial x}{\partial \theta} + \frac{\partial y}{\partial r}\frac{\partial y}{\partial \theta} + \frac{\partial z}{\partial r}\frac{\partial z}{\partial \theta}$

$= (\sin\theta\cos\phi)(r\cos\theta\cos\phi) + (\sin\theta\sin\phi)(r\cos\theta\sin\phi) + \cos\theta(-r\sin\theta)$

$= r\sin\theta\cos\theta - r\sin\theta\cos\theta = 0$;

$g_{13} = \frac{\partial x}{\partial u_1}\frac{\partial x}{\partial u_3} + \frac{\partial y}{\partial u_1}\frac{\partial y}{\partial u_3} + \frac{\partial z}{\partial u_1}\frac{\partial z}{\partial u_3} = \frac{\partial x}{\partial r}\frac{\partial x}{\partial \phi} + \frac{\partial y}{\partial r}\frac{\partial y}{\partial \phi} + \frac{\partial z}{\partial r}\frac{\partial z}{\partial \phi}$

$= (\sin\theta\cos\phi)(-r\sin\theta\sin\phi) + (\sin\theta\sin\phi)(r\sin\theta\cos\phi) + \cos\theta(0)$

$= -r\sin^2\theta\sin\phi\cos\phi + r\sin^2\theta\sin\phi\cos\phi = 0$

and $g_{23} = \frac{\partial x}{\partial u_2}\frac{\partial x}{\partial u_3} + \frac{\partial y}{\partial u_2}\frac{\partial y}{\partial u_3} + \frac{\partial z}{\partial u_2}\frac{\partial z}{\partial u_3} = \frac{\partial x}{\partial \theta}\frac{\partial x}{\partial \phi} + \frac{\partial y}{\partial \theta}\frac{\partial y}{\partial \phi} + \frac{\partial z}{\partial \theta}\frac{\partial z}{\partial \phi}$

$= (r\cos\theta\cos\phi)(-r\sin\theta\sin\phi) + (r\cos\theta\sin\phi)(r\sin\theta\cos\phi) + (-r\sin\theta)(0)$

$= -r^2\sin\theta\sin\phi\cos\theta\cos\phi + r^2\sin\theta\sin\phi\cos\theta\cos\phi = 0$

Since a coordinate system is said to be orthogonal if $g_{ij} = 0,\ \forall i \neq j$.

Hence, spherical coordinate system is orthogonal because g_{12}, g_{13} and g_{23} are zero.

Hello IGNOU Student,

Do you want to get more marks which means good job, and better career opportunities?
Are you confused about where to study?
Do You know Gullybaba / GPH book is the only company started 15 years back by the Ex-IGNOU student and now provides No.1 IGNOU Self-help books across the globe?

We have created these ***Notes*** specially to help IGNOU Students.

We strongly recommend to read from ***GPH Books*** which contain complete material for exam preparation with previous year's question papers solutions.

You can order GPH Books on Gullybaba.com. Pay by "Cash on Delivery", Credit Card, Paytm, or Online Transfer and get home delivery by Govt. Postal Dept. after Lockdown.

Chapter 4

Integration of Scalar and Vector Fields

AN OVERVIEW

Integrals find many applications in physics. For example, the work done by a force or the magnetic field due to a current-carrying conductor can be expressed as a line integral. The flux of a magnetic field can be expressed as a surface integral.

A line integral (sometimes called a path integral) is the integral of some function along a curve. One can integrate a scalar-valued function along a curve, obtaining for example, the mass of a wire from its density. One can also integrate a certain type of vector-valued functions along a curve. These vector-valued functions are the ones where the input and output dimensions are the same and we usually represent them as vector fields.

Integration of a vector with respect to a scalar: If $\vec{a}$ (t) is a vector function of a scalar variable t, then $\frac{d}{dt}\vec{a}(t)=\vec{b}(t)$ and $\int \vec{b}(t)dt=\vec{a}(t)+\vec{c}$ where $\vec{c}$ is a constant vector. For two vectors $\vec{V}_1(t)$ and $\vec{V}_2(t)$ of the scalar t, we have

$\int\left[p\vec{V}_1(t)\pm q\vec{V}_2(t)\right]dt=p\int \vec{V}_1(t)dt\pm q\int \vec{V}_2(t)dt$ where p and q are constants.

Double Integral: The double integral can be defined in a manner analogous to that used for a single integral. We subdivide the region R by drawing lines parallel to x and y-axes. We number the rectangles that are within R from 1 to n. Now, let us consider a point P, in the *i*th rectangle. Let the value of the function at that point be ϕ_i. Now, we form the sum $S_n=\sum_{i=1}^{n}\phi_i \Delta A_i$ where ΔA_i is the area of the *i*th rectangle and n is a positive integer. We take this sum for larger and larger values of n. Then the rectangles become smaller and as n goes to infinity, the length of the maximum diagonal of the rectangles approaches zero and the value of ϕ_i may be considered as constant at all points within the *i*th rectangle.

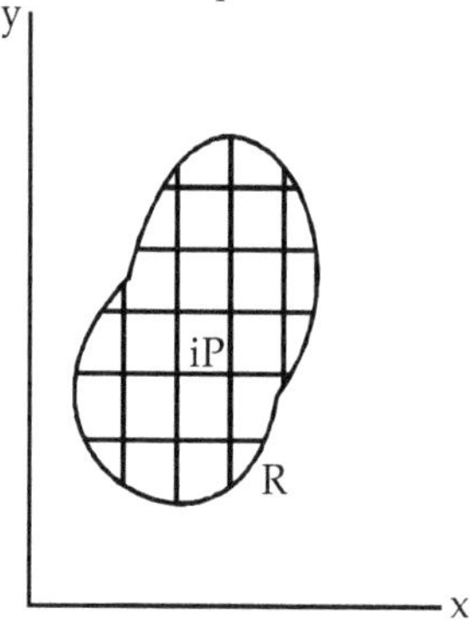

Fig. 4.1

If $\phi(x,y)$ is continuous in R, the limit of S_n, as *n* tends to infinity, is finite and its value is independent of the choice of the sub-divisions. This limit is called the double integral of $\phi(x,y)$ over the region R.

Thus, $\lim_{n\to\infty}\sum_{i=1}^{n}\phi_i \Delta A_i=\iint_R \phi(x,y)dx\,dy=\iint_R \phi(x,y)\,dA$ where dA = dx dy

Properties of double integrals: Let ϕ_1 and ϕ_2 be the functions of x and y, defined and continuous in a region R. Then

(a) $\iint_R k\phi_1 dxdy=k\iint_R \phi_1 dxdy$ where k is a constant,

(b) $\iint\limits_R k(\phi_1 + \phi_2)dxdy = k\iint\limits_R \phi_1 dxdy + k\iint\limits_R \phi_2 dxdy$

and (c) $\iint\limits_R \phi_1 dxdy = \iint\limits_{R_1} \phi_1 dxdy + \iint\limits_{R_2} \phi_1 dxdy$

where R has been subdivided into two regions R_1 and R_2 (fig. 4.2).

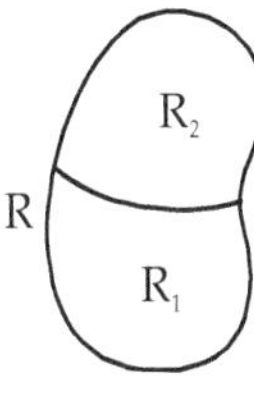

Fig. 4.2

Evaluation of Double Integrals: Double integrals over a region R may be calculated by way of evaluating two successive integrations. The first integration is performed with respect to one of the variables, keeping the other variable constant. Then the double integral reduces to an ordinary definite integral, which can be easily evaluated.

Triple Integrals: Let us consider a function $\psi(x,y,z)$ defined in a bounded closed region T in space.

Let us consider a point in the *i*th parallelepiped. Let the value of the function be ψ_i. Then we form the sum $S_n = \sum_{i=1}^{n} \psi_i \Delta V_i$ where ΔV_i is the volume of the *i*th parallelepiped. We take this sum for larger and larger positive integers n, so that the parallelepipeds become smaller and smaller and lengths of the edges of the largest parallelepiped of subdivision approach zero as n goes to infinity. In this case, the value of the function ψ_i may be considered to be same at all points with the parallelepiped.

If $\psi(x,y,z)$ is continuous in the region of space T, the limit of S_n as *n* tends to infinity is finite and its value is independent of the subdivisions. This limit is called the triple integral of $\psi(x,y,z)$ over the region T.

Thus, $\lim\limits_{n\to\infty} \sum_{i=1}^{n} \psi_i \Delta V_i = \iiint\limits_T \psi(x,y,z)dxdydz = \iiint\limits_T \psi(x,y,z)dV$ where dV = dxdydz.

Line integral of a field: Let $\vec{F}(\vec{r})$ be a continuous vector point function and $\vec{r}$ = f (t) be a continuously differentiable curve. Let $\frac{d\vec{r}}{ds}$ be the unit vector function along the tangent at P. Then the component of the vector function along this tangent at P is $\vec{F}.\frac{d\vec{r}}{ds}$.

For point on the curve, it is a function of s. Then $\int_C \vec{F}\cdot\frac{d\vec{r}}{ds}ds = \int_C \vec{F}\cdot d\vec{r}$ is called the tangent line integral of $\vec{F}(\vec{r})$ along the curve C.

If the path C over which the integration is performed is made up of a number of pieces $C_1, C_2, ..., C_n$ laid end to end, then the integral over the composite path C is the sum of the integrals over the pieces which make it up: $\int_C \vec{F}\cdot d\vec{r} = \int_{C_1} \vec{F}\cdot d\vec{r} + \int_{C_2} \vec{F}\cdot d\vec{r} + ... + \int_{C_n} \vec{F}\cdot d\vec{r}$.

Since $\vec{F}\cdot d\vec{r}$ is scalar, this is the ordinary line integral of elementary calculus.

In component forms F_1, F_2, F_3 along the co-ordinate axes which are functions of x,y,z, this line integral is written as

$$\int_C \vec{F}\cdot d\vec{r} = \int_C \left(F_1\hat{i} + F_2\hat{j} + F_3\hat{k}\right)\cdot\left(\hat{i}dx + \hat{j}dy + \hat{k}dz\right) = \int_C \left(F_1dx + F_2dy + F_3dz\right).$$

This form is frequently used to evaluate the line integrals.

If the curve C is given by the parametric equations

$x = x\ (t), y = y\ (t), z = z\ (t)$

then we may write $\int_C \vec{F}\cdot d\vec{r} = \int_{t_1}^{t_2}\left(F_1(t)\frac{dx}{dt} + F_2(t)\frac{dy}{dt} + F_3(t)\frac{dz}{dt}\right)dt$,

where t_1 and t_2 are the values of the parameters at A and B, two points on the curve.

Note: If P and Q are the two points joined by a curve C, then, in general, the value of the line integral $\int_C \vec{F}\cdot d\vec{r} = \int_C \left(F_1 dx + F_2 dy + F_3 dz\right)$ depends not only on the end points P and Q of the path C but also on C.

The line integral is said to be independent of path in R, if for every pair of end points P and Q in R the value of the integral is the same for all paths C to R starting from P and ending at Q.

Line Integral Independent of Path: If $\vec{F}$ be continuous vector function in region R of space, the line integral $\int_C \vec{F}\cdot d\vec{r}$ is independent of the path C in R joining P and Q if and only if $\vec{F}$ = grad ϕ, where $\phi(x,y,z)$ is a single valued scalar-function having continuous first partial derivatives in R.

Proof: Suppose $\vec{F} = \text{grad}\ \phi = \nabla\phi$ in R.

Let two points P and Q in R be joined by a path C in R. Then we have

$$\int_C \vec{F}\cdot d\vec{r} = \int_C \nabla\phi d\vec{r} = \int\left(\frac{\partial\phi}{\partial x}\hat{i}+\frac{\partial\phi}{\partial y}\hat{j}+\frac{\partial\phi}{\partial z}\hat{k}\right)\left(dx\hat{i}+dy\hat{j}+dz\hat{k}\right)$$

$$=\int_C\left(\frac{\partial\phi}{\partial x}dx+\frac{\partial\phi}{\partial y}dy+\frac{\partial\phi}{\partial z}dz\right)=\int_C d\phi=\int_P^Q dQ=[\phi]_P^Q=\phi(Q)-\phi(P).$$

Thus, the line integral depends on points P and Q and not the path joining them. But this is true only if $\phi(x,y,z)$ is single valued at P and Q.

Conversely, Let the line integral $\int_S \vec{F}\cdot d\vec{r}$ be independent of the path C joining any two points $P(x_0,y_0,z_0)$ and $Q(x,y,z)$ in R. Assume that A is fixed. Let $\phi(x,y,z)=\int_P^Q \vec{F}\cdot d\vec{r}=\int_P^Q\left(\vec{F}\cdot\frac{d\vec{r}}{ds}\right)ds.$

Differentiating both sides, with respect to s, we get

$$\frac{d\phi}{ds}=\vec{F}\cdot\frac{d\vec{r}}{ds}, \text{ but } \frac{d\phi}{ds}=\frac{\partial\phi}{\partial x}\cdot\frac{dx}{ds}+\frac{\partial\phi}{\partial y}\cdot\frac{dy}{ds}+\frac{\partial\phi}{\partial z}\cdot\frac{dz}{ds}$$

$$=\left(\frac{\partial\phi}{\partial x}\hat{i}+\frac{\partial\phi}{\partial y}\hat{j}+\frac{\partial\phi}{\partial z}\hat{k}\right)\cdot\left(\frac{dx}{ds}\hat{i}+\frac{dy}{ds}\hat{j}+\frac{dz}{ds}\hat{k}\right)=\nabla\phi\cdot\frac{d\vec{r}}{ds}$$

$$\therefore\ \vec{F}\cdot\frac{d\vec{r}}{ds}=\nabla\phi\cdot\frac{d\vec{r}}{ds}\quad\left(\vec{F}-\nabla\phi\right)\cdot\frac{d\vec{r}}{ds}=0.$$

The result is true irrespective of the path joining P and Q that is, irrespective of the direction of $\frac{d\vec{r}}{ds}$ which is tangent vector to C.

Hence, $\nabla\phi-\vec{F}=0$, i.e. $\nabla\phi=\vec{F}$.

Conservative Force Field: If the work done by a force field in taking a particle from one point to another depends only on its initial and final positions and is independent of the intermediate path, then the force field is conservative. Otherwise, it is called non-conservative. The gravitational force between any two bodies is conservative.

Now, consider A and B are two points in the field of a conservative force $\vec{F}$.

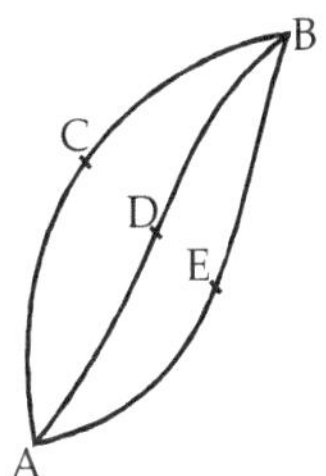

Fig. 4.3

So, according to the definition of a conservative force, we must have

$$\int_{ACB} \vec{F}\cdot d\vec{r} = \int_{ADB} \vec{F}\cdot d\vec{r} = \int_{AEB} \vec{F}\cdot d\vec{r}$$

This means that $\vec{F}.d\vec{r}$ may be expressed as the differential of a scalar function of position coordinates only. So, we may write that $\vec{F}.d\vec{r} = -dU$. where $U = U(x,y,z)$. We have brought the negative sign on the right hand side so that U may be identified with the potential energy (P.E.) of the particle in the given force field.

Surface Integrals of a Field: Let $\vec{r} = f(u,v)$ be a surface which possesses continuous first order partial derivatives and let $\vec{F}(r)$ be a continuous vector point function.

Consider any portion S of the surface (closed or not, plane or not). Let the surface be divided into a number of sub-portions $\delta S_1, \delta S_2, \delta S_3, ...\delta S_n, ...$ and let us consider the sub-surface δS_i. Let A_i be a point in this sub-surface and let $\hat{n}$ be the unit normal vector to the sub-surface at A_i drawn on the side of S.

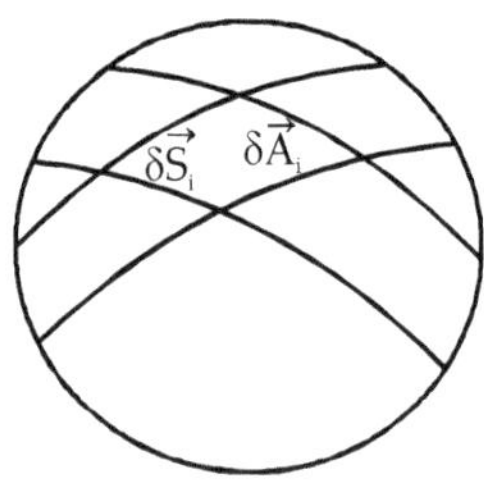

Fig. 4.4

Then δa_i the vector arc of the subsurface, is given by $\delta\vec{a}_i = \hat{n}_i \delta S_i$.

Therefore, $\Sigma\vec{F}(A_i)\cdot\delta\vec{a}_i = \Sigma F(A_i)\cdot\hat{n}_i\,\delta S_i$. ...(i)

where summation is to be taken on the various sub-surfaces in which the surface S has been divided.

If the number of sub-surfaces, $i \to \infty$ and $\delta S_i \to 0$ limit of (i) is called the normal surface integral of $\vec{F}(\vec{r})$ over S and is denoted by $\int_S \vec{F}(\vec{r})\cdot d\vec{a} = \int_S \vec{F}(\vec{r})\cdot\hat{n}\,dS$ or simply by $\int_S \vec{F}\cdot d\vec{a} = \int_S \vec{F}\cdot\hat{n}\,dS$.

Note 1: The normal surface integral $\int_S \vec{F}\cdot d\vec{a}$ of a continuous vector point function $\vec{F}$ over a closed surface S is called the flux of $\vec{F}$ across S.

Note 2: The Cartesian formula for the surface integral is

$$\int_S \int (F_1\,dy\,dz + F_2\,dz\,dx + F_3\,dx\,dy) \qquad ...(ii)$$

where F_1, F_2, F_3 are functions of x,y,z and components of F along co-ordinates axes.

Formula (2) is also equivalent to

$$\iint\left[F_1\frac{\partial(y,z)}{\partial(u,v)}+F_2\frac{\partial(z,x)}{\partial(u,v)}+F_3\frac{\partial(x,y)}{\partial(u,v)}\right](du\,dv)$$

integrated over the region in the u, v plane which corresponds to the surface S given by $\vec{r}=\vec{f}(u,v);\frac{\partial(y,z)}{\partial(u,v)}$, etc. are the Jacobians.

Volume Integrals of a Field: Let $F(\vec{r})$ be a continuous vector point function and a volume V be enclosed by a surface $\vec{r}=\vec{f}$ (u,v). Let the given volume V be divided into elements of volume $\delta v_1, \delta v_2, \delta v_3, \ldots, \delta v_i, \ldots$ Take a particular element δv_i, and take A_i and point on it. Now, consider the sum

$$\sum \vec{F}(A_i)\delta v_i \qquad \ldots(iii)$$

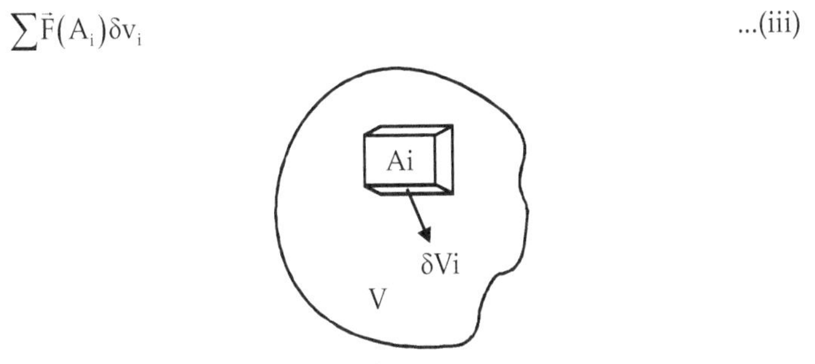

Fig. 4.5

where the summation is to be taken on all the sub-regions.

If i, the number of volume elements $\to\infty$ and $\delta v_i \to 0$ for each i, the limit of eq. (iii) is denoted as $\int_V \vec{F}(\vec{r})\,dv$ or simple $\int_V \vec{F}dv$.

In rectangular Cartesian co-ordinate, it is given by

$$\hat{i}\iiint_V F_1\,dx\,dy\,dz+\hat{j}\iiint_V F_2\,dx\,dy\,dz+\hat{k}\iiint_V F_3\,dx\,dy\,dz.$$

Gauss' Divergence Theorem: It states that the normal surface integral of a vector function $\vec{F}$ over the boundary of a closed region is equal to the volume integral of div $\vec{F}$ taken throughout the region.

In symbols it may be stated as follows: If $\vec{F}$ be a continuously differentiable vector point function in a region V and S is a closed surface enclosed the region V, then $\int_S \vec{F}.\hat{n}\,dS=\int_V \text{div}\vec{F}\,dv$ where $\hat{n}$ is the unit outward drawn normal vector to the surface S.

Proof: Let us assume that the region V is divided into sub–regions V_i such that it is possible to choose co-ordinate axes in sub a way that lines parallel to z-axis or y-axis cut the boundary surface S_i only in two points.

Let R be the projection of the region V_i on the OXY plane. Any point A on R may be taken as (x,y,0). Line through (x,y,0) and parallel to z-axis meets the boundary S into two points P and Q.

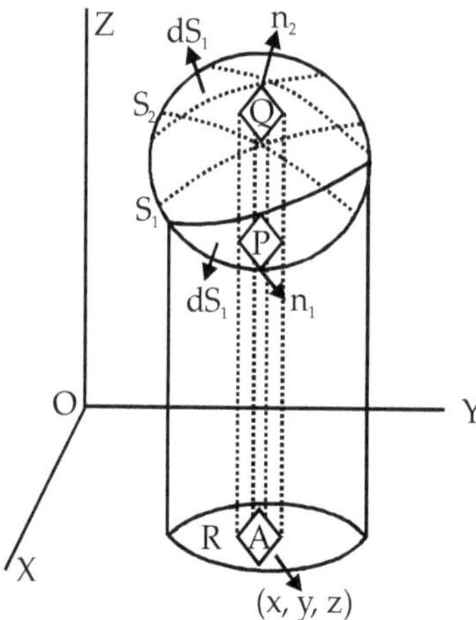

Fig. 4.6

Then Q and P may be taken as x, y, ϕ (x, y) and x, y, ψ (x, y), where $\phi \geq \psi$.

$$\text{Now } \iiint_{V_1} \frac{\partial F_3}{\partial z} dx\,dy\,dz = \iint_R \left[\int_{\psi}^{\phi} \cdot \frac{\partial F_3}{\partial z} dz \right] dx\,dy$$

$$= \iint_R \left[F_3(x,y,\phi) - F_3(x,y,\psi) \right] dx\,dy = \iint_R F_3(x,y,\phi)\,dx\,dy - \iint_R F_3(x,y,\psi)\,dx\,dy \quad ...(iv)$$

Let the parts of the surface corresponding to $z = \phi(x,y)$ and $z = \psi(x,y)$ be denoted by S_1 and S_2 respectively.

Let $\hat{n}$ be the outwards drawn unit normal vector at any point S. Then $\vec{F}\,dS = dS\cos\gamma = dx\,dy$, where γ is the angle to the normal makes with the axis of z. Therefore, $\iint_R F_3(x,y,\phi)\,dx\,dy = \int_{S_1} F_3\,\hat{n}\cdot\hat{k}\,dS$ ...(v)

and $\iint_R F_3(x,y,\psi)\,dx\,dy = -\int_{S_2} F_3\,\hat{n}\cdot\hat{k}\,dS$ ...(vi)

for the outward drawn normal at any point of S_1 will be in the opposite direction of the normal at the corresponding point of S_2.

From (v) and (vi), (iv) becomes

$$\iiint_{V_i} \frac{\partial F_3}{\partial z} dx\,dy\,dz = \int_{S_1} F_3 \hat{n}\cdot\hat{k}\,dS + \int_{S_2} F_3 \hat{n}\cdot\hat{k}\,dS$$

$$= \int_{S_i} F_3 \hat{n}\cdot\hat{k}\,dS \qquad \text{...(vii)}$$

Similarly, it can be proved that $\iiint_{V_i} \frac{\partial F_2}{\partial y} dx\,dy\,dz = \int_{S_i} F_2 \hat{n}\cdot\hat{j}\,dS$ ...(viii)

$$\iiint_{V_i} \frac{\partial F_1}{\partial x} dx\,dy\,dz = \int_{S_i} F_1 \hat{n}\cdot\hat{i}\,dS \qquad \text{...(ix)}$$

Adding (vii), (viii) and (ix) we get

$$\iiint\left(\frac{\partial F_1}{\partial x} + \frac{\partial F_2}{\partial y} + \frac{\partial F_3}{\partial z}\right) dx\,dy\,dz = \int_{S_i}\left(F_1\hat{i} + F_2\hat{j} + F_3\hat{k}\right)\cdot\hat{n}\,dS$$

or $\int_{V_i} \text{div}\,\vec{F}\,dv = \int \vec{F}\cdot\hat{n}\,dS.$

Applying this theorem to each sub-region and adding, we get

$\int_V \text{div}\,\vec{F}\,dv = \int \vec{F}\cdot\hat{n}\,dS.$

Stokes's Theorem: It states that the line integral of a vector function $\vec{F}$ around any closed curve is equal to the surface integral of the curve $\vec{F}$ taken over any surface of which the curve is a bounding edge.

In symbols it may be stated as follows:

If $\vec{F}$ is any continuously differentiable vector function and S is a surface enclosed by a curve C, then $\int_C \vec{F}\cdot d\vec{r} = \iint_S \hat{n}\cdot\text{curl}\,\vec{F}\,dS,$

where $\hat{n}$ is the unit normal vector at any point of S and is drawn in the sense in which a right handed screw would move when rotated in the sense of description of C.

Stokes's Theorem for a Plane:

In Cartesian coordinates

$$\int_C \vec{F}\cdot d\vec{r} = \iint_C\left(\hat{i}\,F_1 + \hat{j}\,F_2 + \hat{k}\,F_3\right)\cdot\left(\hat{i}\,dx + \hat{j}\,dy + \hat{k}\,dz\right) = \int_C\left(F_1 dx + F_2 dy\right)$$

as we are dealing only for a plane, i.e., dz = 0. Again since $\hat{n}$ is the same as $\hat{k}$, we have $\int_C \text{curl}\,\vec{F}\cdot\hat{n}\,dS = \int \text{curl}\,\vec{F}\cdot\hat{k}\,dS = \iint_S\left(\frac{\partial F_2}{\partial y} - \frac{\partial F_1}{\partial y}\right) dx\,dy.$

Let us assume that region S is divided into sub-regions S_i such that any line parallel to any co-ordinate axis meets C_i in at the most two points. Let C_1 be included between the lines x = a, x = b.

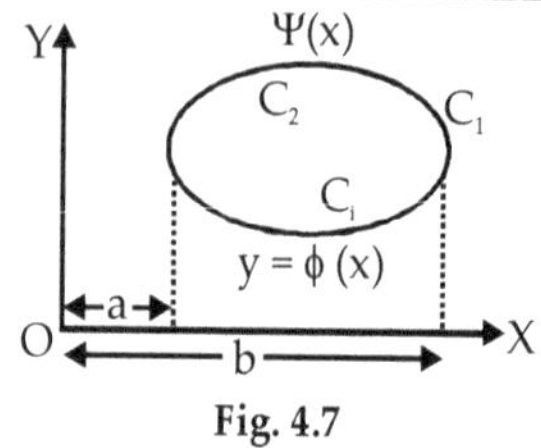

Fig. 4.7

Let any line parallel to y-axis meet C_i in the points whose y-coordinates are given by $y=\psi(x), y=\phi(x)$ such that $\psi(x)\geq\phi(x)$. Thus, the boundary of the curve C_i is divided into two arcs C_1 and C_2.

Now $\iint_{S_i}\frac{\partial F_i}{\partial y}dx\,dy=\int_a^b\left[\int_{y=\phi}^{y=\psi}\frac{\partial F_1}{\partial y}\right]dx$

$$=\int_a^b\left[F_1(x,y)\right]_{y=\phi(x)}^{y=\psi(x)}dx=\int_a^b\left[F_1\{x,\psi(x)\}-F_1\{x,\phi(x)\}\right]dx$$

$$=\int_a^b\left[F_1\{x,\psi(x)\}\right]dx-\int_a^b F_1\{x,\phi(x)\}\,dx$$

$$=-\int_b^a F_1\{x,\psi(x)\}\,dx-\int_a^b F_1\{x,\phi(x)\}\,dx$$

$$=-\int_{C_2}F_1(x,y)\,dx-\int_{C_1}F_1(x,y)\,dx=-\int_{C_i}F_i(x,y)\,dx \quad ...(x)$$

Similarly, it can be shown that $\iint_{S_i}\frac{\partial F_2}{\partial y}dx\,dy=\int_{C_i}f_2(x,y)dy$. ...(xi)

Therefore, from (x) and (xi), we have

$$\int_{C_i}(F_2\,dy+F_1\,dx)=\iint_{S_i}\left[\frac{\partial\vec{F}_2}{\partial x}-\frac{\partial\vec{F}_1}{\partial y}\right]dx\,dy \quad ...(xii)$$

Applying this theorem to each sub-region and adding we get

$$\int_C\left(\vec{F}_2\,dy+\vec{F}_1\,dx\right)=\iint_S\left[\frac{\partial\vec{F}_2}{\partial x}-\frac{\partial\vec{F}_1}{\partial y}\right]dx\,dy$$

(This result is also called the Green's Theorem in a plane.)

i.e. $\int_C\vec{F}\cdot d\vec{r}=\int_S \text{curl}\,\vec{F}\cdot\hat{n}\,dS$

Stokes's Theorem in Space: Let the surface of integration S be given by $\vec{r}=\vec{f}(u,v)$, where (u, v) is a point in a plane with u-axis and v-axis as Cartesian rectangular axes. Then the surface S is the image of a certain region D of the u, v-plane such that to each point (u, v) of D, there corresponds one and only one-point of S. Then,

$$\int \text{curl}\,\vec{F}\cdot\hat{n}\,dS=\iint_S\left(\frac{\partial\vec{F}_3}{\partial y}-\frac{\partial\vec{F}_2}{\partial z}\right)dy\,dz+\left(\frac{\partial\vec{F}_1}{\partial z}-\frac{\partial\vec{F}_3}{\partial x}\right)dz\,dx+\left(\frac{\partial\vec{F}_2}{\partial x}-\frac{\partial\vec{F}_1}{\partial y}\right)dx\,dy$$

$$=\iint_S\left[\left(\frac{\partial\vec{F}_3}{\partial y}-\frac{\partial\vec{F}_2}{\partial z}\right)\frac{\partial(y,z)}{\partial(u,v)}+\left(\frac{\partial\vec{F}_1}{\partial z}-\frac{\partial\vec{F}_3}{\partial x}\right)\frac{\partial(z,x)}{\partial(u,v)}+\left(\frac{\partial\vec{F}_2}{\partial x}-\frac{\partial\vec{F}_1}{\partial y}\right)\frac{\partial(x,y)}{\partial(u,v)}\right]du\,dv$$

...(xiii)

In this integral, the terms involving $\vec{F}_1$ are $\frac{\partial\vec{F}_1}{\partial z}\frac{\partial(z,x)}{\partial(u,v)}-\frac{\partial\vec{F}_1}{\partial y}\frac{\partial(x,y)}{\partial(u,v)}$

$$=-\frac{\partial\vec{F}_1}{\partial z}\frac{\partial(x,z)}{\partial(u,v)}-\frac{\partial\vec{F}_1}{\partial y}\frac{\partial(x,y)}{\partial(u,v)}-\frac{\partial\vec{F}_1}{\partial x}\frac{\partial(x,x)}{\partial(u,v)},\text{ the last term being zero}$$

$$=-\frac{\partial\vec{F}_1}{\partial z}\left[\frac{\partial x}{\partial u}\frac{\partial z}{\partial v}-\frac{\partial x}{\partial v}\frac{\partial z}{\partial u}\right]-\frac{\partial\vec{F}_1}{\partial y}\left[\frac{\partial x}{\partial u}\frac{\partial y}{\partial v}-\frac{\partial x}{\partial v}\frac{\partial y}{\partial u}\right]-\frac{\partial\vec{F}_1}{\partial x}\left[\frac{\partial x}{\partial u}\frac{\partial x}{\partial v}-\frac{\partial x}{\partial v}\frac{\partial x}{\partial u}\right]$$

$$=-\frac{\partial x}{\partial u}\left[\frac{\partial F_1}{\partial z}\frac{\partial z}{\partial v}+\frac{\partial F_1}{\partial y}\frac{\partial y}{\partial v}+\frac{\partial F_1}{\partial x}\frac{\partial x}{\partial v}\right]+\frac{\partial x}{\partial v}\left[\frac{\partial F_1}{\partial z}\frac{\partial z}{\partial u}+\frac{\partial F_1}{\partial y}\frac{\partial y}{\partial u}+\frac{\partial F_1}{\partial x}\frac{\partial x}{\partial u}\right]$$

$$=-\frac{\partial x}{\partial u}\frac{\partial F_1}{\partial v}+\frac{\partial x}{\partial v}\frac{\partial F_1}{\partial u}=\frac{\partial F_1}{\partial u}\frac{\partial x}{\partial v}-\frac{\partial F_1}{\partial v}\frac{\partial x}{\partial u}$$

Similarly, the terms involving F_2 and F_3 are respectively

$$\frac{\partial F_2}{\partial u}\frac{\partial y}{\partial v}-\frac{\partial F_2}{\partial v}\frac{\partial y}{\partial u},\frac{\partial F_3}{\partial u}\frac{\partial z}{\partial v}-\frac{\partial F_3}{\partial v}\frac{\partial z}{\partial u}.$$

Hence, R.H.S. of (xiii) is

$$\iint_D\left[\left(\frac{\partial F_1}{\partial u}\frac{\partial x}{\partial v}-\frac{\partial F_1}{\partial v}\frac{\partial x}{\partial u}\right)+\left(\frac{\partial F_2}{\partial u}\frac{\partial y}{\partial v}-\frac{\partial F_2}{\partial x}\frac{\partial y}{\partial u}\right)+\left(\frac{\partial F_3}{\partial u}\frac{\partial z}{\partial v}-\frac{\partial F_3}{\partial v}\frac{\partial z}{\partial u}\right)\right]du\,dv$$

By Stokes's Theorem in plane,

$$\int_D\left(\frac{\partial F_1}{\partial u}\frac{\partial x}{\partial v}-\frac{\partial F_1}{\partial v}\frac{\partial x}{\partial u}\right)du\,dv=\int_{\Gamma_1}\left(F_1\frac{\partial x}{\partial u}du+F_1\frac{\partial x}{\partial v}dv\right)=\int_{C_1}F_1\,dx$$

and similarly other two terms.

Therefore, $\int_{S_1}\text{curl}\,\vec{F}\cdot\hat{n}\,dS=\int_{C_1}(F_1dx+F_2dy+F_3dz)=\int_C\vec{F}\cdot d\vec{r}$

Applying this theorem to each region and adding we get

$\iint_S\text{curl}\,\vec{F}\cdot\hat{n}\,dS=\int_C\vec{F}\cdot d\vec{r}$

Green's Theorem: It states that if ϕ and ψ are scalar point functions which together with their derivatives in any direction are uniform and continuous within the region V bounded by a closed surface S, then

$\int_V(\phi\nabla^2\psi-\psi\nabla^2\phi)dv=\int_S(\phi\nabla\psi-\psi\nabla\phi)\cdot\hat{n}\,dS.$

Proof: From Divergence theorem, we have $\int_S\vec{F}\cdot\hat{n}\,dS=\int_V\text{div}\,\vec{F}dv.$

Substituting $\phi\nabla\psi$ for $\vec{F}$, we get

$\int_S\phi\nabla\psi\cdot\hat{n}\,dS=\int_V\text{div}(\phi\nabla\psi)\,dv$ ...(xiv)

Also div $(\phi\nabla\psi)=\nabla\cdot(\phi\nabla\psi)=\nabla\phi\cdot\nabla\psi+\phi\nabla\cdot\psi$ ...(xv)

Therefore, using (xv), (xiv) becomes

$$\int_S \phi\nabla\psi\cdot\hat{n}\,dS = \int_V \nabla\phi\cdot\nabla\psi\,dv + \int_V \phi\nabla^2\psi\,dv \qquad ...(xvi)$$

i.e. $$\int_V \nabla\phi\nabla\psi\,dv = \int_S \psi\nabla\phi\cdot\hat{n}\,dS - \int_V \phi\nabla^2\psi\,dv \qquad ...(xvii)$$

Interchanging ϕ and ψ in (xvi), we get

$$\int_S \psi\nabla\phi\cdot\hat{n}\,dv = \int_V \nabla\psi\cdot\nabla\phi\,dv + \int_V \psi\nabla^2\phi\,dv \qquad ...(xviii)$$

Subtracting (xviii) from (xvi) we obtain

$$\int_S (\phi\nabla\psi - \psi\nabla\phi)\cdot\hat{n}\,dS = \int_V (\phi\nabla^2\psi - \psi\nabla^2\phi)\,dv \qquad ...(xix)$$

The result (xix) is referred to as Green's Theorem.

Note: The first member of (xxix) may also be written as $\int\left(\phi\frac{\partial\psi}{\partial n} - \psi\frac{\partial\phi}{\partial n}\right)dS$ where $\frac{\partial\psi}{\partial n}$ denotes the derivative of ψ in the direction of the outward drawn normal to the surface of the region, i.e. $\nabla\psi = \frac{\partial\psi}{\partial n}\hat{n}, \nabla\phi = \frac{\partial\phi}{\partial n}\hat{n}$.

Thus, from (xix), the Green's Theorem can also be stated as

$$\int_V (\phi\nabla^2\psi - \psi\nabla^2\phi)dv = \int_S \left(\phi\frac{\partial\psi}{\partial n} - \psi\frac{\partial\phi}{\partial n}\right)dS.$$

Solved Practical Problems

Q1. The force acting on a particle of constant mass *m* is given in terms of *t* by $\vec{F} = b(\cos\omega t\,\hat{i} + \sin\omega t\,\hat{j})$. If the particle is initially at rest at the origin, compute its velocity as a function of *t*.

Ans. From Newton's second law, the acceleration of the particle is

$$\frac{d\vec{v}}{dt} = \vec{f}(t) = \frac{\vec{F}}{m} = \frac{b}{m}\cos\omega t\,\hat{i} + \frac{b}{m}\sin\omega t\,\hat{j}$$

We know that $$\frac{d\vec{a}(t)}{dt} = \vec{b}(t) \qquad ...(i)$$

and $$\int\left[p\vec{V}_1(t) + q\vec{V}_2(t)\right]dt = p\int\vec{V}_1(t)dt + q\int\vec{V}_2(t)dt \qquad ...(ii)$$

From (i) and (ii), we get $\vec{v}(t) = \frac{b}{m}\left[\hat{i}\int\cos\omega t\,dt + \hat{j}\int\sin\omega t\,dt\right]$

These are ordinary integrals and can be readily evaluated to give

$$\vec{v}(t) = \frac{b}{m}\left[\hat{i}\frac{\sin\omega t}{\omega} + \hat{j}\left(-\frac{\cos\omega t}{\omega}\right)\right] + \vec{c}_1$$

We now have to determine $\vec{c}_1$.

Since, the particle is at rest initially, we have $\vec{v}(0)=\vec{0}$. So,

$$\vec{0}=\frac{b}{m\omega}\left(-\hat{j}\right)+c_1$$

$$\therefore \quad \vec{c}_1=\frac{b}{m\omega}\hat{j}$$

Hence, $\vec{v}(t)=\dfrac{b}{m\omega}\left[\sin\omega t\,\hat{i}+\left(1-\cos\omega t\right)\hat{j}\right]$

Q2. In free space, a transverse electromagnetic (EM) wave propagating in the x-direction has an electric field $\vec{E}=E_0\cos\frac{2\pi}{\lambda}(ct-x)\hat{j}$ and a magnetic induction field $\vec{B}=B_0\cos\frac{2\pi}{\lambda}(ct-x)\hat{k}$. Here c and λ are respectively the velocity and the wavelength of the EM-wave and $E_0=B_0c$. The energy flowing through a volume V per unit time is given by $U=\frac{V}{2}\left(\vec{E}.\vec{D}+\vec{B}.\vec{H}\right)$, where $\vec{D}=\varepsilon_0\vec{E}$ and $B=\mu_0\vec{H}$. Here ε_0 and μ_0 are the permittivity and the magnetic permeability, respectively of free space and c can be expressed as $c=\frac{1}{\sqrt{\varepsilon_0\mu_0}}$.

Compute the total energy flowing through V during one complete cycle of EM oscillation if its time period is T.

Ans. The energy flow during time dt will be given by U dt. So the total energy will be the definite integral of U from t = 0 to t = T, i.e.

$$U_0=\int_0^T U\,dt=\frac{V}{2}\int_0^T\left(\vec{E}.\vec{D}+\vec{B}.\vec{H}\right)dt=\frac{V}{2}\left(I_E+I_B\right)$$

where $I_E=\int_0^T \vec{E}.\vec{D}\,dt$ and $I_B=\int_0^T \vec{B}.\vec{H}\,dt$.

Both I_E and I_B are integrals of the type I_1. So we shall first evaluate the scalar products.

$$\vec{E}=E_0\cos\frac{2\pi}{\lambda}(ct-x)\hat{j}\quad \vec{D}=\varepsilon_0\vec{E}=\varepsilon_0E_0\cos\frac{2\pi}{\lambda}(ct-x)\hat{j}$$

$$\therefore\ \vec{E}.\vec{D}=\varepsilon_0E_0^2\cos^2\frac{2\pi}{\lambda}(ct-x)$$

Similarly, we can show that $\vec{B}.\vec{H}=\dfrac{B_0^2}{\mu_0}\cos^2\dfrac{2\pi}{\lambda}(ct-x)$

$$\therefore\ U_0 = \frac{V}{2}\left(\varepsilon_0 E_0^2 + \frac{B_0^2}{\mu_0}\right) I$$

where $I = \int_0^T \cos^2 \frac{2\pi}{\lambda}(ct - x)\,dt = \frac{T}{2}\ \therefore\ U_0 = \frac{VT}{4}\left(\varepsilon_0 E_0^2 + \frac{B_0^2}{\mu_0}\right)$

Again $B_0^2 = \frac{E_0^2}{c^2} = \varepsilon_0\mu_0 E_0^2\left(\because\ c = \frac{1}{\sqrt{\varepsilon_0\mu_0}}\right)\ \therefore\ \frac{B_0^2}{\mu_0} = \varepsilon_0 E_0^2.$

Hence, $U_0 = \frac{VT}{2}\varepsilon_0 E_0^2$

Q3. The mass of the bob of the simple pendulum shown in given figure is m. It executes small oscillations (i.e. its angular amplitude does not exceed 4°) in the xy plane. Using the result $\tau = \frac{d\vec{L}}{dt}$, where τ and $\vec{L}$ are respectively the torque and angular momentum of the bob about the origin, show that $\vec{L} = m\sqrt{l^3 g}\ \theta_0 \sin\left(\sqrt{\frac{g}{l}}\,t\right)\hat{k} + \vec{L}_0$, where $\vec{L} = \vec{L}_0$ at $t = 0$. It is given that the time-variation of the angular displacement of the bob can be expressed as $\theta = \theta_0 \cos\frac{2\pi t}{T}$, where $T = 2\pi\sqrt{\frac{l}{g}}$

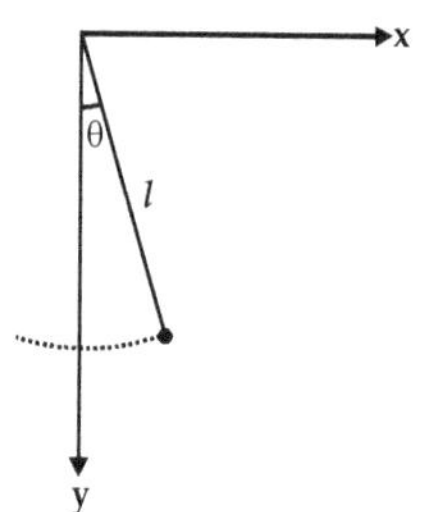

Ans.

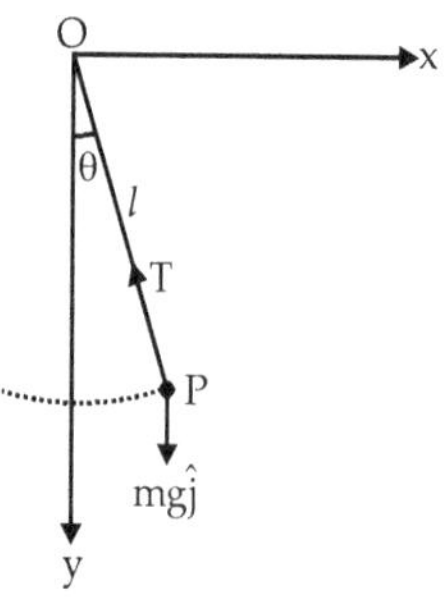

Fig. 4.8

We know that $\tau = \vec{r} \times \vec{F} = \overrightarrow{OP} \times mg\hat{j}$

The component of $\overrightarrow{OP}$ along y-direction is $l\cos\theta$ and that along x-direction is $l\sin\theta$. So, $\overrightarrow{OP} = l\sin\theta\,\hat{i} + l\cos\theta\,\hat{j}$

$$\therefore\ \tau = \left(l\sin\theta\hat{i} + l\cos\theta\hat{j}\right) \times mg\,\hat{j} = mgl\sin\theta\hat{k}\ \ (\because\ \hat{i}\times\hat{j} = \hat{k} \text{ and } \hat{j}\times\hat{j} = 0)$$

If θ is small, $\sin\theta \approx \theta$. Hence, $\tau = mgl\theta\hat{k}$ or $\tau = \frac{d\vec{L}}{dt} = mgl\theta_0 \cos\frac{2\pi}{T}t\hat{k}$

$$\text{Hence, } \vec{L} = \hat{k}(mgl\theta_0)\int \cos\frac{2\pi t}{T}dt = \hat{k}\frac{T}{2\pi}mgl\theta_0 \sin\frac{2\pi t}{T} + \vec{C},$$

where $\vec{C}$ is constant vector of integration.

It is given that $\vec{L} = \vec{L}_0$ at $t = 0$. On applying this condition, we get

$$\vec{L}_0 = \vec{0} + \vec{C}\ \Rightarrow\ \vec{C} = \vec{L}_0$$

Again, as $T = 2\pi\sqrt{\frac{l}{g}}$, we have $\frac{T}{2\pi} = \sqrt{\frac{l}{g}}$

$$\therefore\ \vec{L} = \left[m\sqrt{l^3 g}\ \theta_0 \sin\left(\sqrt{\frac{g}{l}}\,t\right)\right]\hat{k} + \vec{L}_0$$

Q4. The product of inertia of a lamina in the xy-plane about the x and y-axes is given by $I_{xy} = I_{yx} = \iint_R \sigma xy\,dxdy$ where R is the region of space covered by the lamina and σ is the mass per unit area of the lamina. Determine I_{xy} for the rectangle shown in given figure.

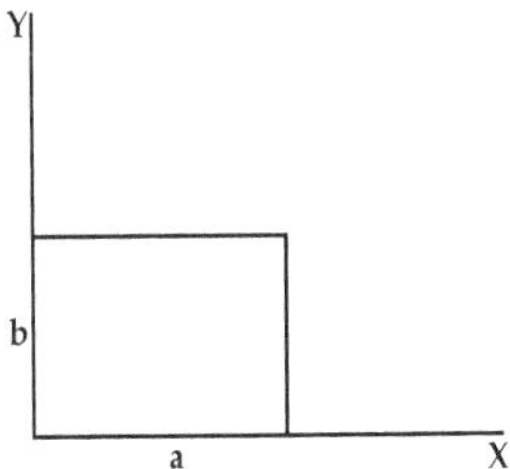

Ans. Here, $I_{xy} = \int_0^a\int_0^b \frac{m}{ab}xy\,dxdy$ where m is the mass of the rectangle.

$$\therefore\ I_{xy} = \frac{m}{ab}\int_0^a\left(\int_0^b xydy\right)dx$$

Now, for evaluating the inner integral, we have to treat x as constant.

$$\therefore\ \int_0^b xydy = \left|\frac{xy^2}{2}\right|_0^b = \frac{xb^2}{2}.$$

Hence, $I_{xy} = \frac{m}{ab}\int_0^a x\frac{b^2}{2}dx = \frac{mb}{2a}\int_0^a x\ dx = \frac{mb}{2a}\left|\frac{x^2}{2}\right|_0^a = \frac{mb}{2a}\frac{a^2}{2} = \frac{mab}{4}$.

Q5. Write down the expression for an element of area of the spherical shell of following figure in spherical polar coordinates and calculate its moment of inertia about any diameter. The mass of the shell is M and its radius R.

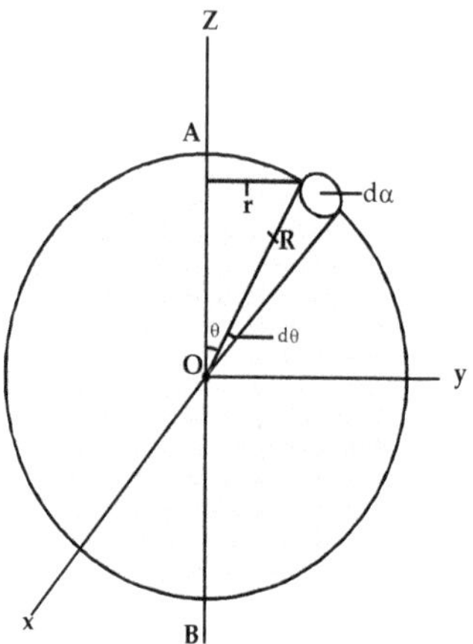

Ans. Let us take the z-axis along the diameter AB about which we intend to calculate I. We take an element of area, $d\alpha$, on the shell included between the polar angles θ and $\theta + d\theta$ and the azimuthal angles ϕ and $\phi + d\phi$. We know that $d\alpha = (Rd\theta)(R\sin\theta\, d\phi)$

Now $dm = \sigma d\alpha$, where σ, the mass per unit area is $\frac{M}{4\pi R^2}$.

Hence, we can write $dm = \frac{M}{4\pi R^2}R^2 \sin\theta d\theta d\phi = \frac{M}{4\pi}\sin\theta d\theta d\phi$

From given figure, it is evident that $r = R\sin\theta$ so that

$$I = \int_{\theta=0}^{\pi}\int_{\phi=0}^{2\pi}(R\sin\theta)^2\frac{M}{4\pi}\sin\theta d\theta d\phi$$

$$\text{Now, } I = \frac{MR^2}{4\pi}\int_0^{2\pi}\left(\int_0^{\pi}\sin^3\theta d\theta\right)d\phi$$

$$\text{Since, } \int_0^{\pi}\sin^3\theta\, d\theta = \frac{4}{3}$$

$$\therefore I = \frac{MR^2}{4\pi}\frac{4}{3}\int_0^{2\pi}d\phi = \frac{MR^2}{3\pi}2\pi = \frac{2}{3}MR^2.$$

Q6. Determine the gravitational potential due to a solid sphere of mass M and radius a at a point (i) outside the sphere and (ii) inside the sphere.

Ans.

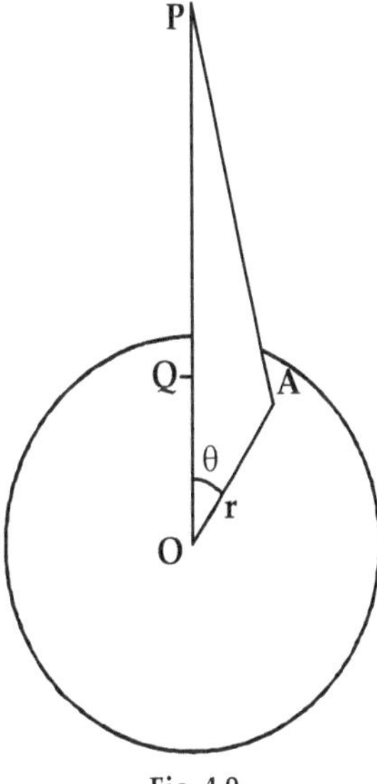

Fig. 4.9

In Fig. 4.91, O is the centre of the sphere. P and Q are, respectively, an external and an internal point. Here O, P and Q are collinear. Since a sphere is symmetrical about its centre, the potential depends only on the distance of the observation point from the centre of the sphere. It is independent of its position. In other words, the potential due to the sphere at all external points which lie on a sphere of radius OP and centre at O will be equal to that at P. Likewise, the potential at all internal points lying on a sphere of radius OQ and centre at O will be equal to that at Q.

Now let us consider an infinitesimal volume element dV of the sphere at A, where OA = r and $\angle AOP = \theta$. Here OP is take to be the polar axis and the volume element dV is included between r and r + dr, θ and θ + dθ, ϕ and $\phi + d\phi$. In other words, $dV = r^2 \sin\theta \, dr \, d\theta \, d\phi$

Now, let r' and R be the distances of the field point from A and O, respectively. Hence, in case (i), $r' = AP$, $R = OP$ and in case (ii), $r' = AQ$, $R = OQ$.

We will note that in case (i) $R > a$ and in case (ii) $R < a$.

The gravitational potential due to the volume element dV at any point at a distance r' from it is given by $d\phi = -\frac{G\rho\, dV}{r'}$

where ρ is the density of the material of the sphere and is given by

$\rho = \frac{M}{\frac{4}{3}\pi a^3} = \frac{3M}{4\pi a^3}$ Since $r' = \sqrt{r^2 + R^2 - 2rR\cos\theta}$, we can write

$$d\phi = -\frac{G\rho\, r^2 \sin\theta\, dr\, d\theta\, d\phi}{\sqrt{r^2 + R^2 - 2rR\cos\theta}} \text{ so that } \phi = \int_{r=0}^{a}\int_{\theta=0}^{\pi}\int_{\phi=0}^{2\pi} -\frac{G\rho\, r^2 \sin\theta\, dr\, d\theta\, d\phi}{\sqrt{r^2 + R^2 - 2rR\cos\theta}}$$

We now separate out the triple integral into three integrals with respect to ϕ, θ and r, i.e. $\phi = -G\rho \int_{r=0}^{a} r^2 dr \int_{\theta=0}^{\pi} \frac{\sin\theta\, d\theta}{\sqrt{r^2 + R^2 - 2rR\cos\theta}} \int_{\phi=0}^{2\pi} d\phi$

The ϕ-integral is quite simple and its value is 2π. The result of the θ-integral is a function of r, say $f(r)$. Then, we have $\phi = -2\pi G\rho \int_0^a r^2 f(r)\, dr$,

where $f(r) = \int_{\theta=0}^{\pi} \frac{\sin\theta\, d\theta}{\sqrt{r^2 + R^2 - 2rR\cos\theta}}$

So far as the evaluation of f(r) is concerned, we have to remember that θ is the only variable quantity. Anything other than θ should be considered as constant. We now introduce a change of variable by writing

$$\sqrt{r^2 + R^2 - 2rR\cos\theta} = u \text{ or } r^2 + R^2 - 2rR\cos\theta = u^2$$

Taking differentials on both sides, we get

$$2Rr\sin\theta d\theta = 2u du \text{ or } \frac{\sin\theta\, d\theta}{u} = \frac{du}{Rr}$$

when $\theta = \pi$, $\cos\theta = -1$, and $u^2 = (r + R)^2$, i.e. $u = R + r$

when $\theta = 0$, $\cos\theta = 1$ and $u^2 = (r - R)^2$

Thus $\theta = 0$ will correspond to u = R – r for R > r and r – R for R < r. Now, as r ranges from 0 to a for case (i), R > r always, so that u = R - r for $\theta = 0$. But case (ii) is a little tricky.

$$\left.\begin{array}{l} \text{For } 0 < r < R, \quad R > r \quad \text{and} \quad u = R - r \\ \text{and for } R < r < a, \quad R < r \text{ and } u = r - R \quad \text{for } \theta = 0. \end{array}\right\}$$

Now let us take up calculation of ϕ for case (i)

$$f(r) = \int_{R-r}^{R+r} \frac{du}{Rr} = \frac{1}{Rr}\left[(R+r)-(R-r)\right] = \frac{2}{R}$$

$$\therefore\ \phi = -2\pi\, G\rho \int_0^a \frac{2r^2}{R} dr = -\frac{4\pi G\rho}{R}\int_0^a r^2 dr = -\frac{4\pi G\rho}{R}\frac{a^3}{3}$$

$$\therefore\ \phi = -\frac{GM}{R}\left(\because M = \frac{4\pi a^3}{3}\rho\right)$$

Now, $f(r) = \frac{2}{R}$ for $R > r$ and $f(r) = \int_{r-R}^{r+R} \frac{du}{Rr}$ for $R < r$

i.e. $f(r) = \frac{1}{Rr}[(r+R)-(r-R)] = \frac{2}{r}$ for $R < r$

Now, $\phi = -2\pi\, G\rho \int_0^a r^2 f(r)\, dr$

$$= -4\pi\, G\rho\left[\frac{1}{R}\frac{R^3}{3} + \left(\frac{a^2}{2} - \frac{R^2}{2}\right)\right] = -2\pi\, G\rho\left(a^2 - \frac{R^2}{3}\right)$$

On putting $\rho = \frac{3M}{4\pi a^3}$, we get

$\phi = -\frac{GM}{2a^3}(3a^2 - R^2)$ when the field point is inside the sphere.

Q7. A two-dimensional force field is defined as $\vec{F} = \frac{k\left(x\hat{j} - y\hat{i}\right)}{x^2 + y^2}$ where k is a constant. Compute the work done by this force in taking a particle from point P(1,0) to Q(0,1) shown in following figure along the straight line PQ.

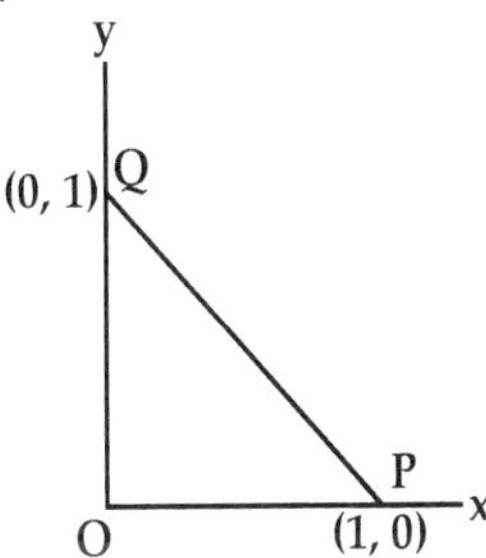

Ans. In order to evaluate the integral, we have to express $\vec{F}$ and $d\vec{r}$ as a function of the same parameter, say t. The equation of PQ is $x + y = 1$.

In going from P to Q, x changes from 1 to 0 and y changes from 0 to 1. This can be expressed in the parametric form as x = t, y=1 – t, where t goes from 1 to 0.

$$\text{Now, } \vec{r} = x\hat{i} + y\hat{j} = t\hat{i} + (1-t)\hat{j}$$

$$\therefore\ d\vec{r} = dt\,\hat{i} - dt\,\hat{j} = (\hat{i} - \hat{j})dt \text{ and } \vec{F} = k\frac{t\hat{j} + (t-1)\hat{i}}{t^2 + (1-t)^2}$$

$$\therefore\ \vec{F}.d\vec{r} = \frac{k\left[(t-1)\hat{i} + t\hat{j}\right].(dt\,\hat{i} - dt\,\hat{j})}{t^2 + (1-t)^2} = k\frac{(t-1)dt - t\,dt}{2t^2 - 2t + 1} = -\frac{k\,dt}{2t^2 - 2t + 1}$$

Hence, the work done is given by

$$W = \int_1^0 -\frac{kdt}{2t^2 - 2t + 1} = k\int_0^1 \frac{dt}{2t^2 - 2t + 1} = \frac{k\pi}{2}$$

Q8. Prove that $\int_A^B \vec{F}.d\vec{r} = T_B - T_{A,}$ where T_A and T_B are the K.Es of the particle at A and B, respectively.

Ans. We know that $\vec{F} = m\frac{d\vec{v}}{dt}, d\vec{r} = \frac{d\vec{r}}{dt}dt = \vec{v}\,dt$

$$\therefore\ \vec{F}.d\vec{r} = m\frac{d\vec{v}}{dt}.\vec{v}\,dt$$

$$\text{Now, we know that } \frac{d\vec{v}}{dt}.\vec{v} = \frac{d}{dt}\left(\frac{v^2}{2}\right)$$

$$\therefore\ \vec{F}\,.\,d\vec{r} = m\frac{d}{dt}\left(\frac{v^2}{2}\right)dt = d\left(\frac{mv^2}{2}\right)$$

$$\therefore\ \int_A^B \vec{F}.d\vec{r} = \int_A^B d\left(\frac{1}{2}mv^2\right) = \frac{1}{2}mv_B^2 - \frac{1}{2}mv_A^2.$$

where v_A and v_B are the magnitudes of the velocity of the particle at A and B, respectively.

Now, as K.E. $= \frac{1}{2}mv^2$, we get $\int_A^B \vec{F}\,.\,d\vec{r} = T_B - T_A$.

Q9. Evaluate $\oiint_S \hat{r}.d\vec{S}$ where S is the surface of a sphere of radius R.

Ans.

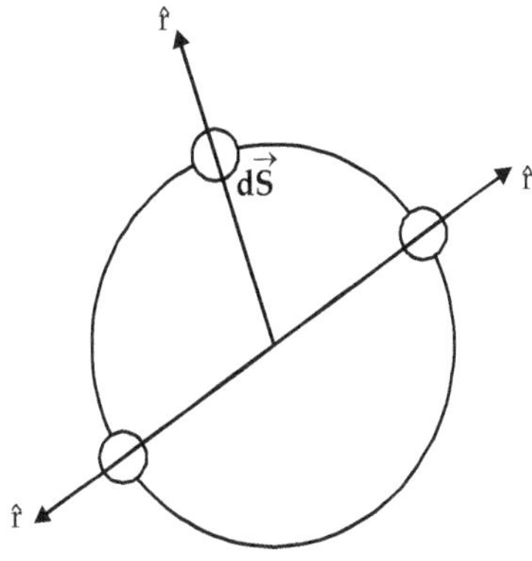

Fig. 4.10

In fig. 4.10, since $d\vec{S}$ points along the outward drawn normal, it points along $\hat{r}$ at every point on the sphere so that $dS = \hat{r}\, dS$

$$\therefore \hat{r}.d\vec{S} = \hat{r}.dS\hat{r} = dS(\hat{r}.\hat{r}) = dS \quad (\because \hat{r}.\hat{r} = 1)$$

Hence, $\oiint_S \hat{r}.d\vec{S} = \oiint_S dS = S$, which is the surface area of the sphere.

Thus, $\oiint_S \hat{r} . d\vec{S} = 4\pi R^2$

Q10. Evaluate $\iiint_V \nabla . \hat{r}\, dV$, what is the volume of a sphere of radius R.

Ans. For evaluating $\nabla . \hat{r}$, we shall use the expression of $\nabla . A$ in spherical polar coordinates.

As $A_\theta = A_\phi = 0$, the calculation will be simplified considerably. We have $A_r = 1$

$$\therefore \nabla . \hat{r} = \frac{1}{r^2}\frac{d}{dr}(r^2) = \frac{1}{r^2}2r = \frac{2}{r}$$

Now, an element of the volume of the sphere included between r, r + dr, θ, θ + dθ and φ, φ + dφ is given by $dV = r^2 \sin\theta\, d\theta\, d\phi\, dr$, where $0 \le r \le R,\ 0 \le \theta \le \pi$ and $0 \le \phi \le 2\pi$.

$$\therefore \iiint_V \nabla . \hat{r}\, dV = \int_{r=0}^{R} dr \int_{\theta=0}^{\pi} d\theta \int_{\phi=0}^{2\pi} d\phi \left(\frac{2}{r} r^2 \sin\theta\right)$$

$$= \left(\int_0^R 2r dr\right)\left(\int_0^\pi \sin\theta\, d\theta\right)\left(\int_0^{2\pi} d\phi\right) = R^2 \times 2 \times 2\pi = 4\pi R^2$$

Q11. Evaluate $\int_C \vec{F}\cdot d\vec{r}$, where $\vec{F} = x^2y^2\hat{i} + y\hat{j}$ and the curve C is $y^2 = 4x$ in the xy-plane from (0,0) to (4,4).

Ans. For the curve $C \equiv y^2 - 4x = 0$, x and y both vary from 0 to 4.

$$\int_C \vec{F}\cdot d\vec{r} = \int_C \left(x^2y^2\hat{i} + y\hat{j}\right)\cdot\left(\hat{i}dx + \hat{j}dy\right) = \int_C x^2y^2dx + \int_C y\,dy$$

Now C is $y^2 = 4x$, therefore

$$\int_C x^2y^2dx = \int_0^4 4x^3dx = \left[x^4\right]_0^4 = 256,$$

and $\int_C y\,dy = \int_0^4 y\,dy = \left[\frac{1}{2}y^2\right]_0^4 = 8.$

Therefore, $\int_C \vec{F}\cdot d\vec{r} = 256 + 8 = 264.$

Q12. Evaluate $\int_C \vec{F}\cdot d\vec{r}$, where $\vec{F} = xy\hat{i} + yz\hat{j} + zx\hat{k}$ and curve C is $\vec{r} = \hat{i}t + \hat{j}t^2 + \hat{k}t^3$, t varying from -1 to + 1.

Ans. We have $\frac{d\vec{r}}{dt} = \hat{i} + 2t\hat{j} + 3t^2\hat{k}$

$$\therefore \int_C \vec{F}\cdot d\vec{r} = \int_{-1}^{+1} \vec{F}\cdot\frac{d\vec{r}}{dt}dt = \int_{-1}^{+1}\left(xy\hat{i} + yz\hat{j} + zx\hat{k}\right)\cdot\left(\hat{i} + 2t\hat{j} + 3t^2\hat{k}\right)dt$$

$$= \int_{-1}^{+1}\left(xy + 2yzt + 3zxt^2\right)dt.$$

But from $\vec{r} = \hat{i}t + \hat{j}t^2 + \hat{k}t^3$ we have $x = t, y = t^2, z = t^3$.

Substituting these values of x, y, z in the line integral, we get

$$\int_C \vec{F}\cdot d\vec{r} = \int_{-1}^{+1}\left(t^3 + 2t^6 + 3t^6\right)dt = \left[\frac{t^4}{4} + \frac{5t^7}{7}\right]_{-1}^{1} = \frac{10}{7}.$$

Q13. Evaluate $\int_C \vec{F}\cdot d\vec{r}$, where $\vec{F} = \left(x^2 + y^2\right)\hat{i} - 2xy\hat{j}$, curve C is the rectangle in the x-plane bounded by y = 0, x = a, y = b, x = 0.

Ans. We have $\int_C \vec{F}\cdot d\vec{r} = \int_C \left\{\left(x^2 + y^2\right)\hat{i} - 2xy\hat{j}\right\}\cdot\left\{\hat{i}\,dx + \hat{j}\,dy\right\}$

$$= \int_C\left[\left\{x^2 + y^2\right\}dx - \left\{2xy\,dy\right\}\right]$$

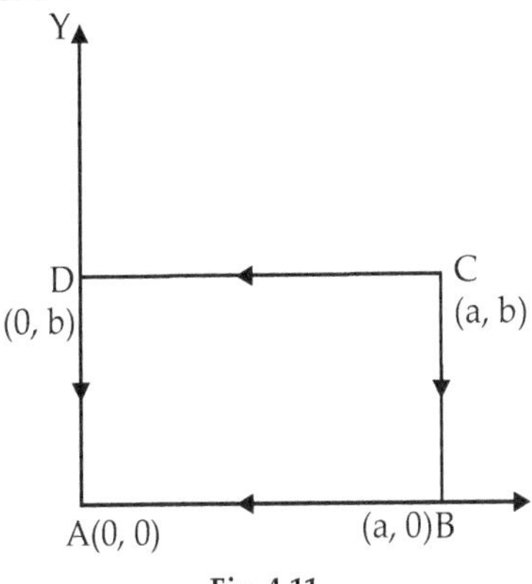

Fig. 4.11

On the part AB of the curve, $y = 0, \therefore dy = 0$.

On BC, $x = a, \therefore dx = 0$

on CD, $y = b, \therefore dy = 0$

on DA, $x = 0, \therefore dx = 0$.

$$\therefore \int \vec{F}\cdot d\vec{r} = \int_0^a x^2\,dx - 2a\int_0^b y\,dy + \int_a^0 (x^2+b^2)dx + \int_b^0 0\,dy$$

$$= \left[\frac{x^3}{3}\right]_0^a - 2a\left[\frac{y^2}{2}\right]_0^b + \left[\frac{x^3}{3}+b^2x\right]_a^0 = \frac{1}{3}a^3 - ab^2 - \left(\frac{1}{3}a^3 + b^2a\right) = -2ab^2.$$

Q14. Evaluate $\int_C \vec{F}\cdot d\vec{r}$, where $\vec{F} = xy\,\hat{i} + (x^2+y^2)\hat{j}$, curve C is the arc of $y = x^2 - 4$ from (2, 0) to (4, 12) in the xy-plane.

Ans. For the given curve C, x varies from 2 to 4 and y varies from 0 to 12.

$$\therefore \int_C \vec{F}\cdot d\vec{r} = \int_C \left\{xy\,\hat{i} + (x^2+y^2)\hat{j}\right\}\cdot\left\{\hat{i}\,dx + \hat{j}\,dy\right\} = \int_C \left\{xy\,dx + (x^2+y^2)\,dy\right\}$$

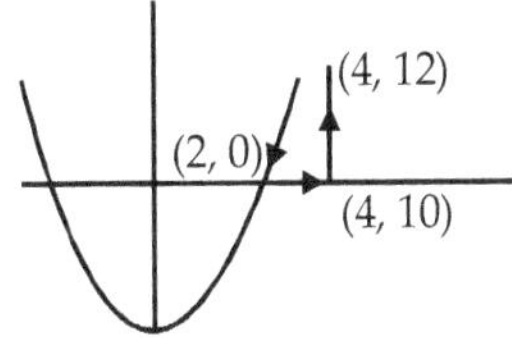

Fig. 4.12

Along the curve $y = x^2 - 4$ or $x^2 = y + 4$, above result

$$= \int_2^4 x(x^2-4)dx + \int_0^{12}(y+4+y^2)dy = \left[\frac{1}{4}x^4 - 2x^2\right]_2^4 + \left[\frac{1}{2}y^2 + 4y + \frac{1}{3}y^3\right]_0^{12}$$

$$= (64 - 32 - 4 + 8) + (72 + 48 + 576) = 732$$

Q15. Evaluate $\int_S \left(yz\hat{i} + zx\hat{j} + xy\hat{k}\right) dS$, where S is the surface of the sphere $x^2 + y^2 + z^2 = 1$ in the first octant.

Ans. Let $f = x^2 + y^2 + z^2 - 1$, so that $\frac{\partial f}{\partial x} = 2x, \frac{\partial f}{\partial y} = 2y, \frac{\partial f}{\partial z} = 2z$

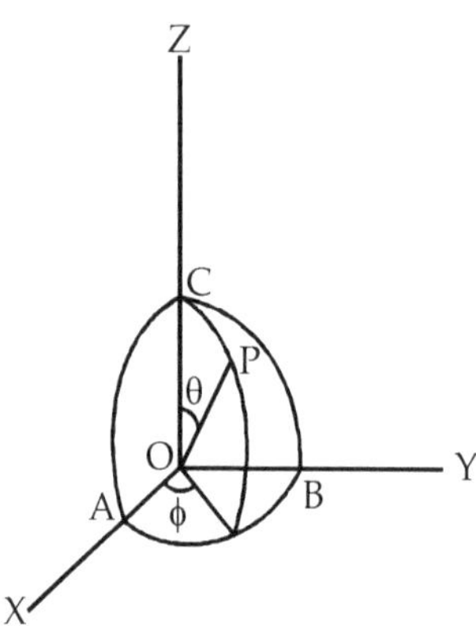

Fig. 4.13

Therefore, $\hat{n} = \frac{\text{grad} f}{|\text{grad} f|} \frac{\nabla f}{|\nabla f|} = \frac{\hat{i}\frac{\partial f}{\partial x} + \hat{j}\frac{\partial f}{\partial y} + \hat{k}\frac{\partial f}{\partial z}}{\sqrt{\left[\left(\frac{\partial f}{\partial x}\right)^2 + \left(\frac{\partial f}{\partial y}\right)^2 + \left(\frac{\partial f}{\partial z}\right)^2\right]}}$

$$= \frac{2\left(x\hat{i} + y\hat{j} + z\hat{k}\right)}{\sqrt{4\left(x^2 + y^2 + z^2\right)}} = x\hat{i} + y\hat{j} + z\hat{k}, \text{ as } x^2 + y^2 + z^2 = 1.$$

Q16. If S is any closed surface enclosing a volume V and $\vec{F} = x\hat{i} + 2y\hat{j} + 3z\hat{k}$, prove that $\iint_S \vec{F} \cdot \hat{n}\, dS = 6V$.

Ans. Here $\vec{F} = x\hat{i} + 2y\hat{j} + 3z\hat{k}$.

$$\therefore \text{div } \vec{F} = \nabla \cdot \vec{F} = \left(\hat{i}\frac{\partial}{\partial x} + \hat{j}\frac{\partial}{\partial y} + \hat{k}\frac{\partial}{\partial z}\right) \cdot \left(x\hat{i} + 2y\hat{j} + 3z\hat{k}\right)$$

$$= \frac{\partial x}{\partial x} + \frac{\partial(2y)}{\partial y} + \frac{\partial(3z)}{\partial z} = 1 + 2 + 3 = 6$$

$\therefore$ By Gauss's Divergence Theorem, we have

$$\iint_S \vec{F} \cdot \hat{n}\, dS = \iiint_V \text{div}\,\vec{F}\, dv = \iiint_V 6\, dv = 6V.$$

Q17. Show that $\int_S \left(ax\hat{i}+by\hat{j}+cz\hat{k}\right)\cdot\hat{n}\,dS=\frac{4}{3}\pi(a+b+c)$, where S is the surface of the sphere $x^2+y^2+z^2=1$.

Ans. Here $\vec{F}=ax\hat{i}+by\hat{j}+cz\hat{k}$, so that

$$\text{div}\,\vec{F}=\nabla\cdot\vec{F}=\left(\hat{i}\frac{\partial}{\partial x}+\hat{j}\frac{\partial}{\partial y}+\hat{k}\frac{\partial}{\partial z}\right)\cdot\left(ax\hat{i}+by\hat{j}+cz\hat{k}\right)$$

$$=\frac{\partial}{\partial x}(ax)+\frac{\partial}{\partial y}(by)+\frac{\partial}{\partial z}(cz)=a+b+c.$$

Hence, by the Gauss's Divergence Theorem, the given integral is

$$=\int_V \text{div}\left(ax\hat{i}+by\hat{j}+cz\hat{k}\right)dv=\int_V(a+b+c)dv=(a+b+c.)\int_V dv$$

$=(a+b+c)V$, where $V=\frac{4}{3}\pi=$ volume of the sphere of unit radius.

$$=\frac{4}{3}(a+b+c)\pi.$$

Q18. Evaluate $\int\left(\hat{i}x+\hat{j}y+\hat{k}z\right)\cdot\hat{n}\,dS$, where S denotes the surface of the cube bounded by the planes x = 0, x = a, y = 0, y = a, z = 0, z = a by the application of Gauss's theorem.

Ans. Here $\vec{F}=\hat{i}x+\hat{j}y+\hat{k}z$.

Now, $\text{div}\,\vec{F}=\frac{\partial}{\partial x}(x)+\frac{\partial}{\partial y}(y)+\frac{\partial}{\partial z}(z)=3$, volume of the cube $=a^3$

Therefore, by Gauss's Theorem

$$\int\vec{F}\cdot\hat{n}\,dS=\int_S\left(\hat{i}x+\hat{j}y+\hat{k}z\right)\cdot\hat{n}\,dS=\int_V \text{div}\,\vec{F}\,dv=3\int_V dv=3V=3a^3.$$

Q19. Find $\int_S \hat{n}\cdot\vec{F}\,dS$, where $\vec{F}=x\hat{i}-y\hat{j}+\left(z^2-1\right)\hat{k}$ and S is the cylinder formed by the surface $z=0, z=1, x^2+y^2=4$.

Ans. Here $\vec{F}=x\hat{i}-y\hat{j}+\left(z^2-1\right)\hat{k}$

$$\therefore \text{div}\,\vec{F}=\frac{\partial}{\partial x}(x)+\frac{\partial}{\partial y}(-y)+\frac{\partial}{\partial z}\left(z^2-1\right)=1-1+2z=2z.$$

Here x lies between -2 and 2, y lies between $-\sqrt{4-x^2}$ to $\sqrt{4-x^2}$ and z lies between 0 to 1.

$$\therefore \int_S \hat{n}.\vec{F}\, dS = \int_V \text{div}\,\vec{F}\, dS$$

$$= \int_{x=-2}^{2}\int_{y=-\sqrt{4-x^2}}^{\sqrt{4-x^2}}\int_{z=0}^{1} 2z\,dx\,dy\,dz = \int_{x=-2}^{2}\int_{y=-\sqrt{4-x^2}}^{\sqrt{4-x^2}}\left[z^2\right]_0^1 dx\,dy$$

$$= \int_{-2}^{2}\int_{-\sqrt{4-x^2}}^{\sqrt{4-x^2}} dx\,dy = 2\int_{-2}^{2}\sqrt{4-x^2}\,dx = 2\left[\frac{1}{2}x\sqrt{4-x^2} + \frac{1}{2}(4)\sin^{-1}\frac{x}{2}\right]_{-2}^{2}$$

$$= 4\left[\sin^{-1}1 + \sin^{-1}1\right] = 4\left[\frac{1}{2}\pi + \frac{1}{2}\pi\right] = 4\pi.$$

Q20. Show that $\int_s \hat{n}.dS = 0$ over a closed surface.

Ans. Let $\vec{a}$ be any arbitrary constant vector. Then

$$\vec{a}.\int_S \hat{n}\, dS = \int_S \vec{a}.\hat{n}\, dS = \int_V \text{div}\,\vec{a}\, dv \qquad ..(i)$$

by the divergence theorem. But

$\text{div}\vec{a} = \nabla.\vec{a} = 0$, as $\vec{a}$ is a constant vector.

Therefore $\vec{a}.\int_S \hat{n}.dS = 0$ from (1),

Since $\vec{a}$ is arbitrary, $\int_S \hat{n}\, dS = 0$.

Q21. Prove that $\oint_C \phi\nabla\psi\bullet d\vec{r} = -\oint_C \psi\nabla\phi\bullet d\vec{r}$.

Ans. By Stoke's theorem, we have

$\oint_C \nabla(\phi\psi)\bullet d\vec{r} = \iint_S\left[\text{curl grad}(\phi\psi)\right]\bullet\hat{n}\, dS = 0$, since curl grad $(\phi\psi) = \vec{0}$.

But $\nabla(\phi\psi) = \phi\nabla\psi + \psi\nabla\phi$.

$\therefore \oint_C (\phi\nabla\psi + \psi\nabla\phi)\bullet d\vec{r} = 0$ or $\oint_C \phi\nabla\psi\bullet d\vec{r} = -\oint_C \psi\nabla\phi\bullet d\vec{r}$.

Q22. Prove that $\oint_C \phi\nabla\psi\bullet d\vec{r} = \iint_S[\nabla\phi\times\nabla\psi]\bullet\hat{n}\, dS$.

Ans. By Stoke's theorem, we have

$$\oint_C \phi\nabla\psi\bullet d\vec{r} = \iint_S[\nabla\times(\phi\nabla\psi)]\bullet\hat{n}\, dS = \iint_S\left[\nabla\phi\times\nabla\psi + \phi\,\text{curl grad}\,\psi\right]\bullet\hat{n}\, dS$$

$= \iint_S[\nabla\phi\times\nabla\psi]\bullet\hat{n}\, dS$, since curl grad $\psi = \vec{0}$.

Q23. Show that $\oint_C \phi\nabla\phi\bullet d\vec{r} = 0$, C being a closed curve.

Ans. Applying Stoke's theorem to the vector function $\phi\nabla\phi$, we have

$$\oint_C (\phi\nabla\phi)\bullet d\vec{r} = \iint_S[\text{curl}(\phi\nabla\phi)]\bullet\hat{n}\, dS = \iint_S\left[\phi\,\text{curl}\nabla\phi + \nabla\phi\times\nabla\phi\right]\bullet\hat{n}\, dS$$

$= \iint_S \vec{0} \cdot \hat{n}\, dS$ [$\because$ $\text{curl}\, \nabla\phi = \vec{0}$ and $\nabla\phi \times \nabla\phi = \vec{0}$] $= 0.$

Q24. Prove that $\oint_C \phi\, d\vec{r} = \iint_S d\vec{S} \times \nabla\phi$.

Ans. Let $\vec{A}$ be any arbitrary constant vector. Let $\vec{F} = \phi\vec{A}$.

Applying Stoke's theorem for $\vec{F}$, we get $\oint_C \vec{F} \cdot d\vec{r} = \iint_S \left[\nabla \times (\phi\vec{A})\right] \cdot \hat{n}\, dS$

$= \iint_S \left[\nabla\phi \times \vec{A} + \phi\, \text{curl}\, \vec{A}\right] \cdot d\vec{S} = \iint_S (\nabla\phi \times \vec{A}) \cdot d\vec{S}$, since curl $\vec{A} = 0$.

$\therefore \oint_C (\phi\vec{A}) \cdot d\vec{r} = \iint_S \vec{A} \cdot (d\vec{S} \times \nabla\phi)$

or $\vec{A} \cdot \oint_C \phi\, d\vec{r} = \vec{A} \cdot \iint_S d\vec{S} \times \nabla\phi$ or $\vec{A} \cdot \left[\oint_C \phi\, d\vec{r} - \iint_S d\vec{S} \times \nabla\phi\right] = 0.$

Since $\vec{A}$ is an arbitrary vector, therefore we must have

$\oint_C \phi\, d\vec{r} = \iint_S d\vec{S} \times \nabla\phi.$

Q25. By Stoke's theorem prove that div curl $\vec{F} = 0$.

Ans. Let V be any volume enclosed by a closed surface.

Then by divergence theorem $\iiint_V \nabla \cdot (\text{curl}\, \vec{F})\, dV = \iint_S (\text{curl}\, \vec{F}) \cdot \hat{n}\, dS.$

Divide the surface S into two portions S_1 and S_2 by a closed curve C. Then

$$\iint_S (\text{curl}\, \vec{F}) \cdot \hat{n}\, dS = \iint_{S_1} (\text{curl}\, \vec{F}) \cdot \hat{n}\, dS_1 + \iint_{S_2} (\text{curl}\, \vec{F}) \cdot \hat{n}\, dS_2. \quad \text{...(i)}$$

By Stoke's theorem, right hand side of (i) is $= \oint_C \vec{F} \cdot d\vec{r} - \oint_C \vec{F} \cdot d\vec{r} = 0.$

Negative sign has been taken in the second integral because the positive directions about the boundaries of the two surfaces are opposite.

$\therefore \iiint_V \nabla \cdot (\text{curl}\, \vec{F})\, dV = 0.$

Now this equation is true for all volume elements V.

Therefore we have $\nabla \cdot (\text{curl}\, \vec{F}) = 0$ or div curl $\vec{F} = 0$.

Q26. By Stoke's theorem prove that curl grad $\phi = \vec{0}$.

Ans. Let S be any surface enclosed by a simple closed curve C. Then by Stoke's theorem, we have $\iint_S (\text{curl grad}\, \phi) \cdot \hat{n}\, dS = \oint_C \text{grad}\, \phi \cdot d\vec{r}.$

Now

$$\text{grad } \phi \cdot d\vec{r} = \left(\frac{\partial\phi}{\partial x}\hat{i} + \frac{\partial\phi}{\partial y}\hat{j} + \frac{\partial\phi}{\partial z}\hat{k}\right) \cdot \left(dx\,\hat{i} + dy\,\hat{j} + dz\,\hat{k}\right) = \frac{\partial\phi}{\partial x}dx + \frac{\partial\phi}{\partial y}dy + \frac{\partial\phi}{\partial z}dz = d\phi.$$

$$\therefore \oint_C \text{grad}\phi \cdot d\vec{r} = \oint_C d\phi = [\phi]_A^A, \text{ where A is any point on } C = 0.$$

Therefore, we have $\iint_S (\text{curl grad}\,\phi) \cdot \hat{n}\, dS = 0.$

Now this equation is true for all surface elements S.

Therefore, we have curl grad $\phi = \vec{0}$.

Q27. Verify Stoke's theorem for $\vec{F} = y\,\hat{i} + z\,\hat{j} + x\,\hat{k}$ where S is the upper half surface of the sphere $x^2 + y^2 + z^2 = 1$ and C is its boundary.

Ans. The boundary C of S is a circle in the xy-plane of radius unity and centre origin. The equations of the curve C are $x^2 + y^2 = 1$, $z = 0$. Suppose $x = \cos t, y = \sin t, z = 0, 0 \le t < 2\pi$ are parametric equation of C. Then

$$\oint_C \vec{F} \cdot d\vec{r} = \oint_C \left(y\,\hat{i} + z\,\hat{j} + x\,\hat{k}\right) \cdot \left(dx\,\hat{i} + dy\,\hat{j} + dz\,\hat{k}\right)$$

$$= \oint_C (y\,dx + z\,dy + x\,dz) = \oint_C y\,dx, \text{ since on C, } z = 0 \text{ and } dz = 0$$

$$= \int_0^{2\pi} \sin t \frac{dx}{dt} dt = \int_0^{2\pi} -\sin^2 t\, dt$$

$$= -\frac{1}{2}\int_0^{2\pi} (1 - \cos 2t) dt = -\frac{1}{2}\left[t - \frac{\sin 2t}{2}\right]_0^{2\pi} = -\pi. \qquad \text{...(i)}$$

Now, let us evaluate $\iint_S \text{curl}\,\vec{F} \cdot \hat{n}\, dS$.

$$\text{We have, curl } \vec{F} = \nabla \times \vec{F} = \begin{vmatrix} \hat{i} & \hat{j} & \hat{k} \\ \frac{\partial}{\partial x} & \frac{\partial}{\partial y} & \frac{\partial}{\partial z} \\ y & z & x \end{vmatrix} = -\hat{i} - \hat{j} - \hat{k}.$$

If S_1 is the plane region bounded by the circle C, then by an application of divergence theorem, we have $\iint_S \text{curl}\,\vec{F} \cdot \hat{n}\, dS = \iint_{S_1} \text{curl}\,\vec{F} \cdot \hat{k}\, dS$

$$= \iint_{S_1} \left(-\hat{i} - \hat{j} - \hat{k}\right) \cdot \hat{k}\, dS = \iint_{S_1} (-1)\, dS = -\iint_{S_1} dS = -S_1.$$

But S_1 = area of a circle of radius $1 = \pi(1)^2 = \pi$.

$$\therefore \iint_S \text{curl}\,\vec{F} \cdot \hat{n}\, dS = -\pi. \qquad \text{...(ii)}$$

Hence, from (i) and (ii), the theorem is verified.

Q28. Verify Stoke's theorem for $\vec{F} = (2x - y)\hat{i} - yz^2\,\hat{j} - y^2 z\,\hat{k}$, where S is the upper half surface of the sphere $x^2 + y^2 + z^2 = 1$ and C is its boundary.

Ans. The boundary C of S is a circle in the xy-plane of radius unity and centre origin. Suppose $x = \cos t, y = \sin t, z = 0, 0 \le t < 2\pi$ are parametric equations of C. Then

$$\oint_C \vec{F}\cdot d\vec{r} = \oint_C \left[(2x-y)\hat{i} - yz^2\hat{j} - y^2 z\,\hat{k}\right]\cdot\left(dx\,\hat{i} + dy\,\hat{j} + dz\,\hat{k}\right)$$

$= \oint_C \left[(2x-y)dx - yz^2 dy - y^2 z\,dz\right] = \oint_C (2x-y)dx$, since $z = 0$ and $dz = 0$

$$= \int_0^{2\pi} (2\cos t - \sin t)\frac{dx}{dt}dt = -\int_0^{2\pi} (2\cos t - \sin t)\sin t\,dt$$

$$= -\int_0^{2\pi}\left[\sin 2t - \frac{1}{2}(1 - \cos 2t)\right]dt = -\left[-\frac{\cos 2t}{2} - \frac{1}{2}t + \frac{1}{2}\frac{\sin 2t}{2}\right]_0^{2\pi}$$

$$-\left[\left(-\frac{1}{2} + \frac{1}{2}\right) - \frac{1}{2}(2\pi - 0) + \frac{1}{4}(0-0)\right] = \pi \qquad \text{...(i)}$$

and $(\nabla \times \vec{F}) = \begin{vmatrix} \hat{i} & \hat{j} & \hat{k} \\ \dfrac{\partial}{\partial x} & \dfrac{\partial}{\partial y} & \dfrac{\partial}{\partial z} \\ 2x - y & -yz^2 & -y^2 z \end{vmatrix}$

$$= (-2yz + 2yz)\hat{i} - (0-0)\hat{j} + (0+1)\hat{k} = \hat{k}.$$

Let S_1 be the plane region bounded by the circle C. If S' is the surface consisting of the surfaces S and S_1, then S' is a closed surface.

∴ By an application of Gauss divergence theorem, we have

$$\iint_{S'} \text{curl } \vec{F}\cdot\hat{n}\,dS = 0$$

or $\iint_S \text{curl } \vec{F}\cdot\hat{n}\,dS + \iint_{S_1} \text{curl } \vec{F}\cdot\hat{n}\,dS = 0$ [∵ S' consists of S and S_1]

or $\iint_S \text{curl } \vec{F}\cdot\hat{n}\,dS - \iint_{S_1} \text{curl } \vec{F}\cdot\hat{k}\,dS = 0$ [∵ on S_1, $\hat{n} = -\hat{k}$]

or $\iint_S \text{curl } \vec{F}\cdot\hat{n}\,dS = \iint_{S_1} \text{curl } \vec{F}\cdot\hat{k}\,dS.$

$$= \iint_{S_1} \hat{k}\cdot\hat{k}\,dS = \iint_{S_1} dS = S_1 = \pi. \qquad \text{...(ii)}$$

Note that S_1 = area of a circle of radius $1 = \pi(1)^2 = \pi$.

Hence, from (i) and (ii), Stoke's theorem is verified.

Q29. Verify Stoke's theorem for the vector $\vec{F} = z\hat{i} + x\hat{j} + y\hat{k}$ taken over the half of the sphere $x^2 + y^2 + z^2 = a^2$ lying above the xy-plane.

Ans. Here S be the surface of the sphere $x^2 + y^2 + z^2 = a^2$ lying above the xy-plane and let the curve C be the boundary of this surface. Obviously, the curve C is a circle in the xy-plane of radius a and centre origin and its equations are $x^2 + y^2 = a^2, z = 0$. Suppose $x = a\cos t, y = a\sin t, z = 0, 0 \le t < 2\pi$ are parametric equations of C.

By Stoke's theorem, we have $\oint_C \vec{F} \cdot d\vec{r} = \iint_S (\text{curl}\,\vec{F}) \cdot \hat{n}\, dS$. ...(i)

Let us verify (i).

We have $\oint_C \vec{F} \cdot d\vec{r} = \oint_C (z\hat{i} + x\hat{j} + y\hat{k}) \cdot (dx\,\hat{i} + dy\,\hat{j} + dz\,\hat{k})$

$= \oint_C (z\,dx + x\,dy + y\,dz) = \oint_C x\,dy$, since on C, $z = 0$ and $dz = 0$

$$= \int_0^{2\pi} a\cos t \cdot \frac{dy}{dt} dt = \int_0^{2\pi} a\cos t . a\cos t\, dt = a^2 \int_0^{2\pi} \cos^2 t\, dt$$

$$= \frac{a^2}{2} \int_0^{2\pi} (1 + \cos 2t) dt = \frac{a^2}{2} \left[t + \frac{\sin 2t}{2} \right]_0^{2\pi} = \frac{a^2}{2} \cdot 2\pi = \pi a^2. \quad \text{...(ii)}$$

Now let us find $\iint_S (\text{curl}\,\vec{F}) \cdot \hat{n}\, dS$.

We have, $\text{curl}\,\vec{F} = \begin{vmatrix} \hat{i} & \hat{j} & \hat{k} \\ \frac{\partial}{\partial x} & \frac{\partial}{\partial y} & \frac{\partial}{\partial z} \\ z & x & y \end{vmatrix} = \hat{i} + \hat{j} + \hat{k}.$

If $\hat{n}$ is a unit vector along outward drawn normal at any point (x, y, z) on the surface S, i.e., the surface $\phi(x, y, z) \equiv x^2 + y^2 + z^2 = a^2$, then

$$\hat{n} = \frac{\nabla\phi}{|\nabla\phi|} = \frac{2x\hat{i} + 2y\hat{j} + 2z\hat{k}}{\sqrt{(4x^2 + 4y^2 + 4z^2)}} = \frac{x\hat{i} + y\hat{j} + z\hat{k}}{a}, \text{ since on S, } x^2 + y^2 + z^2 = a^2.$$

$$\therefore \iint_S (\text{curl}\,\vec{F}) \cdot \hat{n}\, dS = \iint_S (\hat{i} + \hat{j} + \hat{k}) \cdot \left(\frac{x\hat{i} + y\hat{j} + z\hat{k}}{a} \right) dS = \frac{1}{a} \iint_S (x + y + z)\, dS.$$

To evaluate it, we shall use polar spherical coordinates (r, θ, ϕ).

We have $z = r\cos\theta, x = r\sin\theta\cos\phi, y = r\sin\theta\sin\phi$.

Here r = a.

$\therefore x = a\sin\theta\cos\phi,\ y = a\sin\theta\sin\phi,\ z = a\cos\theta.$

Also, dS = an elementary area on the surface of the sphere at the point $(a, \theta, \phi) = a\,d\theta . a\sin\theta\, d\phi = a^2 \sin\theta\, d\theta\, d\phi$.

$\therefore \iint_S (\text{curl } \vec{F}) \cdot \hat{n} \, dS$

$= \frac{1}{a}\int_{\theta=0}^{\pi/2}\int_{\phi=0}^{2\pi} (a \sin\theta\cos\phi + a \sin\theta \sin\phi + a \cos\theta) a^2 \sin\theta \, d\theta \, d\phi$

$= a^2 \int_{\theta=0}^{\pi/2}\int_{\phi=0}^{2\pi} (\sin^2\theta\cos\phi + \sin^2\theta \sin\phi + \cos\theta \sin\theta) d\theta \, d\phi$

$= a^2 \int_{\theta=0}^{\pi/2} \left[\sin^2\theta\sin\phi - \sin^2\theta \cos\phi + \phi\cos\theta \sin\theta\right]_{\phi=0}^{2\pi} d\theta$

$= a^2 \int_{\theta=0}^{\pi/2} 2\pi \cos\theta \sin\theta \, d\theta = 2\pi a^2 \cdot \frac{1}{2} = \pi a^2.$ ...(iii)

From (ii) and (iii), we have, $\oint_C \vec{F} \cdot d\vec{r} = \iint_S (\text{curl } \vec{F}) \cdot \hat{n} \, dS.$

This verifies Stoke's theorem.

$= \frac{1}{2}\int_C x^2 d\left(\frac{y}{x}\right) = \frac{1}{2}\int_C x^2 dt$, as $y = tx = \frac{1}{2}\int_C \frac{9a^2t^2dt}{(1+t)^2} = 9a^2\left[-\frac{1}{3(1+t^2)}\right]_0^1 = \frac{3}{2}a^2.$

Q30. Find the work done when a force $\vec{F} = (x^2 - y^2 + x)\hat{i} - (2xy + y)\hat{j}$ moves a particle in xy-plane from (0, 0) to (1, 1) along the parabola $y^2 = x$.

Ans. Let C denotes the arc of the parabola $y^2 = x$ from the point (0, 0) to the point (1, 1). The parametric equations of the parabola $y^2 = x$ can be taken as $x = t^2, y = t$. At the point (0, 0), $t = 0$ and at the point (1, 1), $t = 1$. The required work done

$= \int_C \vec{F} \cdot d\vec{r} = \int_C \left\{(x^2 - y^2 + x)\hat{i} - (2xy + y)\hat{j}\right\} \cdot (dx \, \hat{i} + dy \, \hat{j})$

$= \int_C \left[(x^2 - y^2 + x)dx - (2xy + y)dy\right]$

$= \int_{t=0}^{1}\left[(x^2 - y^2 + x)\frac{dx}{dt} - (2xy + y)\frac{dy}{dt}\right] dt$

$= \int_0^1 \left[t^4 - t^2 + t^2).2t - (2t^3 + t).1\right] dt$

$= \int_0^1 \left[2t^5 - 2t^3 - t\right]dt = \left[2\cdot\frac{t^6}{6} - 2\cdot\frac{t^4}{4} - \frac{t^2}{2}\right]_0^1 = \frac{1}{3} - \frac{1}{2} - \frac{1}{2} = -\frac{2}{3}.$

Q31. Using divergence theorem evaluate $\iint_S \vec{F} \cdot \hat{n} \, dS$ where $\vec{F} = 4xz\hat{i} - y^2\hat{j} + yz\hat{k}$ and S is the surface of the cube bounded by $x = 0, x = 1, y = 0, y = 1, z = 0$ and $z = 1$. $\hat{n}$ is the unit vector normal to the surface S. [June-2011, Q.No.-2]

Ans. By gauss divergences theorem,

$\iint_S \vec{F} \cdot \hat{n} \, dS = \iiint_V \nabla \cdot \vec{F} \, dV$, where V is the volume enclosed by the surface S

$$= \iiint_V \left[\frac{\partial}{\partial x}(4xz) + \frac{\partial}{\partial y}(-y^2) + \frac{\partial}{\partial z}(yz)\right] dV$$

$$= \iiint_V (4z - 2y + y)\, dV = \iiint_V (4z - y) dx\, dy\, dz$$

$$= \int_{x=0}^{1}\int_{y=0}^{1}\int_{z=0}^{1} (4z - y) dx\, dy\, dz$$

$$= \int_{x=0}^{1}\int_{y=0}^{1}\left[2z^2 - yz\right]_{z=0}^{1} dx\, dy = \int_{x=0}^{1}\int_{y=0}^{1}(2 - y) dx\, dy$$

$$= \int_{x=0}^{1}\left[2y - \frac{y^2}{2}\right]_{y=0}^{1} dx = \int_0^1\left[2 - \frac{1}{2}\right]dx = \frac{3}{2}\int_0^1 dx = \frac{3}{2}.$$

Q32. The electric field due to a point charge q, at a point whose position vector with respect to the location of q is $\vec{r}$, is given by $\vec{E} = \frac{kq}{r^3}\vec{r}$ $(r \neq 0)$ where k is a constant dependent on the nature of the medium. Determine the flux of $\vec{E}$ through a sphere of radius a whose centre is at the position of the charge q.

[Dec-2011, Q.No.-2]

Ans.

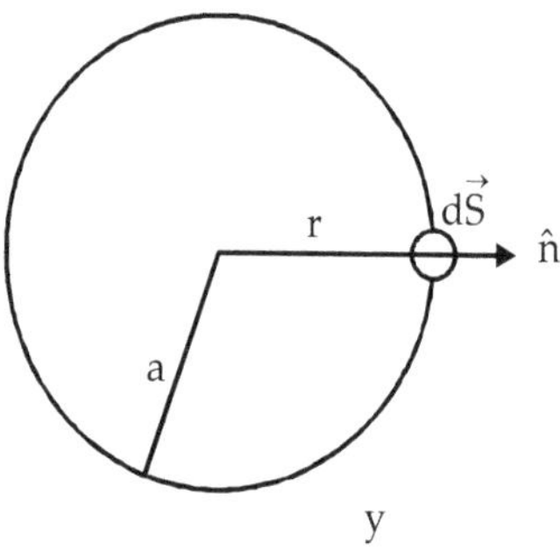

Fig. 4.14

The required surface integral is $\oiint_S \vec{E}\,.\,d\vec{S}$, where S is the surface of the sphere of radius a. Here $\vec{E} = \frac{kq}{r^3}\vec{r} = \frac{kq}{r^3}r\hat{r} = \frac{kq}{r^2}\hat{r}$

Contributions to a surface integral come from the surface only. So we have to know $\vec{E}$ on the surface of the sphere, which is $\frac{kq}{a^2}\hat{r}$

Again, we know that $d\vec{S} = dS\,\hat{n}$

Now, at every point on the sphere $\hat{n} = \hat{r}$

$\therefore d\vec{S} = dS\hat{r}$

Hence, the required flux $= \oiint_S \frac{kq}{a^2}\hat{r}\cdot dS\,\hat{r}$

$= \oiint_S \frac{kq}{a^2} dS \quad (\because \hat{r}.\hat{r} = 1)$

$= \frac{kq}{a^2}\oiint_S dS \quad (\because$ k, q and a are constants)

Now, $\oiint_S dS$ is the surface area of the sphere $= 4\pi a^2$.

Therefore, flux $= \frac{kq}{a^2} 4\pi a^2 = 4\pi\, kq$

Q33. Find the work done in moving a particle once around a circle C in the xy-plane, if the circle has centre at the origin and radius 2 and if the force field $\vec{F}$ is given by $\vec{F} = (2x - y + 2z)\hat{i} + (x + y - z)\hat{j} + (3x - 2y - 5z)\hat{k}$.

Ans. In the xy-plane, we have z = 0. Therefore

$\vec{F} = (2x - y)\hat{i} + (x + y)\hat{j} + (3x - 2y)\hat{k}$.

The circle C is given by $x^2 + y^2 = 4$ or $x = 2\cos t, y = 2\sin t$.

$\therefore \vec{r} = x\hat{i} + y\hat{j} = 2\cos t\,\hat{i} + 2\sin t\,\hat{j}$.

$\therefore \frac{d\vec{r}}{dt} = -2\sin t\,\hat{i} + 2\cos t\,\hat{j}$.

Also $\vec{F} = (4\cos t - 2\sin t)\hat{i} + (2\cos t + 2\sin t)\hat{j} + (6\cos t - 4\sin t)\hat{k}$.

In moving around the circle once t will vary from 0 to 2π.

Therefore, the required work done is $= \int_C \vec{F}\cdot d\vec{r} = \int_0^{2\pi} \vec{F}\cdot\frac{d\vec{r}}{dt}dt$

$= \int_0^{2\pi} \left[-2\sin t(4\cos t - 2\sin t) + 2\cos t(2\cos t + 2\sin t)\right] dt$

$= \int_0^{2\pi} \left[4(\sin^2 t + \cos^2 t) - 4\sin t\cos t\right] dt$

$= \int_0^{2\pi} (4 - 4\sin t\cos t)\, dt = \left[4t - 2\sin 2t\right]_0^{2\pi} = 8\pi.$

Q34. Evaluate $\int_C (\sin x + \cos y) ds$, where C is the line segment from (0, 0) to $(\pi, 2\pi)$.

Ans. The line segment from (0, 0) to $(\pi, 2\pi)$ is given by

$x = t,\ y = 2t,\ 0 \le t \le \pi$

$$\therefore \int_C (\sin x + \cos y) ds = \int_0^\pi (\sin t + \cos 2t)\sqrt{1+4}\, dt$$

$$= \sqrt{5}\int_0^\pi (\sin t + \cos 2t) dt = \sqrt{5}\left[-\cos t + \frac{\sin 2t}{2}\right]_0^\pi$$

$$= \sqrt{5}\left[-\cos\pi + \cos 0 + \frac{\sin 2\pi}{2} - \frac{\sin 0}{2}\right]_0^\pi = \sqrt{5}[1+1+0+0] = 2\sqrt{5}$$

Q35. Calculate the work done by a force $F = (4x^2y, 2xy^2)$ in moving a particle from (0, 0) to (1, 1) along $y = x^2$.

Ans. Here we consider, $C: x = t,\ y = t^2,\ 0 \le t \le 1$.

$$\therefore \text{Work done} = \int_C 4x^2y\,dx + 2xy^2\,dy$$

$$= \int_0^1 4t^4 dt + \int_0^1 2t^5 dt = \frac{4}{5} + \frac{2}{6} = \frac{17}{15}$$

Q36. Calculate the work done by the force $F = (xy, y^2)$ in moving a particle along a piecewise smooth curve $C = C_1 \cup C_2 \cup C_3 \cup C_4$, where

$$C_1 = \{(t,0) \mid 0 \le t \le 1\}$$

$$C_2 = \{(1,t) \mid 0 \le t \le 1\}$$

$$C_3 = \{(1-t,1) \mid 0 \le t \le 1\}$$

$$C_4 = \{(0,1-t) \mid 0 \le t \le 1\}$$

Ans. Here, $\int_C xy\,dx + y^2 dy = \int_{C_1} xy\,dx + y^2 dy + \int_{C_2} xy\,dx + y^2 dy$

$$+ \int_{C_3} xy\,dx + y^2 dy + \int_{C_4} xy\,dx + y^2 dy.$$

Now, $\int_{C_1} xy\,dx + y^2 dy = 0.$ [Here, $y = 0$]

$\int_{C_2} xy\,dx + y^2 dy = \int_0^1 t^2 dt$, since $x = 1$, and hence $dx = 0$. $= \frac{1}{3}$

$$\int_{C_3} xy\,dx + y^2dy = -\int_0^1 (1-t)\,dt, \text{ since } dx = -dt \text{ and } dy = 0.$$

$$= -\left[t - \frac{t^2}{2}\right]_0^1 = -1 + \frac{1}{2} = \frac{-1}{2}.$$

$$\int_{C_4} xy\,dx + y^2dy = -\int_0^1 (1-t)^2dt, \text{ since } dx = 0 \text{ and } dy = -dt$$

$$= -\int_0^1 \left(1 + t^2 - 2t\right)dt = -\left[t + \frac{t^3}{3} - t^2\right]_0^1 = -\left[1 + \frac{1}{3} - 1\right] = \frac{-1}{3}$$

$$\therefore \int_C xydx + y^2dy = \frac{-1}{2}$$

Q37. Verify Green's theorem for $\int_C (y^2 - x^2)dx + (x^2 + y^2)dy$, if C is the boundary of the region D, bounded by $y = 0,\ x = 3,\ y = x$ in the first quadrant.

Ans. Here, D is the region as

$\{x, y \mid 0 \le x \le 3,\ 0 \le y \le x\}$

Now, According to Green theorem

$$\int_C Pdx + Qdy = \iint_D \left(\frac{\partial Q}{\partial x} - \frac{\partial P}{\partial y}\right) dx\,dy$$

where, $P = y^2 - x^2$; $\dfrac{\partial P}{\partial y} = 2y$

$Q = x^2 + y^2$; $\dfrac{\partial Q}{\partial x} = 2x$

Hence, $\displaystyle\int (y^2 - x^2)\,dx + (x^2 + y^2)dy = 2\int_0^3\int_0^x (x - y)dy\,dx = 2\int_0^3 x[y]_0^x - \left[\frac{y^2}{2}\right]_0^x dx$

$$= 2\int_0^3 \left(x^2 - \frac{x^2}{2}\right)dx = 2\left[\frac{\left[x^3\right]_0^3}{3} - \frac{\left[x^3\right]_0^3}{6}\right] = 2\left[9 - \frac{9}{2}\right] = 9$$

Q38. Use Green's theorem to evaluate the area enclosed by the ellipse $\dfrac{x^2}{4} + \dfrac{y^2}{9} = 4$

Ans. Here, the parametric equation of the ellipse can be written as

$x = 2\cos t, y = 3\sin t, \qquad 0 \le t \le 2\pi$

Hence, the area enclosed by the ellipse is:

$$A=\frac{1}{2}\int_C x\,dy-y\,dx=\frac{1}{2}\int_0^{2\pi} x\frac{dy}{dt}dt-y\frac{dx}{dt}dt$$

$$=\frac{1}{2}\int_0^{2\pi}(2\cos t.3\cos t+3\sin t.2\sin t)dt=\frac{6}{2}\int_0^{2\pi}dt=6\pi$$

Q39. Calculate the work done by the force $F=(-4xy,8y)$ in moving a particle along $y=x^2$ from (0, 0) to (2, 4).

Ans. Here we consider, $C:x=t,y=t^2,0\le t\le 2$

$\therefore$ Work done= $\int_c -4xy\,dx+8y\,dy$

$$=\int_0^2 -4t^3dt+\int_0^2 8t^2dt=\frac{-4\left[t^4\right]_0^2}{4}+\frac{8\left[t^3\right]_0^2}{3}=-16+\frac{64}{3}=\frac{16}{3}$$

Q40. Calculate the surface integral of a vector $\vec{A}=x\,\hat{i}+2y\,\hat{j}+3z\,\hat{k}$ over the surface of a sphere of radius 2 by using Gauss's divergence theorem. **[June-2012, Q.No.-2]**

Ans. Here $\vec{A}=x\,\hat{i}+2y\,\hat{j}+3z\,\hat{k}$

$$\therefore \text{div}\vec{A}=\nabla\cdot\vec{A}=\left(\hat{i}\frac{\partial}{\partial x}+\hat{j}\frac{\partial}{\partial y}+\hat{k}\frac{\partial}{\partial z}\right).\left(x\,\hat{i}+2y\,\hat{j}+3z\,\hat{k}\right)$$

$$=\frac{\partial x}{\partial x}+\frac{\partial(2y)}{\partial y}+\frac{\partial(3z)}{\partial z}=1+2+3=6$$

$\therefore$ By Gauss's Divergence theorem, we have

$$\iint_S \vec{A}.\hat{n}\,ds=\iiint_V \text{div}\,\vec{A}\,dx=\iiint_V 6dv=6V$$

Here, V is the volume of a sphere of radius 2:

$$\therefore V=\frac{4}{3}\pi(2)^3=\frac{4}{3}\pi\times 8=\frac{32}{3}\pi$$

Therefore, $\iint_S \vec{A}.\hat{n}\,ds=6V=\frac{6\times 32\pi}{3}=64\pi$.

Q41. Calculate the work done in going from (1,1) to (3, 3) along the path $x = y$ by the force $\vec{F}=(x-y)\hat{i}+(x+y)\hat{j}$. **[Dec-2012, Q.No.-2]**

Ans. Let C denotes the path x = y from point (1, 1) to (3, 3). The parametric equation of x = y can be taken as x = t, y = t. At the point (1, 1), t = 1 and at the point (3, 3), t = 3.

Now, the required work done is $w = \int_c \vec{F}.d\vec{r}$

$$= \int_c \left[(x-y)\hat{i} + (x+y)\hat{j}\right].\left(dx\,\hat{i} + dy\,\hat{j}\right)$$

$$= \int_c \left[(x-y)dx + (x+y)dy\right] = \int_1^3 \left[(x-y)\frac{dx}{dt} + (x+y)\frac{dy}{dt}\right]dt$$

$$= \int_1^3 \left[(t-t).1 + (t+t).1\right]dt = \int_1^3 2t\,dt = 2\int_1^3 t\,dt = 2\left[\frac{t^2}{2}\right]_1^3 = 2\left[\frac{9}{2} - \frac{1}{2}\right] = 8$$

Q42. Using Stokes' theorem show that if the work done by a force along a closed path is zero, the curl of the force field is zero.

[Dec-2012, Q.No.-2]

Ans. Let a force $\vec{F}\left(F_1\hat{i} + F_2\hat{j} + F_3\hat{k}\right)$ act upon a particle, which is displaced along a given path C in space from the point P of which the position vector is $\vec{r}$. Then $\frac{d\vec{r}}{ds}$ is a unit vector along the tangent at P to C in the direction of increasing. The component of $\vec{F}$ along the tangent is $\vec{F}.\frac{d\vec{r}}{ds}$.

$\therefore$ Work done by $\vec{F}$ along the tangent to C $= \vec{F}.\frac{d\vec{r}}{ds}ds = \vec{F}.d\vec{r}$

$\therefore$ Total work done $= \int_c \vec{F}.d\vec{r} = \int_c \left(F_1dx + F_2dy + F_3dz\right)$

If the algebraic sum of work done by a number of forces in bringing the body to its original configuration is zero, the system of forces is said to be conservative.

By Stokes's theorem, we see that if $\vec{F}.d\vec{r}$ i.e., work done is zero then curl $\vec{F} = 0$.

Here condition of $\vec{F}$ to be conservative is curl $\vec{F} = \nabla \times \vec{F} = \vec{0}$.

Q43. Determine the work done by the force $\vec{F} = y^2x\hat{i} + xy\hat{j}$ in moving a particle along the curve $y^2 = 4x$ from (0, 0) and (1, 2).

[June-2013, Q.No.-1(d)]

Ans. Let C denotes the arc of the parabola $y^2 = 4x$ from the point (0, 0) to the point (1, 2).

The parametric equations of the parabola $y^2 = 4x$ can be taken as $x = t^2$, $y = 2t$. At the point (0, 0), $t = 0$ and at the point (1, 2), $t = 1$.

The required work done is $\int_C \vec{F}.d\vec{r} = \int_C \left\{y^2x\hat{i} + xy\hat{j}\right\}.\left(dx\hat{i} + dy\hat{j}\right)$

$$= \int_C \left\{y^2xdx + xydy\right\} = \int_{t=0}^{1}\left[y^2x\frac{dx}{dt} + xy\frac{dy}{dt}\right]dt$$

$$= \int_{t=0}^{1}\left[\left(4t^2\right)\left(t^2\right)(2t) + \left(t^2\right)(2t)(2)\right]dt = \int_{t=0}^{1}\left(8t^5 + 4t^3\right)dt$$

$$= 4\int_{t=0}^{1}\left(2t^5 + t^3\right)dt = 4\left[\frac{2t^6}{6} + \frac{t^4}{4}\right]_0^1 = 4\left[\frac{t^6}{3} + \frac{t^4}{4}\right]_0^1 = 4\left[\frac{1}{3} + \frac{1}{4}\right] = 4\left[\frac{4+3}{12}\right] = \frac{7}{3}$$

For excellent score, read only GPH book.

Chapter 5

Basic Concepts of Probability Theory

An Overview

Probability is used to describe an attitude of mind towards some proposition of whose truth we are not certain. The proposition of interest is usually of the form "Will a specific event occur?" The attitude of mind is of the form "How certain are we that the event will occur?" The certainty, we adopt, can be described in terms of a numerical measure and this number, between 0 and 1, we call probability. The higher the probability of an event, the more certain we are that event will occur. Thus, **probability** in an applied sense is a measure of the confidence a person has that a (random) event will occur.

Sample Space: The set of all possible outcomes of an experiment is called the sample space for that experiment. For example, in a single throw of a dice, the sample space is (1, 2, 3, 4, 5, 6).

Sample Point: Each outcome in a sample space is known as the sample point. For example, if we toss a coin, the sample space has two sample points: $\Omega = \{H, T\}$. If we toss two coins then the sample space has four sample points or elements: $\Omega = \{(HH), (HT), (TH), (TT)\}$

Discrete Sample Space: A sample space containing a finite number of points is called a discrete sample space.

For example, $\Omega = \{(x, y) | x^2 + y^2 = 4\}$

Event of a Sample Space: The collection of all events of a random experiment is called the event of a sample space.

For example, The sample space of the experiment "Tossing of two coins " is: $\Omega = \{HH, HT, TH, TT\}$

The event of getting at least one head is the set $\{HH, HT, TH\}$, which is a subset of Ω.. Similarly, $\{HH\}$ and $\{TT\}$ are also events of getting 2 heads and 2 tails respectively.

Simple Event: Such events, which contain only one sample point, are called simple events. For example, $\{HH\}, \{TT\}$ are simple events.

Algebra of events: Let ς be a fixed sample space. Imagine that the (conceptual) experiment underlying ς is being performed. The phrase "the event E occurs" would mean that the experiment results in an outcome that is included in the event E. Similarly, non-occurrence of the event E would mean that the experiment results into an outcome that is not an element of the event E. Thus, the collection of all sample points that are not included in the event E is also an event that is complementary to E and is denoted as E^c. The event E^c is therefore the event which contains all those sample points of ς which are not in E. As such, it is easy to see that the event E occurs if and only if the event E^c does not take place. The events E and E^c are complementary events and taken together they comprise the entire sample space, i.e. $E \cup E^c = \varsigma$.

Since ς is an event that consists of all the sample points. Hence, its complement is an empty set in the sense that it does not contain any sample point and is called the null event, usually denoted as ϕ so that $\varsigma^c = \phi$.

Consider the event E that the three tosses produce at least one head. Thus, $E=\{s_1,s_2,s_3,s_4,s_5,s_6,s_7\}$ so that the complementary event $E^c=\{s_8\}$, which is the event of not scoring a head at all.

Let us now consider two events E and F. We write $E \cup F$, read as **E "union" F,** to denote the collection of sample points, which are responsible for occurrence of either E or F or both. Thus, $E \cup F$ is a new event and it occurs if and only if either E or F of both occur, i.e. if and only if at least one of the events E or F occurs. Generalising this idea, we can define a new event $\cup_{j=1}^{k} E_j$, read as **"union" of the k events** $E_1, E_2, ..., E_k$, as the event that consists of all sample points that are in at least one of the events $E_1, E_2, ..., E_k$ and it occurs if and only if at least one of the events $E_1, E_2, ..., E_k$, occurs.

Again, let E and F be two given events. We write $E \cap F$, read as **E "intersection" F**, to denote the collection of sample points any of whose occurrence implies the occurrence of both E and F. Thus, $E \cap F$ is a new event and it occurs if and only if both the events E and F occur. Generalising this idea, we can define a new event $\cap_{j=1}^{k} E_j$ read as "intersection" of the k events $E_1, E_2, ..., E_k$, as the event that consists of sample points that are common to each of the events $E_1, E_2, ..., E_k$ and it occurs only if all the k events $E_1, E_2, ..., E_k$ occur simultaneously.

Mutually Exclusive Event: Two events are said to be mutually exclusive events, if the occurrence of one event implies no possibility of occurrence of the other event. For example, in throwing an unbiased dice, the occurrence of the number at the top prevents the occurrence of other numbers on it.

Probability of an Event: If there are n elementary events associated with a random experiment and m of them are favourable to an event A, then the probability of happening or occurrence of A is denoted by P (A) and is defined as the ratio $\frac{m}{n}$.

Thus, $P(A) = \frac{m}{n}$

If P (A) = 1, then A is called the certain event and A is called an impossible event if P (A) = 0.

Also, $P(A)+P(\bar{A})=1$

The odds in favour of occurrence of the event A are defined by m: (n – m), i.e. $P(A):P(\bar{A})$ and the odds against the occurrence of A are defined by (n - m): m, i.e. $P(\bar{A}):P(A)$.

$P(C)=4/6=2/3.$

Multiplication Rule: If an operation can be performed in m ways and a second independent operation can be performed in n ways for each of the m ways, the two operations can be performed together in mn ways.

Permutations: A permutation is an arrangement of all or a part of a set of objects and the number of permutations of n distinct object is n!.

To generalise this result, let us consider the set $B=\{b_1,b_2,....,b_n\}$

Suppose we form samples of size 2, (b_i,b_j) by choosing elements from the set B. It is easy to check that this number is n^2, provided

- repetition of elements is allowed, i.e. samples like $(b_1,b_1),(b_2,b_2),...$ are included in the count.
- samples (b_i,b_j) and (b_j,b_i) for $i=j$ are counted different.

By induction, for samples of size r, the total number of such samples is n^r

This is an important result and can be stated as follows:

The number of ways of drawing a group of r objects (red balls in a box) out of a total of n objects (balls of red, blue and green colour) when repetition (replacement of balls drawn once) is permitted is n^r.

However, if samples made up of identical elements are ignored, the number of samples of size two will be $n(n-1)$. From this we can say that the number of samples of size r without repetition is

$$n(n-1)...(n-r+1)=\frac{n!}{(n-r)!}$$

This is called the number of permutations of n different objects taken r at a time. We represent this by the symbol ${}^nP_r\left[=n!/(n-r)!\right]$.

Note: The number of permutations of n objects of which n_1, are of one kind, n_2 are of second kind, .. n_k of kth kind is $\frac{n!}{n_1!n_2!n_3!.....n_k!}$

In short from, we express this as $\binom{n}{n_1, n_2, \ldots. n_k}$

Combinations: In many problems we are interested in the number of ways of selecting r objects from n without regard to order. These selections are called combinations. The number of such combinations is $\frac{n!}{r!(n-r)!}$. It is denoted by $\binom{n}{r, n-r}$ or simply $\binom{r}{n}$

We may, therefore, conclude that

The number of combinations of n objects taken r at a time is $^nC_r = \binom{n}{r} = \frac{n!}{r!(n-r)!}$

Theorems of Probability: Some important laws and theorems, which frequently simplify the computations of probabilities in complex situations, are as follows:

(a) Theorem of Total Probability

If two events A and B are mutually exclusive, exhaustive and equally likely, then the occurrence of either A or B, ($A \cup B$) is given by the sum of their probability. Thus, P ($A \cup B$)=P (A) + P (B)

This is also known as the Addition Theorem.

Proof: Let us assume that a random experiment has n possible outcomes which are mutually exclusive, exhaustive and equally likely. While m_1 of them are favourable to A; m_2 are favourable to B. By the classical definition of probability $P(A) = m_1/n$ and $P(B) = m_2/n$.

Since A and B are mutually exclusive and exhaustive, the number of events favourable to the event ($A \cup B$) is given by $m_1 + m_2$, therefore,

$$P(A \cup B) = (m_1 + m_2)/n = (m_1/n) + (m_2/n) = P(A) + P(B) \text{ (proved)}$$

Deduction from Theorem of Total Probability

Theorem of Complementary Event

If A denotes the occurrence of the event A, the A^c (read as 'compliment of A') denotes non- occurrence of the event A and $P(A) = 1 - P(A^c)$.

Since A and A^c are mutually exclusive and exhaustive events, $S = \{A, A^c\}$. Applying the theorem of total probability we get,

$$P(S) = P(A) + P(A^c) = 1 \text{ or } P(A^c) = 1 - P(A)$$

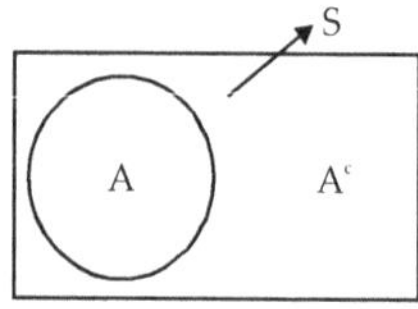

Fig. 5.1

See that this theorem is very intuitive. If the probability of getting head while tossing an unbiased coin is.05 then the probability of getting a tail is obviously 1-.05=.05.

Extension of Total Probability Theorem

The theorem of total probability could be extended to any number of mutually exclusive events. If the events $A_1, A_2, A_3, \ldots\ldots, A_k$ are mutually exclusive, then the probability of occurrence of any one of them $\left(U^k_{i=1} A_i\right)$ is given by the sum of their probabilities.

$$P\left(U^k_{i=1} A_i\right) = P(A_1) + P(A_2) + P(A_3) + \ldots\ldots\ldots\ldots + P(A_k)$$

Theorem of Total Probability with Mutually Non-exclusive Events

The probability of occurrence of at least one of the events A and B (which are not necessarily mutually exclusive) is given by

$$P(A \cup B) = P(A) + P(B) - P(A \cap B)$$

The symbol '$\cap$' means 'and', i.e. $(A \cap B)$ means the occurrence of the event A and B, whereas '$\cup$' means 'or', i.e. $(A \cup B) \Rightarrow$ the occurrence of either the event A or the event B.

Proof: The occurrence of the event $(A \cup B)$ is analogous to the occurrence of any of the following three mutually exclusive events:

$$(A \cap B^c), (A^c \cap B) \text{ and } (A \cap B).$$

In terms of Venn figure,

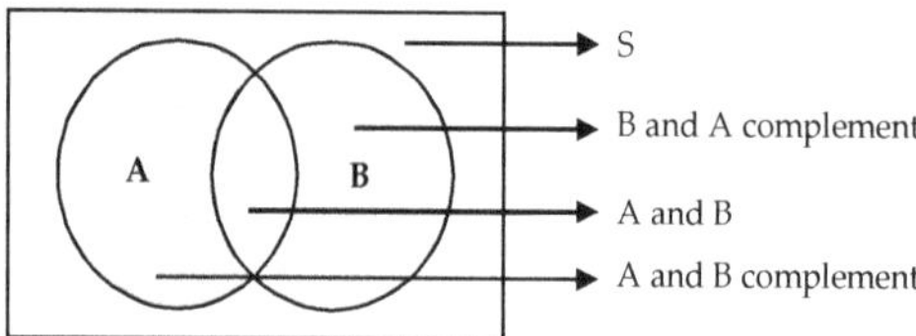

Fig. 5.2

Therefore, using the definition of total probability, we get

$$P(A \cup B) = P(A \cap B^c) + P(A^c \cap B) + P(A \cap B) \qquad \ldots \text{(i)}$$

Again, the occurrence of A is analogous to the occurrence of any one of the following two mutually exclusive events $P(A \cap B)$ and $P(A \cap B^c)$, Thus, we get

$$P(A) = P(A \cap B) + P(A \cap B^c) \qquad \text{...(ii)}$$

Similarly, for B

$$P(B) = P(B \cap A) + P(B \cap A^c) \qquad \text{... (iii)}$$

Using (1), (2), (3) we can derive that

$P(A \cup B) = P(A) + P(B) - P(A \cap B)$ (proved).

[The above result could be extended to three events A, B, C, which are not mutually exclusive]

$$P(AUBUC) = P(A) + P(B) + P(C) - P(A \cap B) - P(A \cap C) - P(C \cap B)$$
$$+P(A \cap B \cap C)$$

In the following figure, we illustrate the situation.

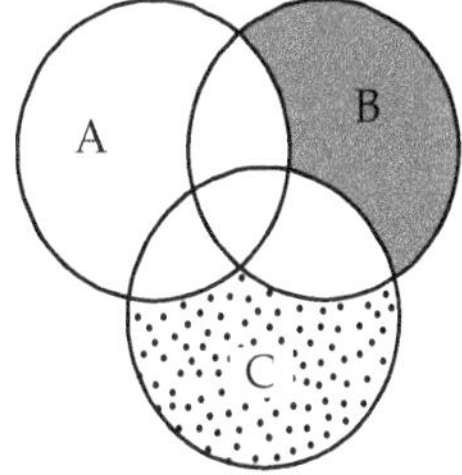

Fig. 5.3

In this context, we mention that there are two standard result in the theory of probability

(1) $P(A \cup B) \le P(A) + P(B)$ ....Boole's inequality

(2) $P(A \cap B) \ge P(A) + P(B) - 1$ ....Bonferroni's inequality

(b) Theorem of Compound Probability

The probability of occurrence of the event A and B simultaneously is given by the product of the probability of the event A and conditional probability of the event B given that A has actually occurred, which is denoted by P(A/B). P(A/B) is given by the ratio of the number of events favourable to the event A and B to the number of events favourable to the event A. Symbolically, $P(A \cap B) = P(A) \times P(B/A)$.

Proof: Suppose a random experiment has n mutually exclusive, exhaustive and equally likely outcomes among which m_1, m_2 and m_{12} are favourable to the events A, B and $(A \cap B)$ respectively.

$$P(A\cap B)=m_{12}/n=m_1/n\times m_{12}/m_1 \;=P(A)\times P(B/A)\text{ (proved).}$$

This theorem is also known as the multiplication theorem.

Deductions from Theorem of Total Probability

The occurrence of one event, say, B may be associated with the occurrence or non-occurrence of another events say, A. This in turn implies that we can think of B to be composed of two mutually exclusive events $(A\cap B)$ and $(A^c\cap B)$. Applying the theorem of total probability

$$P(B)=P(A\cap B)+P(A^c\cap B)=P(A)\times P(B/A)+P(A^c)\times P(B/A^c)$$

[using theorem of compound probability]

Extension of Compound Probability Theorem

The above theorem can be extended to include the cases when there are three or more events. Suppose there are three events A, B and C, then

$$P(A\cap B\cap C)=P(A)\times P(B/A)\times P(C/(A\cap B))$$

and so on for more than three events.

Conditional Probability: The probability of the happening of an event A when the event B has already happened is called the conditional probability and is denoted by P(A/B).

Similarly, P(B/A) means the probability of the happening of an event B when the event A has already happened.

Independent Events: Two events are said to be independent, if the probability of the occurrence of one event will not affect the probability of the occurrence of the second event. Independent events are those events whose probabilities are in no way affected by the occurrence of any other even preceding, following or occurring at the same time.

Two events A and B are said to be independent if and only if

$P(A\cap B)=P(A)P(B)$ which implies that

$P(A/B)=P(A)$ and $P(B/A)=P(B)$

Generalised Theorem of Total Probability: If $\{E_1,E_2,...E_n\}$ constitute a **partition** of the sample space Ω such that $P(E_i)\neq 0$ for $i=1,2,....,n$, then for any event A of Ω $P(A)=\sum_{i=1}^{n}P(E_i)P(A|E_i)=\sum_{i=1}^{n}P(E_i\cap A)$

Bayes' Theorem: Bayes' theorem (also known as Bayes' rule) is a useful tool for calculating conditional probabilities. Bayes' theorem can be stated as follows:

Let $A_1, A_2, ..., A_n$ be a set of mutually exclusive events that together form the sample space S. Let B be any event from the same sample space, such that P(B) > 0. Then, $P(A_k|B) = \frac{P(A_k \cap B)}{P(A_1 \cap B) + P(A_2 \cap B) + ... + P(A_n \cap B)}$

Invoking the fact, that $P(A_k \cap B) = P(A_k)P(B|A_k)$ Bayes' theorem can also be expressed as:

$$P(A_k|B) = \frac{P(A_k)P(B|A_k)}{P(A_1)P(B|A_1) + P(A_2)P(B|A_2) + ... + P(A_n)P(B|A_n)}$$

Random Variables: In probability and statistics, a **random variable** or **stochastic variable** is, roughly speaking, a variable whose value results from the measurement of a quantity that is subject to variations due to chance (i.e. randomness, in a mathematical sense). As opposed to normal mathematical variables, a random variable conceptually does not have a single, fixed value (even if unknown); rather, it can take on a set of possible different values, each with an associated probability.

Random variables can be classified as either *discrete* (i.e. it may assume any of a specified list of exact values) or as *continuous* (i.e. it may assume any numerical value in an interval or collection of intervals). The mathematical function describing the possible values of a random variable and their associated probabilities is known as a probability distribution. The realisations of a random variable, i.e. the results of randomly choosing values according to the variable's probability distribution are called random variables.

A random variable's possible values might represent the possible outcomes of a yet-to-be-performed experiment or an event that has not happened yet, or the potential values of a past experiment or event whose already-existing value is uncertain (e.g. as a result of incomplete information or imprecise measurements). They may also conceptually represent either the results of an "objectively" random process (e.g. rolling a die), or the "subjective" randomness that results from incomplete knowledge of a quantity. The meaning of the probabilities assigned to the potential values of a random variable is not part of probability theory itself, but instead related to philosophical arguments over the interpretation of probability. The mathematics works the same regardless of the particular interpretation in use.

Probability Distribution function: If X is a discrete random variable and the value of its probability at the point t is given by $f(t)$, then the function given by $F(x)=\sum_{x\le t} f(t)$ for $-\infty \le x \le \infty$.

It is called the distribution function or the cumulative distribution of X and is given by the summation of the probabilities if the random variable X takes values less than x.

The density function of a discrete random variable satisfies following conditions:

(a) $f(-\propto)=0, F(\propto)=1$

(b) If $a<b$, then $F(a)\le F(b)$ where a and b are any real number.

If X is a continuous random variable and the value of its probability density at the point t is given by $f(t)$, then the function given by $F(x)=P(X\le x)=\int_{\propto}^{x} f(t)dt$ is called the distribution function. The distribution function of a continuous random variable has the same nice properties as that of a discrete random variable, viz.

(a) $f(-\propto)=0, F(\propto)=1$

(b) If $a<b$ then $F(a)\le F(b)$ where a and b are any real number

(c) Furthermore, it follows directly from the definition that $P(a\le x\le b)=F(b)-F(a)$, where a and b are real constants with $a\le b$.

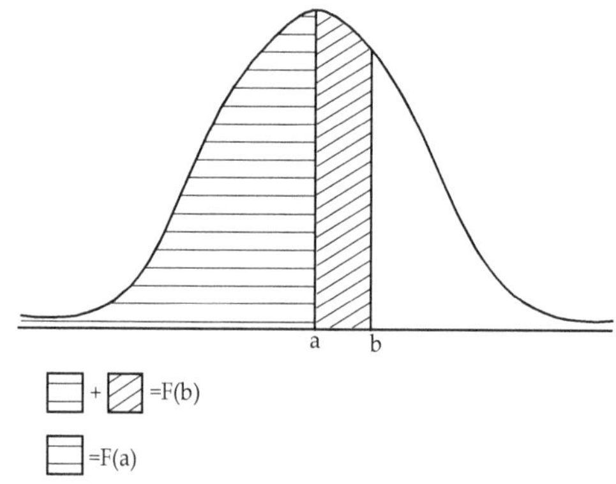

Fig. 5.4

(d) $f(x)=\frac{d}{dx}F(x)$ where the derivatives exist.

Mathematical Expectation: Suppose x is a discrete random variable which takes the values $x_1, x_2, \ldots, x_n$, with respective probabilities $p_1, p_2, \ldots, p_n$ so that $p_1 + p_2 + \ldots + p_n = 1$.

The mathematical expectation of x or the expected value of x, denoted by E(x), is defined as $E(x) = p_1x_1 + p_2x_2 + \ldots + p_nx_n = \sum_{i=1}^{n} p_ix_i$.

We have $E(x) = \frac{\Sigma p_ix_i}{\Sigma p_i}$, since $\Sigma p_i = 1$.

If p_i is replaced by f_i, it follows that

$E(x) = \text{Mean} = \bar{x}$.

If $\phi(x)$ is a single-valued function of a discrete random variable x which takes the values $\phi(x_1), \phi(x_2), \ldots, \phi(x_n)$ when x takes the values $x_1, x_2, \ldots, x_n$ with respective probabilities $p_1 + p_2 + \ldots + p_n$, where $\Sigma p_i = 1$, then the expected value of $\phi(x)$ is defined as

$$E[\phi(x)] = p_1\phi(x_1) + p_2\phi(x_2) + \ldots + p_n\phi(x_n) = \sum_{i=1}^{n} p_i\phi(x_i).$$

Some Properties of Expectation

If x is a discrete random variable and a is a constant, then

(i) $E(a) = a$,

(ii) $E(ax) = aE(x)$,

(iii) $E(x - \bar{x}) = 0$,

(iv) $Var(ax) = a^2Var(x)$,

(v) $Var(x) = E(x^2) - [E(x)]^2$,

(vi) $|E(x)| \le E(|x|)$.

Law

(i) The mathematical expectation of sum of several random variables is equal to the sum of the mathematical expectation of the random variables, i.e. E(a+b+c+d+.........) = E(a)+E(b)+E(c)+E(d)+........., where a, b, c, d represent random variables.

(ii) The expectation of the product of two independent random variables is equal to the product of their expectations, i.e. $E(xy) = E(x)E(y)$ where x and y are two independent random variables.

Variance: If X is a discrete random variable, which assumes values $x_1, x_2, x_3, \ldots, x_n$ with the respective probabilities $p_1, p_2, \ldots, p_n$, then variance of X is defined as $Var(X) = p_1(x_1 - \bar{X})^2 + p_2(x_2 - \bar{X})^2 + \ldots.. + p_n(x_n - \bar{X})^2$

$$\Rightarrow Var(X) = \sum_{i=1}^{n} p_i(x_i - \bar{X})^2, \text{ where } \bar{X} = \sum_{i=1}^{n} p_ix_i \text{ is the mean of X.}$$

Now, $\mathrm{Var}(X)=\sum_{i=1}^{n}p_i\left(x_i-\bar{X}\right)^2 \Rightarrow \mathrm{Var}(X)=\sum_{i=1}^{n}p_i\left(x_i^2-2x_i\bar{X}+\bar{X}^2\right)$

$$\Rightarrow \mathrm{Var}(X)=\sum_{i=1}^{n}p_ix_i^2-2\bar{X}\left(\sum_{i=1}^{n}p_ix_i\right)+\bar{X}^2\left(\sum_{i=1}^{n}p_i\right)$$

$$\Rightarrow \mathrm{Var}(X)=\sum_{i=1}^{n}p_ix_i^2-2\bar{X}.\bar{X}+\bar{X}^2 \quad [\because \sum_{i=1}^{n}p_i=1]$$

$$\Rightarrow \mathrm{Var}(X)=\sum_{i=1}^{n}p_ix_i^2-\bar{X}^2 \Rightarrow \mathrm{Var}(X)=\sum_{i=1}^{n}p_ix_i^2-\left(\sum_{i=1}^{n}p_ix_i\right)^2$$

Thus, $\mathrm{Var}(X)=\sum_{i=1}^{n}p_ix_i^2-\left(\sum_{i=1}^{n}p_ix_i\right)^2$ or $\mathrm{Var}(X)=E\left(X^2\right)-\{E(X)\}^2$

Standard Derivation: The positive square root of the variance is called the standard deviation of X. Hence, standard deviation $=\sqrt{\mathrm{Var}(X)}$

Covariance: The covariance between random discrete variables X and Y, denoted by Cov(X, Y) is defined as $\mathrm{Cov}(X,Y)=\sum_i f(x_i,y_i)\left(x_i-\langle X\rangle\right)\left(y_i-\langle Y\rangle\right)$.

An alternative, and more often used, formula for covariance of two random variables X and Y with means $\bar{X}$ and $\bar{Y}$, respectively is given by

$\mathrm{Cov}(X,Y)=E(XY)-\bar{X}\bar{Y}$

Correlation Coefficient: The covariance between two random variables gives information about the nature of their relationship, its magnitude does not suggest anything about the strength of the relationship, since Cov (X, Y) is not scale free. However, we can determine the strength of such relationship by means of correlation coefficient, r_{XY}. It is defined as

$$r_{XY}=\frac{\mathrm{Cov}(X,Y)}{\sqrt{\mathrm{Var}(X)\mathrm{Var}(Y)}}=\frac{\mathrm{Cov}(X,Y)}{\sigma_X\sigma_Y}$$

Solved Practical Problems

Q1. What is the probability that all three children in a family have different birthdays? (Assume, 1 year = 365 days).

Ans. The first child may be born on any of 365 days of the year; the second also on any of the 365 days, and similarly the third child. Hence, the total number of possible ways in which the three children have birthdays is

$365 \times 365 \times 365$. These cases are mutually exclusive, exhaustive and equally likely. As regards the number of favourable cases out of these, we note that the first child may have any of the 365 days of the year as its birthday. In order that the second child has a birthday different from that of the first, it should have been born on any of the 364 remaining days of the year; Similarly, the 3rd should be born on any of the remaining 363 days. So, the number of cases favourable to the event "different birthdays" is $365 \times 364 \times 363$.

$$\therefore p = \frac{365 \times 364 \times 363}{365 \times 365 \times 365} = 0.992$$

Q2. In simultaneous toss of two coins, find the probability of getting: (i) 2 heads (ii) exactly one head (iii) exactly 2 tails (iv) exactly one tail (v) no tails.

Ans. The sample space associated to the given random experiment is given by $S = |HH, HT, TH, TT|$

Clearly, there are 4 elements in S.

$\therefore$ Total number of elementary events = 4.

(i) There is only one elementary event, i.e. HH favourable to the given event. So, required probability $= \frac{1}{4}$.

(ii) We observe that exactly one head can be obtained in two ways: HT or, TH. So, favourable number of elementary events = 2.

Hence, required probability $= \frac{2}{4} = \frac{1}{2}$.

(iii) Exactly 2 tails can be obtained in one way, i.e. TT.

So, favourable number of elementary events = 1.

Hence, required probability $= \frac{1}{4}$.

(iv) Exactly one tail can be obtained in one of the following two ways:

HT, TH. So, favourable number of elementary events = 2.

Hence, required probability $= \frac{2}{4} = \frac{1}{2}$.

(v) There is only one elementary event, viz. HH favourable to the event "getting no tails"

So, required probability $= \frac{1}{4}$.

Q3. What is the probability that a number selected from the number 1, 2, 3,..., 25, is prime number, when each of the given numbers is equally likely to be selected?

Ans. Let S be the sample space associated with the given experiment and A be the event "selecting a prime number". Then,

S = (1, 2, 3,..., 25) and A = (2, 3, 5, 7, 11, 13, 17, 19, 23)

$\therefore$ Total number of elementary events = 25

Favourable number of elementary = 9

Hence, required probability = $\frac{9}{25}$.

Q4. The probability that at least one of the events A and B occurs is 0.6. If A and B occur simultaneously with probability 0.2, then find $P(\bar{A})+P(\bar{B})$.

Ans. We have,

P (At least one of the events A and B occurs) = 0.6, i.e. $P(A \cup B) = 0.6$

and, P (A and B occur simultaneously) = 0.2, i.e. $P(A \cap B) = 0.2$

Now, $P(A \cup B) = P(A) + P(B) - P(A \cap B) \Rightarrow 0.6 = P(A) + P(B) - 0.2$

$\Rightarrow 0.6 = 1 - P(\bar{A}) + 1 - P(\bar{B}) - 0.2 \Rightarrow 0.6 = 2 - 0.2 - \left[P(\bar{A}) + P(\bar{B})\right]$

$\Rightarrow 0.6 = 1.8 - \left[P(\bar{A}) + P(\bar{B})\right] \Rightarrow P(\bar{A}) + P(\bar{B}) = 1.8 - 0.6 = 1.2$

Q5. If $P(A) = 1/2, P(B) = 1/3, P(A \cap B) = 1/4$, find $P(A^c), P(A \cup B), P(A/B), P(A^c \cap B), P(A^c \cap B^c), P(A^c \cup B)$.

Ans. Given, $P(A) = 1/2, P(B) = 1/3, P(A \cap B) = 1/4$

Hence, $P(A^c) = 1 - P(A) = 1 - 1/2 = 1/2$

$P(A \cup B) = P(A) + P(B) - P(A \cap B) = 1/2 + 1/3 - 1/4 = 7/12$

$P(A/B) = P(A \cap B)/P(B) = (1/4)/(1/3) = 3/4$

$P(A^c \cap B) = P(A^c) \times P(B/A^c) = 1/2 \times 1/2.3 = 1/12$

$P(A^c \cap B^c) = P(A \cup B)^c = 1 - P(A \cup B) = 1 - 7/12 = 5/12$

and $P(A^c \cup B) = P(A^c) + P(B) - P(A^c \cap B)$

$= 1/2 + 1/3 - 1/12 = 9/12 = 3/4.$

Q6. Prove that if A and B are independent events, then A^c and B^c are two independent events.

Ans. To show that A^c and B^c are independent, we need to show $P(A^c)P(B^c) = P(A^c \cap B^c)$.

Since, $P(A^c)P(B^c) = [1-P(A)][1-P(B)] = 1-P(A)-P(B)+P(A)P(B)$

Because A and B are assumed to be independent, $P(A)P(B) = P(A \cap B)$, Hence, $P(A^c)P(B^c) = 1-P(A)-P(B)+P(A \cap B)$

The rule for unions states that $P(A \cup B) = P(A)+P(B)-P(A \cap B)$, Thus,

$P(A^c)P(B^c) = 1-P(A \cup B)$

$= P\left((A \cup B)^c\right)$ [complement rule]

$= P(A^c \cap B^c)$ [De Morgan's Law]

Q7. Events A and B are such that $P(A) = \frac{1}{2}, P(B) = \frac{7}{12}$ and P (not A or not B) = $\frac{1}{4}$. State whether A and B are independent?

Ans. We have,

P (not A or not B) = $\frac{1}{4}$

$$\Rightarrow P\left(\bar{A} \cup \bar{B}\right) = \frac{1}{4} \Rightarrow P\left(\overline{A \cap B}\right) = \frac{1}{4} \Rightarrow 1 - P(A \cap B) = \frac{1}{4} \Rightarrow P(A \cap B) = \frac{3}{4}$$

Clearly, $P(A \cap B) \neq P(A)P(B)$.

So, A and B are not independent events.

Q8. In a bolt factory, machines A, B and C manufacture respectively 25%, 35% and 40% of the total bolts. Of their output 5, 4 and 2 % are respectively defective bolts. A bolt is drawn at random from the product. What is the probability that the bolt drawn is defective?

Ans. Let E_1, E_2, E_3 and A be the events defined as follows:

E_1 = the bolts is manufactured by machine A;

E_2 = the bolts is manufactured by machine B;

E_3 = the bolts is manufactured by machine C,

and, A = the bolt is defective.

Then, $P(E_1) = \frac{25}{100} = \frac{1}{4}, P(E_2) = \frac{35}{100}, P(E_3) = \frac{40}{100}$

$P(A/E_1)$=Probability that the bolt drawn is defective given the condition that it is manufactured by machine A = 5/100

Similarly, we have $P(A/E_2)=\frac{4}{100}$ and $P(A/E_3)=\frac{2}{100}$

Using the law of total probability, we have

$P(A)=P(E_1)P(A/E_1)+P(E_2)P(A/E_2)+P(E_3)P(A/E_3)$

$=\frac{25}{100}\times\frac{5}{100}+\frac{35}{100}\times\frac{4}{100}+\frac{40}{100}\times\frac{2}{100}=0.0345$

Q9. Four coins are tossed. What is the expectation of number of heads?

Ans. Let x be the number of heads.

We have $P(x=4)=\frac{1}{2}\times\frac{1}{2}\times\frac{1}{2}\times\frac{1}{2}=\frac{1}{16}$,

Now $P(x=3)=\frac{{}^4C_3}{16}=\frac{4}{16}=\frac{1}{4}$, $P(x=2)=\frac{{}^4C_2}{16}=\frac{6}{16}=\frac{3}{8}$,

$P(x=1)=\frac{{}^4C_1}{16}=\frac{4}{16}=\frac{1}{4}$, $P(x=0)\frac{{}^4C_0}{16}=\frac{1}{16}$

The probability distribution of x is

x:	0	1	2	3	4
p:	$\frac{1}{16}$	$\frac{1}{4}$	$\frac{3}{8}$	$\frac{1}{4}$	$\frac{1}{16}$.

Hence, $E(x)=0.\frac{1}{16}+1.\frac{1}{4}+2.\frac{3}{8}+3.\frac{1}{4}+4.\frac{1}{16}=2.$

Q10. A factory has two machines A and B. Past records show that the first machine produces 30% of output and the second machine produces 70% of the output. Further, 5% and 3% of the products produced by the first machine and the second machine respectively are defective item was produced by the first machine or the second machine. Hence, find out the probability of defective item being produced by machine A or machine B.

Ans. The output of first machine is denoted by P(A):

P(A) = 0.30

The output of second machine is denoted by P(B):

P(B) = 0.70

The probability of the defective items by first machine:

P(C/A) = 0.05

Similarly, the probability of the defective item by second machine is given by P(C/B) = 0.03

Bayes' Theorem of probability:

$$P(A/C)=\frac{P(C/A)\times P(A)}{P(C/A)\times P(A)+P(C/B)\times P(B)}$$

where, P(A/C) is the probability of single piece defective being produced by the machine A.

Similarly, $$P(B/C)=\frac{P(C/B)\times P(B)}{P(C/B)\times P(B)+P(C/A)\times P(A)}$$

where, P(B/C) is the probability of single piece defective being produced by the machine B.

$$\therefore P(A/C)=\frac{0.05\times 0.3}{0.05\times 0.3+0.03\times 0.7}=\frac{0.015}{0.015+0.021}=0.4167$$

$$\text{and } P(B/C)=\frac{0.03\times 0.7}{0.03\times 0.7+0.5\times 0.03}=\frac{0.021}{0.015+0.021}=0.5833$$

The probability of defective item being produced by machine A is 0.4167, whereas, the probability of defective item being produced by machine B is 0.5833.

Q11. A market survey was conducted in four cities to find out the preference for brand A soap. The responses are shown below:

	Delhi	Kolkata	Chennai	Mumbai
Yes	45	55	60	50
No	35	45	35	45
No opinion	5	5	5	5

(a) What is the probability that a consumer selected at random, preferred brand A?

(b) What is the probability that a consumer preferred brand A and was from Chennai?

(c) What is the probability that a consumer preferred brand A, given that he was from Chennai?

(d) Given that a consumer preferred brand A, what is the probability that he was from Mumbai?

Ans. The information from responses during market survey is as follows:

	Delhi	Kolkata	Chennai	Mumbai	Total
Yes	45	55	60	50	210
No	35	45	35	45	160
No opinion	5	5	5	5	20
Total	85	105	100	100	390

Let X denote the event that a consumer selected at random preferred brand A. Then,

(a) The probability that a consumer selected at random preferred brand A is P(X) = 210/390 = 0.5384

(b) The probability that a consumer preferred brand A and was from Chennai (C) is $P(X \cap C) = 60/390 = 0.1538$

(c) The probability that a consumer preferred brand A, given that he was from Chennai is

$$P(M \mid X) = \frac{P(M \cap X)}{P(X)} = \frac{50/390}{210/390} = \frac{0.128}{0.538} = 0.238$$

(d) The probability that a consumer belongs to Mumbai, given that he preferred brand A is

$$P(M \mid X) = \frac{P(M \cap X)}{P(X)} = \frac{50/390}{210/390} = \frac{0.128}{0.538} = 0.238$$

Q12. Find the expected value and variance of the following data:

Book sold Per Day (x)	0	1	2	3	4	5	6
P(x)	0.02	0.10	0.21	0.32	0.20	0.09	0.06

Ans. Calculation of expected value and variance

x	p(x)	xp(x)
0	0.02	0
1	0.10	0.10
2	0.21	0.42
3	0.32	0.96
4	0.20	0.80
5	0.09	0.45
6	0.06	0.36
		$E(x) = \mu = \Sigma xp(x) = 3.09$

x	$x-\mu$	$(x-\mu)^2$	p(x)	$(x-\mu)^2 p(x)$
0	–3.09	9.55	0.02	0.191
1	–2.09	4.37	0.10	0.437
2	–1.09	1.19	0.21	0.25
3	–0.09	0.01	0.32	0.003
4	0.91	0.83	0.20	0.166
5	1.91	3.65	0.09	0.328
6	2.91	8.47	0.06	0.508
				$\sigma^2 = \Sigma(x-\mu)^2 p(x) = 1.883$

Hence, the expected value and variance of the following data are 3.09 and 1.883 respectively.

Q13. A subcommittee of 6 members is to be formed out of a group consisting of 7 men and 4 ladies. Calculate the probability that the sub-committee will consist of (a) exactly 2 ladies and (b) atleast 2 ladies.

Ans. (a) Exactly 2 ladies mean 2 ladies and 4 men

2 ladies out of 4 can be in ${}^4C_2$ ways

4 men out of 7 can be in ${}^7C_4$ ways

6 members out of 11 can be in ${}^{11}C_6$ ways

$$\therefore \text{Required probability} = \frac{{}^4C_2 \times {}^7C_4}{{}^{11}C_6} = \frac{6 \times 35}{462} = \frac{210}{462} = 0.455$$

(b) At least 2 ladies

Probability of 2 ladies and 4 men$= \frac{{}^4C_2 \times {}^7C_4}{{}^{11}C_6}$

Probability of 3 ladies and 3 men$= \frac{{}^4C_3 \times {}^7C_3}{{}^{11}C_6} = \frac{4 \times 35}{462} = 0.303$

Probability of 4 ladies and 2 men$= \frac{{}^4C_4 \times {}^7C_2}{{}^{11}C_6} = \frac{1 \times 21}{462} = 0.045$

$\therefore$ Required probability $= 0.455 + 0.303 + 0.045 = 0.803$

Q14. A bag contains 8 red balls and 5 white balls. Two successive draws of 3 balls are made without replacement. Find the probability that the first drawing will give 3 white balls and the second 3 red balls.

Ans. Total balls in a bag = 8+5=13

3 balls can be drawn out of 13 balls in ${}^{13}C_3$ ways and 3 white balls can be drawn out of 5 white balls in ${}^5C_3$ ways.

Hence, the probability of drawing 3 white balls $= P(3W) = \frac{{}^5C_3}{{}^{13}C_3}$

After the first draw, balls left are 10.

Now, 3 balls can be drawn out of 10 balls in ${}^{10}C_3$ ways and 3 red balls can be drawn out of 8 balls in ${}^8C_3$ ways.

Probability of drawing 3 red balls $= \frac{{}^8C_3}{{}^{10}C_3}$

Since, both the events are dependent, the required probability is:

$$P(3W \text{ and } 3R) = \frac{{}^5C_3}{{}^{13}C_3} \times \frac{{}^8C_3}{{}^{10}C_3} = \frac{5}{143} \times \frac{7}{15} = \frac{7}{429}.$$

Q15. A student takes a multiple-choice test composed of 100 questions, each with six possible answers. If, for each question, he rolls a fair die to determine the answer to be marked, what is the probability that he answers 20 questions rightly?

Ans. Obviously, the total number of ways in which he can answer all the 100 questions is $6 \times 6 \times 6 \times ... \times 6 = 6^{100}$. He can choose the 20 questions to be answered correctly in ${}^{100}C_{20}$ ways. For wrong answers, he can answer each of the 80 questions in 5 ways while each of the 20 questions has one corrected answer so that each such question can be answered correctly in only one way. Thus, exactly 20 questions can be answered correctly and hence the remaining 80 are answered wrongly in ${}^{100}C_{20}1^{20}5^{80}$ ways. Therefore, P(20 equations are answered $\text{correctly}) = {}^{100}C_{20}1^{20}5^{80}/6^{100}$ $= {}^{100}C_{20}(1/6)^{20}(5/6)^{80}$.

Q16. How many times should an unbiased coin be tossed in order that the probability of observing at least one head is equal to or greater than 0.9?

Ans. Suppose n is the required number. The probability of no head at all in these n tosses is $(1/2)^n$, so that the probability of at least one head is $1-(1/2)^n$. We need to determine n such that $1-(1/2)^n \geq 0.9$ i.e. $(1/2)^n \leq 0.1$ i.e. $n\log(1/2) \leq \log(1/10)$ i.e. $-n\log 2 \leq -1$ i.e. $n \geq (1/\log 2)3.32$. Thus, we shall take n as 4.

Q17. A blood disease is present in 12% of a population and is not present in the remaining 88%. An imperfect clinical test successfully detects the disease and with probability 0.90. Thus, if a person has the disease in the serious form, the probability is 0.9 that the test will be positive and it is 0.1, if the test is negative. Moreover, among the unaffected persons, the probability that the test will be positive is 0.05.

(a) A person selected at random from the population is given the test and the result is positive. What is the probability that this person has the disease?

(b) What is the probability that the test correctly detects the disease?

Ans. Let E be the event that a person has the disease and F be the event that the blood test is positive. From the given data, we note that

$P(E)=0.12, P(E^c)=0.88, P(F|E)=0.90, P(F^c|E)=0.10, P(F|E^c)=0.05$

(a) We are required to compute $P(E|F)$.

By definition, $P(E|F)=\dfrac{P(E\cap F)}{P(F)}$.

We have, $P(E\cap F)=P(F|E)P(E)=(0.90)(0.12)=0.108$

Also, $P(F)=P(F\cap E)+P(F\cap E^c)=P(F|E)P(E)+P(F|E^c)P(E^c)$

$=(0.90)(0.12)+(0.05)(0.88)=0.108+0.044=0.152$

Hence, the required conditional probability $P(E|F)=0.108/0.152=0.7105$.

(b) Let G be the event that the test correctly detects the disease. Then G will consists of all those who actually have the disease and their blood test is positive and also those who do not have the disease and their blood test is negative.

Then we can write $G=(E\cap F)\cup(E^c\cap F^c)$

so that $P(G)=P(E\cap F)+P(E^c\cap F^c)$

Now

$P(E^c\cap F^c)=P(F^c|E^c)P(E^c)=\{1-P(F|E^c)\}P(E^c)=(0.95)(0.88)=0.836$

Thus, $P(G)=0.108+0.836=0.944$

Q18. A person is known to hit the target in 3 out of 4 shots, whereas another person is known to hit the target in 2 out of 3 shots. Find the probability of the target being hit at all when they both try?

Ans. The probability that the first person hits the target = $\dfrac{3}{4}$

The probability that the second person hits the target = $\dfrac{2}{3}$

The events are not mutually exclusive because both of them may hit the target.

P(A and B) = P(A) · P(B) since A and B are independent events.

The required probability = $\left(\dfrac{3}{4}+\dfrac{2}{3}\right)-\left(\dfrac{3}{4}\times\dfrac{2}{3}\right)$.

Here we have applied the theorem *P*(*A* or *B*) = *P*(*A*) + *P*(*B*) – *P*(*A* and *B*).

Q19. A bag contains 5 white and 3 black balls. Two balls are drawn at random one after the other without replacement. Find the probability that both balls drawn are black.

Ans. Probability of drawing a black ball in the first attempt is $P(A)=\dfrac{3}{5+3}=\dfrac{3}{8}$

Probability of drawing the second black ball given that the first ball drawn is black

$$P(B/A)=\frac{2}{5+2}=\frac{2}{7}$$

The probability that both balls drawn are black is given by $P(A and B)=P(A)\times P(B/A)=\frac{3}{8}\times\frac{2}{7}=\frac{3}{28}$.

Q20. In a post office, three clerks are assigned to process incoming mail. The first clerk, B_1, processes 40%, the second clerk, B_2, processes 35% and the third clerk B_3, processes 25% of the mail. The first clerk has an error rate of 0.04, the second has an error rate of 0.06 and the third has an error rate of 0.03. A mail selected at random from a day's output is found to have an error. The postmaster wishes to know the probability that the mail was processed by the first, second or third clerk, respectively.

Ans. Let 'A' denote the event that a mail containing an error is selected at random and B_1, B_2, and B_3, be the event that the mail was processed by the first, second and third clerk, respectively. We want to compute the conditional probabilities:

$P(B_1/A)$, $P(B_2/A)$, $P(B_3/A)$

From the information given we have,

$P(B_1) = 0.40$, $P(B_2) = 0.35$ and $P(B_3) = 0.25$

We are also given the information that the conditional probabilities observing a record with an error, given that it was processed by one of the three clerk are:

$P(A/B_1) = 0.04$, $P(A/B_2) = 0.06$ and $P(A/B_3) = 0.03$

Use Bayes' formula to obtain the desired probabilities:

$$P(B_1/A)=\frac{P(B_1)P(A/B_1)}{P(B_1)P(A/B_1)+P(B_2)P(A/B_2)+P(B_3)P(A/B_3)}$$

$$P(B_1/A)=\frac{0.40\times0.04}{0.40\times0.04+0.35\times0.06+0.25\times0.03}$$

$$=\frac{0.016}{(0.016+0.0210+0.0075)}=\frac{0.016}{0.0445}=0.36$$

Similarly,

$$P(B_2/A) = \frac{0.021}{0.0445} = 0.47$$

$$P(B_3/A) = \frac{0.0075}{0.0445} = 0.17$$

These probabilities are called posterior probabilities because they were calculated after it was known that the mail was one containing an error.

Q21. Among 1000 applicants for admission to MBA programme in University, 600 were mathematics graduates and 400 were non-mathematics graduates. 30% of mathematics graduates applicants and 5% of non-mathematics graduates obtained admission. If an applicant selected at random is found to have been given admission, what is the probability that s/he is a mathematics graduate?

Ans. Let A = The selected applicant has given admission.

E_1 = The selected applicants is mathematics graduate.

E_2 = The selected applicant is non-mathematics graduate.

Here we apply Bayes Theorem

$$P(E_1) = \frac{600}{1000} = \frac{3}{5}$$

$$P(E_2) = \frac{400}{1000} = \frac{2}{5}$$

$P(A/E_1)$ = Probability that the applicant has given admission, given that he is a mathematics graduate.

$$\frac{30}{100} = \frac{3}{10}$$

$P(A/E_2)$ = Probability that the applicant has given admission, given that he is a non-mathematics graduate.

$$\frac{5}{100} = \frac{1}{20}$$

The applicant obtained admission what is the probability that he is a mathematics graduate = $P(E_1/A)$

By Theorem:

$$P(E_1/A) = \frac{P(E_1) \times P(A/E_1)}{P(E_1) \times P(A/E_1) + P(E_2) \times P(A/E_2)}$$

$$P(E_1/A) = \frac{\frac{3}{5} \times \frac{3}{10}}{\frac{3}{5} \times \frac{3}{10} + \frac{2}{5} \times \frac{1}{20}} = \frac{\frac{9}{50}}{\frac{9}{50} + \frac{1}{50}}$$

$$P(E_1/A) = \frac{9}{10} = 0.9$$

Q22. GPH proposes to form a few committees out of its academic faculty to ensure the progress of its B.Sc. programme. To begin with, it is decided to put mathematics and physics faculty members. If two mathematicians and one physicist are to be nominated, how many committees can be formed if the faculty members of physics and mathematics are 4 and 5, respectively.

Ans. The number of ways of selecting two mathematicians out of five available is $\binom{5}{2} = \frac{5!}{2!\ 3!} = 10$

The number of ways of selecting one physicist out of four is $\binom{4}{1} = \frac{4!}{1!\ 3!} = 4$

Using the multiplication rule with $n_1 = 10$ and $n_2 = 4$, we find that the number of committees that can be formed is $n = n_1 n_2 = 10 \times 4 = 40$

Q23. The probability that a regularly scheduled flight departs on time is $P(D) = 0.83$, the probability that it arrives on time is $P(A) = 0.82$, and the probability that it departs and arrives on time is $P(D \cap A) = 0.78$. Calculate the probability that a plane (i) arrives on time if it departed on time and (ii) departs on time if it arrived on time.

Ans. (i) The probability that the plane arrives on time, given that it departed on time, is $P(A|D) = \frac{P(D \cap A)}{P(D)} = \frac{0.78}{0.83} = 0.94$

(ii) The probability that the plane departs on time, given that it had arrived on time, is $P(D|A) = \frac{P(D \cap A)}{P(A)} = \frac{0.78}{0.82} = 0.95$

Q24. The probability that a person can hit a target is 3/5 and the probability that another person can hit the same target is 2/5. But the first person can fire 8 shots in the time the second person fires 10 shots. They fire together. What is the probability that the second person shoots the target?

Ans. Let E denotes the event of shooting the target, E_1 and E_2 respectively denote the events that the first person and the second person shoot the target. We are given $P\left[E|E_1\right] = \frac{3}{5}$ and $P\left[E|E_2\right] = \frac{2}{5}$.

The ratio of the shots of the first person to those of the second person in the same time is $\frac{8}{10} = \frac{4}{5}$. Thus $P\left[E_1\right] = \frac{4}{5} P\left[E_2\right]$. By Baye's theorem, we get

$$P[E_2|E]=\frac{P[E_2]P[E|E_2]}{P[E_1]P[E|E_1]+P[E_2]P[E|E_2]}=\frac{P[E_2].\frac{2}{5}}{\frac{4}{5}P[E_2].\frac{3}{5}+P[E_2].\frac{2}{5}}$$

$$=\frac{1}{\left(\frac{6}{5}\right)+1}=\frac{5}{11}$$

Q25. Urn-A contains 2 white and 2 black balls. Urn-B contains 3 white and 2 black balls. One ball is transferred from A to B and then one ball is drawn out of B. Find the chance that this ball is white. If this ball turns out to be white, find the probability that the transferred ball was white.

Ans. Let E_1 and E_2 denote the events that the transferred ball from A to B is white and black, respectively.

Let W denotes the event that a white ball is drawn from B. Then

$$P[E_1]=2/4, P[E_2]=2/4, P[W|E_1]=4/6, P[W|E_2]=3/6.$$

$$\therefore \quad P[W]=P[E_1]\,P[W|E_1]+P[E_2]\,P[W|E_2]=\frac{2}{4}.\frac{4}{6}+\frac{2}{4}.\frac{3}{6}=\frac{7}{12}.$$

By Bayes' theorem, we have

$$P[E_1|W]=\frac{P[E_1]P[W|E_1]}{P[E_1]P[W|E_1]+P[E_2]P[W|E_2]}=\frac{(2/4)(4/6)}{(7/12)}=\frac{4}{7}.$$

Q26. Three urns A_1, A_2, A_3 contain respectively 3 red, 4 white, 1 blue; 1 red, 2 white, 3 blue; 4 red, 3 white, 2 blue balls. One urn is chosen at random and a ball is withdrawn. It is found to be red. Find the probability that it came from urn A_2.

Ans. If A_i denotes the ith urn chosen and R denotes the event of withdrawing the red ball, then $P[A_1]=P[A_2]=P[A_3]=1/3$.

Now $P[R|A_1]=3/8, P[R|A_2]=1/6, P[R|A_3]=4/9$.

By Bayes' theorem, we have $P[A_2|R]=\frac{P[A_2]P[R|A_2]}{\sum_{i=1}^{3}P[A_i]\,P[R|A_i]}$

$$=\frac{(1/3)(1/6)}{(1/3)(3/8)+(1/3)(1/6)+(1/3)(4/9)}=\frac{1}{18}\times\frac{216}{71}=\frac{12}{71}.$$

Q27. Suppose that in answering a question in a multiple choice test, an examinee knows the answer with probability p or he guesses with probability 1-p. Assume that the probability of answering a question correctly is unity for an examinee who knows the answer and 1/m for the examinee who guesses, where m is the number of multiple choice alternatives. Show that the probability that an examinee knows the answer to a problem, given that he has correctly answered it, is $\frac{mp}{1+(m-1)p}$.

Ans. Let E_1 denotes the event when the examinee knows the answer, E_2: he guesses the answer and E_3 : he answers correctly. Then

$$P[E_1]=p, P[E_2]=1-p, P[A|E_1]=1 \text{ and } P[A|E_2]=\frac{1}{m}.$$

By Bayes' theorem, the probability that an examinee knows the answer to problem is given by $P[E_1|A]=\frac{P[E_1]P[A|E_1]}{P[E_1]P[A|E_1]+P[E_2]P[A|E_2]}$

$$=\frac{p\,.\,1}{p\,.\,1+(1-p).\frac{1}{m}}=\frac{mp}{mp+1-p}=\frac{mp}{1+(m-1)p}.$$

Q28. A die is thrown as long as necessary for a 6 to turn up. Given that 6 does not turn up at the first throw, what is the probability that more than four throws will be necessary?

Ans. Let A_i be the event that 6 does not turn up at the ith throw, where $i=1,2,3,4.$ Then $P[A_i]=\frac{5}{6}.$

Notice that 'more than four throws are needed, given A_1' means that in the first four throws 6 does not turn up.

The required probability is $P[A_1A_2A_3A_4|A_1]$.

Using multiplication rule, we have

$$P[A_1A_2A_3A_4|A_1]=\frac{P[A_1]P[A_2|A_1]P[A_3|A_1A_2]P[A_4|A_1A_2A_3]}{P[A_1]}$$

$$=P[A_2|A_1]P[A_3|A_1A_2]P[A_4|A_1A_2A_3]=\frac{5}{6}\times\frac{5}{6}\times\frac{5}{6}=\frac{125}{216}.$$

Q29. Consider the experiment of tossing two fair regular tetrahedral (a polyhedron with four faces numbered 1 to 4) and noting the numbers on the downturned faces.

Given three proper events which are pair wise independent but not mutually independent.

Ans. The sample space Ω of the given experiment consists of $4 \times 4 = 16$ outcomes: $\Omega = \left\{ \begin{matrix} (1,1),(1,2),(1,3),(1,4),(2,1),(2,2),(2,3),(2,4), \\ (3,1),(3,2),(3,3),(3,4),(4,1),(4,2),(4,3),(4,4) \end{matrix} \right\}$

We define three events A, B, C as follow:

A: odd downturned face on the first tetrahedron

B: odd downturned face on the second tetrahedron

C: sum of points on two tetrahedral is odd.

Then, $A = \{(1,1),(3,1),(1,2),(3,2),(1,3),(3,3),(1,4),(3,4)\}$

$$\therefore P[A] = \frac{8}{16} = \frac{1}{2},$$

$$B = \{(1,1),(2,1),(3,1),(4,1),(1,3),(2,3),(3,3),(4,3)\}$$

$$\therefore P[B] = \frac{8}{16} = \frac{1}{2},$$

$$C = \{(1,2),(1,4),(2,1),(2,3),(3,2),(3,4),(4,1),(4,3)\}$$

$$\therefore P[C] = \frac{8}{16} = \frac{1}{2}.$$

We have $A \cap B \cap C = \phi$, for if two faces read odd, then their sum cannot be odd.

$$\therefore P[A \cap B \cap C] = 0 \neq P[A]\,P[B]\,P[C] = \frac{1}{8}.$$

Hence A, B, C are not independent.

Now $A \cap B = \{(1,1),(3,1),(1,3),(3,3)\}$

$$\Rightarrow \quad P[A \cap B] = \frac{4}{16} = \frac{1}{4} = P[A]\,P[B],$$

$$B \cap C = \{(2,1),(4,3),(4,1),(2,3)\}$$

$$\Rightarrow \quad P[B \cap C] = \frac{1}{4} = P[B]\,P[C],$$

$$A \cap C = \{(1,2),(3,2),(3,4),(1,4)\}$$

$$\Rightarrow \quad P[A \cap C] = \frac{1}{4} = P[A]\,P[C]$$

Hence, A, B, C are pair wise independent, but not mutually independent.

Q30. A consignment of 15 record players contains 4 defectives. The record players are selected at random, one by one and examined. The ones examined are not put back. What is the probability that the ninth one examined is the last defective?

Ans. Let A be the event of getting exactly 3 defectives in examination of 8 record players and let B be the event that the ninth piece examined is a defective one.

Since it is a problem of sampling without replacement and there are 4 defectives out of 15 record players, we have

$$P(A) = \frac{4C_3 \times 11C_5}{15C_8}$$

Since there is only one defective piece left among the remaining 15 - 8 = 7 record players.

$P(B/A)$ = probability that the ninth examined record player is defective $= \dfrac{1}{7}$

$\therefore$ The required probability $= P(B/A)P(A) = \dfrac{1}{7} \times \dfrac{4C_3 \times 11C_5}{15C_8} = \dfrac{8}{195}$

Q31. Suppose four coins are tossed. Let X designate the number of heads which appear. Calculate $E(X)$. June-2011, Q.No.-3]

Ans. We have $P(X=0) = 1/16, P(X=1) = 1/4, P(X=2) = 3/8$

$P(X=3) = 1/4, P(X=4) = 1/16$

Therefore, $E(X) = 0 \times \left(\dfrac{1}{16}\right) + 1 \times \left(\dfrac{1}{4}\right) + 2 \times \left(\dfrac{3}{8}\right) + 3 \times \left(\dfrac{1}{4}\right) + 4 \times \left(\dfrac{1}{16}\right)$

$$= \frac{1}{4} + \frac{3}{4} + \frac{3}{4} + \frac{1}{4} = 2$$

Q32. Determine the value of the constant K such that the function $f(x)$ defined by

$$f(x) = Kx(1-x), \quad 0 < x < 1$$
$$= 0 \quad , \quad \text{elsewhere.}$$

is a probability density function of some distribution. Also find c.d.f. F(x) and hence evaluate P[x>0.5].

Ans. Since f (x) is p.d.f., we have

$$\int_{-\infty}^{\infty} f(x)dx = 1 \text{ or } K\int_{0}^{1}(x-x^2)dx = 1 \text{ or } K\left(\frac{1}{2}-\frac{1}{3}\right)=1.$$

$$\therefore K = 6$$

The c.d.f. is given by

$$F(x) = \int_{-\infty}^{x} f(x)dx = \int_{-\infty}^{0} f(x)dx + \int_{0}^{x} f(x)dx = 0 + \int_{0}^{x} f(x)dx$$

$$= 6\int_{0}^{x}\left(x-x^2\right)dx = 3x^2 - 2x^3, 0 < x < 1.$$

$$\text{Again } F(x) = \int_{-\infty}^{0} f(x)dx + \int_{0}^{1} f(x)dx + \int_{1}^{x} f(x)dx, \text{ for } x \geq 1$$

$$= 0 + 6\int_{0}^{1}\left(x-x^2\right)dx + 0 = 6\left(\frac{1}{2}-\frac{1}{3}\right) = 1.$$

$$\text{Hence, } F(x) = \begin{cases} 0 & , \text{for } x \leq 0 \\ 3x^2 - 2x^3, & \text{for } 0 < x < 1 \\ 1 & , \text{for } x \geq 1. \end{cases}$$

$$\text{Now, } P\left[X \leq \frac{1}{2}\right] = F\left(\frac{1}{2}\right) = 3\left(\frac{1}{2}\right)^2 - 2\left(\frac{1}{2}\right)^3 = \frac{1}{2}.$$

$$\text{Hence, } P\left[X > \frac{1}{2}\right] = 1 - P\left[X \leq \frac{1}{2}\right] = 1 - \frac{1}{2} = \frac{1}{2}.$$

Q33. A box contains 4 bad and 6 good tubes. Two tubes are drawn from the box at a time. One of them is tested and found to be good. What is the probability that the other one is also good?

[June-2011, Q.No.-3]

Ans. Let A = One of the tubes drawn is good

and B = the other tube is good.

Here, $P(A \cap B) = P$ (both tubes drawn are good) $= \frac{6\,C_2}{10\,C_2} = \frac{1}{3}$

Knowing that one tube is good, the conditional probability that the other tube is also good are given by $P(B|A) = \frac{P(A \cap B)}{P(A)} = \frac{1/3}{6/10} = \frac{5}{9}$.

Q34. If at least one child in a family with two children is a girl, what is the probability that both children are girls?

[Dec-2011, Q.No.-3]

Ans. Let A = at least one child is girl and B = both children are girls

Now $S = \{GG, GB, BG, BB\} \Rightarrow n(S) = 4$

$\Rightarrow \quad A = \{GG, GB, BG\}$ and $B = \{GG\}$

$\Rightarrow \quad n(A) = 3$ and $n(B) = 1$

Now, probability of both children are girls and given that at least one child is girl, is $P(B|A) = \frac{n(A \cap B)}{n(A)} = \frac{1}{3}$.

The Book you can believe most – GPH Book

Chapter 6 Probability Distributions

An Overview

In probability and statistics, a probability distribution assigns a probability to each measurable subset of the possible outcomes of a random experiment, survey, or procedure of statistical inference. Examples are found in experiments whose sample space is non-numerical, where the distribution would be a categorical distribution; experiments whose sample space is encoded by discrete random variables, where the distribution can be specified by a probability mass function; and experiments with sample spaces encoded by continuous random variables, where the distribution can be specified by a probability density function. More complex experiments, such as those involving stochastic processes defined in continuous time, may demand the use of more general probability measures.

The Binomial Distribution: The Binomial distribution is also known as Bernoulli distribution and is associated with the name of Jacob Bernoulli. A Bernoulli process is a random process in which:

- The process is performed under the same conditions for a fixed and finite number of trials, say, n.
- Each trial is independent of other trials, i.e. the probability of an outcome for any particular trial is not influenced by the outcomes of other trials.
- Each trial has two mutually exclusive possible outcomes, such as "success" or "failure", "good" or "defective", "yes" or "no", "hit" or "miss", and so on. The outcomes are usually called success and failure for convenience.
- The probability of success, p, remains constant from trial to trial (so is the probability of failure q, where $q = 1 - p$).

$$P(r) = {}^nC_r p^r q^{n-r}$$

where, P (r) = Probability of r successes in n trials; p = Probability of success; q = Probability of failure $= 1 - p; r =$ No. of success desired; and n = No. of trials undertaken.

The determining equation for ${}^nC_r$ can easily be written as:

$$ {}^nC_r = \frac{n!}{r!(n-r)!}$$

n! can be simplified as follows:

$n! = n(n-1)! = n(n-1)(n-2)! = n(n-1)(n-2)(n-3)!$ and so on.

Hence, the following form of the equations, for carrying out computations of the binomial probability is perhaps more convenient.

$$P(r) = \frac{n!}{r!(n-r)!} p^r q^{n-r}$$

The symbol '!' means 'factorial', which is computed as follows: 5! means $5 \times 4 \times 3 \times 2 \times 1 = 120.$ Mathematicians define 0! as 1.

If n is large in number, say, ${}^{50}C_3$, then we can write (with the help of the above explanation)

$$ {}^{50}C_3 = \frac{50!}{3!(50-3)!} = \frac{(50)(49)(48)(47)!}{3!(47)!} = \frac{50 \times 49 \times 48}{3 \times 2 \times 1} = 19600$$

Similarly, $^{75}C_5 = \frac{75!}{5!(75-5)!} = \frac{(75)(74)(73)(72)(71)(70)!}{5!(70)!}$

$= \frac{75 \times 74 \times 73 \times 72 \times 71}{5 \times 4 \times 3 \times 2 \times 1} = 17259390$

Characteristics of a Binomial Distribution

- The form of the distribution depends upon the parameters 'p' and 'n'.
- The probability that there are 'r' successes in 'n', no. of trials is given by $P(r) = {}^nC_r p^r q^{n-r} = \frac{n!}{r!(n-n)!} p^r q^{n-r}$
- It is mainly applied when the population being sampled is infinite.
- It can also be applied to a finite population, if it is not very small or the units sampled are replaced before the next trial is attempted. The point worth noting is 'p' should remain unchanged.

Measures of Central Tendency and Dispersion for Binomial distribution

The mean of a random variable, say X, which follows binomial distribution is $\mu = n.p$ and variance $\sigma^2 = n.p(1-p) = n.p.q.$

Poisson Distribution: A Poisson distribution is the probability distribution that results from a Poisson experiment. It deals with counting the number of occurrences of a particular event in a specific time interval or region of space. It is used in practice where there are infrequently occurring events with respect to time, volume (similar units), area, etc.

The binomial distribution is determined by two parameters 'p' and 'n'. In a number of cases 'p' (the probability of success) may happen to be very small (even less than 0.01) and the 'n' (the no. of trials) is large enough (like more than 50), so that their product "np" remains a constant, the situation is termed as "Poisson Distribution", and it gives an approximation for binomial probability distribution formula, i.e.

$P(r) = {}^nC_r p^r q^{n-r}$

The Poisson distribution process corresponds to a Bernoulli process with a very large number of trials (n) and a very low probability of success. This would comparatively be simpler in dealing with and is given by the Poisson distribution formula as follows:

$$p(r) = \frac{m^r e^{-m}}{r!}$$

where, p (r) = Probability of successes desired

r = 0, 1, 2, 3, 4, ... ∞ (any positive integer)

e = 2.7183 (the base of natural logarithms)

m = The mean of the Poisson Distribution, i.e. np or the average number of occurrences of an event.

Characteristics of the Poisson distribution

- It is also a discrete probability distribution and it is the limiting form of the binomial distribution.
- The range of the random variable is $0 \le r \le \infty$.
- It consists of a single parameter "m" only. So, the entire distribution can be obtained by knowing this value only.
- It is a positively skewed distribution. The skewness, therefore, decreases when "m" increases.

Measures of Central Tendency and Dispersion for Poisson distribution

In Poisson distribution, the mean (m) and the variance (σ^2) represent the same value, i.e. Mean = variance = np = m or S.D. $(\sigma) = \sqrt{\text{Variance}} = \sqrt{np}$.

Normal Distribution: The normal distribution, also called the normal probability distribution happens to be a most useful theoretical distribution for continuous variables. It is an approximation to binomial distribution. Whether or not p is equal to q, the binomial distribution tends to the form of the continuous curve when n becomes large at least for the material part of the range. In fact, that corresponding between the binomial and the normal curve is surprisingly close even for low values of n provided p and q are fairly near equality. The limiting frequency curve, obtained as n, becomes large and is called the normal frequency curve or simply the normal curve.

The normal curve is represented in several forms. The following is the basic form relating to the curve with mean μ and standard deviation σ.

The Normal Distribution

$$P(X) = \frac{1}{\sigma\sqrt{2\pi}} e^{\frac{-(x-\mu)}{2\sigma^2}}$$

x = Values of the continuous random variable

μ = Mean of the normal random variable

e = Mathematical constant approximated by 2.7183

π = Mathematical constant approximated by 3.1416

$\left(\sqrt{2\pi} = 2.5066\right)$

When we say that curve has unit area we mean total frequency N is equated to 1. To obtain ordinates for a particular distribution, the ordinates given by the above formula multiply by N. The equation to a normal curve corresponding to a particular distribution is given by:

$$y = \frac{N}{\sigma\sqrt{2\pi}} e^{-x^2/2\sigma^2}$$

The quantity $\frac{N}{\sigma\sqrt{2\pi}}$ in the above formula is equal to the maximum ordinate (y_0) of the normal curve corresponding to distribution of stated total frequency N and stated standard deviation σ.

A random variable with any mean and standard deviation can be transformed to a standardised normal variable by subtracting the mean and dividing by the standard deviation. For a normal distribution with mean and standard deviation, the standardised variable z is obtained as:

$$z = \left(\frac{X-\mu}{\sigma}\right)$$

Properties of Normal Distribution

(a) Normal distribution is a continuous probability distribution.

(b) Normal distribution has two parameters, namely, μ and σ.

(c) Mean and standard deviation of a normal distribution is given by μ and σ respectively.

(d) For a normal distribution, the mean, median and mode are the same, as a corollary to the above property; we can say that the first and third quartiles are equidistant from the mean of the normal distribution. Approximately,

$Q_1 = \mu - 0.67 \times \sigma$ and $Q_3 = \mu + 0.67 \times \sigma$

(e) All odd order central moments of the normal distribution are 0.

In general, $\mu_{2r} = 1.3.5.....(2r-1)\sigma^{2r}$ for r = 1,2,3,.........

$\mu_{2r+1} = 0$ for r = 1,2,3,......

(f) The normal distribution is symmetrical as well as mesokurtic and skewness = 0 and kurtosis = 0.

(g) Normal distribution is symmetrical about its mean. The two tails of the distribution are extended to infinity on both sides of the mean. The tails of the distribution never meet the horizontal axis. The maximum ordinate of the p.d.f. is at the mean, which is given by $1/\sigma\sqrt{2\pi}$.

(h) The point of inflection of the normal curve are at $x=\mu+\sigma$ and $x=\mu-\sigma$ respectively. At these two points, normal curve changes its curvature.

(i) If a random variable X follows normal distribution with mean and variance μ and σ respectively, then the random variable $Z=(X-\mu)/\sigma$ is called standard normal variable. It has a density function

$$f(X)=\frac{1}{\sqrt{2\pi}}e^{\frac{-z^2}{2}}dz.................... -\infty<z<\infty$$

The continuous probability distribution defined above is known as standard normal distribution. In fact, this is a special kind of probability distribution with mean zero and standard deviation 1. The approximate area under the standard normal curve is shown in the following figure.

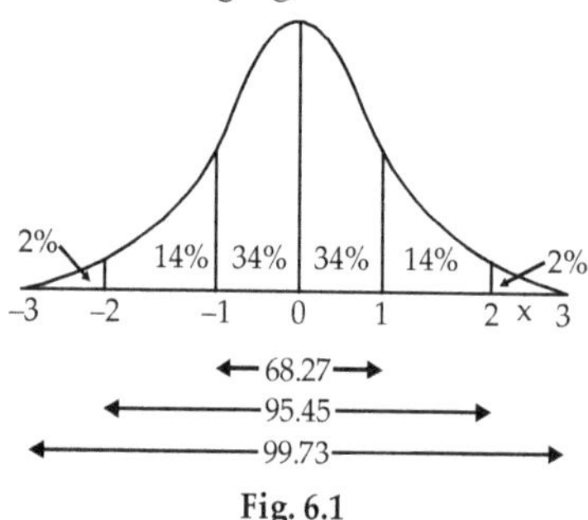

Fig. 6.1

(j) If X and Y are two normal variables with mean μ_1 and μ_2 and standard deviation σ_1 and σ_2, then $(X+Y)$ is also a normal variable with mean $(\mu_1+\mu_2)$ and variance $(\sigma_1{}^2+\sigma_2{}^2)$.

(k) The moment generating function of a normal curve is given by $M_X(t)=e^{\mu t+1/2.\sigma^2 t^2}$

$$M_X(t)=\int_{-\infty}^{\infty}e^{tx}\times\frac{1}{\sigma\sqrt{2\pi}}e^{-1/2\left(\frac{x-\mu}{\sigma}\right)^2}dx$$

The above expression could be written, after some algebraic manipulation, as the follows:

$$M_X(t) = e^{\mu t + \frac{1}{2}(t\sigma)^2} \times \frac{1}{\sigma\sqrt{2\pi}} \int_{-\infty}^{\infty} e^{-1/2\left[\frac{x-(\mu+t\sigma^2)}{\sigma}\right]} dx = e^{\mu t + \frac{1}{2}(t\sigma)^2}$$

$$\left[\text{since } 1/\sigma\sqrt{2\pi} \int_{-\infty}^{\infty} e^{-1/2[\{x-(\mu+t\sigma^2)/\sigma\}]} dx = 1\right]$$

Differentiating $M_x(t)$ with respect to t twice, we can get

$$M'_X(t) = \left(\mu + \sigma^2 t\right) M_X(t)$$

$$M''_X(t) = \left[\left(\mu + \sigma^2 t\right)^2 + \sigma^2\right] M_X(t)$$

Substituting t =0 in the above two equations, we get

$$M'_X(0) = \mu$$

$$M''_X(0) = \mu^2 + \sigma^2 .$$

Therefore, $E(X) = \mu$ and Variance $(X) = \sigma^2$.

The Maxwell-Boltzmann Distribution: This distribution plays a very important role in kinetic theory of gases. The distribution function for the speeds of gaseous molecules is given by

$$f(v)dv = 4\pi\left(\frac{m}{2\pi k_B T}\right)^{3/2} v^2 \exp\left(-\frac{m v^2}{2k_B T}\right) dv, \text{ for } 0 \le v \le \infty$$

where v denotes the speed of a gas molecule, m its mass, T is the absolute temperature and k_B is the Boltzmann constant $\left(1.38 \times 10^{-23} \text{J K}^{-1}\right)$. It is plotted in Fig. 6.2

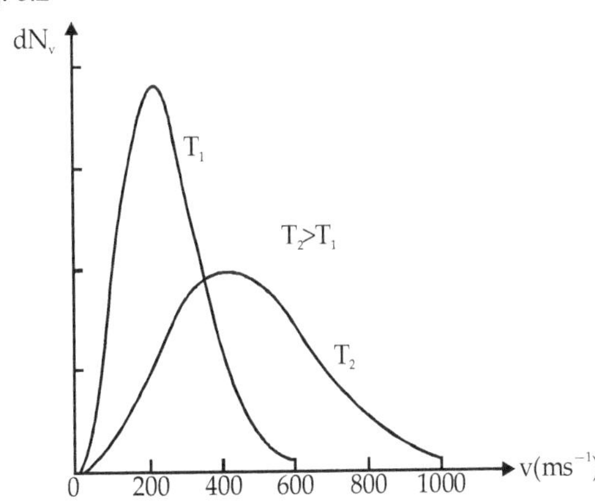

Fig. 6.2: The Maxwell-Boltzmann distribution

The Cauchy Distribution: In this case, the distribution function is $f(x) = \frac{1}{\pi(1+x^2)} \quad -\infty < x < \infty$

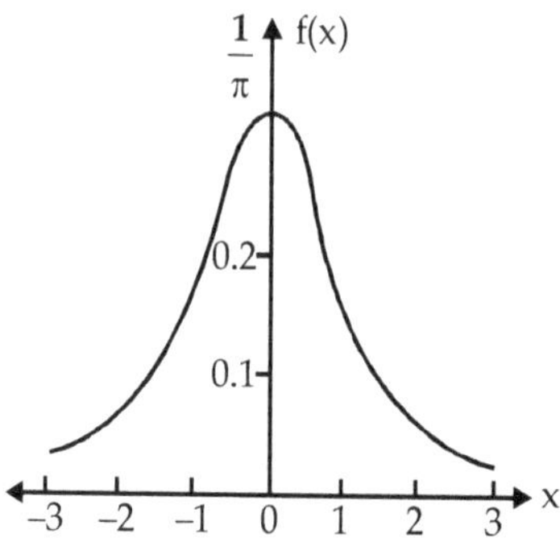

Fig. 6.3: A plot of Cauchy distribution

This distribution, shown in fig. 6.3, occurs in the configuration of atomic spectral lines in classical dispersion theory and NMR studies.

Solved Practical Problems

Q1. Let X be a random variable with p.d.f:

$$f_x(x) = \lambda e^{-\lambda x} I_{(0,\infty)}(x).$$

Find the moment generating function, mean and variance of X.

Ans. The m.g.f. of X is given by $M(t) = E\left[e^{tX}\right] = \int_{-\infty}^{\infty} e^{tx} f_x(x)dx$

$$= \int_0^{\infty} e^{tx} \lambda e^{-\lambda x} dx = \lambda \int_0^{\infty} e^{-(\lambda - t)x} dx, \text{where } \lambda > t$$

$$= -\left(\frac{\lambda}{\lambda - t}\right) \left| e^{-(\lambda - t)x} \right|_0^{\infty}, \text{ for } \lambda > t$$

$$= -\left(\frac{\lambda}{\lambda - t}\right)(0 - 1) = \frac{\lambda}{\lambda - t}; \text{for } \lambda > t.$$

$$\therefore M(t) = \frac{\lambda}{\lambda - t}, \text{for } \lambda > t.$$

Now, $M'(t)=\frac{\lambda}{(\lambda-t)^2}, M''(t)=\frac{2\lambda}{(\lambda-t)^3}$.

$\therefore \mu_1'=M'(t)\Big|_{t=0}=\frac{\lambda}{\lambda^2}=\frac{1}{\lambda},\ \mu_2'=M''(t)\Big|_{t=0}=\frac{2\lambda}{\lambda^3}=\frac{2}{\lambda^2}$.

Hence, Mean of X

$=E[X]=\mu_1'=\frac{1}{\lambda}$ and var $[X]=\mu_2'-(\mu_1')^2=\frac{2}{\lambda^2}-\frac{1}{\lambda^2}=\frac{1}{\lambda^2}$.

Q2. The probability density function of a continuous bivariate distribution is given by

$f(x,y)=x+y, \text{where } 0\le x\le 1, 0\le y\le 1$

= 0, otherwise.

Find the marginal distributions and the correlation coefficient of x and y.

Ans. The marginal distribution of X is $f_x(x)=\int_{-\infty}^{\infty} f(x,y)dy=\int_0^1 (x+y)dy$

$=\left|xy+\frac{1}{2}y^2\right|_0^1=x+\frac{1}{2}$.

$\therefore f_x(x)=x+\frac{1}{2}, 0\le x\le 1$

= 0, otherwise

Similarly, $f_Y(y)=y+\frac{1}{2}, 0\le y\le 1$

= 0, otherwise.

Now, $E[X]=\int_0^1 xf_x(x)dx=\int_0^1 x\left(x+\frac{1}{2}\right)dx=\left|x^3+\frac{x^2}{4}\right|_0^1=\frac{1}{3}+\frac{1}{4}=\frac{7}{12}$.

By symmetry, $E[Y]=E[X]=\frac{7}{12}$.

Now, $E[XY]=\int_0^1\int_0^1 xy(x+y)dxdy=\int_0^1\left(x^2.\frac{1}{2}+x.\frac{1}{3}\right)dx=\frac{1}{6}+\frac{1}{6}=\frac{1}{3}$.

$\therefore \text{cov}(X,Y)=E[XY]-E[X]E[Y]=\frac{1}{3}-\frac{7}{12}\times\frac{7}{12}=-\frac{1}{144}$.

Now, $E\left[X^2\right]=\int_0^1 x^2f_x(x)dx=\int_0^1 x^2\left(x+\frac{1}{2}\right)dx=\frac{1}{4}+\frac{1}{6}=\frac{5}{12}$.

$$\therefore \text{var}[X] = E\left[X^2\right] - \{E[X]\}^2 = \frac{5}{12} - \left(\frac{7}{12}\right)^2 = \frac{11}{144}.$$

By symmetry, var [Y] = $\frac{11}{144}$.

The correlation coefficient of X and Y is given by

$$\rho(X,Y) = \frac{\text{cov}(X,Y)}{\sqrt{\text{var}[X]\text{var}[Y]}} = \frac{-1/144}{\sqrt{11/144 \times 11/144}} = -\frac{1}{11}.$$

Q3. Let the random variable X assume the value r with the probability law: $P(X = r) = q^{r-1}p;\ r = 1,2,3...$

Find the m.g.f. and hence mean and the variance.

Ans. Since, $M_x(t) = E\left(e^{tx}\right)$

$$\text{or } M_x(t) = \sum_{r=1}^{\infty} e^{tr}.q^{r-1}p = \frac{p}{q}\sum_{r=1}^{\infty}\left(qe^t\right)^r = \frac{p}{q}\sum_{r=1}^{\infty}\left(qe^t\right)\left(qe^t\right)^{r-1}$$

$$= \frac{p}{q}qe^t\sum_{r=1}^{\infty}\left(qe^t\right)^{r-1} = pe^t\left[1 + qe^t + \left(qe^t\right)^2 + ...\right]$$

$$\therefore M_x(t) = pe^t\left(1 - qe^t\right)^{-1} = \left(\frac{pe^t}{1 - qe^t}\right).$$

Now $\frac{d}{dt}[M_X(t)] = \frac{pe^t}{\left(1 - qe^t\right)^2}, \frac{d^2}{dt^2}[M_X(t)] = pe^t.\frac{\left(1 + qe^t\right)}{\left(1 - qe^t\right)^3}.$

Putting t = 0 in the above relations, we get

$$\mu_1' = \frac{p}{(1-q)^2} = \frac{1}{p}, \quad (\because p + q = 1)$$

$$\mu_2' = \frac{p(1+q)}{(1-q)^3} = \frac{1+q}{p^2}.$$

Hence, mean = $\mu_1' = 1/p$ and variance $= \mu_2 = \mu_2' - \mu_1'^2 = \frac{1+q}{p^2} - \frac{1}{p^2} = \frac{q}{p^2}.$

Q4. A minimum height is to be prescribed for eligibility to government services such that 60% of the young men will have a fair chance of coming up to that standard. The heights of the young men are normally distributed with mean of 160 cm and standard deviation of 5cm. Determine the minimum height to be prescribed.

Ans. Here if x is the random variable representing the height of students.

μ =160 cm.

σ = 5cm.

We have to include 60% of young men to be eligible. If x_1 is the minimum requirement of heights then from:

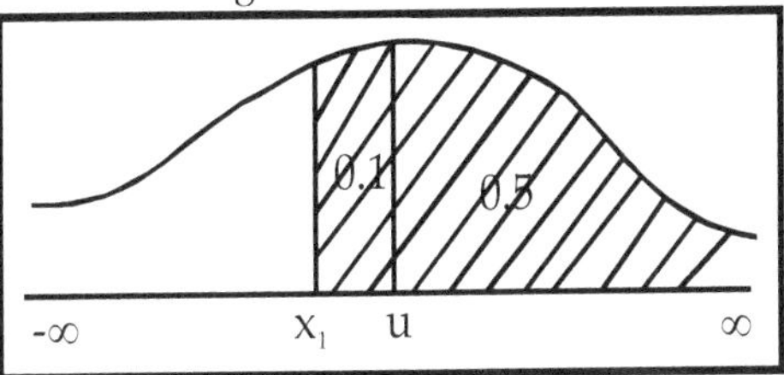

Fig. 6.4

$$P(x_1 < \infty) = 0.6$$

$$P(x,< \mu) = 0.1$$

$$\therefore \; P\left(\frac{x_1 - \mu}{\sigma} < \frac{\mu - \mu}{\sigma}\right) = 0.1$$

$$\therefore P\left(\frac{x - 160}{5} < 0\right) = 0.1$$

From table if $Z_1 = \dfrac{x_1 - 160}{5}$ then $Z_1 = -0.225$.

i.e. $-0.255 = \dfrac{x_1 - 160}{5}$

$\therefore \; x_1 = 160 - 5(0.255) = 158.725$ inches

$\therefore$ The minimum height required is 158.725 inches.

Q5. The number of calories in a salad on the lunch menu is normally distributed with mean 200 and standard deviation 5. Find the probability that the salad you select will contain:

(a) More than 208 calories

(b) Between 190 and 200 calories.

Ans. Let x denote the number of calories in a salad, then $\mu = 200, \sigma = 5$.

(a) **Probability** that salad we select will contain more than 208 calories

$$= P(x > 208) = P\left(\frac{X - \mu}{\sigma} > \frac{208 - \mu}{\sigma}\right)$$

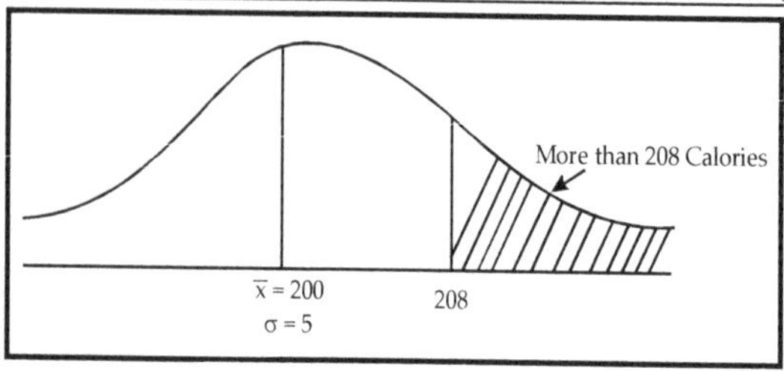

Fig. 6.5

$$= P\left(Z > \frac{208-200}{5}\right) \qquad \left[\because Z = \frac{X-\mu}{\sigma}\right]$$

$$= P\left(Z > \frac{8}{5}\right) = P(Z > 1.6) = 1 - P(Z \le 1.6) = 1 - 0.9452 = 0.0548$$

(b) Probability that the salad we select will contain between 190 and 200 calories $= P(190 < x < 200)$

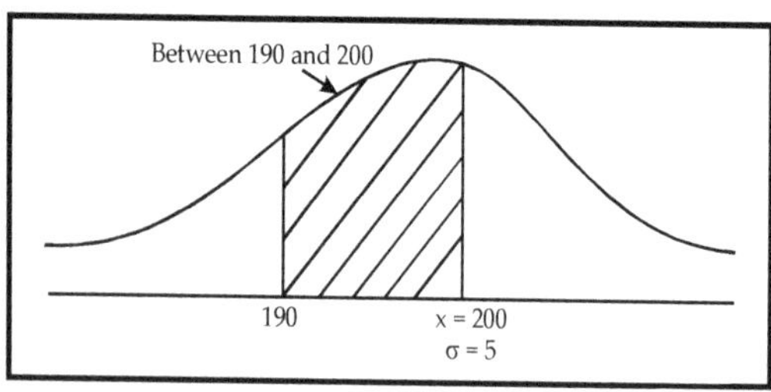

Fig. 6.6

$$= P\left(\frac{190-\mu}{\sigma} < \frac{x-\mu}{\sigma} < \frac{200-\mu}{\sigma}\right) = P\left(\frac{190-200}{5} < z < \frac{200-200}{5}\right)$$

$$= P(-2 < z < 0)$$

$$= P(z \le 0) - P(z \ge -2) = 0.5 - 0.0228 = 0.4772$$

Q6. The mean of a binomial distribution is 40 and standard deviation 6. Calculate n, p and q.

Ans. The Mean of the binomial distribution is given by np and standard deviation by $\sqrt{npq}$.

Since $\sqrt{npq} = 6$; npq=36 and np=40

Therefore, $40q=36 \Rightarrow q=\frac{36}{40}=0.9 \Rightarrow p = 1-q = 1-0.9 = 0.1$

Since, $p = 0.1$, $q = 0.9$ and $npq = 36$

Therefore, $n = \frac{36}{0.1 \times 0.9} = \frac{36}{0.09} = 400$

Hence, for the given question, n = 400, p = 0.1 and q = 0.9.

Q7. The number of defects per unit in a sample of 330 units of manufactured product was found as follows:

No. of defects	No. of units
0	214
1	92
2	20
3	3
4	1

Fit a Poisson distribution to the above given data.

Ans. The mean of the given frequency distribution is:

$$m = \frac{(0\times 214)+(1\times 92)+(2\times 20)+(3\times 3)+(4\times 1)}{214+92+20+3+1} = \frac{145}{330} = 0.439$$

We can write, $P(r) = \frac{0.439^r \times e^{-0.439}}{r!}$ Substituting r = 0, 1, 2, 3, and 4, we get the probabilities for various values of r, as shown below:

$$P(r) = \frac{m^r e^{-m}}{r!} = \frac{0.439^0 \times 2.7183^{-0.439}}{0!} \text{ for } r = 0$$

Thus, the expected frequencies as per Poisson distribution are:

$$= \frac{1(0.6447)}{1} = 0.6447$$

$$N(P_0) = (P_0)\times N = 0.6447 \times 330 = 212.75$$

$$N(P_1) = (P_0)\times m/1 = 212.75 \times 0.439/1 = 93.39$$

$$N(P_2) = (P_1)\times m/2 = 93.39 \times 0.439/2 = 20.49$$

$$N(P_3) = (P_2)\times m/3 = 20.49 \times 0.439/3 = 3.0$$

$$N(P_4) = (P_3)\times m/4 = 3 \times 0.439/4 = 0.33$$

Table 6.1

No. of defects (x)	0	1	2	3	4
Expected frequencies (No. of units) (f)	212.75	93.39	20.49	3.0	0.33

Q8. 2% of the electronic toys produced in a certain manufacturing process turnout to be defective. What is the probability that a

shipment of 200 toys will contain exactly 5 defectives? Also find the mean and standard deviation.

Ans. Here, n = 200;

$$\text{Probability of a defective toy } (P) = \frac{2}{100} = 0.02$$

Since, n is large and p is small, the Poisson distribution is applicable. Apply the formula:

$$P(r) = \frac{m^r e^{-m}}{r!}$$

The probability of 5 defective pieces in 200 toys is given by:

$$P(5) = \frac{m^5 e^{-m}}{5!}, \text{ where } m = np = 200 \times 0.02 = 4;\ e = 2.7183$$

$$\therefore\ P(5) = \frac{(4)^5\,(2.7183)^{-4}}{5 \times 4 \times 3 \times 2 \times 1} = \frac{(1024)\frac{1}{(2.7183)^4}}{120} = \frac{(1024)\,0.0183}{120} = 0.156$$

$$\text{Mean} = np = 200 \times 0.02 = 4;\ \sigma = \sqrt{np} = \sqrt{4} = 2$$

Q9. Find the probability of exactly 4 defective tools in a sample of 30 tools chosen at random by a certain tool producing firm by using (i) Binomial distribution and (ii) Poisson distribution. The probability of defects in each tool is given to be 0.02.

Ans. (i) When Binomial distribution is used, the probability of 4 defectives in 30 tools is given by:

$$P(4) = \left({}^{30}C_4\right)(0.02)^4(0.98)^{26} = 27405 \times 0.00000016 \times 0.59 = 0.00259$$

(ii) When Poisson distribution is used, the probability of 4 defectives in 30 tools is given by:

$$P(4) = \frac{m^4 e^{-m}}{4!}, \text{ where, } m = np = 30\,(0.02) = 0.6; e = 2.7183 (\text{constant})$$

$$\therefore P(4) = \frac{(0.6)^4\,(2.7183)^{-0.6}}{4 \times 3 \times 2 \times 1} = \frac{0.13 \times 0.5488}{24} = 0.00297.$$

Q10. (a) 15,000 students appeared for an examination. The mean marks were 49 and the standard deviation of marks was 6. Assuming the marks to be normally distributed, what proportion of students scored more than 55 marks?

Ans. $Z = \frac{X - \mu}{\sigma}$

$X = 55;\ \mu = 49;\ \sigma = 6$

$$\therefore Z = \frac{55-49}{6} = 1$$

For Z = 1, the area is 0.3413

∴The proportion of students scoring more than 55 marks is (0.5)-(0.3413) = 0.1587 or 15.87%.

(b) If in the same examination, Grade 'A' is to be given to students scoring more than 70 marks, what proportion of students will receive grade 'A'?

Ans. $Z = \frac{X-\mu}{\sigma}$

$X = 70;\ \mu = 49;\ \sigma = 6$

$$\therefore Z = \frac{70-49}{6} = 3.5$$

For Z = 3.5, the area is 0.4998

Therefore, 0.02% (0.5 – 0.4998 = 0.0002 × 100) would score more than 70 marks. Since, there are 15,000 candidates, 3 candidates (15,000 × 0.02% = 3) will receive Grade 'A'.

Q11. In a training programme (self-administered) to develop marketing skills of marketing personnel of a company, the participants indicate that the mean time on the programme is 500 hours and that this normally distributed random variable has a standard deviation of 100 hours. Find out the probability that a participant selected at random will take:

(i) fewer than 570 hours to complete the programme, and

Ans. To get the Z value for the probability that a candidate selected at random will take fewer than 570 hours, we have:

$$Z = \frac{x-\mu}{\sigma} = \frac{570-500}{100} = \frac{70}{100} = 0.7$$

We find a probability of 0.2580 (this probability will lay between the mean, 500 hours and 570 hours). We must add 0.5 to this probability (0.2580) that the random variable will be between the left-hand tail and the mean.

Therefore, we obtain the probability that the random variable will lie between the left-hand tail and 570 hours is 0.7580 (0.5 + 0.2580).

This situation is shown below:

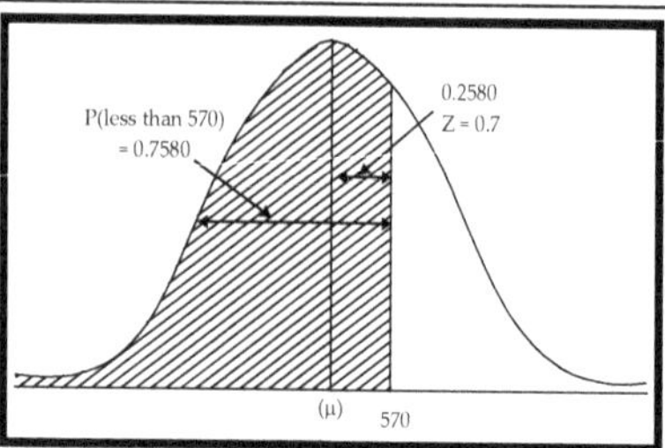

Fig. 6.7

Thus, the probability of a participant taking less than 570 hours to complete the programme is marginally higher than 75%.

(ii) between 430 and 580 hours to complete the programme.

Ans. In order to get the probability of a participant chosen at random, that he will take between 430 and 580 hours to complete the programme, we must, first, compute the Z value for 430 and 580 hours.

$$Z = \frac{X - \mu}{\sigma}$$

$$Z \text{ for } 430 = \frac{430 - 500}{100} = \frac{-70}{100} = -0.7$$

$$Z \text{ for } 580 = \frac{580 - 500}{100} = \frac{80}{100} = 0.8$$

The table shows the probability values of Z values of –0.7 and 0.8 are 0.2580 and 0.2881 respectively. This situation is shown in the following figure:

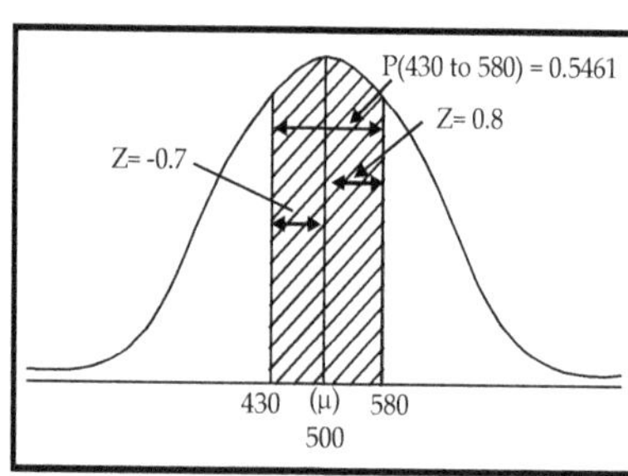

Fig. 6.8

Thus, the probability that the random variables lie between 430 and 580 hours is 0.5461 (0.2580 + 0.2881).

Q12. There are 100 misprints randomly distributed throughout the 100 pages of a book. What probability model is appropriate to describe such a distribution? Using the model, find the probability that a page observed at random will contain at least three mistakes.

Ans. Since 100 misprints are distributed randomly throughout the 100 pages of a book, therefore on an average there is only one mistake on a page. This means, the probability of there being a misprint, p=1/100, is very small and the number of words, n, in 100 pages are very large. Hence, poison distribution is best suited in this case.

Average number of misprints in one page, $\lambda = \pi p = 100 \times (1/100) = 1$.

Therefore, $e^{-\lambda} = e^{-1} = 0.3679$

The probability of at least three misprints in a page is $P(x \geq 3) = 1 - P(x < 3) = 1 - \{P(x=0) + P(x=1) + P(x=2)\}$

$$= 1 - [e^{-\lambda} + \lambda e^{-\lambda} + \frac{1}{2!}\lambda^2 e^{-\lambda}]$$

$$= 1 - \left\{e^{-1} + e^{-1} + \frac{e^{-1}}{2!}\right\} = 1 - 2.5e^{-1} = 1 - 2.5(0.3679) = 0.0802$$

Q13. The concentration of impurities in a semiconductor used in the production of microprocessors for computers is a normally distributed random variable with mean 127 parts per million and standard deviation 22. A semiconductor is acceptable only if its concentration of impurities is below 150 parts per million. What proportion of the semiconductor are acceptable for use?

(The area under the standard normal curve for the value of z = 1.04 is 0.3508)

Ans. Here, X: concentration of impurities in semiconductor

Now, $X - N(\mu = 127, \sigma = 22)$ and we need $P(X < 150)$.

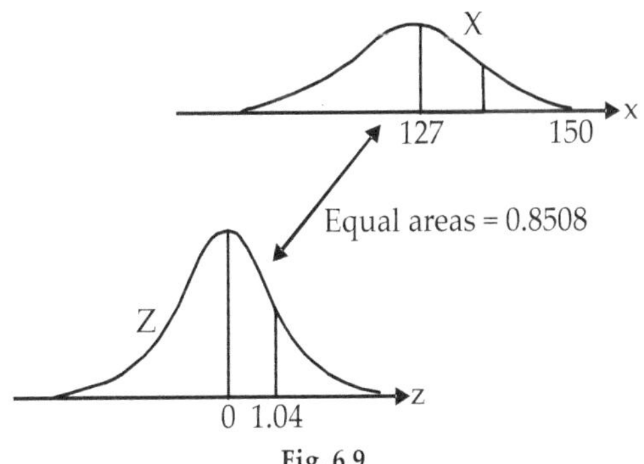

Fig. 6.9

$$P(X < 150) = P\left(\frac{X - \mu}{\sigma} < \frac{150 - \mu}{22}\right) = P\left(Z < \frac{150 - 127}{22}\right)$$

$$= P(Z < 1.04) = 0.5 + 0.3508 = 0.8508$$

Thus, 85.08% of the semiconductors are acceptable for use.

Q14. Suppose x has the following probability distribution.

x	0	1	2	3	4
P(n)	0.2	0.2	0.1	0.3	0.2

Find the mean and variance of the distribution.

Ans. Calculation of mean

x	P(n)	x. P(n)
0	0.2	0
1	0.2	0.2
2	0.1	0.2
3	0.3	0.9
4	0.2	0.8
		$\mu = \sum x.P(n) = 2.1$

Calculation of variance

x	$x-\mu$	$(x-\mu)^2$	P(n)	$(x-\mu)^2.P(n)$
0	–2.1	4.41	0.2	0.882
1	–1.1	1.21	0.2	0.242
2	–0.1	0.01	0.1	0.001
3	0.9	0.81	0.3	0.243
4	1.9	3.61	0.2	0.722
				$\sigma^2 = \sum(x-\mu)^2 P(n) = 2.09$

Hence, the mean and variance of the distribution are 2.1 and 2.09 respectively.

Q15. If X is a random variate which is distributed normally with mean 60 and standard deviation 5, find the probabilities of the following events:

(i) $60 \le X \le 70$, **(ii)** $50 \le X \le 65$, **(iii)** $X > 45$, **(iv)** $X \le 50$.

Ans. It is given that $\mu = 60$ and $\sigma = 5$

(i) Given $X_1 = 60$ and $X_2 = 70$, we can write

$$z_1 = \frac{X_1 - \mu}{\sigma} = \frac{60-60}{5} = 0 \text{ and } z_2 = \frac{X_2 - \mu}{\sigma} = \frac{70-60}{5} = 2$$

$$\therefore P(60 \le X \le 70) = P(0 \le z \le 2) = 0.4772 \text{ (from table).}$$

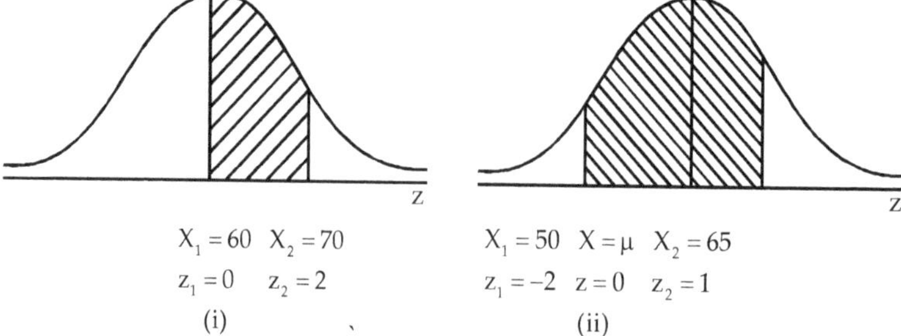

Fig. 6.10

(ii) Here $X_1 = 50$ and $X_2 = 65$, therefore, we can write

$$z_1 = \frac{50-60}{5} = -2 \text{ and } z_2 = \frac{65-60}{5} = 1$$

Hence $P(50 \le X \le 65) = P(-2 \le z \le 1) = P(0 \le z \le 2) + P(0 \le z \le 1)$

$= 0.4772 + 0.3413 = 0.8185$

(iii) $P(X > 45) = P\left(z \ge \frac{45-60}{5}\right) = P(z \ge -3)$

$= P(-3 \le z \le 0) + P(0 \le z \le \infty) = P(0 \le z \le 3) + P(0 \le z \le \infty)$

$= 0.4987 + 0.5000 = 0.9987$

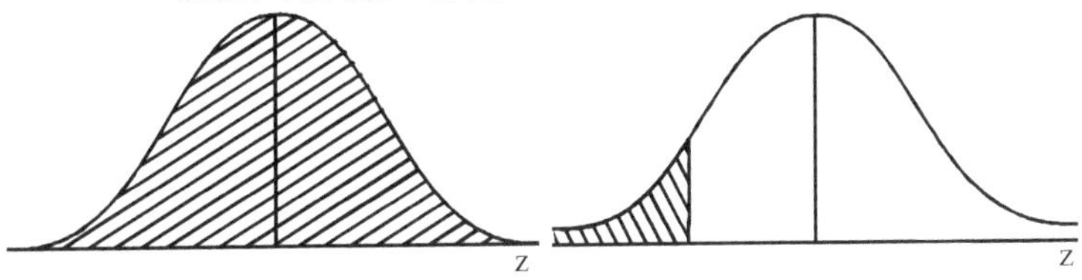

$X = 45$ $X = \mu$

$z = -3$ $z = 0$

(iii)

$X_1 = 50$ $X = \mu$

$z_1 = -2$ $z = 0$

(iv)

Fig. 6.10

(iv) $P(X \le 50) = P\left(z \le \frac{50-60}{5}\right) = P(z \le -2)$

$= 0.5000 - P(-2 \le z \le 0) = 0.5000 - P(0 \le z \le 2)$

$= 0.5000 - 0.4772 = 0.0228$

Q16. As a result of tests on 10,000 electric bulbs manufactured by a company; it was found that the life time of bulbs was normally distributed with an average life of 2040 hours and standard deviation of 60 hours. On the basis of the above information, find out the number of bulbs that are expected to burn for (a) more than 2150 hours and (b) less than 1960 hours. You are given the following information:

Proportion of Area under normal curve

Z	1.23	1.33	1.43	1.63	1.83
Area	0.3907	0.4082	0.4236	0.4484	0.4667

Ans. (a) $\overline{X} = 2040, X = 2150, \sigma = 60$

$$Z = \frac{X - \overline{X}}{\sigma} = \frac{2150 - 2040}{60} = 1.833$$

Area to the right of ordinate at 1.833

$= 0.5 - 0.4667 = 0.0333$

No. of bulbs expected to burn more than 2150 hours

$0.0333 \times 10000 = 333$

(b) $X = 1960, \overline{X} = 2040, \sigma = 60$

$$Z = \frac{1960 - 2040}{60} = 1.333$$

Area to the left of ordinate at 1.333

$= 0.5 - 0.4082 = 0.0918$

No. of bulbs expected to burn less than 1960 hours

$= 0.0918 \times 10000 = 918$

Q17. 15000 students appear in an exam with mean marks 49 and standard deviation 6. Assuming that the marks were normally distributed what proportion of students scoring (a) more than 55 marks (b) more than 70 marks.

Ans. (a) $z = \dfrac{x - \mu}{\sigma}$

$x = 55, \mu = 49, \sigma = 6$

$$z = \frac{55 - 49}{6} = 1$$

The value for z = 1 in normal distribution table (Appendix Table B) is 0.3413.

Hence, the proportion of the students getting marks more than 55 = 0.5-0.3413 = 0.1587

(b) For students scoring more than 70

$$z = \frac{x - \mu}{\sigma}$$

$x = 70, \mu = 49, \sigma = 6$

$$z = \frac{70 - 49}{6} = 3.5$$

The value for z = 3.5 in normal distribution table is 0.4998.

The proportion of students scoring more than 70 is

$0.50 - 0.4998 = 0.0002$ or 3 out of 15000 students score more than 70.

Q18. Two dice are thrown n times. Let X denotes the number of throws in which the number on the first die exceeds the number on the second die. Find (i) the distribution of X, (ii) Mean of X, (iii) Variance of X

Ans. (i) The 15 favourable cases when the number on the first die exceeds the number on the second die are: $(2,1);(3,1),(3,2);(4,1),(4,2),(4,3);$

$$(5,1),(5,2),(5,3),(5,4);(6,1),(6,2),(6,3),(6,4),(6,5).$$

It is clear that X follows Binomial distribution with parameters n and $p=\frac{5}{12}$, where p = probability of success $=\frac{15}{36}=\frac{5}{12}$.

(ii) Mean of $X=E[X]=np=\frac{5n}{12}$.

(iii) Variance of $X=npq=n\times\frac{5}{12}\times\left(1-\frac{5}{12}\right)=\frac{35\,n}{144}$.

Q19. Let X be a random variable having a binomial distribution with parameters n = 25 and p =.2. Evaluate $P\left[X<\mu_X-2\sigma_X\right]$.

Ans. We have $n=25,\ p=\frac{2}{10}=\frac{1}{5},\ q=1-\frac{1}{5}=\frac{4}{5}$.

$$\therefore\ \mu_X=np=25\times\frac{1}{5}=5,\ \sigma_X=\sqrt{npq}=\sqrt{25\times\frac{1}{5}\times\frac{4}{5}}=2.$$

$$\therefore\ P\left[X<\mu_X-2\sigma_X\right]=P\left[X<1\right]=P\left[X=0\right]=q^n=\left(\frac{4}{5}\right)^{25}.$$

Q20. A car hire firm has two cars which it hires out day by day. The number of demands for a car on each day is distributed as Poisson variate with mean 1.5. Calculate the proportion of days on which (i) neither car is used, and (ii) some demand is refused. $\left(e^{-1.5}=0.2231\right)$

Ans. The proportion of days on which there are x demands for a car is given by $P\left[X=x\right]=\frac{e^{-1.5}(1.5)^x}{x!},(\lambda=1.5)$

(i) Proportion of days on which neither car is used is given by $P\left[X=0\right]=e^{-1.5}=0.2231$.

(ii) Proportion of days on which some demand is refused is given by

$$P\left[X>2\right]=1-P\left[X\le 2\right]=1-\left\{P\left[X=0\right]+P\left[X=1\right]+P\left[X=2\right]\right\}$$

$$=1-e^{-1.5}\left(1+1.5+\frac{(1.5)^2}{2!}\right)=1-0.2231\times 3.625=0.19126.$$

Q21. A manufacturer of cotter pins knows that 5% of his product is defective. If he sells cotter pins in boxes of 100 and guarantees that not more than 10 pins will be defective, what is the approximate probability that a box will fail to meet the guaranteed quality?

Ans. We have $n = 100$ and $p = 5\% = 0.05$.

$\therefore\ \lambda = np = 100 \times 0.05 = 5.$

Probability of x defective pins in a box of 100 is

$$P[X = x] = \frac{e^{-5}5^x}{x!}; x = 0,1,2,...$$

Probability that a box will fail to meet the guaranteed quality is

$$P[X > 10] = 1 - P[X \le 10] = 1 - \sum_{x=0}^{10} \frac{e^{-5}5^x}{x!} = 1 - e^{-5}\sum_{x=0}^{10} \frac{5^x}{x!}.$$

Q22. If x is a Poisson variate with parameter m, show that $E\{|x-1|\} = m + 2e^{-m} - 1$.

Ans. Since, $E\{|x-1|\} = \sum_{x=0}^{\infty} P[x].|x-1| = \sum_{x=0}^{\infty} \frac{e^{-m}m^x}{x!}|x-1| = e^{-m} + \sum_{x=2}^{\infty} \frac{e^{-m}m^x}{x!}(x-1)$

$$= e^{-m} + \sum_{x=2}^{\infty} \frac{e^{-m}m^x}{(x-1)!} - \sum_{x=2}^{\infty} \frac{e^{-m}m^x}{x!}$$

$$= e^{-m} + e^{-m}\left[\frac{m^2}{1!} + \frac{m^3}{2!} + \frac{m^4}{3!} + ...\right] - e^{-m}\left[\frac{m^2}{2!} + \frac{m^3}{3!} + ...\right]$$

$$= e^{-m} + me^{-m}\left[m + \frac{m^2}{2!} + \frac{m^3}{3!} + ...\right] - e^{-m}\left[e^m - (1+m)\right]$$

$$= e^{-m} + me^{-m}(e^m - 1) - e^{-m}(e^m - 1 - m)$$

$$= e^{-m} + m - me^{-m} - 1 + e^{-m} + me^{-m} = m + 2e^{-m} - 1.$$

Q23. A telephone switch board handles 600 calls, on an average, during a rush hour. The board can make a maximum of 20 connections per minute. Use the Poisson distribution to evaluate the probability that the board will be overtaxed during any given minute.

Ans. We have $\lambda = \frac{600}{60} = 10$ per minute.

Required probability $= P[X > 20] = 1 - P[X \le 20] = 1 - \sum_{x=0}^{20} \frac{e^{-10}10^x}{x!}.$

Q24. In a normal distribution, 31% of the items are under 45 and 8 % are over 64. Find the mean and s.d. (standard deviation) of the distribution.

Ans. If X is $N(\mu,\sigma^2)$, then we are given

$$P[X<45]=0.31 \text{ and } P[X>64]=.08.$$

$$\Rightarrow P[45<X<\mu]=0.50-0.31=0.19 \text{ and } P[\mu<X<64]=0.42$$

$$\Rightarrow P\left[\frac{45-\mu}{\sigma}<\frac{X-\mu}{\sigma}<0\right]=0.19, \text{ and } P\left[0<\frac{X-\mu}{\sigma}<\frac{64-\mu}{\sigma}\right]=0.42$$

$$\Rightarrow P\left[0<Z<\frac{\mu-45}{\sigma}\right]=0.19 \text{ and } P\left[0<Z<\frac{64-\mu}{\sigma}\right]=0.42$$

$$\Rightarrow \frac{\mu-45}{\sigma}=0.496 \text{ and } \frac{64-\mu}{\sigma}=1.405, \text{ (by table)}$$

Adding, we get $\frac{19}{\sigma}=1.901 \Rightarrow \sigma=10$ (approx.)

and $\mu=45+(0.496)\times 10=50$ (approx.)

Q25. The probability that a person recovers from a serious disease is 0.40. What is the probability that atleast one of the eight persons admitted in a hospital survives?

Ans. It is quite pertinent to assume that the recovery of patients is independent of each other. Thus, we wish to calculate the probability

$$p(X\geq 1)=1-p(X=0)$$

$$=1-\binom{8}{0}(0.40)^0(0.60)^8=1-0.017=0.983$$

Q26. During the Second World War, the number of bomb-hits recorded in each of 576 small areas (of 0.25 sq. km. each) in the south of London are recorded below:

x_i	0	1	2	3	4	5
$f(x_i)$	229	211	93	35	7	1

Does it fit a Poisson distribution?

Ans. We have $m=\frac{537}{576}=0.9323$

The theoretical Poisson frequency distribution is given by $np(x;m)=576\,p(x;0.9323)$

For $x=0,1,2,3,4,$ and 5, the values are 226.74, 211.39, 98.54, 30.62, 7.14 and 1.57, respectively.

Since, these are in excellent agreement with the observed values. Hence, observations fit a Poisson distribution.

Q27. The average number of calls received in a BPO is 4 per minute. Calculate the probability that not more than one call is received during one minute. [June-2012, Q.No.-3]

Ans. Average number of calls received at the BPO = 4

Now, we need to find that the probability that not more than one call is received during one minute.

So, we have $P(x,m)=\dfrac{e^{-m}m^x}{x!}$

where $m=4,\ x=1$

$$\therefore \qquad P(1,4)=\frac{e^{-4}\times(4)^1}{1!}=\frac{0.0183\times 4}{1}\Rightarrow \quad P(1,4)=0.0732.$$

Q28. A continuous random variable X has the probability distribution

$$\mathbf{P(x)=\frac{1}{\pi(1+x^2)} \quad -1<x<1}$$

$$\mathbf{=0 \qquad otherwise}$$

Calculate its mean. [June-2012, Q.No.-3]

Ans. Given equation is $P(x)=\dfrac{1}{\pi(1+x^2)}$ if $-1<x<1$

$=0$ otherwise

Now, $\displaystyle\int_{-1}^{1}\frac{1}{\pi(1+x^2)}dx=\frac{1}{\pi}\int_{-1}^{1}\frac{1}{1+x^2}dx=\frac{1}{\pi}\left[\tan^{-1}x\right]_{-1}^{1}$

$$=\frac{1}{\pi}\left[\tan^{-1}(1)-\tan^{-1}(-1)\right]=\frac{1}{\pi}\left[\frac{\pi}{4}+\frac{\pi}{4}\right]=\frac{1}{\pi}\left[\frac{2\pi}{4}\right]=\frac{1}{2}$$

$\Rightarrow$ Mean of $X=E[X]=\displaystyle\int_{-1}^{1}x\,P(x)\,dx$

$$\Rightarrow \ =\int_{-1}^{1}x\cdot\frac{1}{\pi(1+x^2)}dx=\frac{1}{\pi}\int_{-1}^{1}\frac{x}{1+x^2}dx$$

Let $1+x^2=t$ if $x=-1\Rightarrow t=2$

$2xdx=dt$ if $x=1\Rightarrow t=2$

$\Rightarrow xdx=dt/2$

$$\Rightarrow\frac{1}{\pi}\int_{-1}^{1}\frac{x}{1+x^2}dx=\frac{1}{\pi}\times\frac{1}{2}\int_{2}^{2}\frac{1}{t}dt=\frac{1}{2\pi}\left[\log t\right]_2^2=\frac{1}{2\pi}(0)=0\Rightarrow \text{ Mean}=0.$$

To get success in your studies, read only GPH Book.

Chapter

7 Applications in Physics

An Overview

Physics is an experimental science. Any hypothesis or theory proposed in physics has to stand the test of observation and experiment. The raw data obtained from observations and experiments has to be analysed and interpreted systematically.

In day-to-day situations where decisions must be made, conclusions and recommendations are often based upon the relationship between two or more variables.

Therefore, in many applied fields, much of the research carried out deals with the problems of trying to discover whether a relationship between variables exists, and, if so, whether it can be identified. The most common procedure for examining relationships between numerical variables is correlation.

The study of regression has special importance in statistical analysis. We know that the mutual relationship between two series is measured with the help of correlation. Under correlation, the direction and magnitude of the relationship between two variables is measured. But it is no possible to make the best estimate of the value of a dependent variable on the basis of the given value of the independent variable by correlation analysis. Therefore, to make the best estimates and future estimation, the study of regression analysis is very important and useful.

Correlation: In our day to day life, we find many examples when a mutual relationship exists between two variables, i.e., with fall or rise in the value of one variable, the fall or rise may take place in the value of other variable. For example, price of commodity rises as the demand for the commodity goes up. Upto a certain time-period, weight of a person increases with the increase in age. Similarly, the temperature rises with the rise in the sunlight. These facts indicate that there is certainly some mutual relationship that exists between the demand for commodity and its price, the age of a person and his weight, and the sunlight and temperature. The correlation refers to the statistical technique used in measured the closeness of the relationship between the variables.

Correlation Coefficient and its Interpretation: Correlation coefficient is said to be a measures of covariance between two series. It is denoted by r. The value of correlation coefficient always lie between or equal to –1 to 1.

The coefficient of correlation measures the degree of relationship between two sets of figures. As the reliability of estimates depends upon the closeness of relationship it is imperative that utmost care be taken while interpreting the value of coefficient of correlation, otherwise fallacious conclusions can be drawn. The following general rules are given which would help in interpreting the value of r:

- When $r = +1$, it means there is perfect positive relationship between the variables.
- When $r = -1$, it means there is perfect negative relationship between the variables.
- When $r = 0$, it means that there is no relationship between the variables, i.e. the variables are uncorrelated.
- The closer r is to +1 or –1, the closer the relationship between the variables and the closer r is to 0, the less close the relationship.
- For testing the significance of the correlation coefficient, given a random sample from a bivariate normal population, if we are to test the hypothesis that the correlation coefficient of the population are uncorrelated, we have to apply the following test.

$$t = \frac{r}{\sqrt{1-r^2}} \times \sqrt{n-2}$$

here t is based on (n – 2) degrees of freedom. If the calculated value of t exceeds t0.05 for (n – 2), d.f., we say that the value of r is significant at 5% level. If t < t0.05 the data are consistent with the hypothesis of an uncorrelated population.

Karl Pearson's Correlation Co-efficient: Karl Pearson defined the correlation coefficient r_{xy} as follows:

$$r_{xy} = \frac{E(x-\bar{x})(y-\bar{y})}{\sqrt{E(x-\bar{x})^2}\sqrt{E(y-\bar{y})^2}} = \frac{\operatorname{cov}(x,y)}{\sigma_x\sigma_y} \text{ or}$$

$$r_{xy} = \frac{E(xy)-E(x)(y)}{\sqrt{E(x^2)-\{E(x)\}^2}\sqrt{E(y^2)-\{E(y)\}^2}}.$$

Other notations of the correlation coefficient between x and y are $\rho_{xy}, \rho(x,y), r(x,y)$ or simply ρ, r.

For a bivariate distribution $(x_i, y_i); i = 1,2,\ldots,n$

The correlation coefficient is defined as $r_{xy} = \dfrac{\sum \frac{1}{n}(x-\bar{x})(y-\bar{y})}{\sqrt{\sum \frac{1}{n}(x-\bar{x})^2 \sum \frac{1}{n}(y-\bar{y})^2}}$

Two variates x and y are said to be uncorrelated if $r_{xy} = 0$ or $\operatorname{cov}(x,y) = 0$.

Scatter Diagram: Scatter diagram is a graphic method of finding out correlation between two variables. By this method, direction of correlation can be ascertained. For constructing a scatter diagram, X-variable is represented on X-axis and the Y-variable on Y-axis. Each pair of values of X and Y series is plotted in two-dimensional space of X–Y. Thus, we get a scatter diagram by plotting all the pair of values. Different points may be scattered in various ways in the scatter diagram whose analysis gives us an idea about the direction and magnitude of correlation in the following ways:

Perfect Positive Correlation (r = +1)

If all points are plotted in the shape of straight line, passing from lower corner of left side to the upper corner at right side, then both series X and Y have perfect positive correlation, as is clear from the [Fig. 7.1] below.

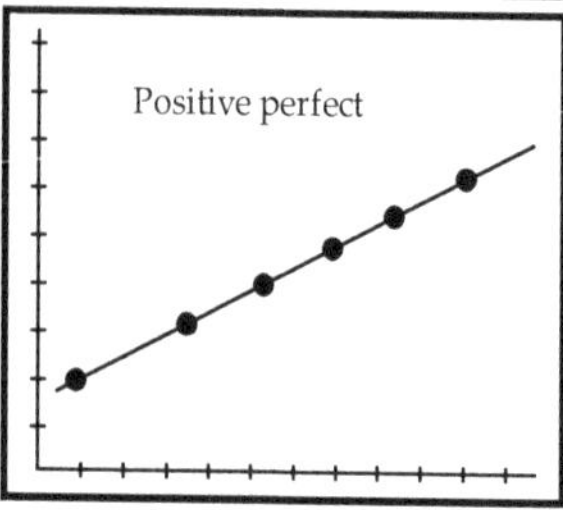

Fig. 7.1: Perfect Positive correlation

Perfect Negative Correlation (r = –1)

When all points lie on a straight line from up to down, then X and Y have perfect negative correlation, as it is clear from the [Fig. 7.2] below.

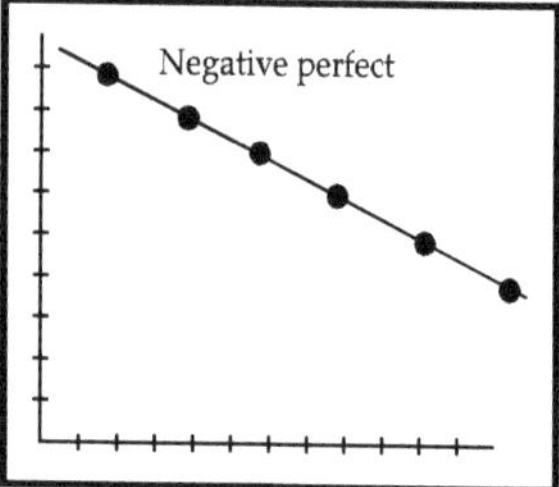

Fig. 7.2: Perfect Negative correlation

High Degree of Positive Correlation (0 < r < 1)

When concentration of points moves from left to right upward and the points are close to each other, then X and Y have high degree of positive correlation, as is clear from the [Fig. 7.3] below.

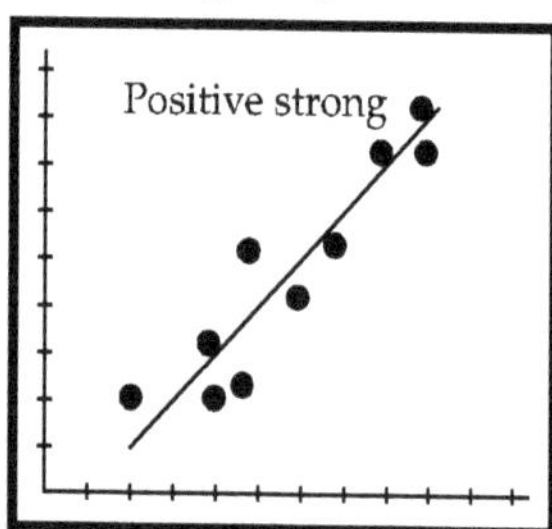

Fig. 7.3: High Degree of Positive Correlation

High Degree of Negative Correlation (r < 0)

When points are concentrated from left to right downward, and the points are close to each other, then X and Y have high degree of negative correlation, as is clear from the [Fig. 7.4] below.

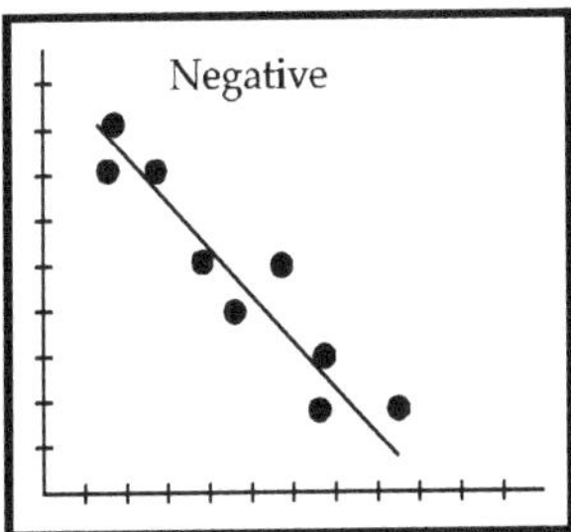

Fig. 7.4: High Degree of Negative Correlation

Zero Correlation (r = 0)

When all the points are scattered in four directions here and there and are lacking in any pattern, then there is absence of correlation as is clear from the [Fig. 7.5] below.

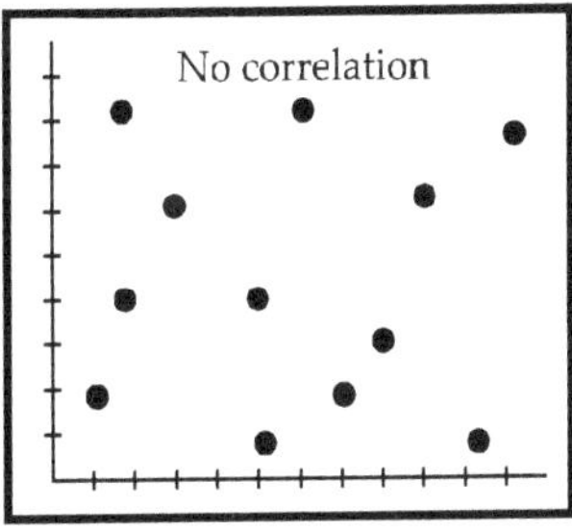

Fig. 7.5: Zero correlation

Regression Analysis and its significance: Regression is the study of nature of relationship between the variables, so that one may be able to predict the unknown value of one variable for a known value of another variable.

If two variables are significantly correlated, and if there is some theoretical basis for doing so, it is possible to predict values of one variable from the other. This observation leads to a very important concept known as 'Regression Analysis'.

Regression analysis, in general sense, means the estimation or prediction of the unknown value of one variable from the known value of the other variable. It is one of the most important statistical tools, which are extensively used in almost all sciences — Natural, Social and Physical. It is specially used in business and economics to study the relationship between two or more variables that are related causally and for the estimation of demand and supply graphs, cost functions, production and consumption functions and so on.

According to M. M. Blair, "Regression analysis is a mathematical measure of the average relationship between two or more variables in terms of the original units of the data."

The study of regression is very useful and important in statistical analysis, which is clear from the following points:

- **Nature of Relationship:** Regression analysis explains the nature of relationship between two variables.
- **Estimation of Relationship:** The mutual relationship between two or more variables can be easily measured by regression analysis.
- **Prediction:** By the regression analysis, the value of a dependent variable can be predicated on the basis of an independent variable. For example, if price of a commodity rises, what will be the probable fall in demand; this can be predicated by regression.
- **Useful in Economic and Business Research:** Regression analysis is very useful in business and economic research. With the help of regression, business and economic policy can be formulated.

The Method of Least Squares: Least Square Method is a statistical technique to determine the line of best fit for a model. It is also known as straight line method. This method is most commonly used in research to estimate the trend of time series data, as it is mathematically designed to satisfy two conditions. They are:

- sum of $(Y-Y_c) = 0$, and
- sum of $(Y-Y_c)^2$ = least

The straight-line method gives a line of best fit on the given data. The straight line, which can satisfy the above conditions and make use of the regression equation is given by: $Y_c = a + bX\,c$

where, 'Y_c' represents the trend value of the time series variable Y, 'a' and 'b' are constant.

Values of which 'a' is the trend value at the point of origin and 'b' is the amount by which the trend value changes per unit of time, and 'X' is the unit of time (value of the independent variable).

The values of constants, 'a' and 'b', are determined by the following two normal equations.

$$\sum Y = Na + b\sum X$$
$$\sum XY = a\sum X + b\sum X^2$$

The process of finding values of constants a and b can be made simple by using a shortcut method, that is, by taking the origin year in such a way that it gives the total of 'X' $\sum X$ equal to 'zero'. This becomes possible if we take the median year as origin period. Thus, the negative values in the first half of the series balance out the positive values in the second half. Thus, the normal equation shall be changed as follows, with reference to $\sum X = 0$.

$$\sum Y = a \text{(as } b\sum X \text{ becomes zero)}$$
$$\sum XY = b\sum X^2 \text{(as } a\sum X \text{ becomes zero)}$$

Therefore, the values of two constants are obtained by the following formula:

$$a = \frac{\sum Y}{N}, \text{ and } b = \frac{\sum XY}{\sum X^2}$$

It is to be noted that when the number of time units involved is even the point of origin will have to be chosen between the two middle time units.

Properties of linear regression: Let us define two regression lines as:

$$\hat{Y}_i - \overline{Y} = b_{yx}\left(X_i - \overline{X}\right) \qquad [Y \text{ on } X] \text{ and}$$
$$\hat{X}_i - \overline{X} = b_{xy}\left(Y_i - \overline{Y}\right) \qquad [X \text{ on } Y]$$

where b_{xy} and b_{yx} are coefficients of regression.

Note the following properties:

(1) If b_{yx} and b_{xy} denote the slopes of the regression lines Y on X and X on Y, then $b_{yx} \times b_{xy} = \gamma^2$, **i.e.** product of coefficients of regression is equal to square of the correlation coefficient.

(2) $b_{yx} = \gamma.\frac{\sigma_y}{\sigma_x}$ and $b_{xy} = \gamma.\frac{\sigma_x}{\sigma_y}$

(3) γ, b_{xy} and b_{yx} all have the same sign. If γ is zero then b_{xy} and b_{yx} are zero.

(4) The angle between the regression lines depends on the correlation coefficient (γ). If $\gamma = 0$, they are perpendicular. If $\gamma = +1$ or -1 they coincide. As γ increases numerically from 0 to 1 or -1, angle between the regression lines starts diminishing from 90° to 0°.

Regression Equation: The equation of the estimated regression line is $\hat{y} = a + bx$ where $b = \frac{n\sum xy - (\sum x)(\sum y)}{n(\sum x^2) - (\sum x)^2}$, $a = \frac{1}{n}(\sum y - b\sum x)$ and n is the number of pairs of data points

Methods of estimation of non-linear equations: All the measures of relationships and dependence of one variable on others are captured only when the relationship is linear. But in practice, mostly, relationships are non-linear. Such relationship may be parabolic, exponential and geometric. We adopt different techniques to estimate them:

(a) Parabolic relationship

Suppose the relationship between two variable is

$$Y = a + bx + cx^2$$

We have data on x pairs of observations $(x_i y_i); i = 1, 2, ..., n.$

Using the method of least squares, the constants a, b, c could be estimated by solving the following 3 equations.

- $\sum_{i=1}^{n} y_i = na + b\sum_{i=1}^{n} x_i + c\sum_{i=1}^{n} x_i^2$ s.
- $\sum_{i=1}^{n} x_i y_i = a\sum_{i=1}^{n} x_i + b\sum_{i=1}^{n} x_i^2 + c\sum_{i=1}^{n} x_i^3$
- $\sum_{i=1}^{n} x_i^2 y_i = a\sum_{i=1}^{n} x_i^2 + b\sum_{i=1}^{n} x_i^3 + c\sum_{i=1}^{n} x_i^4$

(b) Exponential and Geometric Curves

Take the equations of following form:

$y_i = a.b^{x_i}$ (exponential form)

$y_i = a.x_i^b$ (logarithmic form)

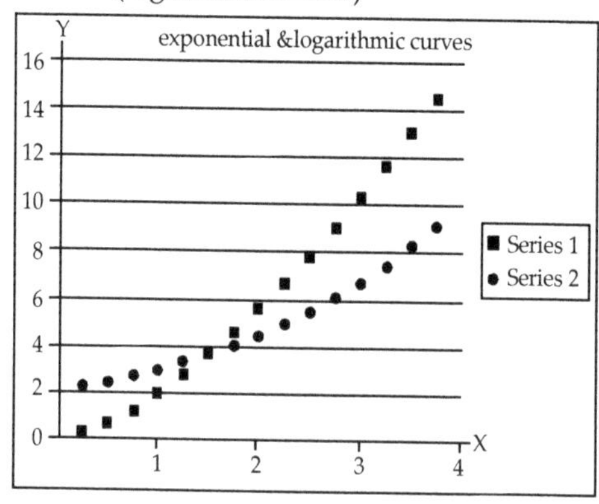

Fig. 7.6

For a = 2, b = 1.5 and x = (.25,.5,.75, 1,.......3.75), Series 1 represents logarithmic curve and Series 2 represents exponential curve.

If we take logarithms of both sides of the exponential and logarithmic forms of equation given above, we get

$\log y_i = \log a + \log bx_i$ and $\log y_i = \log a + b.\log x_i$.

If we assume

$y'_i = \log y_i, \log a = A,$

$x'_i = \log x_i, \log b = B,$

Then the equation reduces to simple bivariate equation of the form

$y'_i = A + B.x_i,$

$y'_i = A + b.x'_i.$

The Standard Error of Estimate: A regression equation, by itself, allows us to make predictions, but it does not provide any information about the accuracy of the predictions. To measures the precision of the regression, it is customary to compute a standard error of estimate.

The standard error of estimate gives a measure of the standard distance between a regression line and actual data points. Conceptually, the standard error of estimate is very much like a standard deviation; both provide a measure of standard distance.

The standard error of estimate measures the accuracy of the estimated figures. The smaller the value of the standard error of the estimate, the closer will be dots to the regression line and the better the estimates based on the equation for this line. If standard error of estimate is zero, then there is no variation about the line and the correlation will be perfect. Thus, with the help of standard error of estimate, it is possible for us to ascertain how good and representative the regression line is as a description of the average relationship between two series.

Types of Errors: There are mainly two types of errors.

(a) Systematic Error: A systematic error is one that is due to a definitely identifiable cause. Under given conditions, it affects a measurement in a regular way. If it is constant it affects all measurements and shifts them by the same magnitude. For example, if the zero reading in a measuring instrument (say, an ammeter) has been wrongly set, there will be a systematic error in the measurements. Again, a stop-watch running slow or fast will produce a systematic error. Systematic error may be subdivided into three kinds:

(i) *Instrument errors* are those resulting from imperfections in a measuring instrument, as due to the stop–watch mentioned above.

(ii) *Natural errors* arise from change in ambient conditions. For example, temperature changes may cause expansion of metals, electrical instruments may be affected by external magnetic fields, and so on.

(iii) *Personal errors* result from the physical limitations of an observer. For example, while measuring the time period of a pendulum, an observer might press the stop–watch a bit early or a bit late.

Systematic errors need not be revealed by repeated observations. The safest course for an experimenter is to regard them as effects to be discovered and eliminated.

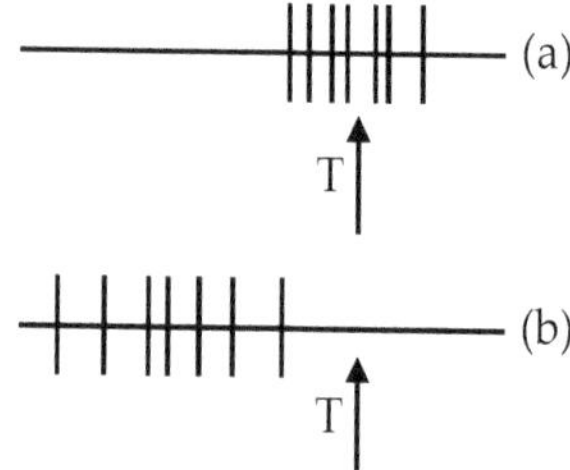

Fig 7.7: (a) Random errors distribution around the true value; (b) combination of systematic and random errors. T indicates the true value.

(b) Random Error: Random errors arise due to unknown reasons, which cannot be controlled by the experimenter. For example, small irregularities in the motion of the pendulum may cause variations in successive measurements and may be regarded as random errors. Random errors are just as likely to be positive as negative and their magnitudes can vary. In the absence of systematic errors, the random errors cause successive readings to spread about the true value of the quantity [Fig. 7.7(a)]. If, in addition, a systematic error is present, the readings spread about some displaced value. [Fig. 7.7 (b)]

Note: A measurement is said to be accurate if it is relatively free from systematic errors; it is said to be precise if the random error is small.

Estimation of Random Errors for a Single Variable: Suppose a physical quantity is measured n times yielding the values $x_1, x_2, \ldots x_n$.

At the outset, let us assume that there is no systematic error in the measurements. Although we have only n actual measurements, let us imagine that we go on making the measurements so that we end up with a large number N. We call this hypothetical set of a very large number of readings a distribution. Our actual set of n measurements should be regarded as a random sample taken from the distribution of N measurements. We then define a function $f(x)$, known as the distribution function, such that $f(x)\,dx$ gives the probability that a single measurement taken at random from the distribution will lie in the interval x and x + dx. In other words, $f(x)$ is a probability distribution.

We know that the most experimental observations obey the normal (or the Gaussian) distribution given by $f(x)=\frac{1}{\sqrt{2\pi}}\frac{1}{\sigma}\exp\left[-\frac{(x-\bar{x})^2}{2\,\sigma^2}\right]$ where x represents the value obtained from a single measurement, $\bar{x}$ represents the mean of the distribution and σ is the standard deviation of the distribution.

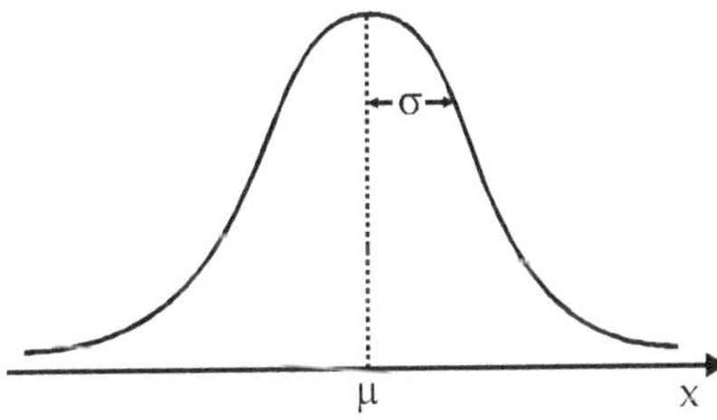

Fig. 7.8: The Gaussian distribution obeyed by most experimental observations

Since the normal curve is symmetric about the mean and its maximum value occurs at $x=\bar{x}$. In other words, the most probable value of x is $\bar{x}$. Thus, the best value of the quantity being measured is the arithmetic mean $\bar{x}$ of the measurements defined as $\bar{x}=\frac{1}{n}\sum x$. The standard deviation σ is a measure of the spread of the observations [Fig. 7.8]. It is called the standard error.

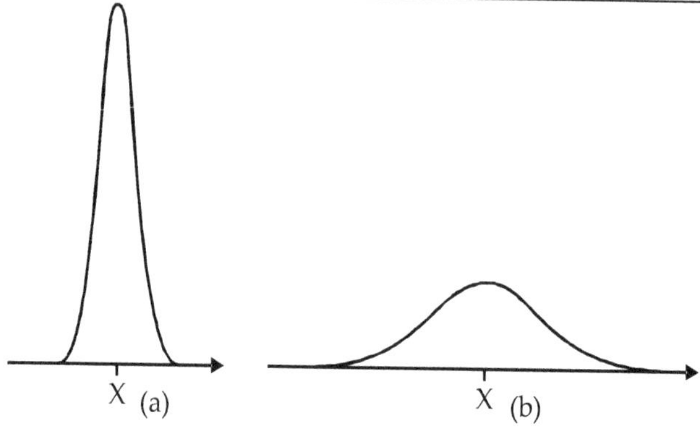

Fig. 7.9: Distribution function for (a) a precise set of measurements has a smaller value of σ; and (b) an imprecise set of measurements has a large value of σ

According to the normal distribution for a set of readings with mean $\bar{x}$, roughly two thirds of the readings should lie between $\bar{x} \pm \sigma$. However, we would note that we are considering a random sample of a limited number (n) of measurements from a large (infinite) number of measurements to which the normal distribution refers. And it is unlikely that the mean of only n values would exactly equal the mean of an infinite number. Moreover, a different sample of n values would in general have a different mean. We, therefore, also need to ask how the means of various samples of n values are distributed. Thus, we define another quantity called the standard error in the mean $\sigma_m : \sigma_m = \frac{\sigma}{\sqrt{n}}$ where σ_m is a measure of how reliably the sample mean indicates the mean of the infinite number. Whereas σ represents the error in a single measurement, σ_m represents the error in the mean of n measurements. The final result of the measurement is written as $x = \bar{x} \pm \sigma_m$. This result implies that, in the absence of systematic error, the probability that the true value of the quantity lies in the range $(\bar{x} \pm \sigma_m)$ is about 2/3.

Determination of σ and σ_m

Consider a set of n measurements $x_1, x_2, \ldots\ldots, x_n$. Let the error in the ith reading be $e_i = x_i - x_t$ ...(i)

where x_t is the true value of the quantity, which is unknown. The error in the mean E_m is

$$E_m = \bar{x} - x_t = \left(\frac{1}{n}\sum x_i\right) - x_t = \frac{1}{n}\sum_i (x_i - x_t) = \frac{1}{n}\sum_i e_i \qquad \text{...(ii)}$$

The best estimate of σ is $\left[(1/n)\sum e_i^2\right]^{1/2}$. But since the errors e_i come from the true value x_t they are not known. A way around this difficulty is provided by introducing the residuals:

The residual d_i of the ith measurement is defined by $d_i = x_i - \bar{x}$ ...(iii)

Unlike the error, the residual is a known quantity and we can relate it to σ and σ_m.

From Eqs. (i) and (ii) we have that $x_i - \bar{x} = e_i - E_m$ ...(iv)

It follows that $\sum d_i^2 = \sum (x_i - \bar{x})^2 = \sum (e_i - E_m)^2 = \sum e_i^2 - 2E_m \sum e_i + nE_m^2$

or $\sum d_i^2 = n\sigma^2 - nE_m^2 \quad \left[\because \sum e_i = \sum (x_i - x_t) = n(\bar{x} - x_t) = nE_m\right]$ ...(v)

Now, from Eq. (ii), $E_m^2 = \frac{1}{n^2}\left(\sum e_i\right)^2 = \frac{1}{n^2}\left[\sum e_i^2 + \sum_{i \neq j} e_i e_j\right] = \frac{\sigma^2}{n} + \frac{1}{n^2}\sum_{i \neq j} e_i e_j$

Thus, Eq. (v) yields $\sum d_i^2 = (n-1)\sigma^2 - \frac{1}{n}\sum_{i \neq j} e_i e_j$

For large values of n, the sum of the cross products of the errors becomes very small compared to $(n-1)\sigma^2$.

Hence, we get $\sigma^2 = \frac{1}{n-1}\sum d_i^2$ ...(vi)

From Eq. $\left(\sigma_m = \frac{\sigma}{\sqrt{n}}\right)$, we obtain $\sigma_m^2 = \frac{1}{n(n-1)}\sum d_i^2$ ...(vii)

So when we are given a sample set of measurements for a single variable, we can reasonably assume that the larger set, from which the sample is taken, follows the normal distribution. Then the mean of the sample ($\bar{x} = \frac{1}{n}\sum x$) is the best value of the unknown magnitude and σ_m gives the standard error of the mean. The final result is quoted as $x = \bar{x} \pm \sigma_m$.

Random Error Estimation for Indirect Measurements: Let us consider the problem of estimating error in a quantity Q which is a function of n other quantities $u_1, u_2, u_3, \ldots, u_n$.

$$Q = Q(u_1, u_2, u_3, \ldots, u_n)$$

The quantities $u_1, u_2, \ldots u_n$ are directly measured. Let the random errors in these quantities be $\pm\Delta u_1, \pm\Delta u_2, \ldots \pm\Delta u_n$. These errors will give rise to a random error, say $Q \pm \Delta Q$ in Q. If the random errors are small, the best value of Q (say $\bar{Q}$) will be that calculated from the mean values of the measured quantities $\bar{u}_1, \bar{u}_2, \ldots \bar{u}_n$. Then, provided that the function $Q(u_1, u_2, \ldots, u_n)$ is continuous, we can make use of the result

$$\Delta Q = \frac{\partial Q}{\partial u_1}\Delta u_1 + \frac{\partial Q}{\partial u_2}\Delta u_2 + \ldots + \frac{\partial Q}{\partial u_n}\Delta u_n \qquad \ldots\text{(viii)}$$

where $\Delta u_1, \Delta u_2, \ldots, \Delta u_n$, represent small deviations from $u_1, u_2, \ldots u_n$, respectively, and ΔQ represents the corresponding deviation of Q from $\bar{Q}$. The partial derivatives $\frac{\partial Q}{\partial u_1}$ etc. are evaluated at the mean values $\bar{u}_1, \bar{u}_2, \ldots$ If a large number N of sets of values of $u_1, u_2, \ldots u_n$ are measured, the standard deviation σ_Q of the resulting N values of Q can be obtained from Eq. (vi) as $\sigma_Q^2 = \frac{1}{N-1}\sum(\Delta Q_i)^2$ where $\Delta Q_i = Q_i - \bar{Q}$, $i = 1, 2, ..N$

Using Eq. (viii), we can write

$$\sigma_Q^2 = \frac{1}{N-1}\sum\left[\frac{\partial Q}{\partial u_1}\Delta u_1 + \frac{\partial Q}{\partial u_2}\Delta u_2 + \ldots + \frac{\partial Q}{\partial u_n}\Delta u_n\right]^2 \qquad \ldots\text{(ix)}$$

When the quantity within the brackets on the right hand side is squared, we get two types of terms:

One kind of terms is squares like $\left[\frac{\partial Q}{\partial u_1}(\Delta u_1)\right]^2$.

The other kind is 'cross' terms like $2\frac{\partial Q}{\partial u_1}\frac{\partial Q}{\partial u_2}\Delta u_1 \Delta u_2$

Since $\Delta u_1, \Delta u_2$, etc. represent normal errors they are just as likely to be positive as negative. So the sum of the large number of cross terms will be close to zero, or in any case much smaller than the sum of the square terms. We can prove this result rigourously for normal distribution provided the variables are independent. Now, we write

$$\sigma_Q^2 = \frac{1}{N-1}\sum\left[\left(\frac{\partial Q}{\partial u_1}\right)^2(\Delta u_1)^2 + \left(\frac{\partial Q}{\partial u_2}\right)^2(\Delta u_2)^2 + \ldots + \left(\frac{\partial Q}{\partial u_n}\right)^2(\Delta u_n)^2\right]$$

$$= \left(\frac{\partial Q}{\partial u_1}\right)^2 \frac{1}{N-1}\sum(\Delta u_1)^2 + \left(\frac{\partial Q}{\partial u_2}\right)^2 \frac{1}{N-1}\sum(\Delta u_2)^2 + \ldots + \left(\frac{\partial Q}{\partial u_n}\right)^2 \frac{1}{N-1}\sum(\Delta u_n)^2$$

Since the partial derivatives are computed at the respective mean values $\bar{u}_1, \bar{u}_2, \ldots$, they are constants and have been taken out of the summation. Now, $\frac{1}{N-1}\sum(\Delta u_i)^2$ is simply $\sigma_{u_i}^2$.

Thus, we obtain $\sigma_Q^2 = \left(\frac{\partial Q}{\partial u_1}\right)^2 \sigma_{u_1}^2 + \left(\frac{\partial Q}{\partial u_2}\right)^2 \sigma_{u_2}^2 + \ldots + \left(\frac{\partial Q}{\partial u_n}\right)^2 \sigma_{u_n}^2$ ...(x)

We can express this result in a compact form as

$$\sigma_Q^2 = \sum\left(\frac{\partial Q}{\partial u_i}\right)^2 \sigma_{u_i}^2 \qquad \text{...(xi)}$$

where the partial derivatives are computed at the mean values $\bar{u}_1, \bar{u}_2, \ldots \bar{u}_n$. In terms of the standard error in the mean, we have

$$\sigma_{\bar{Q}}^2 = \sum\left(\frac{\partial Q}{\partial u_i}\right)^2 \sigma_{\bar{u}_i}^2 \qquad \text{...(xii)}$$

where $\sigma_{\bar{u}_i}$ is the standard error in the mean of u_i. The best value of Q is written as $Q = \bar{Q} \pm \sigma_{\bar{Q}}$ ...(xiii)

Solved Practical Problems

Q1. Find the correlation coefficient between the sales and expenses from the data given below:

Firm:	1	2	3	4	5	6	7	8	9	10
Sales (₹ in Lakh):	50	50	55	60	65	65	65	60	60	50
Expenses (₹ in Lakh):	11	13	14	16	16	15	15	14	13	13

Ans. Calculation of Correlation Coefficient

Firm	Sales X	$x = (X - \bar{X})$	x^2	Expenses Y	$y = (Y - \bar{Y})$	y^2	xy
1	50	−8	64	11	−3	9	+24
2	50	−8	64	13	−1	1	+8
3	55	−3	9	14	0	0	0
4	60	+2	4	16	+2	4	+4
5	65	+7	49	16	+2	4	+14
6	65	+7	49	15	+1	1	+7
7	65	+7	49	15	+1	1	+7
8	60	+2	4	14	0	0	0
9	60	+2	4	13	−1	1	−2
10	50	−8	64	13	−1	1	+8
N = 10	ΣX = 580	Σx = 0	$\Sigma x^2 = 360$	ΣY = 140	Σy = 0	$\Sigma y^2 = 22$	Σxy = 70

$$\bar{X} = \frac{\sum X}{N} = \frac{580}{10} = 58, \bar{Y} = \frac{\sum Y}{N} = \frac{140}{10} = 14$$

$$r = \frac{\sum xy}{\sqrt{\sum x^2 \sum y^2}} = \frac{70}{\sqrt{360 \times 22}} = \frac{70}{88.994} = 0.787$$

Hence, the correlation coefficient between the sales and expenses is 0.787.

Q2. From the following 12 months sample data of a company, estimate the regression lines and also estimate the value of sales when the company decided to spend ₹2,50,000 on advertising during the next quarter.

(₹ in lakh)

Advertisement Expenditure :	0.8	1.0	1.6	2.0	2.2	2.6	3.0	3.0	4.0	4.0	4.0	4.6
Sales:	22	28	22	26	34	18	30	38	30	40	50	46

Ans. Calculations for Least Square Estimates of a Company

Advertising Expenditure : (X)	**Sales (Y)**	X^2	Y^2	XY
0.8	22	0.64	484	17.6
1.0	28	1.00	784	28.0
1.6	22	2.56	484	35.2
2.0	26	4.00	676	52.0
2.2	34	4.84	1156	74.8
2.6	18	6.76	324	46.8
3.0	30	9.00	900	90.0
3.0	38	9.00	1,444	114.0
4.0	30	16.00	900	120.0
4.0	40	16.00	1600	160.0
4.0	50	16.00	2,500	200.0
4.6	46	21.16	2,116	211.6
ΣX=32.8	ΣY=384	ΣX^2=106.96	ΣY^2=13368	ΣXY=1150.0

Now we establish the best regression line (estimated by the least square method).

We know the regression equation of Y on X is:

$$Y-\overline{Y}=b_{yx}\left(X-\overline{X}\right)$$

$$\overline{Y}=\frac{384}{12}=32;\overline{X}=\frac{32.8}{12}=2.733$$

From $Y-\overline{Y}=b_{yx}\left(X-\overline{X}\right)$

$$b_{yx}=\frac{\sum XY-\frac{(\sum X)(\sum Y)}{N}}{\sum X^2-\frac{(\sum X)^2}{N}}$$

$$b_{yx}=\frac{1,150-\frac{(32.8)(384)}{12}}{106.96-\frac{(32.8)^2}{12}}=5.801$$

$$Y-32=5.801(X-2.733)$$

$$Y=5.801X-15.854+32=5.801X+16.146$$

or $Y=16.146+5.801X$

We obtained the regression model of the company for predicting sales which is $Y=16.146+5.801X$

wherein Y = estimated sales for given value of X, and X = level of advertising expenditure.

To find Y, the estimate of expected sales, we substitute the specified advertising level into the regression model. For example, if we know that the company's marketing department has decided to spend ₹2,50,000/- (X = 2.5) on advertisement during the next quarter, the most likely estimate of sales (Y) is:

$$Y=16.1436+5.801(2.5)=30.6455=₹30,64,550.$$

Thus, an advertising expenditure of ₹2.5 lakh is estimated to generate sales for the company to the tune of ₹30,64,550.

Q3. Consider the following data relating to the relationships between expenditure on research and development, and annual profits of a firm during 2007–2013.

Years:	2007	2008	2009	2010	2011	2012	2013
R&D (₹ lakh):	2.5	3.0	4.2	3.0	5.0	7.8	6.5
Profit (₹ lakh):	23	26	32	30	38	46	44

The estimated regression equation in this situation is found to be $Y_c = 14.44 + 4.31X$. Calculate the standard error of estimate.

Ans. Here,

Years	Expenditure on R&D X	Profit Y	Estimating values $Y_c = (14.44 + 4.31X)$	Individual error $(Y - Y_c)$	$(Y - Y_c)^2$
2007	2.5	23	$14.44 + 4.31(2.5) = 25.21$	–2.21	4.88
2008	3.0	26	$14.44 + 4.31(3) = 27.37$	–1.37	1.88
2009	4.2	32	$14.44 + 4.31(4.2) = 32.54$	–0.54	0.29
2010	3.0	30	$14.44 + 4.31(3) = 27.37$	2.63	6.92
2011	5.0	38	$14.44 + 4.31(5) = 35.99$	2.01	4.04
2012	7.8	46	$14.44 + 4.31(7.8) = 48.06$	–2.06	4.24
2013	6.5	44	$14.44 + 4.31(6.5) = 42.46$	1.54	2.37
					$\Sigma(Y - Y_c)^2 = 24.62$

$$\sum(Y - Y_c)^2 = 24.62$$

Now, we can find the standard error of estimate as follows:

$$S_e = \sqrt{\frac{\sum(Y - Y_c)^2}{n}} = \sqrt{\frac{24.62}{7}} = 1.875$$

∴ Standard error of estimate of annual profit is ₹1.875 lakh.

Q4. Fit a second-degree parabola to the following data taking x as the independent variable.

x	1	2	3	4	5	6	7	8	9
y	2	6	7	8	10	11	11	10	9

Ans. The equation of second-degree parabola is given by $y = a + bx + cx^2$ and the normal equations are:

$$\left.\begin{aligned} \sum y &= na + b\sum x + c\sum x^2 \\ \sum xy &= a\sum x + b\sum x^2 + c\sum x^3 \\ \sum x^2y &= a\sum x^2 + b\sum x^3 + c\sum x^4 \end{aligned}\right\} \quad ....(i)$$

Here n = 9. The various sums are appearing in the table as follows:

The main aim of GPH book is to provide knowledge as well as good marks in exams.

x	y	xy	x^2	x^2y	x^3	x^4
1	2	2	1	2	1	1
2	6	12	4	24	8	16
3	7	21	9	63	27	81
4	8	32	16	128	64	256
5	10	50	25	250	125	625
6	11	66	36	396	216	1296
7	11	77	49	539	343	2401
8	10	80	64	640	512	4096
9	9	81	81	729	729	6561
$\sum x = 45$	$\sum y = 74$	$\sum xy = 421$	$\sum x^2 = 285$	$\sum x^2y = 2771$	$\sum x^3 = 2025$	$\sum x^4 = 15333$

Putting these values of $\sum x, \sum y, \sum x^2, \sum xy, \sum x^2y, \sum x^3 \text{ and } \sum x^4$ in equation (i) and solving the equations for a, b and c, we get

$a = -0.923; b = 3.520; c = -0.267.$

Hence, the fitted equation is $y = -0.923 + 3.52x - 0.267x^2$.

Q5. Estimate the regression equation of x on y from the following data:

x	5	3	8	5	10
y	8	11	6	9	8

Ans. Calculation of Regression equation

x	x^2	y	y^2	xy
5	25	8	64	40
3	9	11	121	33
8	64	6	36	48
5	25	9	81	45
10	100	8	64	80
$\sum x = 31$	$\sum x^2 = 223$	$\sum y = 42$	$\sum y^2 = 366$	$\sum xy = 246$

Regression equation of x on y is given by $x = a + by$

The normal equations are:

$\sum x = na + b\sum y$

$\sum xy = a\sum y + b\sum y^2$

Substituting the values, we get

$31 = 5a + 42b$ ...(i)

$246 = 42a + 366b$ ...(ii)

Solving (i) and (ii), we get $a = 15.36$ and $b = -1.09$

Hence, the required regression equation of x on y is given by

$x = 15.36 - 1.09y.$

Q6. Marks obtained by 12 students in the college test (x) and the university test (y) are as follows:

x	41	45	50	68	47	77	90	100	80	100	40	43
y	60	63	60	48	85	56	53	91	74	98	65	43

What is your estimate of the marks a student would have got in the university test if he got 60 in the college test but was ill at the time of the university test?

Ans. For estimating y, we use the regression equation of y on x, viz $y-\bar{y}=b_{yx}(x-\bar{x})$, where $b_{yx}=\text{cov}(x,y)/\sigma_X^2$. Therefore, we have to find $\bar{x},\bar{y},\text{cov}(x,y)$ and σ_x^2.

Calculation for Regression

x	y	X = x−60	Y = y−60	X^2	XY
41	60	−19	0	361	0
45	63	−15	3	225	−45
50	60	−10	0	100	0
68	48	8	−12	64	−96
47	85	−13	25	169	−325
77	56	17	−4	289	−68
90	53	30	−7	900	−210
100	91	40	31	1,600	1,240
80	74	20	14	400	280
100	98	40	38	1,600	1,520
40	65	−20	5	400	−100
43	43	−17	−17	289	289
781	796	61	76	6,397	2,485

Here, $\bar{x}=781/12=65.08$, $\bar{y}=781/12=65.08$,

Since the variance and covariance are unaffected by changes of origin,

$\text{cov}(x,y)=\text{cov}(X,Y)=\Sigma XY/n-(\Sigma X/n)(\Sigma Y/n)$

$=2485/12-(61/12)(76/12)=25184/144$

$\sigma_x^2=\Sigma X^2/n-(\Sigma X/n)^2=6397/12-(61/12)^2=73043/144$

Therefore, $b_{yx}=\dfrac{25184/144}{73043/144}=\dfrac{25184}{73043}=0.345$

Hence, the regression equation is $y-66.33=0.345(x-65.08)$;

i.e. $y=43.88+0.345x$

Now, when $x=60, y=43.88+0.345\times 60=64.58=65(\text{approx.})$

Q7. Given the values of x and y

x	25	25	30	30	16
y	2	3	5	1	8

Regress y on x.

Ans. Calculation of Regression equation

x	y	x^2	y^2	xy
25	2	625	4	50
25	3	625	9	75
30	5	900	25	150
30	1	900	1	30
16	8	256	64	128
$\sum x = 126$	$\sum y = 19$	$\sum x^2 = 3306$	$\sum y^2 = 103$	$\sum xy = 433$

Regression equation of y on x is given by:

$y = a+bx$

The normal equations are:

$\sum y = na + b\sum x$

$\sum xy = a\sum x + b\sum x^2$

Substituting the values, we get

$19 = 5a + 126b$ ...(i)

$433 = 126a + 3306b$ ...(ii)

Solving equation (i) and (ii), we get $a = 12.62$, $b = -0.35$

Hence, the required regression equation of y on x is given by $y = 12.62 - 0.35x$.

Q8. From the following data, obtain the two regression equations Y on X and X on Y:

X	2	4	6	8	10
Y	5	7	9	8	11

Ans. Calculation of Regression equation

x	x^2	y	y^2	xy
2	4	5	25	10
4	16	7	49	28
6	36	9	81	54
8	64	8	64	64
10	100	11	121	110
$\sum x = 30$	$\sum x^2 = 220$	$\sum y = 40$	$\sum y^2 = 340$	$\sum xy = 266$

Regression equation of x on y is given by:

$x = a+by$

The normal equations are:

$\sum x = na + b\sum y$

$\sum xy = a\sum y + b\sum y^2$

Substituting the value, we get

$30 = 5a + 40b$ ...(i)

$266 = 40a + 340b$ ...(ii)

Solving (i) and (ii), we get $a = -4.4$, $b = 1.3$

Hence, the required regression equation of x on y is given by $x = -4.4 + 1.3y$

Now, Regression equation of y on x is given by

$y = a + bx$

where, normal equations are

$\sum y = na + b\sum x$

$\sum xy = a\sum x + b\sum x^2$

Substituting the values, we get

$40 = 5a + 30b$ ...(iii)

$266 = 30a + 220b$ ...(iv)

Solving (iii) and (iv), we get $a = 4.1$, $b = 0.65$

Hence, the required regression equation of y on x is given $y = 4.1 + 0.65x$.

Q9. A hosiery mill wants to estimate how its monthly costs are related to its monthly output rate. For that, the firm collects a data regarding its costs and output for a sample of nine months as given in table below:

Output (tons)	Production cost (thousands of Rupees)
1	2
2	3
4	4
8	7
6	6
5	5
8	8
9	8
7	6

(i) Construct a scatter diagram for the data given above.

Ans. Suppose that x_i denote the output for the ith month and y_i denote the cost for the ith month. Then, we can plot the graph for the pair (x_i, y_i) of the values given in table. The scatter diagram as shown in Fig.

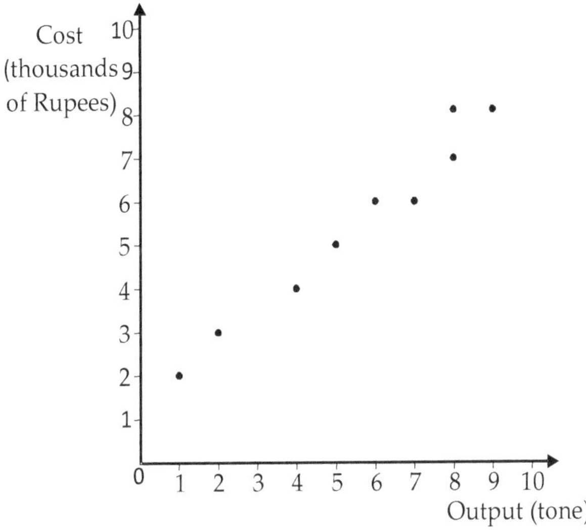

Fig. 7.10: Scatter Diagram

(ii) Calculate the best linear regression line, where the monthly output is the dependent variable and the monthly cost is the independent variable.

Ans. From table, we get that

$$\bar{x} = \frac{\sum_{i=1}^{n} x_i}{n} = \frac{50}{9}$$

$$\bar{y} = \frac{\sum_{i=1}^{n} y_i}{n} = \frac{49}{9}$$

$$\sum x_i^2 = 340$$

$$\sum y_i^2 = 303$$

and $\sum x_i y_i = 319$

Therefore, we get that $\hat{b} = \dfrac{\sum_{i=1}^{n} x_i y_i - n\bar{x}\bar{y}}{\sum_{i=1}^{n} x_i^2 - n\bar{x}^2} \dfrac{9 \times 319 - 50 \times 49}{9 \times 340 - 50^2} \dfrac{421}{560} = 0.752$

Correspondingly, we get $\hat{a} = \dfrac{49}{9} - (0.752) \times \dfrac{50}{9} = 1.266$

Therefore, the best linear regression line is $y = 1.266 + (0.752)x$

(iii) Use this regression line to predict the firm's monthly costs if they decide to produce 4 tons per month.

Ans. If the firms decide to produce 4 tons per month, then one can predict that its cost would be $1.266+(0.752)\times 4=4.274$

Since the costs are measured in thousands of dollars, this means that the total costs would be expected to be ₹4,274.

Q10. An economist wants to estimate the relationship in a small community between a family's annual income and the amount that the family saves. The following data from nine families are obtained:

Annual income (thousands of Rupees)	Annual savings (thousands of Rupees)
12	0.0
13	0.1
14	0.2
15	0.2
16	0.5
17	0.5
18	0.6
19	0.7
20	0.8

Calculate the least-squares regression line, where annual savings is the dependent variable and annual income is the independent variable, and interpret your results.

Ans. Letting x_i be the income (in thousands of dollars) of the ith family, and y_i be the saving (in thousands of Rupees) of the ith family, we find that

$$\sum_{i=1}^{9} x_i y_i = 63.7, \quad \sum_{i=1}^{9} y_i = 3.6 \quad \bar{y} = 0.4,$$

$$\sum_{i=1}^{9} x_i^2 = 2364, \quad \sum_{i=1}^{9} x_i = 144, \quad \bar{x} = 16.$$

Thus, substituting these values, we obtain

$$\hat{b} = \frac{\sum_{i=1}^{n} x_i y_i - n\overline{xy}}{\sum_{i=1}^{n} x_i^2 - n\bar{x}^2} = \frac{63.7 - 9(16)(0.4)}{2364 - 9(16)^2} = \frac{6.1}{60} = 0.1017$$

Consequently, $\hat{a} = \bar{y} - b\bar{x} = 0.4 \times 0.1017(16) = -1.2272$

Thus, the regression line is $y = -1.2272 + 0.1017x$ where both x and y are measured in thousands of Rupees.

The interpretation of this regression line is as follows: On the average, families with zero income would be expected to save -1,227.20. (Negative saving means that a family's consumption expenditure exceeds its income.) An increase in family income of 1,000 is associated with an increase in family saving of 101.70.

Q11. The following table showing the test scores made by salesmen on the intelligence test and their weekly sales:

Salesmen:	1	2	3	4	5	6	7	8	9	10
Test Score:	40	70	50	60	80	50	90	40	60	60
Sale (₹ '000):	2.5	6.0	4.0	5.0	4.0	2.5	5.5	3.0	4.5	3.0

Calculate the regression line of sales on test scores and estimate the probable weekly sales volume if a salesman makes a score of 100.

Ans. Let sales be denoted by Y and test scores by X. We have to fit a regression equation of Y on X, i.e. $Y - \overline{Y} = b_{yx}\left(X - \overline{X}\right)$.

Calculation of Regression Line

Salesmen	Test Score X	$(X-\overline{X})$ x	x^2	Sales Y	$(Y-\overline{Y})$ y	y^2	xy
1	40	–20	400	2.5	–1.5	2.25	+30
2	70	+10	100	6.0	+2.0	4.00	+20
3	50	–10	100	4.0	0	0	0
4	60	0	0	5.0	1.0	1.00	0
5	80	+20	400	4.0	0	0	0
6	50	–10	100	2.5	–1.5	2.25	+15
7	90	+30	900	5.5	+1.5	2.25	+45
8	40	–20	400	3.0	–1.0	1.00	+20
9	60	0	0	4.5	+0.5	0.25	0
10	60	0	0	3.0	–1.0	1.00	0
N = 10	$\Sigma X = 600$	$\Sigma x = 0$	$\Sigma x^2 = 2400$	$\Sigma Y = 40$	$\Sigma y = 0$	$\Sigma y^2 = 14$	$\Sigma xy = 40$

$$\overline{X} = \frac{\sum X}{N} = \frac{600}{10} = 60$$

$$\overline{Y} = \frac{\sum Y}{N} = \frac{40}{10} = 4$$

$$b_{yx} = \frac{\sum xy}{\sum x^2} = \frac{130}{2400} = 0.054$$

$$Y - 4 = 0.054 \times (X - 60)$$

$$Y = 0.76 + 0.054X$$

When X is 100, Y would be

$Y = 0.76 + 0.054(100) = 6.16$

Thus, the most probable weekly sales volume if salesman makes a score of 100 is 6.16 thousand rupees.

Q12. Fit a linear regression of rice yield (X_1 quintals) on the use of fertiliser (X_2 kgs per acre) and the amount of rainfall (X_3 inches), from the following data:

X_1	:	45	50	55	70	75	75	85
X_2	:	25	35	45	55	65	75	85
X_3	:	31	28	32	32	29	27	31

Estimate the yield when $X_2 = 60$ and $X_3 = 25$.

Ans. To simplify calculation work, we change origin of the three variable as $U_1 = X_1 - 65$, $U_2 = X_2 - 55$ and $U_3 = X_3 - 30$.

U_1	U_2	U_3	U_1U_2	U_1U_3	U_2U_3	U_1^2	U_2^2	U_3^2
-20	-30	1	600	-20	-30	400	900	1
-15	-20	-2	300	30	40	225	400	4
-10	-10	2	100	-20	-20	100	100	4
5	0	2	0	10	0	25	0	4
10	10	-1	100	-10	-10	100	100	1
10	20	-3	200	-30	-60	100	400	9
20	30	1	600	20	30	400	900	1
0	0	0	1900	-20	-50	1350	2800	24

Note: Since $\sum U_i = 0, \therefore u_i = U_i - \bar{U}_i = U_i, i = 1,2,3. \left(\because \bar{U}_i = 0\right)$

Hence, $b_{12.3} = \dfrac{1900 \times 24 - (-20)(-50)}{2800 \times 24 - (-50)^2} = 0.689$

$b_{13.2} = \dfrac{(-20) \times 2800 - 1900 \times (-50)}{2800 \times 24 - (-50)^2} = 0.603$

Further, we have

$\bar{X}_1 = \dfrac{\sum U_1}{n} + 65 = 65, \bar{X}_2 = \dfrac{\sum U_2}{n} + 55 = 55$ and $\bar{X}_3 = \dfrac{\sum U_3}{n} + 30 = 30$

and $a_{1.23} = \bar{X}_1 - b_{12.3}\bar{X}_2 - b_{13.2}\bar{X}_3 = 65 - 0.689 \times 55 - 0.603 \times 30 = 9.015$

$\therefore$ The fitted regression of X_1 on X_2 and X_3 is $X_{1c} = 9.015 + 0.689X_2 + 0.603X_3$

The estimate of yield (X_{1c}) when $X_2 = 60$ and $X_3 = 25$ is

$X_{1c} = 9.015 + 0.689 \times 60 + 0.603 \times 25 = 65.43$ quintals.

Q13. Given the following pairs of values of the variable X and Y:

X:	10	20	30	40	50	60
Y:	25	50	75	100	125	150

(i) **Make a Scatter Diagram.**

Ans.

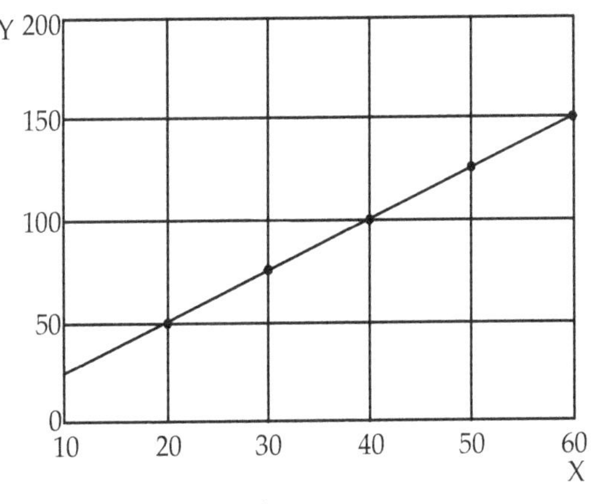

Fig. 7.11

(ii) **Is there any correlation between the variables X and Y?**

Ans. By looking at the scatter diagram, we can say that there is perfect positive correlation between X and Y variables.

Q14. Calculate the coefficient of correlation between age group and rate of mortality from the following data:

Age Group	0-20	20-40	40-60	60-80	80-100
Rate of Mortality	350	280	540	760	900

Ans.

Age group (x)	Rate of mortality (y)	m	$dx = \frac{x-50}{20}$	dx^2	$dy = \frac{y-540}{10}$	dy^2	dxdy
0-20	350	10	–2	4	19	361	–38
20-40	280	30	–1	1	26	676	–26
40-60	540	50	0	0	-	-	0
60-80	760	70	1	1	22	484	22
80-100	900	90	2	4	36	1296	72
			0	10	103	2817	30

$$r = \frac{N\sum dxdy - \sum dx \sum dy}{\sqrt{N\sum dx^2 - \left(\sum dx\right)^2}\sqrt{N\sum dy^2 - \left(\sum dy\right)^2}}$$

$$= \frac{5\times30 - 0\times103}{\sqrt{5\times10-(0)^2}\sqrt{5\times2817-(103)^2}} = \frac{150}{\sqrt{50}\sqrt{3476}} = \frac{150}{416.89} = 0.3598$$

Q15. The resistance of a coil of wire (in Ω) was measured to be 4.615, 4.638, 4.597,4.634, 4.613, 4.623, 4.659, 4.623. Calculate the best value of the resistance and the standard error of the mean.

Ans. We calculate the mean of the sample and the residual of each measurement and use Eqs. $\left(\sigma^2 = \frac{1}{n-1}\sum d_i^2\right)$ and $\left(\sigma_m^2 = \frac{1}{n(n-1)}\sum d_i^2\right)$. The calculations are tabulated below:

$x_i\,(\Omega)$	$d_i = x_i - \bar{x}$	d_i^2
4.615	-0.010	0.000100
4.638	+0.013	0.000169
4.597	-0.028	0.000784
4.634	0.009	0.000081
4.613	-0.012	0.000144
4.623	-0.002.	0.000004
4.659	0.034	0.001156
4.623	-0.002	0.000004
$\bar{x} = 4.625$		$\sum d_i^2 = 0.002442$

Hence,

$$\sigma_m^2 = \frac{1}{56}\times 0.002442 = 0.000044,$$

and $\sigma_m = .007$

Therefore, the best value of the resistance is $(4.625 \pm 0.007)\Omega$

Q16. The combined resistance R of two resistors (of resistance R_1 and R_2) connected in parallel is given by $R = \left(\frac{1}{R_1} + \frac{1}{R_2}\right)^{-1}$. Determine the best value of R, given that $R_1 = (200 \pm 5)\Omega$ and $R_2 = (600 \pm 10)\Omega$.. The errors in R_1 and R_2 are the standard errors in the mean.

Ans. The mean value of R is $\bar{R} = \left(\frac{1}{\bar{R}_1} + \frac{1}{\bar{R}_2}\right)^{-1} = \left(\frac{1}{200} + \frac{1}{600}\right)^{-1} = 150\Omega$

To use eq. ($Q=\bar{Q}\pm\sigma_{\bar{Q}}$), we must calculate $\frac{\partial R}{\partial R_1}$ and $\frac{\partial R}{\partial R_2}$ at $R_1=\bar{R}_1$ and $R_2=\bar{R}_2$:

$$\frac{\partial R}{\partial R_1}=\frac{R_2^2}{(R_1+R_2)^2}=\frac{(600\ \Omega)^2}{(800\ \Omega)^2}=\frac{9}{16} \text{ and } \frac{\partial R}{\partial R_2}=\frac{R_1^2}{(R_1+R_2)^2}=\frac{(200\ \Omega)^2}{(800\ \Omega)^2}=\frac{1}{16}.$$

Hence, eq. ($\sigma_{\bar{Q}}^2=\sum\left(\frac{\partial Q}{\partial u_i}\right)^2\sigma_{\bar{u}_i}^{\ 2}$) gives $\sigma_{\bar{R}}^2=\left(\frac{9}{16}\right)^2(5)^2+\left(\frac{1}{16}\right)^2(10)^2=8$ or $\sigma_{\bar{R}}=3$

Therefore, the best value of R is $(150\pm3)\Omega$..

Q17. The measurement of surface tension, S of water at various temperatures are given in the following table.

T (°C)	**10**	**20**	**30**	**40**	**50**	**60**
S (dynes cm^{-1})	**74.0**	**73.0**	**71.0**	**70.0**	**68.0**	**66.0**

Calculate the correlation coefficient for this data.

[June-2011, Q.No.-4]

Ans.

T (°C)	S (dynes cm^{-1})	$T^2(°C)^2$	$S^2(dynes^2cm^{-2})$	TS(^{0}Cdynescm^{-1})
10	74.0	100	5476.0	740.0
20	73.0	400	5329.0	1460.0
30	71.0	900	5041.0	2130.0
40	70.0	1600	4900.0	2800.0
50	68.0	2500	4624.0	3400.0
60	66.0	3600	4356.0	3960.0
$\sum T$ =210	$\sum S$ = 422	$\sum T^2$ 9100	$\sum S^2$ = 29726.0	$\sum TS$ = 14490.0

With the above results we can compute r_{XY} for the given data:

$$r_{XY}=\frac{6(14490.0)-(210)(422)}{\sqrt{6(9100)-(210)^2}\sqrt{6(29726.0)-(422)^2}}=\frac{-1680}{(102.5)(16.5)}=-0.99$$

Q18. The heat capacity of liquid sulphuric acid was measured at various temperatures yielding the following set of data:

Heat capacity (in cal/°C):	**0.38**	**0.39**	**0.40**	**0.41**	**0.45**	**0.46**
Temperature (in °C)	**50**	**100**	**150**	**200**	**250**	**300**

Compute the correlation coefficient r_{xy}.

Ans. Let X represents the temperature and Y, the heat capacity. We arrange the data in a tabular form and compute r_{XY} as follows:

x(°C)	y(cal/°C)	x^2	y^2	xy
50	0.38	2500	0.1444	19.00
100	0.39	10000	0.1521	39.00
150	0.40	22500	0.1600	60.00
200	0.41	40000	0.1681	82.00
250	0.45	62500	0.2025	112.50
300	0.46	90000	0.2116	138.00
$\sum x = 1050$	$\sum y = 2.49$	$\sum x^2 = 227500$	$\sum y^2 = 1.0387$	$\sum xy = 450.50$

Using $r_{XY} = \dfrac{n\sum(xy) - \sum(x)\sum(y)}{\sqrt{n\sum(x^2) - (\sum x)^2}.\sqrt{n\sum(y^2) - (\sum y)^2}}$ we have

$$r_{XY} = \frac{6(450.50) - (1050)(2.49)}{\sqrt{6(2,27,500) - (1050)^2}\sqrt{6(1.0387) - (2.49)^2}} = \frac{88.5}{512.35 \times 0.179} = 0.96.$$

This suggests a high degree of positive correlation.

Q19. The extension in a material is measured as a function of load in appropriate units and is given by:

Load (x)	**0**	**1**	**2**	**3**	**4**
Extension (y)	**16**	**13**	**10**	**6**	**3**

Obtain the least square fit to the data. [June-2012, Q.No.-4]

Ans. We first prepare table for the calculations.

Load (x)	Extension(y)	xy	x^2	y^2
0	16	0	0	256
1	13	13	1	169
2	10	20	4	100
3	6	18	9	36
4	3	12	16	9
$\sum x = 10$	$\sum y = 48$	$\sum xy = 63$	$\sum x^2 = 30$	$\sum y^2 = 570$

The least square fit line is $\hat{y} = a + bx$

$$\text{where } b = \text{slope of line} = \frac{n\sum xy - \sum x \sum y}{n\sum x^2 - (\sum x)^2} = \frac{5 \times 63 - (10)(48)}{5 \times 30 - (10)^2}$$

$\therefore \quad b = \frac{315-480}{150-100} = \frac{-165}{50} = -3.30$ and $a = \frac{1}{n}\left[\sum y - (b)\sum x\right]$

$= \frac{1}{5}\left[48-(-3.30)\times 10\right] = \frac{1}{5}[48+33] = \frac{81}{5} = 16.20$

Hence, the least square fit to the data is $\hat{y} = a + bx$

$\Rightarrow \quad y = 16.20 - 3.3x$

Q20. The resistance of a coil is measured as a function of temperature and is given by

T (°C) =	40	50	60	70	80
R (Ω) =	6	7	8	9	10

Obtain R = a + bT for the best fit. **[Dec-2012, Q.No.-4]**

Ans.

T(°C)	R(Ω)	$T^2(°C)^2$	$R^2(\Omega^2)$	TR(Ω°C)
40	6	1600	36	240
50	7	2500	49	350
60	8	3600	64	480
70	9	4900	81	630
80	10	6400	100	800
ΣT =300	ΣR =40	ΣT^2 =19000	ΣR^2 =330	ΣTR =2500

Here, n = 5

Now, the regression equation is R = a + bT

Where $b = \frac{5(2500)-(300)(40)}{5(19000)-(300)^2} = \frac{12500-12000}{95000-90000} = \frac{500}{5000} \Rightarrow \quad b = 0.1$

and $a = \frac{1}{5}[40-(0.1)(300)] \Rightarrow \quad a = \frac{1}{5}[40-30.0] \Rightarrow \quad a = \frac{1}{5}[10]$

$\Rightarrow \quad a = 2$

Thus, the equation is R = a + bT ⇒ $\quad R = 2 + 0.1T$

Feedback is the breakfast of Champions.

Ken Blanchard

You can Help other students.
"Inform any error or mistake in this book."

We and Universe
will reward you for Your Kind act.

Email at : feedback@gullybaba.com
or
WhatsApp on 9350849407

Important Formulae

List of Important Formulae

(1) If $\vec{a}$ and $\vec{b}$ are two vectors:

Then $\vec{a} \cdot \vec{b} = a\, b \cos\theta$

and $\vec{a} \times \vec{b} = (a b \sin\theta)\, \hat{c}$

(2) If $\hat{i}, \hat{j}$ and $\hat{k}$ are unit vectors:

Then $\hat{i} \cdot \hat{i} = \hat{j} \cdot \hat{j} = \hat{k} \cdot \hat{k} = 1$

$\hat{i} \cdot \hat{j} = \hat{j} \cdot \hat{k} = \hat{k} \cdot \hat{i} = \hat{j} \cdot \hat{i} = \hat{k} \cdot \hat{j} = \hat{i} \cdot \hat{k} = 0$

and $\hat{i} \times \hat{i} = \hat{j} \times \hat{j} = \hat{k} \times \hat{k} = \vec{0}$

$\hat{i} \times \hat{j} = \hat{k},\ \hat{j} \times \hat{k} = \hat{i},\ \hat{k} \times \hat{i} = \hat{j}$

$\hat{j} \times \hat{i} = -\hat{k},\ \hat{k} \times \hat{j} = -\hat{i},\ \hat{i} \times \hat{k} = -\hat{j}$

(3) Derivative of a vector function $\vec{f}(t)$ with respect to t is:

$$\frac{d\vec{f}(t)}{dt} = \lim_{\Delta t \to 0} \frac{\vec{f}(t+\Delta t) - \vec{f}(t)}{\Delta t}$$

(4) Derivative of a vector function in component form is:

$$\frac{d}{dt}\vec{f}(t) = \frac{df_1(t)}{dt}\hat{i} + \frac{df_2(t)}{dt}\hat{j} + \frac{df_3(t)}{dt}\hat{k}$$

(5) Derivative of the scalar product is:

$$\frac{d}{dt}(\vec{a} \cdot \vec{b}) = \left(\vec{b} \cdot \frac{d\vec{a}}{dt} + \vec{a} \cdot \frac{d\vec{b}}{dt}\right)$$

(6) Derivative of the cross product is:

$$\frac{d}{dt}(\vec{a} \times \vec{b}) = \left(\vec{b} \times \frac{d\vec{a}}{dt} + \vec{a} \times \frac{d\vec{b}}{dt}\right)$$

(7) The partial derivative of a function f (x, y, z, t) with respect to x is:

$$\frac{\partial f}{\partial x} = \lim_{\Delta x \to 0} \frac{f(x+\Delta x, y, z, t) - f(x, y, z, t)}{\Delta x}$$

(8) The gradient of the scalar field f is:

$$\text{grad} f \equiv \nabla f = \frac{\partial f}{\partial x}\hat{i} + \frac{\partial f}{\partial y}\hat{j} + \frac{\partial f}{\partial z}\hat{k}$$

(9) Directional derivative of f is:

$$\frac{\partial f}{\partial s} = \hat{n} \cdot \nabla f$$

(10) Vector Operator:

$$\nabla \equiv \frac{\partial}{\partial x}\hat{i} + \frac{\partial}{\partial y}\hat{j} + \frac{\partial}{\partial z}\hat{k}$$

(11) Divergence of a vector field is:

$$\nabla \cdot \vec{F} = \frac{\partial F_x}{\partial x} + \frac{\partial F_y}{\partial y} + \frac{\partial F_z}{\partial z}$$

(12) Curl of vector field is:

$$\text{Cutl}\,\vec{F} = \vec{\nabla} \times \vec{F} = \begin{vmatrix} \hat{i} & \hat{j} & \hat{k} \\ \frac{\partial}{\partial x} & \frac{\partial}{\partial y} & \frac{\partial}{\partial z} \\ F_x & F_y & F_z \end{vmatrix}$$

(13) Vector Identities following:

(a) grad (uv) = v grad u + u grad v

(b) $\text{grad}(\vec{a} \cdot \vec{b}) = \vec{a} \times \text{curl}\,\vec{b} + \vec{b} \times \text{curl}\,\vec{a} + (\vec{a} \cdot \nabla)\vec{b} + (\vec{b} \cdot \nabla)\vec{a}$

(c) $\text{div}\,(u\vec{a}) = u\,\text{div}\,\vec{a} + \vec{a} \cdot \text{grad}\,u$

(d) $\text{div}(\vec{a} \times \vec{b}) = \vec{b} \cdot \text{curl}\,\vec{a} - \vec{a} \cdot \text{curl}\,\vec{b}$

(e) $\text{curl}\,(u\vec{a}) = \text{grad}\,u \times \vec{a} + u\,\text{curl}\,\vec{a}$

(f) $\text{curl}(\vec{a} \times \vec{b}) = \vec{a}\,\text{div}\,\vec{b} - \vec{b}\,\text{div}\,\vec{a} + (\vec{b} \cdot \nabla)\,\vec{a} - (\vec{a} \cdot \nabla)\vec{b}$

(14) Vector Properties are as follows:

(a) $\text{div}\,\text{grad}\,f = \nabla \cdot (\nabla f) = \frac{\partial^2 f}{\partial x^2} + \frac{\partial^2 f}{\partial y^2} + \frac{\partial^2 y}{\partial z^2} = \nabla^2 f$

(b) $\text{curl grad}\,f = \nabla \times (\nabla f) = \vec{0}$

(c) $\text{div}\,\text{curl}\,\vec{f} = \nabla \cdot (\nabla \times f) = \vec{0}$

(d) $\text{grad div}\,\vec{f} = \text{curl}\,\text{curl}\,\vec{f} + \frac{\partial^2 \vec{f}}{\partial x^2} + \frac{\partial^2 \vec{f}}{\partial y^2} + \frac{\partial^2 \vec{f}}{\partial z^2}$

(15) Non-Cartesian coordinates system:

(i) In plane polar coordinate system

$x = \rho \cos \phi$

$y = \rho \sin \phi$

(b) In cylindrical coordinate system

$$x = \rho \cos \phi$$

$$y = \rho \sin \phi$$

$$z = z$$

we can invert these relations

$$\rho = \sqrt{x^2 + y^2}$$

$$\phi = \tan^{-1}\left(\frac{y}{x}\right)$$

$$z = z$$

(c) In spherical polar coordinate system

$$x = r \sin\theta \cos \phi$$

$$y = r \sin\theta \sin\phi$$

$$z = r \cos \theta$$

we can invert these relations

$$r = \sqrt{x^2 + y^2 + z^2}$$

$$\theta = \tan^{-1}\left(\frac{\sqrt{x^2 + y^2}}{z}\right)$$

and $\phi = \tan^{-1}\left(\frac{y}{x}\right)$

(16) Expressing A Vector in Polar Coordinates:

(a) Cylindrical coordinate system

$$\hat{i} = \cos \phi \, \hat{e}_\rho - \sin\phi \, \hat{e}_\phi$$

$$\hat{j} = \sin\phi \, \hat{e}_\rho + \cos \phi \, \hat{e}_\phi$$

and $\hat{k} = \hat{e}_z$

Conversely

$$\hat{e}_\rho = \cos \phi \, \hat{i} + \sin\phi \, \hat{j}$$

$$\hat{e}_\phi = -\sin\phi \, \hat{i} + \cos \phi \, \hat{j}$$

$$\hat{e}_z = \hat{k}$$

(b) In spherical coordinate system

$$\hat{e}_r = \sin\theta \cos \phi \, \hat{i} + \sin\theta \sin\phi \hat{j} + \cos \theta \, \hat{k}$$

$$\hat{e}_\theta = \cos\theta \cos \phi \, \hat{i} + \cos \theta \sin \phi \, \hat{j} - \sin \theta \, \hat{k}$$

$$\hat{e}_\phi = -\sin\phi\,\hat{i} + \cos\phi\,\hat{j}$$

Conversely

$$\hat{i} = \sin\cos\phi\,\hat{e}_r + \cos\theta\cos\phi\hat{e}_\theta - \sin\phi\,\hat{e}_\phi$$

$$\hat{j} = \sin\theta\sin\phi\hat{e}_r + \cos\theta\sin\phi\hat{e}_\theta + \cos\phi\,\hat{e}_\phi$$

$$\hat{k} = \cos\theta\hat{e}_r - \sin\theta\hat{e}_\theta$$

(17) Differential Element of vector Area $\vec{A}$ is:

$$d\vec{A} = \rho\,d\phi\,dz\,\hat{e}_\rho + d\rho\,dz\,\hat{e}_\phi + \rho d\rho\,\,d\phi\,\hat{e}_z$$

In spherical coordinate system, we can write

$$d\vec{A} = r^2\sin\theta\,d\theta\,d\phi\,\hat{e}_r + r\,\sin\theta\,drd\phi\,\hat{e}_\theta + rd\theta dr\,\hat{e}_\phi$$

In cylindrical and spherical polar coordinates, volume element can be written as

$$dV = \rho\,d\rho\,d\phi\,dz$$

and $dV = r^2 dr\,\sin\theta\,d\theta\,d\phi$

(18) In curvilinear coordinate system:

we have

$$x = x(q_1, q_2, q_3)$$

$$y = y(q_1, q_2, q_3)$$

$$z = z\,(q_1, q_2, q_3)$$

we can invert these relation

$$q_1 = q_1(x, y, z)$$

$$q_2 = q_2(x, y, z)$$

$$q_3 = q_3(x, y, z)$$

(19) Laplace Operator:

$$\nabla^2 f = \frac{1}{h_1 h_2 h_3}\sum_{\substack{i=1 \\ i\neq j\neq k}}^{3}\frac{\partial}{\partial u_i}\left(\frac{h_j h_k}{h_i}\frac{\partial f}{\partial u_i}\right)$$

(20) Standard Results of Integration of vectors:

(a) $\int\left(\frac{d\vec{r}}{dt}\cdot\vec{s}+\vec{r}\cdot\frac{d\vec{s}}{dt}\right)dt=\vec{r}\cdot\vec{s}+c$

where c is constant of integration.

(b) $\int\left(2\vec{r}\cdot\frac{d\vec{r}}{dt}\right)dt=\vec{r}^{2}+c$

(ci) $\int\left(2\frac{d\vec{r}}{dt}\cdot\frac{d^{2}\vec{r}}{dt^{2}}\right)dt=\left(\frac{d\vec{r}}{dt}\right)^{2}+c$

(d) $\int\left(\vec{r}\times\frac{d^{2}\vec{r}}{dt^{2}}\right)dt=\vec{r}\times\frac{d\vec{r}}{dt}+c$

(e) $\int\left(\vec{a}\times\frac{d\vec{r}}{dt}\right)dt=\vec{a}\times\vec{r}+c$

(f) $\int\left(\frac{1}{r}\frac{d\vec{r}}{dt}-\frac{1}{r^{2}}\frac{dr}{dt}\vec{r}\right)dt=\hat{r}+c$

(g) $\int c\,\vec{r}\,dt=c\int\vec{r}\,dt$

where c is constant scalar and $\vec{r}$ a vector function of a scalar t.

(h) $\int(\vec{r}+\vec{s})dt=\int\vec{r}\,dt+\int\vec{s}\,dt$

(21) Gauss's Divergence Theorem:

$$\int_{S}\vec{F}\cdot\hat{n}\,ds=\int_{V}\operatorname{div}\vec{F}\,dv$$

(22) Stokes's Theorem:

$$\int_{C}\vec{F}\cdot d\vec{r}=\iint_{S}\hat{n}\cdot\operatorname{curl}\vec{F}\,dS$$

(23) Green's Theorem:

$$\int_{V}(\phi\nabla^{2}\Psi-\Psi\nabla^{2}\phi)dV=\int_{S}(\phi\nabla\psi-\psi\nabla\phi)\cdot\hat{n}\,dS.$$

(24) Probability of an event A is

$$P(A)=\frac{n(A)}{n(\Omega)}=\frac{\text{number of events}}{\text{number of outcomes}}$$

(25) $^{n}p_{r}=\frac{n!}{(n-r)!}$ **and** $^{n}c_{r}=\frac{n!}{r!(n-r)!}$

(26) Theorem of total Probability is

$$P(E\cup F)=P(E)+P(F)-P(E\cap F)$$

(27) Generalised Theorem of Total Probability is $P(A)=\sum_{i=1}^{n} P(E_i)\,P(A\|E_i)=\sum_{i=1}^{n} P(E_i \cap A)$
(28) Bayes' Theorem: $P(E_i\|A)=\dfrac{P(E_i \cap A)}{\sum_{i=1}^{n} P(E_i \cap A)}=\dfrac{P(E_i)P(A\|E_i)}{\sum_{i=1}^{n} P(E_i)P(A\|E_i)}$
(29) Expectation $E(X)=\langle X\rangle=\int_{-\infty}^{\infty} x\, f(x)dx$
(30) Variance of X is $Var(X)=E(X^2)-[E(X)]^2$
(31) Standard Deviation $=\sqrt{Var(X)}$
(32) Covariance is: $Cov(X,Y)=\sum_{i} f(x_i,y_i)\,(x_i-\langle X\rangle)(y_i-\langle Y\rangle)$
(33)Correlation coefficients: $r_{XY}=\dfrac{Cov(X,Y)}{\sqrt{Var(X)Var(Y)}}$
(34) Binomial Distribution: $f_X(x)\begin{cases} {}^nc_x\, p^x q^{n-x}, & For\, x=0,1,2,...,n \\ 0\quad , & otherwise \end{cases}$
(35) Mean of binomial distribution b (x; n, p) is $E(X)=np$
(36) Variance of the binomial distribution b (x; n, p) is $Var(X)=npq$
(37) Poisson Distribution is $f_X(x)=\begin{cases} \dfrac{e^{-\lambda}\lambda^x}{x!}, & for\, x=0,1,2,.... \\ 0\quad , & otherwise \end{cases}$

(38) Normal Distribution is

$$\phi(x) = \frac{1}{\sigma\sqrt{2\pi}} e^{-\frac{1}{2}\left(\frac{x-\mu}{\sigma}\right)^2}, -\infty < x < \infty$$

(39) The Maxwell – Boltzmann Distribution is

$$f(v)dv = 4\pi\left(\frac{m}{2\pi k_B T}\right)^{3/2} v^2 \exp\left(-\frac{mv^2}{2k_B T}\right)dv, \quad \text{for } 0 \le v \le \infty$$

(40) The Cauchy Distribution:

$$f(x) = \frac{1}{\pi(1+x^2)}, \quad -\infty < x < \infty$$

(41) Regression Equation:

$$\hat{y} = a + bx$$

where

$$a = \frac{1}{n}(\Sigma y - b\Sigma x)$$

and

$$b = \frac{n\Sigma xy - (\Sigma x)(\Sigma y)}{n(\Sigma x^2) - (\Sigma x)^2}$$

(42) The standard error of estimate:

$$S_e = \left[\frac{\Sigma y^2 - a\Sigma y - b\Sigma xy}{n-2}\right]^{1/2}$$

(43) The standard error in a set of n measured values of a single variable is

$$\sigma = \left[\frac{1}{n-1}\Sigma d_i^2\right]^{1/2}$$

(44) The standard error in the mean is

$$\sigma_{\bar{Q}} = \left[\Sigma\left(\frac{\partial Q}{\partial u_i}\right)^2 \sigma_{u_i}^{\ 2}\right]^{1/2}$$

◈◈◈

Hello IGNOU Student,

Do you want to get more marks which means good job, and better career opportunities?
Are you confused about where to study?
Do You know Gullybaba / GPH book is the only company started 15 years back by the Ex-IGNOU student and now provides No.1 IGNOU Self-help books across the globe?

We have created these ***Notes*** specially to help IGNOU Students.

We strongly recommend to read from ***GPH Books*** which contain complete material for exam preparation with previous year's question papers solutions.

You can order GPH Books on Gullybaba.com. Pay by "Cash on Delivery", Credit Card, Paytm, or Online Transfer and get home delivery by Govt. Postal Dept. after Lockdown.

Appendix Tables

Table (A): Binomial Distribution

		p																			
n	r	.01	.05	.10	.15	.20	.25	.30	.35	.40	.45	.50	.55	.60	.65	.70	.75	.80	.85	.90	.95
2	0	.980	.902	.810	.723	.640	.563	.490	.423	.360	.303	.250	.203	.160	.123	.090	.063	.040	.023	.010	.002
	1	.020	.095	.180	.255	.320	.375	.420	.455	.480	.495	.500	.495	.480	.455	.420	.375	.320	.255	.180	.095
	2	.000	.002	.010	.023	.040	.063	.090	.123	.160	.203	.250	.303	.360	.423	.490	.563	.640	.723	.810	.902
3	0	.970	.857	.729	.614	.512	.422	.343	.275	.216	.166	.125	.091	.064	.043	.027	.016	.008	.003	.001	.000
	1	.029	.135	.243	.325	.384	.422	.441	.444	.432	.408	.375	.334	.288	.239	.189	.141	.096	.057	.027	.007
	2	.000	.007	.027	.057	.096	.141	.189	.239	.288	.334	.375	.408	.432	.444	.441	.422	.384	.325	.243	.135
	3	.000	.000	.001	.003	.008	.016	.027	.043	.064	.091	.125	.166	.216	.275	.343	.422	.512	.614	.729	.857
4	0	.961	.815	.656	.522	.410	.316	.240	.179	.130	.092	.062	.041	.026	.015	.008	.004	.002	.001	.000	.000
	1	.039	.171	.292	.368	.410	.422	.412	.384	.346	.300	.250	.200	.154	.112	.076	.047	.026	.011	.004	.000
	2	.001	.014	.049	.098	.154	.211	.265	.311	.346	.368	.375	.368	.346	.311	.265	.211	.154	.098	.049	.014
	3	.000	.000	.004	.011	.026	.047	.076	.112	.154	.200	.250	.300	.346	.384	.412	.422	.410	.368	.292	.171
	4	.000	.000	.000	.001	.002	.004	.008	.015	.026	.041	.062	.092	.130	.179	.240	.316	.410	.522	.656	.815
5	0	.951	.774	.590	.444	.328	.237	.168	.116	.078	.050	.031	.019	.010	.005	.002	.001	.000	.000	.000	.000
	1	.048	.204	.328	.392	.410	.396	.360	.312	.259	.206	.156	.113	.077	.049	.028	.015	.006	.002	.000	.000
	2	.001	.021	.073	.138	.205	.264	.309	.336	.346	.337	.312	.276	.230	.181	.132	.088	.051	.024	.008	.001
	3	.000	.001	.008	.024	.051	.088	.132	.181	.230	.276	.312	.337	.346	.336	.309	.264	.205	.138	.073	.021
	4	.000	.000	.000	.002	.006	.015	.028	.049	.077	.113	.156	.206	.259	.312	.360	.396	.410	.392	.328	.204
	5	.000	.000	.000	.000	.000	.001	.002	.005	.010	.019	.031	.050	.078	.116	.168	.237	.328	.444	.590	.774
6	0	.941	.735	.531	.377	.262	.178	.118	.075	.047	.028	.016	.008	.004	.002	.001	.000	.000	.000	.000	.000
	1	.057	.232	.354	.399	.393	.356	.303	.244	.187	.136	.094	.061	.037	.020	.010	.004	.002	.000	.000	.000
	2	.001	.031	.098	.176	.246	.297	.324	.328	.311	.278	.234	.186	.138	.095	.060	.033	.015	.006	.001	.000
	3	.000	.002	.015	.042	.082	.132	.135	.236	.276	.303	.312	.303	.276	.236	.185	.132	.082	.042	.015	.002

contd.

		p																			
n	**r**	**.01**	**.05**	**.10**	**.15**	**.20**	**.25**	**.30**	**.35**	**.40**	**.45**	**.50**	**.55**	**.60**	**.65**	**.70**	**.75**	**.80**	**.85**	**.90**	**.95**
6	4	.000	.000	.001	.006	.015	.033	.060	.095	.138	.186	.234	.278	.311	.328	.324	.297	.246	.176	.098	.031
	5	.000	.000	.000	.000	.002	.004	.010	.020	.037	.061	.094	.136	.187	.244	.303	.356	.393	.399	.354	.232
	6	.000	.000	.000	.000	.000	.000	.001	.002	.004	.008	.016	.028	.047	.075	.118	.178	.262	.377	.531	.735
7	0	.932	.698	.478	.321	.210	.133	.082	.049	.028	.015	.008	.004	.002	.001	.000	.000	.000	.000	.000	.000
	1	.066	.257	.372	.396	.367	.311	.247	.185	.131	.087	.055	.032	.017	.008	.004	.001	.000	.000	.000	.000
	2	.002	.041	.124	.210	.275	.311	.318	.299	.261	.214	.164	.117	.077	.047	.025	.012	.004	.001	.000	.000
	3	.000	.004	.023	.062	.115	.173	.227	.268	.290	.292	.273	.239	.194	.144	.097	.058	.029	.011	.003	.000
	4	.000	.000	.003	.011	.029	.058	.097	.144	.194	.239	.273	.292	.290	;268	.227	.173	.115	.062	.023	.004
	5	.000	.000	.000	.001	.004	.012	.025	.047	.077	.117	.164	.214	.261	.299	.318	.311	.275	.210	.124	.041
	6	.000	.000	.000	.000	.000	.001	.004	.008	.017	.032	.055	.087	.131	.185	.247	.311	.367	.396	.372	.257
	7	.000	.000	.000	.000	.000	.000	.000	.001	.002	.004	.008	.015	.028	.049	.082	.133	.210	.321	.478	.698
8	0	.923	.663	.430	.272	.168	.100	.058	.032	.017	.008	.004	.002	.001	.000	.000	.000	.000	.000	.000	.000
	1	.075	.279	.383	.385	.336	.267	.198	.137	.090	.055	.031	.016	.008	.003	.001	.000	.000	.000	.000	.000
	2	.003	.051	.149	.238	.294	.311	.296	.259	.209	.157	.109	.070	.041	.022	.010	.004	.001	.000	.000	.000
	3	.000	.005	.033	.084	.147	.208	.254	.279	.279	.257	.219	.172	.124	.081	.047	.023	.009	.003	.000	.000
	4	.000	.000	.005	:018	.046	.087	.136	.188	.232	.263	.273	.263	.232	.188	.136	.087	.046	.018	.005	.000
	5	.000	.000	.000	.003	.009	.023	.047	.081	.124	.172	.219	.257	.279	.279	.254	.208	.147	.084	.033	.005
	6	.000	.000	.000	.000	.001	.004	.010	.022	.041	.070	.109	.157	.209	.259	.296	.311	.294	.238	.149	.051
	7	.000	.000	.000	.000	.000	.000	.001	.003	.008	.016	.031	.055	.090	.137	.198	.267	.336	.385	.383	.279
	8	.000	.000	.000	.000	.000	000	.000	.000	.001	.002	.004	.008	.017	.032	.058	.100	.168	.272	.430	.663
9	0	.914	.630	.387	.232	.134	.075	.040	.021	.010	.005	.002	.001	.000	.000	.000	.000	.000	.000	.000	.000
	1	.083	.299	.387	.368	.302	.225	.156	.100	.060	.034	.018	.008	.004	.001	.000	.000	.000	.000	.000	.000

contd.

		p																			
n	r	.01	.05	.10	.15	.20	.25	.30	.35	.40	.45	.50	.55	.60	.65	.70	.75	.80	.85	.90	.95
9	2	.003	.063	.172	.260	.302	.300	.267	.216	.161	.111	.070	.041	.021	.010	.004	.001	.000	.000	.000	.000
	3	.000	.008	.045	.107	.176	.234	.267	.272	.251	.212	.164	.116	.074	.042	.021	.009	.003	.001	.000	.000
	4	.000	.001	.007	.028	.066	.117	.172	.219	.251	.260	.246	.213	.167	.118	.074	.039	.017	.005	.001	.000
	5	.000	.000	.001	.005	.017	.039	.074	.118	.167	.213	.246	.260	.251	.219	.172	.117	.066	.028	.007	.001
	6	.000	.000	.000	.001	.003	.009	.021	.042	.074	.116	.164	.212	.251	.272	.267	.234	.176	.107	.045	.008
	7	.000	.000	.000	.000	.000	.001	.004	.010	.021	.041	.070	.111	.161	.216	.267	.300	.302	.260	.172	.063
	8	.000	.000	.000	.000	.000	.000	.000	.001	.004	.008	.018	.034	.060	.100	.156	.225	.302	.368	.387	.299
	9	.000	.000	.000	.000	.000	.000	.000	.000	.000	.001	.002	.005	.010	.021	.040	.075	.134	.232	.387	.630
10	0	.904	.599	.349	.197	.107	.056	.028	.014	.006	.003	.001	.000	.000	.000	.000	.000	.000	.000	.000	.000
	1	.091	.315	.387	.347	.268	.188	.121	.072	.040	.021	.010	.004	.002	.000	.000	.000	.000	.000	.000	.000
	2	.004	.075	.194	.276	.302	.282	.233	.176	.121	.076	.044	.023	.011	.004	.001	.000	.000	.000	.000	.000
	3	.000	.010	.057	.130	.201	.250	.267	.252	.215	.166	.117	.075	.042	.021	.009	.003	.001	.000	.000	.000
	4	.000	.001	.011	.040	.088	.146	.200	.238	.251	.238	.205	.160	.111	.069	.037	.016	.006	.001	.000	.000
	5	.000	.000	.001	.008	.026	.058	.103	.154	.201	.234	.246	.234	.201	.154	.103	.058	.026	.008	.001	.000
	6	.000	.000	.000	.001	.006	.016	.037	.069	.111	.160	.205	.238	.251	.238	.200	.146	.088	.040	.011	.001
	7	.000	.000	.000	.000	.001	.003	.009	.021	.042	.075	.117	.166	.215	.252	.267	.250	.201	.130	.057	.010
	8	.000	.000	.000	.000	.000	.000	.001	.004	.011	.023	.044	.076	.121	.176	.233	.282	.302	.276	.194	.07.
	9	.000	.000	.000	.000	.000	.000	.000	.000	.002	.004	.010	.021	.040	.072	.121	.188	.268	.347	.387	.315
	10	.000	.000	.000	.000	.000	.000	.000	.000	.000	.000	.001	.003	.006	.014	.028	.056	.107	.197	.349	.599
11	0	.895	.569	.314	.167	.086	.042	.020	.009	.004	.001	.000	.000	.000	.000	.000	.000	.000	.000	.000	.000
	1	.099	.329	.384	.325	.236	.155	.093	.052	.027	.013	.005	.002	.001	.000	.000	.000	.000	.000	.000	.000
	2	.005	.087	.213	.287	.295	.258	.230	.140	.089	.051	.027	.013	.005	.002	.001	.000	.000	.000	.000	.000

contd.

n	r	p .01	.05	.10	.15	.20	.25	.30	.35	.40	.45	.50	.55	.60	.65	.70	.75	.80	.85	.90	.95
11	3	.000	.014	.071	.152	.221	.258	.257	.225	.177	.126	.081	.046	.023	.010	.004	.001	.000	.000	.000	.000
	4	.000	.001	.016	.054	.111	.172	.220	.243	.236	.206	.161	.113	.070	.038	.017	.006	.002	.000	.000	.000
	5	.000	.000	.002	.013	.039	.080	.132	.183	.221	.236	.226	.193	.147	.099	.057	.027	.010	.002	.000	.000
	6	.000	.000	.000	.002	.010	.027	.057	.099	.147	.193	.226	.236	.221	.183	.132	.080	.039	.013	.002	.000
	7	.000	.000	.000	.000	.002	.006	.017	.038	.070	.113	.161	.206	.236	.243	.220	.172	.111	.054	.016	.001
	8	.000	.000	.000	.000	.000	.001	.004	.010	.023	.046	.081	.126	.177	.225	.257	.258	.221	.152	.071	.014
	9	.000	.000	.000	.000	.000	.000	.001	.002	.005	.013	.027	.051	.089	.140	.200	.258	.295	.287	.213	.087
	10	.000	.000	.000	.000	.000	.000	.000	.000	.001	.002	.005	.013	.027	.052	.093	.155	.236	.325	.384	.329
	11	.000	.000	.000	.000	.000	.000	.000	.000	.000	.000	.000	.001	.004	.009	.020	.042	.086	.167	.314	.569
12	0	.886	.540	.282	.142	.069	.032	.014	.006	.002	.001	.000	.000	.000	.000	.000	.000	.000	.000	.000	.000
	1	.107	.341	.377	.301	.206	.127	.071	.037	.017	.008	.003	.001	.000	.000	.000	.000	.000	.000	.000	.000
	2	.006	.099	.230	.292	.283	.232	.168	.109	.064	.034	.016	.007	.002	.001	.000	.000	.000	.000	.000	.000
	3	.000	.017	.085	.172	.236	.258	.240	.195	.142	.092	.054	.028	.012	.005	.001	.000	.000	.000	.000	.000
	4	.000	.002	.021	.068	.133	.194	.231	.237	.213	.170	.121	.076	.042	.020	.008	.002	.001	.000	.000	.000
	5	.000	.000	.004	.019	.053	.103	.158	.204	.227	.223	.193	.149	.101	.059	.029	.011	.003	.001	.000	.000
	6	.000	.000	.000	.004	.016	.040	.079	.128	.177	.212	.226	.212	.177	.128	.079	.040	.016	.004	.000	.000
	7	.000	.000	.000	.001	.003	.011	.029	.059	.101	.149	.193	.223	.227	.204	.158	.103	.053	.019	.004	.000
	8	.000	.000	.000	.000	.001	.002	.008	.020	.042	.076	.121	.170	.213	.237	.231	.194	.133	.068	.021	.002
	9	.000	.000	.000	.000	.000	.000	.001	.005	.012	.028	.054	.092	.142	.195	.240	.258	.236	.172	.085	.017
	10	.000	.000	.000	.000	.000	.000	.000	.001	.002	.007	.016	.034	.064	.109	.168	.232	.283	.292	.230	.099
	11	.000	.000	.000	.000	.000	.000	.000	.000	.000	.001	.003	.008	.017	.037	.071	.127	.206	.301	.377	.341
	12	.000	.000	.000	.000	.000	.000	.000	.000	.000	.000	.000	.001	.002	.006	.014	.032	.069	.142	.282	.540

contd.

n	r	p: .01	.05	.10	.15	.20	.25	.30	.35	.40	.45	.50	.55	.60	.65	.70	.75	.80	.85	.90	.95
15	0	.860	.463	.206	.087	.035	.013	.005	.002	.000	.000	.000	.000	.000	.000	.000	.000	.000	.000	.000	.000
	1	.130	.366	.343	.231	.132	.067	.031	.013	.005	.002	.000	.000	.000	.000	.000	.000	.000	.000	.000	.000
	2	.009	.135	.267	.286	.231	.156	.092	.048	.022	.009	.003	.001	.000	.000	.000	.000	.000	.000	.000	.000
	3	.000	.031	.129	.218	.250	.225	.170	.111	.063	.032	.014	.005	.002	.000	.000	.000	.000	.000	.000	.000
	4	.000	.005	.043	.116	.188	.225	.219	.179	.127	.078	.042	.019	.007	.002	.001	.000	.000	.000	.000	.000
	5	.000	.001	.010	.045	.103	.165	.206	.212	.186	.140	.092	.051	.024	.010	.003	.001	.000	.000	.000	.000
	6	.000	.000	.002	.013	.043	.092	.147	.191	.207	.191	.153	.105	.061	.030	.012	.003	.001	.000	.000	.000
	7	.000	.000	.000	.003	.014	.039	.081	.132	.177	.201	.196	.165	.118	.071	.035	.013	.003	.001	.000	.000
	8	.000	.000	.000	.001	.003	.013	.035	.071	.118	.165	.196	.201	.177	.132	.081	.039	.014	.003	.000	.000
	9	.000	.000	.000	.000	.001	.003	.012	.030	.061	.105	.153	.191	.207	.191	.147	.092	.043	.013	.002	.000
	10	.000	.000	.000	.000	.000	.001	.003	.010	.024	.051	.092	.140	.186	.212	.206	.165	.103	.045	.010	.001
	11	.000	.000	.000	.000	.000	.000	.001	.002	.007	.019	.042	.078	.127	.179	.219	.225	.188	.116	.043	.005
	12	.000	.000	.000	.000	.000	.000	.000	.000	.002	.005	.014	.032	.063	.111	.170	.225	.250	.218	.129	.031
	13	.000	.000	.000	.000	.000	.000	.000	.000	.000	.001	.003	.009	.022	.048	.092	.156	.231	.286	.267	.135
	14	.000	.000	.000	.000	.000	.000	.000	.000	.000	.000	.000	.002	.005	.013	.031	.067	.132	.231	.343	.366
	15	.000	.000	.000	.000	.000	.000	.000	.000	.000	.000	.000	.000	.000	.002	.005	.013	.035	.087	.206	.463
16	0	.851	.440	.185	.074	.028	.010	.003	.001	.000	.000	.000	.000	.000	.000	.000	.000	.000	.000	.000	.000
	1	.138	.371	.329	.210	.113	.053	.023	.009	.003	.001	.000	.000	.000	.000	.000	.000	.000	.000	.000	.000
	2	.010	.146	.275	.277	.211	.134	.073	.035	.015	.006	.002	.001	.000	.000	.000	.000	.000	.000	.000	.000
	3	.000	.036	.142	.229	.246	.208	.145	.089	.047	.022	.009	.003	.001	.000	.000	.000	.000	.000	.000	.000
	4	.000	.006	.051	.131	.200	.225	.204	.155	.101	.057	.028	.011	.004	.001	.000	.000	.000	.000	.000	.000
	5	.000	.001	.014	.056	.120	.130	.210	.201	.162	.112	.067	.034	.014	.005	.001	.000	.000	.000	.000	.000

contd.

		p																			
n	**r**	**.01**	**.05**	**.10**	**.15**	**.20**	**.25**	**.30**	**.35**	**.40**	**.45**	**.50**	**.55**	**.60**	**.65**	**.70**	**.75**	**.80**	**.85**	**.90**	**.95**
16	6	.000	.000	.003	.018	.055	.110	.165	.198	.198	.168	.122	.075	.039	.017	.006	.001	.000	.000	.000	.000
	7	.000	.000	.000	.005	.020	.052	.101	.152	.189	.197	.175	.132	.084	.044	.019	.006	.001	.000	.000	.000
	8	.000	.000	.000	.001	.006	.020	.049	.092	.142	.181	.196	.181	.142	.092	.049	.020	.006	.001	.000	.000
	9	.000	.000	.000	.000	.001	.006	.019	.044	.084	.132	.175	.197	.189	.152	.101	.052	.020	.005	.000	.000
	10	.000	.000	.000	.000	.000	.001	.006	.017	.039	.075	.122	.168	.198	.198	.165	.110	.055	.018	.003	.000
	11	.000	.000	.000	.000	.000	.000	.001	.005	.014	.034	.067	.112	.162	.201	.210	.180	.120	.056	.014	.001
	12	.000	.000	.000	.000	.000	.000	.000	.001	.004	.011	.028	.057	.101	.155	.204	.225	.200	.131	.051	.006
	13	.000	.000	.000	.000	.000	.000	.000	.000	.001	.003	.009	.022	.047	.089	.146	.208	.246	.229	.142	.036
	14	.000	.000	.000	.000	.000	.000	.000	.000	.000	.001	.002	.006	.015	.035	.073	.134	.211	.277	.275	.146
	15	.000	.000	.000	.000	.000	.000	.000	.000	.000	.000	.000	.001	.003	.009	.023	.053	.113	.210	.329	.371
	16	.000	.000	.000	.000	.000	.000	.000	.000	.000	.000	.000	.000	.000	.001	.003	.010	.028	.074	.185	.440
20	0	.818	.358	.122	.039	.012	.003	.001	.000	.000	.000	.000	.000	.000	.000	.000	.000	.000	.000	.000	.000
	1	.165	.377	.270	.137	.058	.021	.007	.002	.000	.000	.000	.000	.000	.000	.000	.000	.000	.000	.000	.000
	2	.016	.189	.285	.229	.137	.067	.028	.010	.003	.001	.000	.000	.000	.000	.000	.000	.000	.000	.000	.000
	3	.001	.060	.190	.243	.205	.134	.072	.032	.012	.004	.001	.000	.000	.000	.000	.000	.000	.000	.000	.000
	4	.000	.013	.090	.182	.218	.190	.130	.074	.035	.014	.005	.001	.000	.000	.000	.000	.000	.000	.000	.000
	5	.000	.002	.032	.103	.175	.202	.179	.127	.075	.036	.015	.005	.001	.000	.000	.000	.000	.000	.000	.000
	6	.000	.000	.009	.045	.109	.169	.192	.171	.124	.075	.037	.015	.005	.001	.000	.000	.000	.000	.000	.000
	7	.000	.000	.002	.016	.055	.112	.164	.184	.166	.122	.074	.037	.015	.005	.001	.000	.000	.000	.000	.000
	8	.000	.000	.000	.005	.022	.061	.114	.161	.180	.162	.120	.073	.035	.014	.004	.001	.000	.000	.000	.000
	9	.000	.000	.000	.001	.007	.027	.065	.116	.160	.177	.160	.119	.071	.034	.012	.003	.000	.000	.000	.000
	10	.000	.000	.000	.000	.002	.010	.031	.069	.117	.159	.176	.159	.117	.069	.031	.010	.002	.000	.000	.000

contd.

		p																			
n	r	.01	.05	.10	.15	.20	.25	.30	.35	.40	.45	.50	.55	.60	.65	.70	.75	.80	.85	.90	.95
20	11	.000	.000	.000	.000	.000	.003	.012	.034	.071	.119	.160	.177	.160	.116	.065	.027	.007	.001	.000	.000
	12	.000	.000	.000	.000	.000	.001	.004	.014	.035	.073	.120	.162	.180	.161	.114	.061	.022	.005	.000	.000
	13	.000	.000	.000	.000	.000	.000	.001	.005	.015	.037	.074	.122	.166	.184	.164	.112	.055	.016	.002	.000
	14	.000	.000	.000	.000	.000	.000	.000	.001	.005	.015	.037	.075	.124	.171	.192	.169	.109	.045	.009	.000
	15	.000	.000	.000	.000	.000	.000	.000	.000	.001	.005	.015	.036	.075	.127	.179	.202	.175	.103	.032	.002
	16	.000	.000	.000	.000	.000	.000	.000	.000	.000	.001	.005	.014	.035	.074	.130	.190	.218	.182	.090	.013
	17	.000	.000	.000	.000	.000	.000	.000	.000	.000	.000	.001	.004	.012	.032	.072	.134	.205	.243	.190	.060
	18	.000	.000	.000	.000	.000	.000	.000	.000	.000	.000	.000	.001	.003	.010	.028	.067	.137	.229	.285	.189
	19	.000	.000	.000	.000	.000	.000	.000	.000	.000	.000	.000	.000	.000	.002	.007	.021	.058	.137	.270	.377
	20	.000	.000	.000	.000	.000	.000	.000	.000	.000	.000	.000	.000	.000	.000	.001	.003	.012	.039	.122	.358

Table (B): Normal Area Table

	0.00	0.01	0.02	0.03	0.04	0.05	0.06	0.07	0.08	0.09
0.0	0.0000	0.0040	0.0080	0.0120	0.0160	0.0199	0.0239	0.0279	0.0319	0.0359
0.1	0.0398	0.0438	0.0478	0.0517	0.0557	0.0596	0.0636	0.0675	0.0714	0.0753
0.2	0.0793	0.0832	0.0871	0.0910	0.0948	0.0987	0.1026	0.1064	0.1103	0.1141
0.3	0.1179	0.1217	0.1255	0.1293	0.1331	0.1368	0.1406	0.1443	0.1480	0.1517
0.4	0.1554	0.1591	0.1628	0.1664	0.1700	0.1736	0.1772	0.1808	0.1844	0.1879
0.5	0.1915	0.1950	0.1985	0.2019	0.2054	0.2088	0.2123	0.2157	0.2190	0.2224
0.6	0.2257	0.2291	0.2324	0.2357	0.2389	0.2422	0.2454	0.2486	0.2517	0.2549
0.7	0.2580	0.2611	0.2642	0.2673	0.2704	0.2734	0.2764	0.2794	0.2823	0.2852
0.8	0.2881	0.2910	0.2939	0.2967	0.2995	0.3023	0.3051	0.3078	0.3106	0.3133
0.9	0.3159	0.3186	0.3212	0.3238	0.3264	0.3289	0.3315	0.3340	0.3365	0.3389
1.0	0.3413	0.3438	0.3461	0.3485	0.3508	0.3531	0.3554	0.3577	0.3599	0.3621
1.1	0.3643	0.3665	0.3686	0.3708	0.3729	0.3749	0.3770	0.3790	0.3810	0.3830
1.2	0.3849	0.3869	0.3888	0.3907	0.3925	0.3944	0.3962	0.3980	0.3997	0.4015
1.3	0.4032	0.4049	0.4066	0.4082	0.4099	0.4115	0.4131	0.4147	0.4162	0.4177
1.4	0.4192	0.4207	0.4222	0.4236	0.4251	0.4265	0.4279	0.4292	0.4306	0.4319
1.5	0.4332	0.4345	0.4357	0.4370	0.4382	0.4394	0.4406	0.4418	0.4429	0.4441
1.6	0.4452	0.4463	0.4474	0.4484	0.4495	0.4505	0.4515	0.4525	0.4535	0.4545
1.7	0.4554	0.4564	0.4573	0.4582	0.4591	0.4599	0.4608	0.4616	0.4625	0.4633
1.8	0.4641	0.4649	0.4656	0.4664	0.4671	0.4678	0.4686	0.4693	0.4699	0.4706
1.9	0.4713	0.4719	0.4726	0.4732	0.4738	0.4744	0.4750	0.4756	0.4761	0.4767
2.0	0.4772	0.4778	0.4783	0.4788	0.4793	0.4798	0.4803	0.4808	0.4812	0.4817
2.1	0.4821	0.4826	0.4830	0.4834	0.4838	0.4842	0.4846	0.4850	0.4854	0.4857
2.2	0.4861	0.4864	0.4868	0.4871	0.4875	0.4878	0.4881	0.4884	0.4887	0.4890
2.3	0.4893	0.4896	0.4898	0.4901	0.4904	0.4906	0.4909	0.4911	0.4913	0.4916
2.4	0.4918	0.4920	0.4922	0.4925	0.4927	0.4929	0.4931	0.4932	0.4934	0.4936
2.5	0.4938	0.4940	0.4941	0.4943	0.4945	0.4946	0.4948	0.4949	0.4951	0.4952
2.6	0.4953	0.4955	0.4956	0.4957	0.4959	0.4960	0.4961	0.4962	0.4963	0.4964
2.7	0.4965	0.4966	0.4967	0.4968	0.4969	0.4970	0.4971	0.4972	0.4973	0.4974
2.8	0.4974	0.4975	0.4976	0.4977	0.4977	0.4978	0.4979	0.4979	0.4980	0.4981
2.9	0.4981	0.4982	0.4982	0.4983	0.4984	0.4984	0.4985	0.4985	0.4986	0.4986
3.0	0.4987	0.4987	0.4987	0.4988	0.4988	0.4989	0.4989	0.4989	0.4990	0.4990

Question Papers

Mathematical Methods in Physics-I: PHE-4

June, 2011

Note: Attempt all questions. The marks for each question are indicated against it.

Q1. Attempt any three parts:

(a) Show that $(\vec{a}\times\vec{b})\cdot(\vec{c}\times\vec{d}) = (\vec{a}\cdot\vec{c})(\vec{b}\cdot\vec{d}) - (\vec{a}\cdot\vec{d})(\vec{b}\cdot\vec{c})$

Ans. Refer to Chapter-1, Q.No.-24

(b) A particle moves along a curve whose parametric equations are $x = e^{-t}, y = 2\cos 3t, z = 2\sin 3t$, **where** t **is the time. Determine the magnitude of the velocity and acceleration at** $t = 0$.

Ans. Refer to Chapter-2, Q.No.-29.

(c) Given that $\vec{E} = -\vec{\nabla}\Phi$ **and** $\vec{\nabla}\cdot\vec{E} = \rho/\varepsilon_0$. **Determine the electric field** $\vec{E}$ **and the charge distribution** ρ **that corresponds to the potential** $\Phi = k_0(x^2 + y^2 + z^2)$.

Ans. Refer to Chapter-2, Q.No.-11(a).

(d) Express the following vector field in spherical polar coordinates.

$$\vec{F} = \frac{k(x\hat{j} - y\hat{i})}{x^2 + y^2 + z^2}$$

Ans. Refer to Chapter-3, Q.No.-17.

(e) Evaluate $\int_C \vec{F}.d\vec{r}$ **from (0, 0) to (1, 2) for the field** $\vec{F} = 3xy\,\hat{i} - y^2\hat{j}$, **where C is the curve** $y = 2x^2$ **in the xy plane.**

Ans. Same as Chapter-4, Q.No.-11.

Q2. State the divergence theorem. Using divergence theorem evaluate $\iint_S \vec{F}\cdot\hat{n}\,dS$ **where** $\vec{F} = 4xz\,\hat{i} - y^2\,\hat{j} + yz\,\hat{k}$ **and S is the surface of the cube bounded by** $x = 0, x = 1, y = 0, y = 1, z = 0$ **and** $z = 1$. $\hat{n}$ **is the unit vector normal to the surface S.**

Ans. See theorem in Chapter-4 [Gauss' Divergence Theorem]and Q.No.-31

Or

State Stoke's theorem. Show that for a conservative force field $\vec{F}$ curl $\vec{F}$ is zero everywhere.

Ans. See theorem in Chapter-4 [Stokes's Theorem]

We have $\int_{ACB} \vec{F}.d\vec{r} = \int_{ADB} \vec{F}.d\vec{r}$

where $\vec{F}$ is a conservative force field.

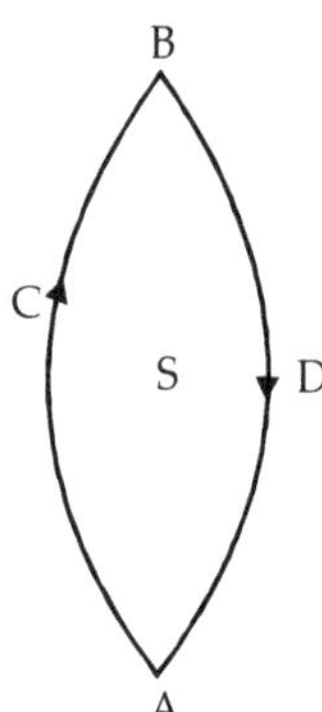

$$\therefore \int_{ACB} \vec{F}.d\vec{r} = -\int_{BDA} \vec{F}.d\vec{r} \text{ or } \int_{ACB} \vec{F}.d\vec{r} + \int_{BDA} \vec{F}.d\vec{r} = 0$$

i.e. $\oint_{ACBDA} \vec{F}.d\vec{r} = 0$

From Stokes' theorem, we know that $\oint_{ACBDA} \vec{F}.d\vec{r} = \iint_S \text{curl}\,\vec{F}.d\vec{S}$

So, $\iint_S \text{curl}\,\vec{F}.d\vec{S} = 0$ But $d\vec{S}$ is arbitrary.

Hence, the integrand is zero.

Hence, curl $\vec{F} = 0$ everywhere in the field.

$\Rightarrow$ $\vec{F}$ curl $\vec{F} = 0$ everywhere.

Q3. Suppose four coins are tossed. Let X designate the number of heads which appear. Calculate E (X).

Ans. Refer to Chapter-5, Q.No.-32

Or

A box contains 4 bad and 6 good tubes. Two tubes are drawn from the box at a time. One of them is tested and found to be good. What is the probability that the other one is also good?

Ans. Refer to Chapter-5, Q.No.-34

Q4. Derive the expression for the mean and variance of the Poisson distribution. $p(x;m) = \dfrac{e^{-m}m^x}{x!} : x = 0,1,2,.....$

Ans. By definition, $E(X) = \sum_{x=0}^{\infty} xp(x;m) = \sum_{x=0}^{\infty} x\dfrac{e^{-m}m^x}{x!} = me^{-m}\sum_{x=1}^{\infty}\dfrac{m^{x-1}}{(x-1)!}$

since $x/x! = 1/(x-1)!$ and $x = 0$ does not yield an acceptable value. Now, the summation term simply defines exp (m).

Substituting this result in the expression for E (X), we get $E(X) = me^{-m}e^{m} = m$ which proves our statement that parameter m signifies the mean of the distribution.

The variance of the Poisson distribution can be computed easily by noting that $\mathrm{Var}(X) = \sum_{x=0}^{\infty} x^2 p(x;m) - [E(X)]^2 = \sum_{x=0}^{\infty} x^2 \dfrac{e^{-m}m^x}{x!} - m^2$

The sum in the first term on the right hand side can be rewritten as

$$\sum_{x=0}^{\infty}[x + x(x-1.)]\frac{e^{-m}m^x}{x!} = \sum_{x=0}^{\infty}\frac{xe^{-m}m^x}{x!} + e^{-m}\sum_{x=0}^{\infty}x(x-1)\frac{e^{-m}m^x}{x!}$$

$$= m + e^{-m}m^2\sum_{x=2}^{\infty}\frac{m^{x-2}}{(x-2)!} = m + m^2e^{-m}e^{m} = m(1+m)$$

Hence, $\mathrm{Var}(X) = m + m^2 - m^2 = m$ and the standard deviation is $\sqrt{m}$.

Or

The measurement of surface tension, S of water at various temperatures are given in the following table.

T (°C)	10	20	30	40	50	60
S (dynes cm^{-1})	74.0	73.0	71.0	70.0	68.0	66.0

Calculate the correlation coefficient for this data.

Ans. Refer to Chapter - 7, Q.No.-17.

"Don't aim for success if you want it;
just do what you love and believe in,
and it will come naturally."

Mathematical Methods in Physics-I: PHE-4

December, 2011

Note: Attempt all questions. The marks for each question are indicated against it.

Q1. Attempt any three parts:

(a) Calculate the area of a parallelogram having diagonals $\vec{A} = 3\,\hat{i} + \hat{j} - 2\,\hat{k}$ and $\vec{B} = \hat{i} - 3\hat{j} + 4\,\hat{k}$.

Ans. Refer to Chapter-1, Q.No.-25

(b) A particle moves along the curve $x = 2t^2, y = t^2 - 4t, z = 3t - 5$, where t is the time. Determine the component of its velocity at t = 1 in the direction $\hat{i} - 3\,\hat{j} + 2\,\hat{k}$.

Ans. Same as Chapter-2, Q.No.-32

(c) Express the force field $\vec{F} = \dfrac{z\,\hat{i} + x\,\hat{j} + y\,\hat{k}}{x^2 + y^2 + z^2}$ in cylindrical polar coordinates.

Ans. Refer to Chapter-3, Q.No.-18

(d) Prove that $\nabla^2\left(\dfrac{1}{r}\right) = 0$.

Ans. Refer to Chapter-2, Q.No.-30.

(e) A two – dimensional force field is defined as $\vec{F} = k\left(x\,\hat{j} - y\,\hat{i}\right)$ where k is a constant. Compute the work done by this force in taking a particle along the straight line x + y = 1.

Ans. Same as Chapter-4, Q.No.-7.

Q2. State divergence theorem. The electric field due to a point charge, q, at a point whose position vector with respect to the location of q is $\vec{r}$, is given by $\vec{E} = \dfrac{kq}{r^3}\,\vec{r}\,(r \neq 0)$ where k is a constant dependent

on the nature of the medium. Determine the flux of $\vec{E}$ through a sphere of radius a, whose centre is at the position of the charge q.

Ans. Refer to Chapter-4 [Gauss' Divergence Theorem] and Chapter-4, Q.No.-32

Or

State stokes theorem. Using Stokes' theorem for the vector field $\vec{A} = \vec{P}(x,y)\,\hat{i} + Q(x,y)\,\hat{j}$, show that

$$\oint_C (Pd\,x + Qd\,y) = \iint_S \left(\frac{\partial Q}{\partial x} - \frac{\partial P}{\partial y}\right) dxdy$$

Ans. Refer to Chapter-4 [Stokes's Theorem]

Q3. If at least one child in a family with two children is a girl, what is the probability that both children are girls?

Ans. Refer to Chapter-5, Q.No.-35.

Or

A continuous random variable x that can assume any value between x = 2 and x = 5 and has a density function $f(x) = k(1+x)$. Find $p(x<4)$.

Ans. By the property of P.d.f.

$\int_{R_x} f(x)dx = 1.$ X takes values between 2 and 5.

$$\therefore \quad \int_2^5 k(1+x)dx = 1$$

$$\text{i.e. } \frac{27}{2}k = 1$$

$$\therefore k = \frac{2}{27}$$

$$\text{Now } p(X<4) = p(2<X<4) = \int_2^4 K(1+x)dx = \frac{16}{27}$$

Q4. Derive the expression for the mean and variance of the Poisson distribution $p(x\,;m) = \dfrac{e^{-m}m^x}{x!}\,; x = 0,1,2,......$

Ans. Refer to June-2011, Q.No.-4.

Or

The following table shows the marks denoted by x and y, respectively, of 10 students in two tests. Obtain the least square regression line of y on x.

x:	6	5	8	8	7	6	10	4	9	7
y:	8	7	7	10	5	8	10	6	8	6

Ans. Same as Chapter-7, Q.No.-10.

Those who try to do Something
and **FAIL**.........
are infinitely better than
those who try to do nothing
and **Succeed**...........

Mathematical Methods in Physics-I: PHE-4

June, 2012

Note: Attempt all questions. The marks for each question are indicated against it.

Q1. Attempt any three parts:

(a) Determine the angle between the vectors

$\vec{A} = -6\hat{i} - 4\hat{j} + 2\hat{k}$ and $\vec{B} = \hat{i} - 2\hat{j} - \hat{k}$

Ans. Refer to Chapter-1, Q.No.-23

(b) Calculate the volume of the parallelepiped formed by the vectors:

$\vec{A} = \hat{i} + 2\hat{j} - \hat{k}$ $\quad \vec{B} = \hat{j} + \hat{k}$ $\quad \vec{C} = \hat{i} - \hat{j}.$

Ans. Same as Chapter-1, Q.No.-16

(c) Determine the unit vector normal to the surface $x^2 + y^2 + z^2 = 3$ at $(1, 1, 1)$.

Ans. Same as Chapter-2, Q.No.-31

(d) A frictionless bead slides down a vertical helix of radius R such that its position vector at time t is given by:

$$\vec{r}(t) = a(\cos\omega t\, \hat{i} + \sin\omega t\, \hat{j}) - \frac{1}{2}gt^2\hat{k}$$

Determine its velocity and acceleration.

Ans. Refer to Chapter-2, Q.No.-36

(e) The cylindrical coordinates $u_1 = \rho, u_2 = \phi, u_3 = z$ are related to the Cartesian coordinates x, y and z as follows:

$x = \rho \cos\phi$ $\quad y = \rho \sin\phi$ $\quad z = z$

Show that the cylindrical coordinate system is orthogonal, i.e., $g_{ij}(i \neq j) = 0$ for all i and j.

Ans. Refer to Chapter-3, Q.No.-7

Q2. **A force acting on a particle is given by: $\vec{F} = -kx\,\hat{i} - ky\,\hat{j}$. Calculate the work done in moving the particle from (1, 1) to (4, 4) along the path $x = y$.**

Ans. Same as Dec.-2012, Q.No.-2

Or

Calculate the surface integral of a vector $\vec{A} = x\,\hat{i} + 2y\,\hat{j} + 3z\,\hat{k}$ over the surface of a sphere of radius 2 by using Gauss's divergence theorem.

Ans. Refer to Chapter-4, Q.No.-40

Q3. **The average number of calls received in a BPO is 4 per minute. Calculate the probability that not more than one call is received during one minute.**

Ans. Refer to Chapter-6, Q. No.-27

Or

A continuous random variable X has the probability distribution

$$P(x) = \frac{1}{\pi\left(1 + x^2\right)} \quad -1 < x < 1$$

$$= 0 \text{ otherwise}$$

Calculate its mean.

Ans. Refer to Chapter-6, Q. No.-28

Q4. **The extension in a material is measured as a function of load in appropriate units and is given by:**

Load (x)	0	1	2	3	4
Extension (y)	16	13	10	6	3

Obtain the least square fit to the data

Ans. Refer to Chapter-7, Q.No.-19

Or

Derive an expression for the mean of the normal distribution

$$n\left(x;\bar{x},\sigma\right) = \frac{1}{\sqrt{2\pi}\,\sigma}\exp\left[-\frac{1}{2}\left(\frac{x-\bar{x}}{\sigma}\right)^2\right]$$

Ans. Since, $E(X) = \dfrac{1}{\sqrt{2\pi}\,\sigma}\displaystyle\int_{-\infty}^{\infty} x \exp\left[-\frac{(x-\mu)^2}{2\sigma^2}\right]dx$ ...(i)

Setting $t = \frac{x-\mu}{\sigma}$ we find that $dx = \sigma\, dt$ and $x = \sigma t + \mu$.

Then Eq. (i) takes the form

$$E(X) = \frac{1}{\sqrt{2\pi}} \int_{-\infty}^{\infty} (\sigma t + \mu) \exp\left(-\frac{t^2}{2}\right) dt$$

$$= \frac{\sigma}{\sqrt{2\pi}} \int_{-\infty}^{\infty} t \exp\left(-\frac{t^2}{2}\right) dt + \frac{\mu}{\sqrt{2\pi}} \int_{-\infty}^{\infty} \exp\left(-\frac{t^2}{2}\right) dt$$

The first integral vanished since t is an odd function and $\frac{t^2}{2}$ is an even function. So the expression for $E(X)$ assumes a compact form:

$$E(X) = \frac{\mu}{\sqrt{2\pi}} \int_{-\infty}^{\infty} \exp\left(-\frac{t^2}{2}\right) dt$$

The right hand side signifies μ times the area under a normal curve with mean zero and variance one.

Hence $E(X) = \mu$ and the variance of the normal distribution is given by

$$Var(X) = \frac{1}{\sqrt{2\pi}\sigma} \int_{-\infty}^{\infty} (x-\mu)^2 \exp\left[-\frac{1}{2}\left(\frac{x-\mu}{\sigma}\right)^2\right] dx$$

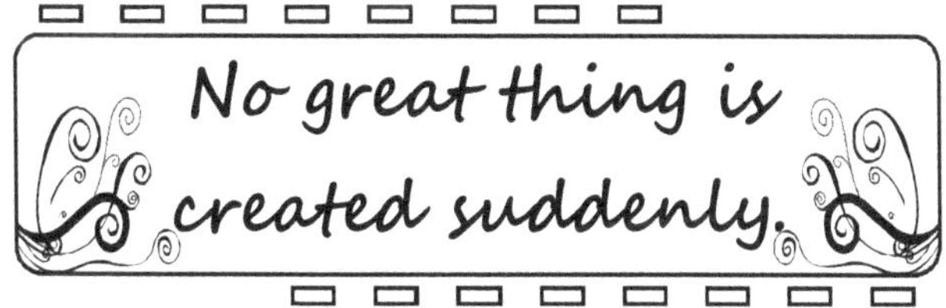

Mathematical Methods in Physics-I: PHE-4

December, 2012

Note: Attempt all questions. The marks for each question are indicated against it.

Q1. Attempt any three parts:

(a) Determine the vector $\vec{A}$ perpendicular to the vectors $\vec{B} = 2\hat{i} + \hat{j} - \hat{k}$ and $\vec{C} = \hat{i} - \hat{j} + \hat{k}$.

Ans. Refer to Chapter-1, Q.No.-26

(b) Show that $(\vec{A} \times \vec{B}).(\vec{A} \times \vec{B}) = A^2B^2 - (\vec{A}\vec{B})^2$.

Ans. Refer to Chapter-1, Q.No.-27

(c) Determine the directional derivative of the scalar field $f = x^2 + yz$ at the point (1, 2, 2) in the direction of the unit vector $\hat{A} = \frac{1}{\sqrt{6}}\left(2\hat{i} + \hat{j} - \hat{k}\right)$.

Ans. Refer to Chapter-2, Q.No.-37

(d) The position vector $\vec{r}$ of particle moving on a curve is given by $\vec{r} = 3t^2\hat{i} + 4t\hat{j} + 2\hat{k}$. Determine the angular momentum of the particle about the origin.

Ans. The angular momentums of the particle is given by equation $\left(\vec{L} = \vec{r} \times m\vec{v}\right)$

Consider, m be the cross of the particle.

Here, The position vector of the particle is $\vec{r} = 3t^2\hat{i} + 4t\hat{j} + 2\hat{k}$

$\therefore$ The velocity of the particle are $\vec{v} = \frac{d\vec{r}}{dt} = \left[\frac{d}{dt}(3t^2)\hat{i} + \frac{d}{dt}(4t)\hat{j} + \frac{d}{dt}(2)\hat{k}\right]$

$= 6t\hat{i} + 4\hat{j}$

Hence, the angular momentum of the particle about the origin is given by:

$$\vec{L} = (m)\left[\left(3t^2\hat{i} + 4t\hat{j} + 2\hat{k}\right) \times \left(6t\hat{i} + 4\hat{j}\right)\right]$$

$$= (m)\left[12t^2\hat{k} - 24t^2\hat{k} + 12t\hat{j} - 8\hat{i}\right]$$

$$= (m)\left[-8\hat{i} + 12t\hat{j} - 12t^2\hat{k}\right]$$

(e) Spherical polar coordinates $u_1 = r, u_2 = \theta, u_3 = \phi$ are related to the Cartesian coordinates x, y and z as follows:

$$x = r\sin\theta\cos\phi \qquad y = r\sin\theta\sin\phi \qquad z = r\cos\theta.$$

Calculate g_{12}, g_{13} and g_{23} to show that the spherical coordinate system is orthogonal.

Ans. Refer to Chapter-3, Q.No.-19

Q2. Calculate the work done in going from (1,1) to (3, 3) along the path $x = y$ by the force $\vec{F} = (x - y)\hat{i} + (x + y)\hat{j}$.

Ans. Refer to Chapter-4, Q.No.-41

Or

Using Stokes' theorem show that if the work done by a force along a closed path is zero, the curl of the force field is zero.

Ans. Refer to Chapter-4, Q. No.-42

Q3. The probability of surviving an attack of dengue is 0.2. What is the probability that at least one person out of 10 suffering from dengue will survive?

Ans. Same as Chapter-6, Q. No.-25

Or

A continuous random variable X lying between 0 and ∞ has the probability distribution $P(x) = e^{-x}$. Obtain $< X^2 >$.

Ans. Notice that $\int_0^\infty e^{-x}\,dx = -\left[e^{-x}\right]_0^\infty = -(0-1) = 1$

Now, $< X^2 > = \int_0^\infty x^2 P(x)\,dx = \int_0^\infty x^2 e^{-x}\,dx$

After solving by Integration by parts, we obtain

$$< X^2 > = -\left[x^2 e^{-x}\right]_0^\infty + 2\int_0^\infty x e^{-x}\,dx = 0 + 2 \times 1 \Rightarrow \qquad < X^2 > = 2.$$

Q4. The resistance of a coil is measured as a function of temperature and is given by

T (°C) =	40	50	60	70	80
R (Ω) =	6	7	8	9	10

Obtain R = a + bT for the best fit.

Ans. Refer to Chapter-7, Q.No.-20

Or

Derive the expression for the mean of a random variable with a Poisson distribution: $P(x;m) = \frac{e^{-m}m^x}{x!}$

Ans. Refer to June-2011, Q.No.-4

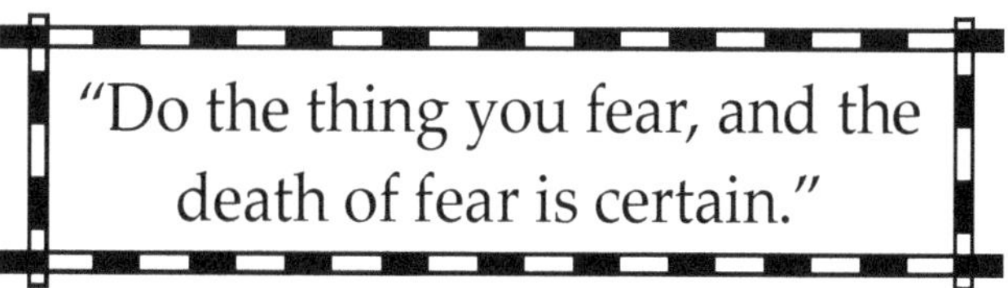

Mathematical Methods in Physics-I: PHE-4

June, 2013

Note: Attempt all questions. The marks for each question are indicated against it.

Q1. Attempt any three parts:

(a) Determine the unit vector perpendicular to the plane formed by the two vectors:

$\vec{a} = 2\hat{i} - \hat{k}, \vec{b} = 3\hat{j} + 2\hat{k}$

Ans. Refer to Chapter-1, Q.No.-28

(b) Obtain the components of acceleration in cylindrical coordinates for a particle moving in space.

Ans. Refer to Chapter-3, Q.No.-6

(c) Obtain the directional derivative of $V = \frac{k}{\left(x^2 + y^2 + z^2\right)^{1/2}}$ at the point (1, 2, 1) in the direction $\hat{n} - \left(\hat{i} + \hat{j} - 2\hat{k}\right) / \sqrt{6}$.

Ans. Same as Chapter-2, Q.No.-8

(d) Determine the work done by the force $\vec{F} = y^2 x\hat{i} + xy\hat{j}$ in moving a particle along the curve $y^2 = 4x$ from (0, 0) and (1, 2).

Ans. Refer to Chapter-4, Q.No.-43

(e) Show that for a vector field $\vec{A}, \vec{\nabla} . \left(\vec{\nabla} \times \vec{A}\right) = 0.$

Ans. Refer to Chapter-2, Page No.-42

Q2. State Gauss's divergence theorem and use it to evaluate $\iint_S \vec{F}.\hat{n}\, ds$ for $\vec{F} = 2xz\hat{i} - z^2\hat{j} + zx\hat{k}$ where s is the surface of a cube bounded by $x = 0, x = 1, y = 0, y = 1, z = 0$ and $z = 1$.

Ans. Same as June-2011, Q.No.-2

Or

Using Stoke's theorem, prove Green's theorem in a plane. $\oint_C [Pdx + Qdy] = \iint_R \left(\frac{\partial Q}{\partial x} - \frac{\partial P}{\partial y}\right) dx\,dy$**, where R is a region of the xy-plane bounded by a simple closed curve C.**

Ans. Refer to Dec-2011, Q.No.-2

Q3. Write down an expression for the binomial distribution function b(x; n, p). Hence find mean and variance of a binomial random variable X.

Ans. Refer to Chapter-6 [Binomial Distribution]

Or

The number of bomb-hits recorded in each of the 550 small areas in a city are recorded below:

x_i	0	1	2	3	4
$f(x_i)$	224	206	88	30	2

Does it fit a Poisson distribution?

Ans. Same as Chapter-6, Q.No.-26

Q4. Determine the expectation value of x for the probability density function $f(x) = axe^{-bx}, 0 < x < \infty$**.**

Ans. Given that $f(x) = axe^{-bx}, 0 < x < \infty$.

Hence, expectation value $E[x] = a\int_0^\infty x.xe^{-bx}dx = a\int_0^\infty x^2e^{-bx}dx$

$$= a\left[\frac{x^2e^{-bx}}{-b} - \frac{2xe^{-bx}}{b^2} - \frac{2e^{-bx}}{b^3}\right]_0^\infty \text{ which does not exist.}$$

Therefore, expectation value does not exist.

Or

The heat capacity of liquid sulphuric acid was measured at various temperatures yielding the following set of data:

X-Temp ($^\circ C$):	50	100	150	200	250
Y-Heat capacity (in cal/$^\circ C$):	0.38	0.39	0.41	0.43	0.45

Compute the correlation coefficient r_{XY}.

Ans. Same as Chapter-7, Q.No.-18

Mathematical Methods in Physics-I: PHE-4

December, 2013

Note: Attempt all questions. The marks for each question are indicated against it. You may use log tables or calculators. Symbols have their usual meanings.

Q1. Attempt any three parts:

(a) Determine the volume of the parallelepiped formed by $\vec{r}_1 = 2\hat{i} + 4\hat{j} - 5\hat{k}$, $\vec{r}_2 = \hat{i} + 2\hat{j} + 3\hat{k}$, $\vec{r}_3 = \hat{i} + \hat{j}$.

(b) A particular electromagnetic field in free space is given by $E_x = 0$, $E_y = E_0 \sin(kx + \omega t)$, $E_z = 0$ $B_x = 0$, $B_y = 0$, $B_z = -E_0 \sin(kx + \omega t)$. Obtain the relation between ω and k for which the following equation holds:

$$\vec{\nabla} \times \vec{E} = -\frac{1}{c}\frac{\partial \vec{B}}{\partial t}$$

(c) The position vector of a particle of mass m is $\vec{r} = x\vec{i} + y\vec{j} + z\vec{k}$. Obtain its angular momentum $\left(\vec{r} \times m\vec{v}\right)$ in cylindrical coordinates.

(d) Show that for a scalar field $\phi(x,y,z)$, $\vec{\nabla} \times \left(\vec{\nabla}\phi\right) = \vec{0}$

(e) If $\vec{F} = xy\,\vec{i} - z\,\vec{j} + x^2\vec{k}$ and C is the curve $x = t^2, y = 2t, z = t^3$ from t = o to t = 1, evaluate the integral $\int_C \vec{F} \cdot d\vec{r}$

Q2. State Stoke's theorem and evaluate the integral $\int_S \vec{A} . d\vec{s}$ for $\vec{A} = (2x - y)\hat{i} - yz^2\hat{j} - y^2 z\hat{k}$, where S is the upper half surface of the sphere $x^2 + y^2 + z^2 = 1$.

Or

Use Green's theorem:

$\oint_C Pdx + Qdy = \iint_R \left(\frac{\partial Q}{\partial x} - \frac{\partial P}{\partial y}\right) dxdy$ where R is a region in xy-plane bounded by a simple closed curve C, to evaluate $\oint_C [(y - \sin x)dx + \cos x dy]$, where c is a triangle OAB such that the co-ordinates of O, A and B are respectively (0, 0), $\left(\frac{\pi}{2}, 0\right)$ and $\left(\frac{\pi}{2}, 1\right)$.

Q3. In an objective type examination, 10 questions are true-false type. Calculate the probability of guessing at least 8 correct answers.

Or

Let y designate the number of tails which appear when 3 coins are tossed. Calculate E(y).

Q4. The Maxwell-Boltzmann distribution of velocity υ, of particles each of mass m, is given by

$$f(\upsilon) = 4\pi\left(\frac{m}{2\pi k_B T}\right)^{3/2} \upsilon^2 \exp\left(-\frac{m\upsilon^2}{2k_B T}\right);$$

$0 \le \upsilon \le \alpha$, where T is the temperature and k_B is the Boltzmann constant. Show that the mean velocity,

$$\bar{\upsilon} = \sqrt{\frac{8k_B T}{m\pi}}.$$

Or

The pressure of a gas corresponding to various volume V is measured, yielding the following data:

V (cm^3)	50	60	70	90	100
p (kg cm^{-2})	65	50	40	25	10

Fit the data to the equation $pV^\gamma = c$.

◈◈◈

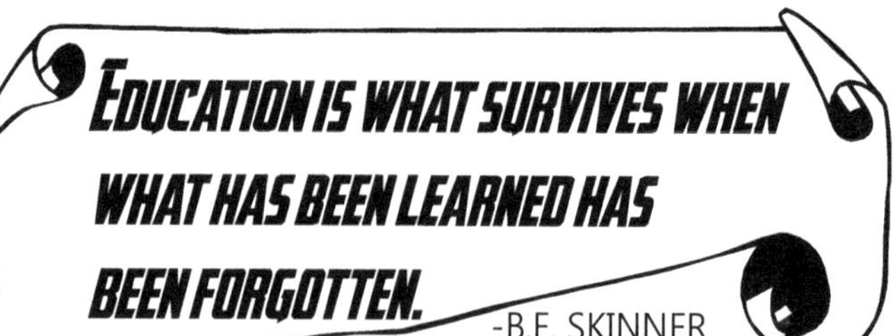

Mathematical Methods in Physics-I: PHE-4

June, 2014

Note: Attempt all questions. The marks for each question are indicated against it. Symbols have their usual meaning. You may use a log table or calculator.

Q1. Answer any three parts:

(a) Three vectors $\vec{a}$, $\vec{b}$ and $\vec{c}$ are given by

$$\vec{a} = 2\hat{i} + 4\hat{j} + \hat{k}$$

$$\vec{b} = 7\hat{i} + 4\hat{j} + 2\hat{k}$$

$$\vec{c} = 4\hat{i} + 3\hat{j} + \hat{k}$$

Determine the angle between the vectors $(\vec{b} - \vec{a})$ and $(\vec{c} - \vec{a})$.

(b) Obtain the unit vector normal to the surface of a cone $z^2 = 4(x^2 + y^2)$ at the point (1, 0, 2).

(c) The spherical polar coordinates $u_1 = r$, $u_2 = \theta$ and $u_3 = \phi$ are related to the cartesian coordinates x, y, z as follows:

$$x = r\sin\theta\cos\phi$$

$$y = r\sin\theta\sin\phi$$

$$z = r\cos\theta$$

Show that the spherical polar coordinate system is orthogonal.

(d) Compute $(\vec{A} \times \vec{B}) \cdot (\vec{C} \times \vec{D})$ for the vectors

$$\vec{A} = \hat{i} + 2\hat{j}$$

$$\vec{B} = -3\hat{i} + 2\hat{j}$$

$$\vec{C} = 2\hat{i} + 3\hat{j} + 4\hat{k}$$

$\vec{D} = 6\hat{i} - 7\hat{j} + 2\hat{k}$

(e) The position vector $\vec{r}(t)$ of a particle of mass m is moving on a curve given by

$\vec{r}(t) = 3t^2\hat{i} + 6t\hat{j} + 7\hat{k}$

Determine the angular momentum of the particle about the origin.

Q2. Obtain the work done by the force

$\vec{F} = z\hat{i} + x\hat{j} + y\hat{k}$

in moving a particle along the curve x=cos t, y = sin t, z = 3t for $(0 \le t \le 2\pi)$.

Or

State Gauss's divergence theorem and use it to evaluate the surface integral $\int_S \vec{A} \cdot d\vec{S}$ over a spherical surface of radius 2 units, for

$\vec{A} = 7x\hat{i} - z\hat{k}$.

Q3. The probability of a successful brain operation is 0.2. What is the probability that at least one person out of 10 undergoing the operation will survive?

Or

The probability distribution for a continuous random variable X lying between $0 \le X \le \infty$ is e^{-X}. Calculate the mean <X> and the variance σ.

Q4. Resistance of a coil at different temperatures is measured. The data is given below:

T (°C)	40°	50°	60°	70°	80°
R (Ω)	1.2	1.3	1.4	1.6	1.7

Obtain the equation R = a + bT for the best fit.

Or

Obtain the value of $E(X^2)$ for the Poisson distribution:

$p(x;m) = \frac{e^{-m}}{x!} m^x$.

Mathematical Methods in Physics-I: PHE-4

December, 2014

Note: Attempt all questions. The marks for each question are indicated against it. Symbols have their usual meaning. You may use log tables or a calculator.

Q1. Answer any three parts:

(a) Determine the vector $\vec{A}$ normal to the vectors, $\vec{B}$ and $\vec{C}$ given by

$$\vec{B} = 2\hat{i} + 3\hat{j} + 5\hat{k}$$

$$\vec{C} = \hat{i} - 3\hat{j} + \hat{k}$$

(b) Obtain the directional derivative of $f(x,y,z) = 2x^2 + 3y^2 + z^2$ at the point (2, 1, 3) in the direction of the vector $\vec{a} = \hat{i} - 2\hat{k}$.

(c) A force $\vec{F} = 3\hat{i} - 6\hat{k}$ acts along a line passing through the point P(0, –1, 4). Determine the torque about the point Q(4, 6, –1).

(d) The cylindrical coordinates $u_1 = \rho, u_2 = \phi, u_3 = z$ are related to the Cartesian coordinates x, y and z as follows:

$$x = \rho\cos\phi, \quad y = \rho\sin\phi, \quad z = z$$

Obtain the square of the arc element given by

$$ds^2 = g_{11}(du_1)^2 + g_{22}(du_2)^2 + g_{33}(du_3)^2$$

(e) Define polar and axial vectors. Give one example of each.

Q2. Calculate the work done in moving a particle from (1, 1) to (3, 3) along the path x = y by the force

$$\vec{F} = (x + 2y)\hat{i} + (3x - y)\hat{j}$$

Or

State Stokes' theorem. Using Stokes' theorem evaluate the line integral $\oint \vec{F} \cdot \vec{dl}$ where $\vec{F} = y\hat{i} + z^3 x\hat{j} - yz^3\hat{k}$ over a circle of radius 2 parallel to the x – y plane at z = 3.

Q3. An unbiased coin is tossed 10 times. Calculate the probability of getting at least 8 heads.

Or

The probability distribution for a continuous variable $0 \le x \le L$ is given by $P(x) = \frac{2}{L}\sin^2\frac{\pi x}{L}$. Calculate <x>.

Q4. The radius of a capillary tube is measured 6 times to obtain the following data:

0.0461 mm

0.0464 mm

0.0460 mm

0.0463 mm

0.0461 mm

0.0459 mm

Obtain the best value of the radius and standard error in the mean.

Or

Show that the binomial distribution $b(n;x,p)$ tends to the Poisson's distribution

$$p(x;m) = \frac{e^{-m}m^x}{x!}; \quad x = 0,1,2,....$$

In the limit $n \to \infty$ but np remaining constant.

A good education is the greatest gift you can give yourself or anyone else.

(Mahtab Narsimhan)

Mathematical Methods in Physics-I: PHE-4

June, 2015

Note: Attempt all questions. The marks for each question are indicated against it. Symbols have their usual meanings. You may use log tables or non-programmable calculators.

Q1. Attempt any three parts:

(a) Vectors $\vec{a}$ and $\vec{b}$ are given by $\vec{a} = \hat{i} + 2\hat{j} + 3\hat{k}$ and $\vec{b} = 2\hat{i} + 3\hat{j} + 4\hat{k}$

Calculate (i) the angle between $\vec{a}$ and $\vec{b}$ and (ii) the projection of the vector $\vec{a} + \frac{1}{2}\vec{b}$ onto $\vec{a}$.

(b) Show that $\vec{\nabla} \cdot (\vec{\nabla} \times \vec{F}) = 0$ for a vector field $\vec{F}$.

(c) Consider a force $\vec{F} = -x\hat{i} + y\hat{j} + z\hat{k}$ N, acting at a point $P(7\hat{i} + 3\hat{j} + \hat{k})$ m. What is the torque (in Nm) about the origin?

(d) Calculate the work done in moving a particle in a force field given by

$\vec{F} = 3xy\hat{i} - 5z\hat{j} + 10x\hat{k}$ along the curve C defined by $x = t^2 + 1;\ y = 2t^2;\ z = t^3$ from $t = 1$ to $t = 2$.

(e) The nuclear force between two neutrons in a nucleus is described by the Yukawa potential

$$U(r) = -U_0 \frac{r_0}{r} \exp\left(-\frac{r}{r_0}\right)$$

Where r is the distance between neutrons and U_0 and r_0 are constants. Determine the force $\vec{F}(r) = -\vec{\nabla}U(r)$

Q2. Evaluate $I_{xy} = \iint\limits_{R} \sigma xy\, dx\, dy$ for a square plate of side L and mass m. σ is mass density of the plate and R is the region of space covered by it.

Or

State divergence theorem. Evaluate the surface integral $I = \oiint\limits_{S} \vec{a} \cdot d\vec{S}$, where

$\vec{a} = (y - x)\hat{i} + y\hat{j} + (z + x^2)\hat{k}$ and S is the closed surface of the sphere $x^2 + y^2 + z^2 = a^2$.

Q3. There are 20 computers in a store. Among them, 15 are new and 5 are refurbished, but these are indistinguishable. Six computers are selected at random from this store and purchased for a lab. Compute the probability that among the chosen computers, two are refurbished.

Or

A biased dice has probabilities $P(x_i) = \frac{p}{2}, p, p, p, p, 2p$ of showing $x_i = 1, 2, 3, 4, 5, 6,$ respectively. Calculate E(X) and E(X²) for this distribution.

Q4. Derive the expressions for the mean and variance of the normal distribution with mean μ and variance σ^2 given by

$$n(x;\mu,\sigma) = \frac{1}{\sqrt{2\pi}} \cdot \frac{1}{\sigma} \exp\left[-\frac{1}{2}\left(\frac{x-\mu}{\sigma}\right)^2\right] \quad -\infty < x < \infty$$

Or

The heat capacity of liquid sulphuric acid was measured at various temperatures yielding the following set of data:

Heat capacity (in cal C^{-1})	Temperature (in °C)
0.38	50
0.39	100
0.40	150
0.41	200
0.45	250
0.46	300

Compute the correlation coefficient r_{xy}.

Mathematical Methods in Physics-I: PHE-4

December, 2015

Note: Attempt all questions. The marks for each question are indicated against it. Symbols have their usual meanings. You may use log tables or non-programmable calculations.

Q1. Attempt any three parts:

(a) Determine the volume of a parallelepiped, whose three sides are given to be

$\vec{a} = 2\hat{i} + 3\hat{j} - 4\hat{k}$, $\vec{b} = \hat{i} + 2\hat{j} - \hat{k}$ and $\vec{c} = 2\hat{i} + 3\hat{j} + 4\hat{k}$.

(b) Show that $\vec{\nabla} \cdot (\phi \vec{A}) = (\vec{\nabla}\phi) \cdot \vec{A} + \phi(\vec{\nabla} \cdot \vec{A})$ for a scalar field ϕ and a vector field $\vec{A}$.

(c) Determine the values of the constants a, b and c such that the vector field

$\vec{A} = (x + 2y + az)\hat{i} + (bx - 3y - z)\hat{j} + (4x + cy + 2z)\hat{k}$ is irrotational.

(d) If $\vec{A} = (3x^2 + 6y)\hat{i} - 14yz\hat{j} + 20xz^2\hat{k}$, evaluate $\int_c \vec{A} \cdot \vec{dr}$ along the straight line paths from (0, 0, 0) to (1, 1, 0), and then from (1, 1, 0) to (1, 1, 1).

(e) If $\vec{r} = x\hat{i} + y\hat{j} + z\hat{k}$, show that $\vec{\nabla} r^n = n r^{n-2} \vec{r}$

Q2. State divergence theorem. Using it, evaluate $\oiint_S \vec{F} \cdot d\vec{S}$ where $\vec{F} = 4xz\hat{i} - y^2\hat{j} + yz\hat{k}$ and S is the surface of the cube bounded by the planes x = 0, x = 1, y = 0, y = 1, z = 0, z = 1.

Or

Using Green's theorem, evaluate

$\oint_C [(3x + 4y)dx + (2x - 3y)dy]$ where C is a circle of radius 2 with its centre at the origin of the xy plane.

Q3. There are two groups: a group of 5 boys and another of 10 girls. First, one of the groups – the boys or the girls – is selected. Then one child from among that group is selected. What is the probability that a girl will be selected?

Or

A random variable X has the following density function

$$f(x) = \begin{cases} \alpha e^{-\alpha x} & , \quad x \geq 0 \\ 0 & , \quad x < 0 \end{cases}$$

Determine the variance of this distribution, given that the mean is $\frac{1}{\alpha}$.

Q4. A mass M is suspended from the centre of a steel bar supported at its ends. The depression y is measured by means of a dial height indicator. The following readings are obtained:

M (kg)	0	1	2	3	4
y (μm)	1600	1300	950	600	250

Calculate the best value of the slope and the standard error of estimate for y.

Or

Two types of e-mails arrive independently and at random: external e-mails at a mean rate of one every five minutes and internal e-mails at a mean rate of two every five minutes. Calculate the probability of receiving two or more e-mails in any two-minute interval.

Education is the passport to the future,
for tomorrow belongs to those...
who prepare for it today.

Mathematical Methods in Physics-I: PHE-4

June, 2016

Note: Attempt all questions. The marks for each question are indicated against it. Symbols have their usual meanings.

Q1. Attempt any three parts:

(a) Determine a unit vector normal to the plane formed by the vectors $\vec{A} = 2\hat{i} + \hat{j} - \hat{k}$ and $\vec{B} = \hat{i} - \hat{j} + \hat{k}$.

(b) Determine the directional derivative of f(x, y, z) = xy + z^2 at the point (1, 0, 2) along the vector $\vec{A} = 2\hat{i} + \hat{j} + 3\hat{k}$.

(c) Show that for a vector field $\vec{A}(x,y,z), \vec{\nabla}.(\vec{\nabla} \times \vec{A}) = 0$.

(d) The relations between the spherical polar coordinates r, θ and ϕ and the Cartesian coordinates x, y and z are given by: $x = r \sin\theta \cos\phi; y - r \sin\theta \sin\phi$ and $z = r \cos\theta$. Calculate g_{ij} for all i, j and show that the spherical coordinate system is orthogonal.

(e) The position vector of a particle of mass m moving along a curve is given by

$$\vec{r} = ut\hat{i} + at^2\hat{j} + s_0\hat{k}$$

Calculate the velocity and angular momentum of the particle about the origin.

Q2. Calculate the work done by a force

$$\vec{F} = (x + 2y)\hat{i} + (2x - y)\hat{j}$$

in moving a particle along a circle of radius 3 with its centre at the origin and lying in the x-y plane. State Gauss's divergence theorem. Using the divergence theorem, evaluate the surface integral $\int_S \left(2x\hat{i} + 4y\hat{j} - 3z\hat{k}\right).d\vec{S}$ over the surface of a cube of side 2.

Q3. An unbiased dice is tossed 5 times. Calculate the probability of getting at least 3 sixes.

Or

A random variable x lying between 0 and $1\left(0 \leq x \leq 1\right)$ has the probability density function p(x) = $3x^2$. Calculate the mean <x> and the variance σ.

Q4. When a resistance is measured six times, the following data is obtained:

R (in Ω): 0.0461, 0.0464, 0.0460, 0.0463, 0.0461 and 0.0459.

Obtain the best value of the resistance and the standard error of the mean.

The surface tension of a liquid is measured as a function of temperature. In appropriate units, the measured values are as given below:

Temp. (T)	0°	10°	20°	30°	40°
Surface Tension (σ)	80	72	60	55	50

Obtain the least square fit

$\sigma = \sigma_0 + \alpha T$

to the data.

Mathematical Methods In Physics-I: PHE-4

December, 2016

Note: Attempt all questions. The marks for each question are indicated against it. Symbols have their usual meanings.

Q1. Attempt any three parts:

(a) Calculate the volume of a parallelopiped formed by the vectors $\vec{A} = 2\hat{i} + \hat{j} - 4\hat{k}$; $\vec{B} = 2\hat{i} - \hat{j}$ and $\vec{C} = 2\hat{i} + \hat{j} + \hat{k}$.

Ans. Given

$$\vec{A} = 2\hat{i} + \hat{j} + 4\hat{k}$$

$$\vec{B} = 2\hat{i} + \hat{j}$$

$$\vec{C} = 2\hat{j} + \hat{k}$$

Thus, the volume of the parallelopiped is equal to

$$\left(\vec{A}\,\vec{B}\,\vec{C}\right) = \begin{vmatrix} 2 & 1 & 4 \\ 2 & 1 & 0 \\ 0 & 2 & 1 \end{vmatrix}$$

$= 2\,(1 - 0) - 1\,(2 - 0) + 4\,(4 - 0)$

$= 2 - 2 + 16$

$= 16$ cubic units.

(b) Construct a unit vector normal to the surface $x^2 + y^2 + 3xyz = 4$ at the point (1, 0, 1).

Ans. Same as Chapter-2, Q.No.-31.

(c) Define polar and axial vectors. Give one example of each.

Ans. Refer to Chapter-1 (Polar and axial vectors), Page No.-17.

(d) The force $\vec{F} = \left(\hat{i} + 2\hat{j} + 3\hat{k}\right)N$ acts at a point P(3, 0, 4). Determine the torque about the origin.

Ans. Same as Chapter-1, Q.No.-10(b).

(e) (x, y, z) and (u_1, u_2, u_3) are the respective cartesian and curvilinear coordinates of a point which are related by

$$x = 2u_1 - u_2 + 3u_3$$

$$y = u_1 + 2u_2 + 3u_3$$

$$z = u_1 - u_2$$

Calculate g_{ij} for all i and j. Is the system (u_1, u_2, u_3) orthogonal?

Ans. Same as Chapter-3, Q.No.-7.

Q2. **State Stokes' theorem. Using Stokes' theorem evaluate the line integral $\oint_C \vec{F}.\vec{dl}$, where C is a circle of radius 3 which is parallel to the x-y plane at z = 3 and $\vec{F} = y\hat{i} + 9x\hat{j} - 3xy\hat{k}$.**

Ans. Refer to Chapter-4 (Stokes' theorem), Page No.-99 and same as Chapter-4, Q.No.-33.

Or

A force $\vec{F} = -2x\hat{i} - 3y\hat{j}$ acts on a particle. Calculate the work done against the force in taking the particle from the origin to the point (5, 5) along the path x = y.

Ans. Same as Chapter-4, Q.No.-41.

Q3. **A continuous random variable x such that $0 \le x \le \pi$ has the probability distribution function:**

$$P(x) = \frac{2}{\pi}\sin^2 x.$$

Calculate the mean <x>.

Ans. Same as Chapter-6, Q.No.-1.

Or

The probability of surviving in an accident on a highway is 0.7. Calculate the probability that 2 people out of 10 involved in accidents will survive.

Ans. Same as Chapter-6, Q.No.-25.

Q4. **The number of $\alpha-$particles emitted from a radioactive sample per minute is recorded to be 2016, 1953, 2130, 2511, 1890, 2220 in six samples. Calculate the best value and standard error of the mean.**

Ans. Same as Chapter-15, Q.No.-7.

Or

Resistance of a coil is measured as a function of temperature in an experiment. The following data was obtained:

Temperature (T°)	40°	50°	60°	70°	80°
Resistance (R)	0.6	0.7	0.8	0.9	1.0

Obtain the least square fit

$R = R_0 + \sigma T$ to the data.

Ans. Same as Chapter-7, Q.No.-20

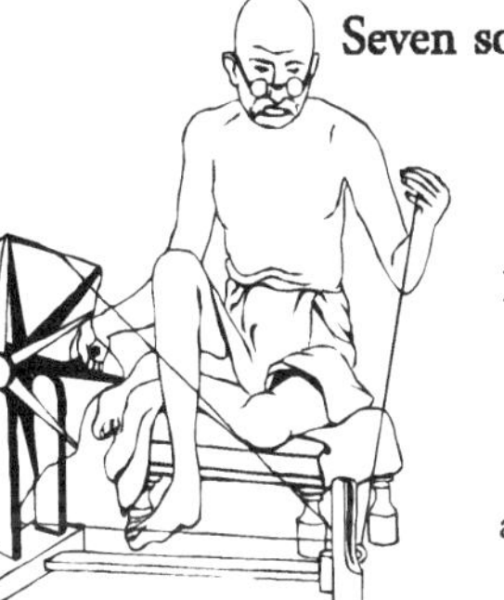

Seven social sins: Politics without principles,

wealth without work,

pleasure without conscience,

knowledge without character,

commerce without morality,

science without humanity,

and worship without sacrifice.

Mathematical Methods In Physics-I: PHE-4

June, 2017

Note: Attempt all questions. The marks for each question are indicated against it. Symbols have their usual meanings. You may use log tables or non-programmable calculators.

Q1. Attempt any three parts:

(a) Determine the volume of a parallelepiped whose three adjacent sides are given by $\vec{a}=2\hat{i}-4\hat{k}, \vec{b}=\hat{i}+2\hat{j}-\hat{k}$ and $\vec{c}=2\hat{i}-3\hat{j}+4\hat{k}$.

Ans. Refer to Chapter-1, Q.No.-16

(b) A rigid body is rotating with an angular speed of 3.0 rad s^{-1} about an axis OL= $2\hat{i}-2\hat{j}+\hat{k}$, where O is the origin. Determine the velocity of the body at the point P(4, 1, 2).

Ans. Axis of rotation is given by,

$$OL = 2\hat{i}-2\hat{j}+\hat{k}, \ \omega = 3.0 \text{ rad } s^{-1}$$

Obviously, the unit vector $\hat{n}$ in the direction of

$$2\hat{i}-2\hat{j}+\hat{k} = \frac{(2\hat{i}-2\hat{j}+\hat{k})}{|2\hat{i}-2\hat{j}+\hat{k}|} = \frac{(2\hat{i}-2\hat{j}+\hat{k})}{3}$$

Angular velocity $\vec{\omega}$ of the rigid body $= 3\hat{n} = 3\left[\frac{(2\hat{i}-2\hat{j}+\hat{k})}{3}\right] =$ $2\hat{i}-2\hat{j}+\hat{k}$

Let the point (4, 1, 2) whose velocity is desired to be determined by P. Then its position vector w.r.t. the origin (which is given as point on the axis) is given by

$$\vec{r} = 4\hat{i}+\hat{j}+2\hat{k}$$

Hence, if $\vec{v}$ be the velocity of pt. P, we have $\vec{v}=\vec{\omega}\times\vec{r}$

$$= \left(2\hat{i} - 2\hat{j} + \hat{k}\right) \times \left(4\hat{i} + \hat{j} + 2\hat{k}\right)$$

$$= \begin{vmatrix} i & j & k \\ 2 & -2 & 1 \\ 4 & 1 & 2 \end{vmatrix} = (-4-1)\,i - (4-4)\hat{j} + (2+8)\hat{k}$$

$$= -5\hat{i} + 10\hat{k}$$

(c) **A particle moves along a curve whose parametric equations are $x = 3t^2, y = t^2 - 2t, z = t^3$, where the parameter t is time. Calculate its velocity and acceleration at t = 2 s.**

Ans. Let $\bar{r}(t) = x\hat{i} + y\hat{j} + z\hat{k} = 3t^2\hat{i} + \left(t^2 - 2t\right)\hat{j} + t^3\hat{k}$

The velocity $\bar{v}(t) = \dfrac{d\bar{r}}{dt} = 6t\hat{i} + (2t-2)\hat{j} + 3t^2\hat{k}$

and the acceleration $\vec{a}(t)$ of the particle at time *t* is

$$a(t) = \frac{d^2\bar{r}}{dt^2} = 6\hat{i} + 2\hat{j} + 6t\hat{k}$$

At $t = 2, \left(\dfrac{d\bar{r}}{dt}\right)_{t=2} = 12\hat{i} + 2\hat{j} + 12\hat{k}$, and $\left(\dfrac{d^2\bar{r}}{dt^2}\right)_{t=2} = 6\hat{i} + 2\hat{j} + 12\hat{k}$

(d) **Calculate a unit vector normal to the surface**

$x^3 + y^3 + 3xyz = 3$ at the point (1, 2, – 1).

Ans. Refer to Chapter-2, Q.No.-31

(e) **Prove that:**

$$\nabla^2\left(r^n\right) = n\,(n+1)\,r^{n-2}$$

Ans. Refer to Chapter-2, Q.No.-24(i)

Q2. Using the line integral, calculate the work done by the force $\vec{F} = (2y+3)\hat{i} + xz\hat{j} + (yz - x)\hat{k}$ when it moves a particle from the point (0, 0, 0) to the point (2, 1, 1) along the curve $x = 2t^2, y = t, z = t^3$.

Ans. Let C denotes the arc of given curve from point (0, 0, 0) to the point (2, 1, 1). The parametric equation is given as $x = 2t^2, y = t, z = t^3$

At the point (0, 0, 0), t= 0 and at the point

(2, 1, 1) , t = 1

The required work done

$$= \int_C \vec{F} \cdot d\vec{x} = \int_C \left\{ (2y+3)\,\hat{i} + xz\ \hat{j} + (yz - x)\,\hat{k} \right\}\ \left(dx\,\hat{i} + dy\,\hat{j} + dz\,\hat{k} \right)$$

$$= \int_C (2y+3)\,dx + xz\,dy + (yz-x)dz$$

$$= \int_{t=0}^{1} \left[(2y+3)\frac{dx}{dt} + x = \frac{dy}{dt} + (yz-x)\frac{dz}{dt} \right] dt$$

$$= \int_0^1 \left[(2t+3)\cdot 4t + \left(2t^2 \cdot t^3\right)\cdot 1 + \left(t \cdot t^3 - 2t^2\right)\cdot 3t^2 \right] dt$$

$$= \int_0^1 \left[8t^2 + 12t + 2t^5 + 3t^6 - 6t^4 \right] dt$$

$$= \int_0^1 \left[12t + 8t^2 - 6t^4 + 2t^5 + 3t^6 \right] dt$$

$$= \left[12 \cdot \frac{t^2}{2} + 8 \cdot \frac{t^3}{3} - 6 \cdot \frac{t^5}{5} + 2 \cdot \frac{t^6}{6} + 3 \cdot \frac{t^7}{7} \right]_0^1$$

$$= \frac{6}{1} + \frac{8}{3} - \frac{6}{5} + \frac{1}{3} + \frac{3}{7}$$

$$= \frac{630 + 280 - 126 + 35 + 45}{105}$$

$$= \frac{990 - 126}{105}$$

$$= \frac{864}{105}$$

Or

Using Stokes' theorem, evaluate the integral $\int_C \vec{A}.d\vec{l}$, where $\vec{A} = z^2\,\hat{j} + yz\hat{k}$ and C is a closed path in the yz-plane joining the points O(0, 0, 0), P(0, 3, 0) and Q(0, 3, 1).

Ans. The closed path will be a triangle in yz plane—

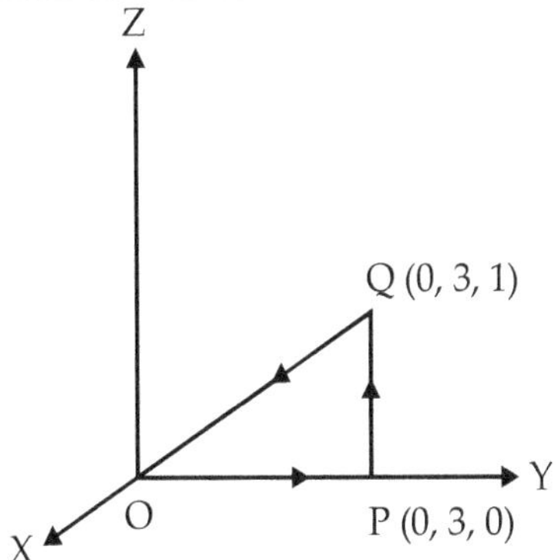

Now,

$$\vec{A} = z^2\,\hat{j} + yz\,\hat{k}$$

$$\text{So,}\quad \text{curl A} = \begin{vmatrix} \hat{i} & \hat{j} & \hat{k} \\ \frac{\partial}{\partial x} & \frac{\partial}{\partial y} & \frac{\partial}{\partial z} \\ 0 & z^2 & yz \end{vmatrix} = -z\,\hat{i}$$

Since, the path C is traversed an anticlockwise, we have $d\vec{l} = dl\hat{i}$. Moreover, as l lies on the, yz plane,

$$dl = dydz.$$

$$\therefore\ d\vec{l} = dy\,dz\,\hat{i}$$

$$\therefore\ \text{curl}\ \vec{A}.d\vec{l} = -z\hat{i}.dydz\,\hat{i} = -zdydz$$

$$\text{and}\ \int_C \vec{A}.d\vec{l} = \iint_l \text{Curl}\ \vec{A}.d\vec{l}$$

$$= -\iint_S zdy\ dz = -\int_0^3 dy\left(\int_0^{y/3} = zdz\right)$$

$$= -\int_0^3 \left[\frac{z^2}{z}\right]_0^{\frac{y}{3}} dy = -\int_0^3 \frac{y^2}{18}dy$$

$$= -\frac{1}{18}\left[\frac{y^3}{3}\right]_0^3$$

$$= -\frac{1}{18} \times \frac{27}{3}$$

$$= -\frac{9}{18} = -\frac{1}{2}$$

Q3. A class in probability theory consists of 6 boys and 4 girls. An examination is conducted and the students are ranked according to their marks. Assuming that no two students obtain the same score, what is the probability that girls receive the top four scores?

Ans. Since each ranking corresponds to a particular ordered arrangement of the 10 students, thus total number of different rankings = 10!

Since there are 4! possible rankings among the girl students and 6! possible rankings among the boy students, so the total number of ways in which the four girls can receive the top rankings

$$= 4! \times 6!$$

Hence the desired probability $= \frac{4! \times 6!}{10!} = \frac{4 \times 3 \times 2 \times 1}{10 \times 9 \times 8 \times 7} = \frac{1}{210}$

Or

Calculate the probability of getting 3 heads when an unbiased coin is tossed five times.

Ans. fair coin is tossed 5 times, $p(H) = \frac{1}{2}$, $P(T) = \frac{1}{2}$

$$P\text{ (Exactly 3 Heads)} = {}^5C_3 \times \left(\frac{1}{2}\right)^3 \left(\frac{1}{2}\right)^2$$

$$= \frac{5!}{3! \times 2!} \times \frac{1}{8} \times \frac{1}{4}$$

$$= \frac{5 \times 4 \times 3 \times 2 \times 1}{3 \times 2 \times 2} \times \frac{1}{32}$$

$$= \frac{10}{32}$$

$$= \frac{5}{16}$$

Q4. Determine the constants a and b such that the curve $y = ae^{bx}$ is the 'best fit' for the following data:

x:	2	4	6	8	10
y:	4.0777	11.084	30.128	81.897	222.62

Ans. The curve is $y = ae^{bx}$. Taking logarithm both sides, we obtain

$ln\, y = ln\, a + bx$

or, $Y = A + bx$,

where, $Y = ln\, y$ and $A = ln\, a$

We formulate the following table:

x	Y= *ln* y	x^2	xY
2	1.405	4	2.810
4	2.405	16	9.620
6	3.405	36	20.430
8	4.405	64	35.240
10	5.405	100	54.050
Total 30	17.025	220	122.150

Substituting for $\Sigma x, \Sigma Y, \Sigma x^2$ and ΣxY in the normal equations for the straight line $Y = A + bx$, we obtain

$5\,A + 30\,b = 17.025$

$17.025\,A + 220\,b = 122.50$

Solving for A and b, we obtain $A = 0.405$ and $b = 0.5$, and further from $A = 0.405$, we obtain $a = e^{0.405} = 1.499$. Thus the curve is $y = 1.499\, e^{0.5x}$

Or

Derive the expressions of the mean and variance of the following distribution

$$\mathbf{f(x) = \frac{1}{\sqrt{2\pi\sigma}} \exp\left(-\frac{x^2}{2\sigma^2}\right), -\infty < x < \infty.}$$

Ans. $f(x) = \frac{1}{\sqrt{2\pi\sigma^2}} \exp\left(-\frac{x^2}{2\sigma^2}\right)$ (given)

Since $E(x) = \int_{-\infty}^{\infty} x\, f(x)\, dx$

$$\therefore E(x) = \int_{-\infty}^{\infty} x \left[\frac{1}{\sqrt{2\pi\sigma^2}} \exp\left(-\frac{x^2}{2\sigma^2}\right)\right] dx$$

$$=\frac{1}{\sqrt{2\pi\sigma^2}}\int_{-\infty}^{\infty} x\left[\exp\left(-\frac{x^2}{2\sigma^2}\right)\right]dx \qquad \text{...... (i)}$$

Setting $t=\frac{x}{\sigma}$, we find that $dx = \sigma\, dt$ and $x=\sigma t$

$$\therefore E(X)=\frac{1}{\sqrt{2\pi}}\int_{-\infty}^{\infty} t\left[\exp\left(-\frac{t^2}{2}\right)\right]dt$$

Since t is an odd function and $\frac{t^2}{2}$ is an even function, so the integral vanished and $E(X)=0$

So the mean of the given distribution is 0. Now, the variance of the normal distribution is given by-

$$\text{Var }(X) = \int_{-\infty}^{\infty}(x-\mu)^2 f(x)dx$$

But $\mu=0$

$$\therefore \text{Var}(X)=\int_{-\infty}^{\infty} x^2\ f(x)dx$$

$$=\frac{1}{\sqrt{2\pi\sigma^2}}\int_{-\infty}^{\infty} x^2\left[\exp\left(-\frac{x^2}{2\sigma^2}\right)\right]dx$$

Setting $\frac{x}{\sigma}=t,\ dx=\sigma\ dt$ and $x=\sigma t$

$$\Rightarrow \text{Var}(X)=\frac{1}{\sqrt{2\pi\,\sigma^2}}\int_{-\infty}^{\infty}\sigma^2 t^2\left[\exp\left(-\frac{1}{2}t^2\right)\right]\sigma\ dt$$

$$=\frac{\sigma^2}{\sqrt{2\pi\sigma^2}}\int_{-\infty}^{\infty} t^2\left[\exp\left(-\frac{1}{2}t^2\right)\right]\sigma\ dt$$

$$=\frac{\sigma^2}{\sqrt{2\pi}}\int_{-\infty}^{\infty} t\times\left[t\cdot\exp\left(-\frac{1}{2}t^2\right)\right]dt$$

Let t = f (t) and $-\exp\left(-\frac{1}{2}t^2\right)=g(t)$

Then $f'(t)=1$ and $g'(t)=t\exp\left(-\frac{1}{2}t^2\right)$

Then $\text{Var}(X) = \frac{\sigma^2}{\sqrt{2\pi}} \int_{-\infty}^{\infty} f(t)\, g'(t)\, dt$

$$= \lim_{n\to\infty} \frac{\sigma^2}{\sqrt{2\pi}} \int_{-n}^{n} f(t)\, g'(t)\, dt$$

Now $\int_{-n}^{n} f(t)\, g'(t) dt = f(n)\, g(n) - f(-n)\, g(-n) - \int_{-n}^{n} f'(t) g(t)\, dt$

Here, $f(t) = t,\ f'(t) = 1$

$$g(t) = \left(-e^{-\frac{t^2}{2}}\right), \quad g'(t) = te^{-\frac{t}{2}}$$

$$\therefore \int_{-n}^{n} f(t)\, g'(t)\, dt = n\left(-e^{-\frac{t^2}{2}}\right) - (-n)\left(e^{-\frac{(-n)^2}{2}}\right) - \int_{-n}^{n} -e^{\frac{-t^2}{2}}\, dt$$

$$= \left(-n\frac{1}{e^{\frac{n^2}{2}}}\right) + \left(-n\frac{1}{e^{\frac{n^2}{2}}}\right) + \int_{-n}^{n} e^{\frac{-t^2}{2}}\, dt$$

$$= \left(-2n\frac{1}{e^{\frac{n^2}{2}}}\right) + \int_{-n}^{n} e^{\frac{-t^2}{2}}\, dt$$

$$\therefore \text{Var}(X) = \frac{\sigma^2}{\sqrt{2\pi}} \lim_{n\to\infty} \left[\left(-2n\frac{1}{e^{\frac{n^2}{2}}}\right) + \int_{-n}^{n} e^{\frac{-t^2}{2}}\, dt\right]$$

$$= \frac{\sigma^2}{\sqrt{2\pi}} \left[-2n\frac{1}{e^{\frac{n^2}{2}}}\right]_{-\infty}^{\infty} + \frac{\sigma^2}{\sqrt{2\pi}} \int_{-\infty}^{\infty} e^{-\frac{t^2}{2}}\, dt$$

$$= 0 + \frac{\sigma^2}{\sqrt{2\pi}} \int_{-\infty}^{\infty} e^{-\frac{t^2}{2}}\, dt$$

$$= \sigma^2 \int_{-\infty}^{\infty} \frac{1}{\sqrt{2\pi}} e^{\frac{-t^2}{2}}\, dt$$

which is σ^2 times the area under a normal curve with variance'1'.

Hence $\text{Var}(X) = \sigma^2 \times 1 = \sigma^2$

Mathematical Methods In Physics-I: PHE-4

December, 2017

Note: Attempt all questions. The marks for each question are indicated against it. Symbols have their usual meanings. You may use log tables or non-programmable calculators.

Q1. Answer any three parts:

(a) If $\vec{A} = 5\hat{i} + \hat{j} - 3\hat{k}$ and $\vec{B} = 2\hat{i} - 2\hat{j} - 7\hat{k}$, determine $\vec{A} + \vec{B}$. Also find a vector of magnitude six units long in the direction of $\vec{A}$.

(b) Consider a force $\vec{F} = 20\,(6\hat{i} - \hat{j} + \hat{k})\,N$ acting at a point $P\,(-3\hat{i} + \hat{j} + 5\hat{k})\,m$. What is the torque (in Nm) at point P about the origin?

(c) Determine the angle between the tangents to the curve $\vec{r} = t^2\,\hat{i} + 2t\,\hat{j} - t^3\,\hat{k}$ at the points $t = \pm 1$.

(d) Determine the directional derivative of the scalar field $\phi(x, y, z) = xy^2 + yz^3$ at the point (2, −1, 1) in the direction of the vector $\hat{i} + 2\hat{j} + 2\hat{k}$.

(e) If $f = (x^2 + y^2 + z^2)^n$,

determine n if $\vec{\nabla} \cdot (\vec{\nabla} f) = 0$.

Q2. A vector field is given by

$\vec{F} = (\sin y)\,\hat{i} + x\,(1 + \cos y)\,\hat{j}$. Evaluate the line integral over a circular path given by $x^2 + y^2 = a^2, z = 0$.

Or

State Gauss's divergence theorem. Using it evaluate

$$\iint_S \vec{F}\cdot\vec{d}S,$$

where $\vec{F} = x^3\hat{i} + y^3\hat{j} + z^3\hat{k}$ and S is the surface of the sphere $x^2 + y^2 + z^2 = a^2$.

Q3. The probability that a certain component survives a given shock is $3/5$. Calculate the probability that 2 of the next 4 components tested survive.

Or

The life of a component X has the probability density function

$$f(x) = \begin{cases} 2e^{-2x}, & \text{for} \quad x > 0 \\ 0, & \text{for} \quad x \le 0 \end{cases}$$

Calculate the probabilities that it will take on a value between (i) 1 and 3, and (ii) greater than 0.5.

Q4. Obtain the regression equation which is the best fit for the following data:

x	2	3	4	5	6	7
y	3.0	5.0	5.5	6.0	8.0	9.5

Or

Obtain the mean and variance of the Poisson distribution

$$p(x; m) = \frac{e^{-m} m^x}{x!}, x = 0, 1, 2, \dots.$$

Mathematical Methods In Physics-I: PHE-4

June, 2018 (Sample Paper)

Note: Attempt all questions. You may use log tables or calculators. Symbols have their usual meanings.

Q1. Answer any three parts:

(a) Calculate the area of a parallelogram having diagonals $\vec{A} = 3\hat{i} + \hat{j} - 2\hat{k}$ and $\vec{B} = \hat{i} - 3\hat{j} + 4\hat{k}$.

Ans. Refer to Chapter-1, Q.No.-25 (Pg. No.-31)

(b) A particle moves along a curve whose parametric equations are $x = e^{-t}$, $y = 2\cos 3t$, $z = 2\sin 3t$, where t is the time. Determine the magnitude of the velocity and acceleration at $t = 0$.

Ans. Refer to Chapter-2, Q.No.-29 (Pg. No.-59)

(c) Find a unit normal vector to the level surface $x^2y + 2xz = 4$ at the point (2, –2, 3).

Ans. Refer to Chapter-2, Q.No.-31 (Pg. No.-60)

(d) Express the following vector field in spherical polar coordinates

$$\vec{F} = \frac{k(x\hat{j} - y\hat{i})}{x^2 + y^2 + z^2}$$

Ans. Refer to Chapter-3, Q.No.-17 (Pg. No.-88)

(e) Find the directional derivative of $V = \frac{k}{(x^2 + y^2 + z^2)^{1/2}}$ at the point (3, 4, 0) in the direction $\hat{n} = \frac{1}{\sqrt{6}}(\hat{i} + \hat{j} - 2\hat{k})$.

Ans. Refer to Chapter-2, Q.No.-8 (Pg. No.-47)

Q2. Using stokes' theorem show that if the work done by a force along a closed path is zero, the curl of the force is zero.

Ans. Refer to Chapter-4, Q.No.-42 (Pg. No.-127)

Or

Using divergence theorem to evaluate $\iint_S \vec{F} \cdot \hat{n} ds$ where $\vec{F} = 4xz\,\hat{i} - y^2\,\hat{j} + yz\,\hat{k}$ and S is the surface of the cube bounded by $x = 0, x = 1, y = 0, y = 1, z = 0$ and $z = 1$. $\hat{n}$ is the unit vector normal to the surface S.

Ans. Refer to Chapter-4, Q.No.-31 (Pg. No.-121)

Q3. **A bag contains 8 red balls and 5 white balls. Two successive draws of 3 balls are made without replacement. Find the probability that the first drawing will give 3 white balls and the second 3 red balls.**

Ans. Refer to Chapter-5, Q.No.-14 (Pg. No.-147)

Or

If at least one child in a family with two children is a girl, what is the probability that both children are girls?

Ans. Refer to Chapter-5, Q.No.-34 (Pg. No.-158)

Q4. **The probability density function of a continuous bivariate distribution is given by f (x, y) = x + y, where $0 \le x \le 1,\ 0 \le y \le 1 = 0$, otherwise find the marginal distributions and the correlation coefficient of x and y.**

Ans. Refer to Chapter-6, Q.No.-2 (Pg. No.-167)

Or

Estimate the regression equation of x on y from the following data:

x	5	3	8	5	10
y	8	11	6	9	8

Ans. Refer to Chapter-7, Q.No.-5 (Pg. No.-201)

Mathematical Methods In Physics-I: PHE-4

June, 2018

Note: Attempt all questions. The marks for each question are indicated against it. You may use log tables or calculators. Symbols have their usual meanings.

Q1. Answer any three parts:

(a) Calculate the volume of a parallelopiped having sides

$\vec{a} = \hat{i} + 2\hat{j} + 3\hat{k}$,

$\vec{b} = 2\hat{i} + 2\hat{j} - \hat{k}$ and

$\vec{c} = 2\hat{i} + \hat{j} - 2\hat{k}$.

(b) Show that for a scalar field ϕ (x, y, z),

$\vec{\nabla} \times \vec{\nabla}\phi = 0$.

(c) Define a solenoidal vector field. Determine the constant 'a' so that the vector field $\vec{A} = (2x+3y)\hat{i} + (y-3z)\hat{j} + (x+az)\hat{k}$ is solenoidal. Show that $\vec{A}$ is not conservative.

(d) Express $\vec{v} = \dfrac{y\hat{i} - x\hat{j}}{x^2 + y^2}$ in cylindrical polar coordinates.

(e) Determine the unit tangent vector at a point on the curve C defined by

$\vec{r} = xy\hat{i} - z\hat{j} + x^2\hat{k}$, where

$x = t^2, y = 2t$, and $z = t^3$.

Q2. State Stokes' theorem and use it to obtain the value of curl $\vec{B}$, starting from Ampere's law, $\oint_l \vec{B}.\, d\vec{l} = \mu_0 I$, where l defines the periphery of surfaces.

Or

Calculate the work done by the force $\vec{F} = z\hat{i} + x\hat{j} + y\hat{k}$ moving a particle along the curve x = cos t, y = sin t and z = 3t for $0 \leq t < 2\pi$.

Q3. Determine the mean and variance of the normal distribution defined by $\frac{1}{\sqrt{2\pi}}\exp\left(\frac{-x^2}{2}\right)$.

Or

A student measures temperature (in °C) of a body and obtains five values at different times in an experiment : 25, 27, 26, 28, 24. Calculate the arithmetic mean and its standard error.

Q4. Calculate the probability of getting 3 heads in a toss of 5 ideal coins.

Or

The average number of phone calls received by a telephone exchange per minute between 2 a.m. and 3 a.m. is 2. Identify the probability distribution that applies in this case. Calculate the probability that during one minute, chosen at random, there will be one incoming phone call.

◈◈◈

I grew up in a physical world, and I speak English. The next generation is growing up in a digital world, and they speak social.

Mathematical Methods In Physics-I: PHE-4
December, 2018

Note: Attempt all questions. The marks for each question are indicated against it. You can use a calculator or log tables. Symbols have their usual meanings.

Q1. Answer any three parts:

(a) Determine the unit vector normal to the plane formed by the vectors $\vec{a} = 2\hat{i} - \hat{k}$ and $\vec{b} = 3\hat{j} + 2\hat{k}$.

(b) Calculate the work done by a force $\vec{F} = xy^2\hat{i} + xy\hat{j}$ in moving a particle along the curve $y^2 = 4x$ from (0, 0) to (1, 2).

(c) The position vector of a particle moving in space is $\vec{r} = x\hat{i} + y\hat{j} + z\hat{k}$. Obtain expression for components of its velocity in cylindrical coordinates.

(d) Calculate the directional derivative of $V = \dfrac{A}{\left[x^2 + y^2 + z^2\right]^{1/2}}$ at the point (4, 4, 7) in the direction $\hat{n} = \dfrac{1}{\sqrt{6}}\left(\hat{i} + \hat{j} - 2\hat{k}\right)$.

(e) Prove that for a vector field $\vec{A}(x,y,z) = A_1\hat{i} + A_2\hat{j} + A_3\hat{k}$ and a scalar field $\phi(x, y, z)$:

$$\vec{\nabla}.\left(\phi\vec{A}\right) = \phi\vec{\nabla}.\vec{A} + \vec{A}.\vec{\nabla}\phi$$

Q2. State Stokes' theorem. Use it for the vector field $\vec{A} = P(x,y)\hat{i} + Q(x,y)\hat{j}$ to show that $\oint_c (P\,dx + Q\,dy) = \iint_S \left(\dfrac{\partial Q}{\partial x} - \dfrac{\partial P}{\partial y}\right) dx\,dy$

Or

State Gauss's divergence theorem. The electric field due to a point charge, q, at a point whose position vector with respect to the location of q is $\vec{r}$ is given by $\vec{E} = \dfrac{kq}{r^3}\vec{r}, (r \neq 0)$, where k is a constant, which depends on the nature of the medium. Calculate the flux of $\vec{E}$ through a sphere of radius a, whose centre is at the position of the charge q.

Q3. The probability that a molecule has speeds between v and v + dv is given by Maxwell-Boltzmann distribution of speeds. For gas molecules of mass m, it is given by

$$f(v) = 4\pi\left(\frac{m}{2\pi k_B T}\right)^{3/2} v^2 e^{-mv^2/2k_B T} \quad 0 \le v \le \infty$$

where T is temperature. Show that

$$\bar{v} = \sqrt{\frac{8k_B T}{m\pi}}$$

Or

The marks obtained by 6 students in two class tests denoted by x and y, are as follows :

X	6	5	8	10	4	9
Y	8	6	7	10	6	8

Obtain the least square regression line of y on x.

Q4. A continuous random variable can assume any value between 2 and 5. If its density function f(x) = k(1 + x), calculate p(x < 4).

Or

The probability of success in a sequence of 300 independent trials is $\frac{3}{4}$. Assuming that the trials form a normal distribution, calculate the mean and the standard deviation of the distribution.

Mathematical Methods In Physics-I: PHE-4
June, 2019

Note: Attempt all questions. The marks for each question are indicated against it. You can use a calculator or log tables. Symbols have their usual meanings.

Q1. Answer any three parts:

(a) If $\vec{a} = 2\hat{i} + \hat{j} - 3\hat{k}$ and $\vec{b} = \hat{i} - 2\hat{j} + \hat{k}$, determine a vector of magnitude 4 units, perpendicular to both $\vec{a}$ and $\vec{b}$.

(b) Obtain the directional derivative of $\Phi = x^2yz + xz^2$ at the point (1, 2, −1) in the direction of $\hat{i} - \hat{j} + 3\hat{k}$.

(c) Show that for any vector field $\vec{A}$, $\vec{\nabla}.(\vec{\nabla} \times \vec{A}) = 0$.

(d) Using the parametric representation, calculate the work done in moving a particle once around a circle in the xy plane. It is given that the circle has its centre at the origin and radius 2 units, and the force field is :

$$\vec{F} = (2x - y)\hat{i} + (x + 2y)\hat{j}.$$

(e) Determine the square of the arc element for the orthogonal curvilinear coordinate system whose coordinates (u, v, w) are related to the cartesian coordinates as follows :

$$x = \frac{1}{2}(u^2 - v^2); y = uv; z = w.$$

Q2. Answer any one part :

(a) Using Green's theorem evaluate the integral $\oint_C (y^3dx - x^3dy)$ where C is a circle of radius two units with its centre at the origin.

(b) State Gauss's theorem. Using Gauss's theorem evaluate the integral

$$\oiint_R (3x\hat{i} + 2y\hat{j}).d\vec{S}$$

where R is the sphere defined by $x^2 + y^2 + z^2 = 9$.

Q3. Answer any one part :

(a) The probability that a certain item produced in a factory is defective is 0.36. Assuming a normal distribution, calculate its mean and standard deviation in a random sample of 400 items.

(b) Measurements of the diameter X of wires manufactured in a factory have the probability distribution $f(x) = \begin{cases} \dfrac{4}{\pi\left(1+x^2\right)} & \text{for } 0 < x < 1 \\ 0 & \text{elsewhere} \end{cases}$

Calculate the expectation value of X.

Q4. Answer any one part :

(a) The diffusion time in hours for a silicon wafer and the resulting sheet resistance are given as follows :

Diffusion time	0.60	1.1	1.6	2.0	2.5
Resistance	84.0	90.0	91.0	93.0	92

Obtain the equation of the regression line for this data.

(b) The probability distribution of the binomial random variable X representing the number of successes in n independent trials is given by :

$b(x;\ n,\ p) = {}^nC_x p^x q^{n-x}, n = 0, 1, 2, \ldots n$. Show that the mean of the binomial distribution is np.

Mathematical Methods In Physics-I: PHE-4

December, 2019

Note: (i) Answer all questions.(ii) The marks for each question are indicated against it.(iii) The marks for each question are indicated against it.

Q1. Attempt any three parts:

(a) Determine the projection of the vector $\vec{a} = 4\hat{i} - 3\hat{j} + \hat{k}$ on the line passing through the points (2, 3, –1) and (–2, –4, 3).

(b) Determine the direction in which the rate of change of the scalar field $\phi = 2xz - y^2$ will be maximum at the point (1, 1, 2). What is the magnitude of this maximum rate of change?

(c) If $\vec{v} = \vec{w} \times \vec{r}$, prove that $\vec{w} = \frac{1}{2}(\vec{\nabla} \times \vec{v})$ where $\vec{w}$ is a constant vector.

(d) Calculate the work done by a force field $\vec{F} = 3xy\,\hat{i} - 2y^2\hat{j}$ in moving a particle along the curve C in the xy plane given by $y = 2x^2$ from (0, 0) to (1, 2).

(e) Determine the curl of the following vector field in cylindrical coordinates.

$$\vec{F} = p^2\hat{e}_\rho + z\sin\phi\hat{e}_\phi + 2z\cos\phi\hat{e}_z$$

(2) Answer any one part.

(a) Using Stoke's theorem evaluate $\int_C \vec{F}\, d\vec{l}$ where $\vec{F} = y\hat{i} + xz\hat{j} + \hat{k}$ and C is a circle of unit radius in the xy plane with its centre at the origin.

(b) A solid cube with a uniform density ρ and side of length one unit is placed with one corner at the origin and the three adjacent edges along the Cartesian coordinate axes. Determine the moment of inertia of the cube about the x-axis, defined by $I = \rho\iiint_V (y^2 + z^2)dV$.

(3) Answer any one part.

(a) The probability that a certain part of an instrument survives a given shock is $\frac{2}{3}$. Calculate the probability that I of the next 4 parts survives the shock.

(b) The probability distribution function for a random variable X is given by

$$f(x)=\begin{cases}\frac{C}{\sqrt{x}} & \text{for } 0<x<4 \\ 0 & \text{elsewhere}\end{cases}$$

Determine the value of C.

Q4. Answer any one part.

(a) In a laboratory experiment, the time period of a pendulum is measured by five students as 3.9s, 3.5s, 3.7s, 3.4s and 3.5s, respectively. Calculate the best value of the time period and the standard error of the mean.

(b) Derive the expression for the mean and variance of Poisson distribution defined by

$$p(x;m)=\frac{e^{-m}m^{x}}{x!};\ x=0,1,2,...$$

www.ingramcontent.com/pod-product-compliance
Ingram Content Group UK Ltd.
Pitfield, Milton Keynes, MK11 3LW, UK
UKHW021932200726
13853UKWH00010B/442